ROUND-THE-WORLD
FLIGHTS

THIRD EDITION

ROUND-THE-WORLD
FLIGHTS

THIRD EDITION

CARROLL V. GLINES

Brassey's, Inc.
Washington, D.C.

Third Edition Copyright © 2003 by Carroll V. Glines

First Edition © 1982 by Van Nostrand Reinhold
Second Edition © 1990 by Aero, an imprint of Tab Books, a division of McGraw-Hill, Inc.

Library of Congress Cataloging-in-Publication Data

Glines, Carroll V., 1920–
    Round-the-world flights / Carroll V. Glines.—3rd ed.
        p. cm.
    Includes bibliographical references (p.) and index.
    ISBN 1-57488-448-4 (pbk. : alk. paper)
    I. Flights around the world.   I. Title.
G445.G54   2003
629.13'09—dc21   2002156210

Printed in the United States of America on acid-free paper that meets the American National Standards Institute Z39-48 Standard.

Brassey's, Inc.
22841 Quicksilver Drive
Dulles, Virginia 20166

10 9 8 7 6 5 4 3 2 1

CONTENTS

ACKNOWLEDGMENTS

Although I had written a number of books on aviation subjects, this one presented an interesting challenge. When I was researching for the first edition of this work, I thought that only a very few flights had been made around the world and that my problem would be finding enough interesting material to compose a book-length manuscript. The more I researched, however, the more evidence I found that many pilots since the invention of the flying machine had thought about defying the odds of making a successful global flight and a surprising number had succeeded. I then had to choose those flights that represented significant aviation "firsts" or had established speed records recognized by the record-keeping authorities for various categories of aircraft. Now, in the new millennium, I find that many more pilots have taken their dream flights and more are planning them as this edition goes to press. An exclusive organization for those who have successfully completed world flights, called Earthrounders, has been formed and promises to meet regularly in different world cities to keep track of those who share this experience.

While risks still exist, the chances of successfully circumnavigating the globe are so improved that the trip can be made today with more assurance of success than ever before. This is possible because of advanced cockpit instrumentation, more dependable engines, improved navigation facilities, satellite communications, availability of airports, and timely, reliable weather reporting and forecasting.

I am grateful for the information provided by the pilots whose stories appear here, and for those who verified the facts through interviews and correspondence and provided photographs. Of special help were members of the Earthrounders, especially Margi Moss and Claude Meunier, and the staff of the National Aeronautic Association, who not only made their files available but also encouraged me to continue my quest for information despite the difficulties sometimes involved in separating truth from fiction.

My thanks are also extended to the public relations staff members of the sponsors of some of the flights who delved into their historical files to provide factual material and photographs. I am especially indebted to Mrs. Ann Whyte, former historian of Pan American World Airways, the once giant airline that set so many aviation precedents. I am also grateful to the late James A. Arey, former head of Pan Am's public relations department, for including me on the passenger manifest of the airline's two record-setting world flights of 1976 and 1977.

Since the first edition of this book was published in 1982 and the second in 1990, dozens more pilots have realized their dream of completing a world flight. It is interesting to note their varied motives for accepting the risks of aircraft malfunctions, braving diverse weather conditions, and facing the frustrations of obtaining clearances for overflights and landings in foreign countries. A few wanted to better a world speed record in their class of aircraft. Some wanted to do it for the brief fame that it brought them. Others just had a keen desire to see if they could do it and sought neither fame nor fortune. But all who succeeded gained the personal satisfaction of having been particularly privileged to view other places and cultures from the skies and thus had their lives and spirits enriched as never before.

INTRODUCTION

It was inevitable. When the flying machine reached the point where it could span distances of a few miles, some intrepid airman would look at the globe and consider circling it by air. However, it was the men of the sea who were the first to consider the challenge. Christopher Columbus and others had theorized that the world is round and thus could be circumnavigated. But it was Ferdinand Magellan, a Portuguese sea captain, who was first to try. Snubbed by his own king, he persuaded Charles I of Spain to sponsor a trip in search of the Spice Islands by sailing west. On September 20, 1519, he set sail from Spain with 280 men in five ships, and headed southwest across the South Atlantic. Passing through the strait at the tip of South America that now bears his name, he reached the ocean, which he named "Pacific." Along the way, one ship was lost in a storm, and another turned back to Spain. Sailing northwest, the three remaining ships arrived at the Philippine Islands in March 1521.

Unfortunately, Magellan never returned to his adopted homeland: he got involved in a tribal war and was killed in the islands at Mactan on April 27, 1521. Sebastian del Cano assumed command. He ordered one ship burned and sent another back east to assure that at least one of the ships would return to Spain. That ship was captured by the Portuguese and most of the crew were killed. Del Cano sailed west in his flagship *Victoria* with 18 men aboard, rounded the Cape of Good Hope, and arrived in Spain on September 6, 1522, to complete the first circumnavigation of the globe. It had taken the survivors of Magellan's crew 1,083 days to complete the voyage.

The second world circumnavigation was made by Francis Drake, an Englishman, who departed Plymouth, England, on December 13, 1577, in the *Golden Hind* with six ships under his command. Five ships turned back at the Strait of Magellan while Drake continued westward. He returned to England with gold and spices on September 26, 1580, to become the first sea captain to circle the globe.

The next celebrated world voyage was that of Capt. James Cook, an

Englishman. He sailed from Dover, England, on August 25, 1768, and returned three years later on July 13, 1771.

Perhaps one of the most daring sailors to complete such a global journey was Joshua Slocum, who was born in Nova Scotia in 1844 and became an American citizen. At age 51, he rebuilt an old 37-foot oyster boat, named it *Spray*, and left Boston harbor on April 24, 1895. He started alone heading eastward but turned around when warned of pirates in the Mediterranean and headed westward. He sailed around South America, across the Pacific, around Australia and Africa's Cape of Good Hope, and arrived at Newport, Rhode Island, on June 27, 1898, more than three years later. He had traveled 46,000 miles to firmly establish himself as the first to sail around the world alone.

Slocum's feat was outdone by Francis Chichester who sailed alone on his 66-foot ketch *Gypsy Moth* from Plymouth, England, in 1966. He made a world voyage almost without stopping until he had to repair the steering mechanism at Sydney, Australia. He spent 226 days at sea and returned to Plymouth on May 26, 1967.

Others have tried to have their names placed in the seafaring record books for solo world circling. Chay Blyth, an Englishman, sailed east to west aboard the ketch *British Steel* in 1971, completing the voyage in 302 days. A Frenchman, Alain Colas, sailed his trimaran *Manureva* in 1973 around the three great capes in only 129 days. The first woman to sail around the world alone is Lisa Clayton, who took her steel-hulled *Spirit of Birmingham* from Dartmouth, England, in September 1994 and returned 285 days later. Jonathan Sanders, an Englishman, made his mark by making five solo circumnavigations, one of them a nonstop triple world trip alone between May 1986 and March 1988 during which he covered 80,000 miles.

Probably the first person to circle the earth in a deliberate attempt to set a record was Nellie Bly, a newspaperwoman who had become well known for her exposés of social conditions in the United States in the nineteenth century. Born Elizabeth Cochran on May 5, 1867, she took the name Nellie Bly as a pen name when she began writing for the *Pittsburgh* (Pa.) *Dispatch*. In 1887, she pretended insanity and had herself committed to an insane asylum. Her series of articles on conditions in the asylum, published in the *New York World*, made her famous. Joseph Pulitzer, publisher of the *World*, in a continued effort to outdo his competitors with sensational and unusual news accounts, had been impressed by Jules Verne's novel *The Tour of the World in Eighty Days*, which had been published in 1872. Would Nellie like to try to beat Phineas Fogg's fictional record of circumnavigating the globe in 80 days by using available commercial transportation?

Nellie, an aggressive reporter, saw the opportunity of a lifetime. She studied shipping schedules and in mid-November 1889, with a minimum of baggage, left New York. She crossed the Atlantic and the Mediterranean, proceeding to Aden, Colombo, Singapore, Hong Kong, Tokyo, and San Francisco. She returned to New York on January 25, 1890, 72 days, 6 hours, and 11 minutes after departing. Pulitzer gave much front-page space to Nellie's description of her adventures by train, ship, ricksha, and sampan, keeping public attention focused on her trip. Clothes, games, songs, and dances were dedicated to her; parades were held in her honor; and toys were named after her. She later wrote three books, one of them *Nellie Bly's Book: Around the World in Seventy-Two Days*.

The publicity given Nellie's feat encouraged others. George Francis Train duplicated her feat in 1890, establishing a new mark of 67 days. Charles Fitzmorris, chief of police in Chicago, left the city in 1901 and returned 60 days, 13 hours, and 29 minutes later to brief acclaim. By now, the fever had caught on. J. W. Willis Sayre, of Seattle, became the first to make the trip in less than 60 days when, in 1903, he set a new mark of 54 days, 9 hours, and 42 minutes. That year Henry Frederick bested Sayre's mark by a mere two hours and 40 minutes. In 1907, a new record was set by Colonel Burnley-Campbell of Great Britain (40 days, 9 hours, and 30 minutes), which was broken four years later by Andre Jaeger-Schmidt, a one-legged French newspaperman and adventurer, who circled the globe in 39 days, 19 hours, 42 minutes, and 38 seconds.

The publicity given these trips, however brief, continued to fascinate the few Americans who could afford the trip and who wanted the fame anticipated in setting a new record. John Henry Mears, a New York theatrical producer and writer, carefully analyzed world shipping schedules and, in 1913, went around the world in 35 days, 21 hours, and 36 minutes. Mears has the distinction of being the first circumnavigator to fly, the airplane then being only a decade old. He flew for only 40 miles, however, sitting on the wing and clinging to the struts and wires, but it was enough to make his trip forever different from all the others. It isn't known whether the publicity given Mears on this trip inspired others, but in February 1914, the Bureau of Aeronautics of the Panama-Pacific Exposition Company announced sponsorship of a race around the world "by aeroplane." The race was to start and end in San Francisco; the starting date was set for May 1915. The company offered $150,000 to the winners and sought an additional subscription of $150,000 from interested parties. Confidence that the trip could be made entirely by air is evident in this excerpt from *Aero and Hydro* magazine: "Considerable discussion has been launched as to the possibility of accomplishing the voyage within the prescribed limit of 90 days, traveling only by some sort of motored aero vehicle for the entire distance, but . . . it is more than probable that the trip will be made by some individual before the date set for the start

of the race. To win the race, and the Exposition's cash prize of $100,000,
. . . it will be necessary to average nearly 250 miles a day. The world's
record for one day's flying is 1,350 miles."

The only restrictions were that the course outlined by the race's organizers had to be followed within the 90-day period and the entire distance
had to be by aircraft. The race, scheduled to start in May 1915, was to be
flown from San Francisco eastward, with stops at Reno, Nevada; Cheyenne, Wyoming; Kansas City; St. Louis; Chicago; and New York. "The
flight across the Atlantic Ocean is conceded to be the most formidable
feature of the race," *Aero and Hydro* said. "It will be essayed from Belle
Isle, a small point between Newfoundland and Labrador. Cape Farewell,
Greenland, the next stop, is 610 miles away. From Cape Farewell to Reykjavik, Iceland, is 670 miles. One more jump to Stornoway, in the Hebrides, a distance of 570 miles, and the Atlantic will have been crossed."

The route from Iceland included stops at Edinburgh, London, Paris,
Berlin, Warsaw, St. Petersburg, and Moscow, "and along the Trans-
Siberian Railway down into Manchuria and Korea, and across into
Japan." The optimism of the race's planners is also evident in this statement: "From northern Japan to Kamchatka, with varying routes across
the little gap which separates Asia from North America, no obstacle likely
to be met is insurmountable. Then Vancouver, B.C., Seattle and Tacoma,
Portland, Oregon, and San Francisco again and the world will have been
circled." The prize money was to be split three ways—$100,000 to the
winner, $30,000 for second place, and $20,000 for third.

There is no available record that indicates what happened to these
grandiose plans, but they never materialized. Apparently, the planners
were not familiar with the logistical and governmental requirements that
had to be met. The route of the flight would have taken the entrants over
numerous uninhabited areas, as well as areas where no airplane had ever
been. Airfields, if they existed at all, were usually a parade ground, park,
or polo field. Since motor vehicles were rare, gasoline would be in short
supply or nonexistent at many of the stops projected. In short, the world
wasn't yet ready for a round-the-world race entirely by airplane.

World War I canceled any thought of flying around the world, but the
war did have one beneficial effect: aircraft, engines, and facilities all
improved rapidly in the Northern Hemisphere. Thousands of pilots were
trained, though few saw action. But a desire to fly an "aeroplane" was
instilled in the minds of many trained pilots, and it could not be long
denied.

Shortly after the war two private organizations dedicated to the
growth of aviation, the Aero Club of America and the Aerial League of
America, joined forces. In 1919, they appointed a commission to make a
survey "for the special purpose of ascertaining the extent of interest in

civilian aeronautics throughout the United States." A number of "aeronautic authorities" were selected to make the survey, and the group traveled by Pullman car to 49 cities. The commission concluded that the nation was indeed interested in aviation. "The extensive use of planes for transportation, surveying, passenger-carrying and other useful purposes in the middle [west] and northwest was a revelation even for the aeronautic authorities in the party," according to *Flying*, the official journal of the two organizations. "A number of people, including some railroad magnates who were interested in establishing aerial transportation lines, actually went begging for quotations on large aeroplanes and dirigibles which would have given the aeronautics industry business amounting to over $20 million had the manufacturers been able to give quotations and make deliveries."

The commission's report noted that several national and international contests were scheduled for the year 1920, with more than $2 million in prizes offered. Typical was a prize of $100,000 announced by the Aero Club of America, "to be awarded to the person who evolves and demonstrates the first heavier-than-air aircraft which will rise from and land on the ground vertically and will, in other words, make it possible to rise from and land on the roof of a medium-size house," according to *Flying*. The prize was offered by the French millionaire Andre Michelin to the first aviator or designer to "(1) rise vertically from the ground; (2) to possess the greatest possible range of speed up to 124 miles per hour; and (3) land vertically within a radius of five meters."

This interest encouraged the commission members to expand their survey. The Aero Club and the Aerial League appointed a special three-man commission to tour the world and organize "The First Aerial Derby Around the World." The group traveled (mostly by ship, never by air) more than 40,000 miles and visited 32 countries. Twenty-seven new Aero Clubs were organized in other nations as they passed through. When the commission reached Paris, May 20, 1920, it was dissolved by mutual consent. In its place, The World's Board of Aeronautical Commissions, Inc. was established "to perpetuate the work of the Commission which organized the first aerial derby around the world." The board was "to act in an advisory capacity to all interested in aviation throughout the world, to advance it as rapidly as possible, and to encourage aerial navigation in all parts of the world."

Rules for the derby were drawn up. They reflected an optimism about the future of aviation that was based on the fact that a few aircraft had already flown great distances without refueling and now seemed reliable enough to make such an arduous trip. The aspirations of the two aviation organizations were never realized. The world was not yet ready for such an undertaking. In fact, they were not realized until the early 1920s, when the U.S. Army Air Service decided to focus world attention on American air power by embarking on a world flight (see Chapter 1). Even so, only two aircraft made the journey, which took 175 days. This success gave rise to a new urge to better the record by whatever means, including the airplane.

Although attempts to be the fastest around the world by land and sea briefly received considerable publicity, those made largely or solely by air are the subject of this book. In racing against time, fliers had to contend with the vagaries of the world's weather, since any flight would encounter weather conditions that, at the least, were cause for concern and, at the most, were extremely dangerous, or fatal, to an airplane and its passengers.

The success of any world flight depends on aircraft, engine, instrument reliability, and the navigation skill of the pilot. The fact that modern aircraft now circle the earth with no difficulty is a tribute to the many anonymous engineers, scientists, and pioneer aviators who chipped away at the barriers to safe flight and gave us what today is the most reliable, efficient, and safe means of mass transportation the world has yet known. To no small extent is this due to the feats of the men and women whose stories appear in the following pages.

1

FIRST FLIGHT ROUND
THE WORLD

"Would you do it again?" a newsman asked Army lieutenant Lowell H. Smith as he climbed down from the open cockpit of his Douglas World Cruiser at Seattle's airport. "We wouldn't do it again for a million dollars—unless we were ordered to," Smith replied.

It was the first flight around the world. On September 28, 1924, two of the originally four aircraft and three of four two-man crews had officially completed the flight, landing at Sand Point, near Seattle. Six of the eight Army Air Service fliers who had left Sand Point 175 days earlier had covered 26,345 miles in 15 days, 11 hours, and 7 minutes. They had touched down in 29 countries, survived 5 forced landings, lost 2 planes, and burned out 17 Liberty engines. Until 2000, no one has duplicated their feat of circumnavigating the globe in an open-cockpit, single-engine aircraft.

Although aviation had just celebrated the twentieth anniversary of the Wright brothers' first flight, flying was still in a trial-and-error period. U.S. military pilots were being encouraged to bring public attention to the airplane's potential by breaking speed, distance, and altitude records. When the attempt was announced in 1923, its avowed purpose was to "point the way for all nations to develop aviation commercially and to secure for our country the honor of being the first to [circle] the globe entirely by air."

It was a noble objective, but there was more to the idea than that. American military aviation had been neglected. Although the United States then held 33 of the 42 world aviation records, there was no national program of research and development in either commercial or military aviation. Few new models of aircraft were being produced, and other

1

countries had vowed to take aviation leadership away from the United States.

It is uncertain who first thought of sending the army pilots on their around-the-world flight. The chief of the Air Service, Maj. Gen. Mason M. Patrick and his deputy, Brig. Gen. Billy Mitchell, endorsed the plan and got it approved by the War Department. They obtained the cooperation of the Navy Department, the U.S. Bureau of Fisheries, and the Coast Guard. The three essential elements of success were the fliers, the type of aircraft selected (five, including one prototype, were built to Air Service specifications), and logistic support at all 52 foreign stops planned.

The selection of pilots was as careful as selection for promotion to higher rank. Orders came down through channels: All pilots who wanted to be considered for a round-the-world flight were to complete a questionnaire that included the question, "Why should you be selected for this flight?" One of the pilots subsequently chosen, Lt. (later Maj. Gen.) Leigh Wade, recalls answering "past experience." The number of applicants was reduced to 50, then 25, then 15. Seven names were forwarded to General Patrick, who selected four. Besides Wade, Maj. Frederick L. Martin (the flight leader), and First Lieutenants Lowell H. Smith and Erik Nelson were chosen.

Each pilot was given the opportunity to select a "mechanician." Martin chose Sgt. Alva L. Harvey, Smith chose Lt. Leslie P. Arnold, Nelson selected Lt. John Harding, and Wade asked for Sgt. Henry H. Ogden. The eight men were sent to Langley Field, in Virginia, for intensive training in aerial navigation, meteorology, and first aid. While there, the pilots flew the prototype of the World Cruiser, a converted Navy torpedo bomber fitted with pontoons. None had seaplane experience.

Meanwhile, Erik Nelson helped choose the Douglas model for the flight, and he nursed the four Cruisers through the production line at the Santa Monica plant. The pilots tested them as they came off the line and promptly named them for American cities related to the four cardinal points of the compass. Martin chose *Seattle;* Smith, *Chicago;* Nelson. *New Orleans;* and Wade, *Boston.* Once the planes were ready, they were flown to Sand Point, Seattle, the official starting point. It took three weeks to assemble equipment, study maps, convert from wheels to pontoons, and make test flights. In the meantime, the headquarters of the Navy, Coast Guard, and Bureau of Fisheries radioed their people and told them to provide logistical support for the Air Service crews. Men were dispatched to the numerous stops en route to stockpile supplies and establish radio communications. The Navy was instructed to provide most of the support, which was divided roughly into two segments, through Asian waters and across the Atlantic from England westward. The Coast Guard promised to make two ships available to aid the flight in the area of

Alaska, as did the Bureau of Fisheries. As it turned out, this interagency cooperation proved vital to the safe return of the airmen.

On April 5, 1924, all was declared ready for departure. But, on takeoff, Major Martin, in the *Seattle*, dug a prop tip in the water and damaged it. He also punctured a pontoon on a buoy. Both prop and pontoon were quickly changed, and the four aircraft left Sand Point the next day. At first though, Wade found he couldn't get off the water with his load and had to discard a rifle, some clothing, and an anchor. He departed later and made his way alone to Prince Rupert, British Columbia, 650 miles away. When Wade arrived, he saw that the *Seattle* lay damaged in the harbor. Major Martin had leveled off too high and stalled in with a bone-jarring crunch. The left outer wing struts and guy wires were broken. Fortunately, local carpenters were able to shape new struts and rewire the wings.

U.S. Army Service pilots and mechanics pose for an official photo before the 1924 world flight. Left to right: Maj. F. L. Martin, Sgt. Alva L. Harvey, Lt. Leigh Wade, Sgt. H. H. Ogden, Lt. Lowell Smith, Sgt. Arthur Turner, Lt. Erik Nelson, and Lt. John Harding. Sergeant Turner was replaced by Lt. Leslie P. Arnold, a pilot, just before the start. (U.S. Air Force photo)

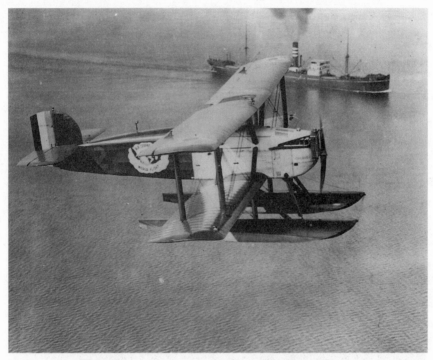

Awkward-looking by today's standards, the sturdily built *Chicago* and the *New Orleans* were the first aircraft to fly entirely around the world. The flight took 175 days. One aircraft crashed in Alaska; the other was abandoned at sea after it was damaged. (U.S. Air Force photo)

Martin's second mishap wasn't his last. Departing from Sitka, where the *Boston* and the *New Orleans* had nearly been lost in the harbor due to high winds, he and Sergeant Harvey were forced down on the leg between Seward and Chignik by an engine crankcase rupture. After a cold night adrift in the harbor at Cape Igvak, the *Seattle* was towed to Kanatak by a Coast Guard cutter and there repaired. Meanwhile, the other planes had gone on to Dutch Harbor in the Aleutians, where they were told to await the *Seattle*. Martin never caught up. On April 30, blinded by wind-driven fog, he crashed into a mountain on the Bering Sea side of the Alaska Peninsula. Both Martin and Harvey survived. After 10 tortuous days, they made their way to a fishing village, where they eventually were picked up by a Navy destroyer. Lieutenant Smith was named flight leader, and the three remaining planes were told to continue.

From Dutch Harbor, the route was to Atka and Attu, through spring williwaws that attack the Aleutians with unmatched fury. Rain, snow, and sleet pelted the three remaining planes as they plodded toward Atka.

Maj. Frederick L. Martin, commander of the world flight, and Sgt. Alva L. Harvey, just after their arrival at Port Moller on the Alaska Peninsula. Their aircraft had crashed into a mountainside in bad weather. (U.S. Air Force photo)

In the harbor at Nazan, the wind whipped the waves so furiously that it became impossible even to board the planes, let alone fly them. The six fliers were landlocked for the next six days before departing for Attu, the last island in the Aleutian chain. The 555-mile hop against driving winds took nearly eight hours.

The next leg was supposed to be from Attu to Paramushiro, in the Kuriles. Although the nearest land en route was the Komandorskie Islands, which belonged to the U.S.S.R., no diplomatic clearance to land had been granted the fliers. Nevertheless, if the going got too rough, they planned to land in Soviet waters. A Bureau of Fisheries vessel would serve as lighthouse and fuel depot.

This forethought paid off. Faced with strong head winds, the pilots landed near the U.S. vessel in the harbor of Nicholski and were promptly intercepted by a group of non-English-speaking fishermen who rowed out to meet them. Though cordial, they said, through an interpreter, that the pilots could not be invited ashore unless permission was granted from Moscow. Permission never came; next morning, the Americans departed for Japan.

They made six stops in Japan, all overflowing with formalities, good food, and sight-seeing. "At one stop, much to our dismay," General Wade recalled, "28 days of receptions had been planned. We compromised and boiled everything down to three days to give us time for engine changes and repairs."

The stopover in Japan by American planes flying from North America gave the United States a little-known aviation first: the Americans were the first to fly across the Pacific and thus link the Asian and North American continents by air.

While the Americans were completing the first quarter of their journey, pilots from five other countries—Argentina, France, Great Britain, Italy, and Portugal—were trying to beat them. Victims of inadequate logistics, all of the competitors failed.

Enjoying the fruits of good planning and maintenance, the six airmen flew down the lower edge of Asia via Shanghai, along the coast of French Indochina, across the tip of Siam, and up the Burma coast to Calcutta. Each landing was a new experience, with new hazards and dangers. Typical was the landing in the Yangtze-Kiang River at Shanghai. The harbor master, not knowing how much space the World Cruisers needed, had cleared the river for miles. The result was one of the world's largest sea-traffic jams.

While the wide sea-lane helped the pilots in landing, takeoff was a different matter. An old Chinese superstition says that the devil follows each sampan as it starts out in the morning. To cut the devil off, each skipper tries to steer across the bow of a larger moving vessel. As the Americans tried to take off, one at a time, the taxiing planes apparently served that purpose. All three pilots had to maneuver far down the river to find sufficient takeoff room.

As the planes edged south, both engines and pilots began to show the effects of tropical Asia. Although engines were throttled back, they still overheated. Exhaust pipes burned out with uncomfortable regularity. The crews discarded their heavy winter flying clothes and put on lightweight materials. It was the typhoon season, and each leg along southeast Asia was a test of their flying skill and luck. So were unknown floating hazards, which lurked just beneath the water on every takeoff and landing.

It was inevitable that engine problems would seriously hamper the mission. As they flew around the Gulf of Tonkin, Smith's engine began to overheat. He headed for a small lagoon near Hue and landed. Wade and Nelson circled overhead to be sure Smith and Arnold were safe, then went on to Touraine, a few miles away. During the next 70 hours, Lieutenant Nelson, with help from the natives, made a night trek through the jungle to the lagoon and arranged to have the *Chicago* towed upriver to Hue. Meanwhile, an engine that had been sent ahead to Saigon was brought by truck and boat to meet them. The old engine was removed and the new one installed: Smith continued to Saigon.

Saigon marked the southernmost latitude of the flight. The worst was yet to come, however. Heat and humidity took their toll on aircraft and men. Smaller fuel loads and longer takeoff runs from rivers crowded with all kinds of boats continually hampered them; but they persisted, flying from Saigon to Bangkok across the Malay Peninsula to Rangoon. This course was chosen, despite the fact that pontoons were attached, in order to save 800 miles around the peninsula.

Small mishaps continued to threaten one or another crew member. At Rangoon, Arnold almost drowned, Smith collapsed with dysentery, and Nelson's plane was rammed by a sampan. These obstacles were overcome, and the fliers continued on to Calcutta by way of Akyab, Burma, and Chittagong (then in India, now in Pakistan).

Their arrival in Calcutta marked 81 days and 11,232 miles of aerial circumnavigation. It also marked the end of overwater flight until the leg over the North Atlantic. The pontoons were removed and replaced by wheels—not an easy task, considering the time and place. Their maintenance area was The Maidan, a famous park in Calcutta. It was the only place with enough clearance for aircraft and equipment. The six Americans made their own repairs. The transformation from floats to wheels and the other maintenance work took three days. Smith broke a rib when he fell from the upper wing of his plane.

As much as anything, Smith's injury accounts for Wade's decision to take on Linton O. Wells as a passenger. Wells was not a stowaway, as was later reported. Wells was an Associated Press correspondent who had been reporting the crossing of the Pacific. Ordered to Calcutta for a follow-up story, he was to return to his Tokyo office once the flight departed. But Wells believed the big story of the flight lay ahead, and he pleaded to be taken along. "We sympathized with him," Wade told the author, "but gave him a flat 'no.' The . . . weather dictated [that] we keep the planes as light as possible. He didn't give up easily, though, and I finally gave in. His argument that he could fill in on the work shift for the injured Smith made sense." As it turned out, Wells tagged along for the next 2,000 miles. It wasn't until they reached Karachi, India, that an official War Department message denying Wells permission to fly caught up with them.*

The flight over India to Karachi was memorable for the 120-degree heat, goggle-pitting sandstorms, and near loss of the *New Orleans*. About an hour out of Karachi, with its Royal Air Force repair depot, *New Orleans's* engine blew apart. Despite three exploded pistons, broken connecting rod and wrist pin, and other damage, Nelson kept his oil-covered plane airborne and brought it in safely. The men arrived in Karachi on July 4. After three 16-hour workdays, the expedition departed and flew along the rugged coastline to Chahbar and Bandar Abbas, in Persia. The next day, July 8, after a grueling 10 hours and 35 minutes in the air, they reached Baghdad, some 920 miles away.

To reach Aleppo, Syria, the aviators followed the Euphrates valley. Any hope of a respite at Aleppo was dashed when a dinner given by their Turkish hosts lasted until 2:00 A.M. A tired group of fliers left at six, reaching Constantinople at 1:40 P.M. The fame of the American fliers preceded them and grew at each stop. The price of fame was increasingly time-consuming receptions and banquets. At Constantinople, officials had planned four days of festivities, but the men prevailed on their hosts to cut this to two days.

En route to Paris, they stopped to refuel at Bucharest, Budapest, and Vienna. On the morning of July 14, the fliers were airborne early, confident that they would reach Paris in time for the Bastille Day celebration. They were dog-tired and were looking forward to a few days' rest.

Thirty minutes after leaving Vienna, they flew into heavy rain and low clouds. They swooped below the clouds, following the Danube past Linz, then following a meandering course through mountain passes via Munich. A quick refueling was made at a small field near Strasbourg, in France. Of their arrival in Paris, Wade later said: "Near the city a flight of eight French aircraft intercepted us and gave escort to Le Bourget Field. . . . We landed at 5:15 on Bastille Day to an overwhelming welcome. . . . It took us an hour just to get free from the handshaking crowd."

---

* Wells later set a record as a passenger. See Chapter 2.

Arriving exhausted, they wanted nothing more than a soft bed; but it wasn't to be. First came small receptions, then press interviews, radio broadcasts, autograph seekers, and a stop at the Folies Bergere. They all fell soundly asleep during the show. Upon reaching their hotel, they hung this sign on each door: "Please do not wake us until 9 tomorrow unless the hotel is on fire and not then unless the firemen have given up all hope."

The 215-mile leg from Paris to London was made along a commercial air route that linked the two cities. The fliers had a mixture of escorts: French, English, military, civilian, and photographic. Their stay in London was brief, just long enough for them to receive an official welcome from the British government and to learn that the British world flier, Stuart MacLaren, who had been reported lost, was safe.

The fliers arrived at their next stop, Brough-on-the-Humber, 17 days ahead of schedule, which gave them ample time to overhaul their aircraft—install new engines, replace the wheels with pontoons, and otherwise prepare for what was considered the most treacherous leg—the

One of the World Cruisers has an engine change at Brough-on-the-Humber, England. The wheels were exchanged here for pontoons before attempting the flight across the North Atlantic. (U.S. Air Force photo)

North Atlantic. Meanwhile, T.P. Magruder, commander of the U.S. Navy's Light Cruiser Division Scouting Fleet, was positioning two light cruisers and two destroyers at Edinburgh to guard the flight. He also fanned destroyers and light cruisers out along the route. The ships stretched from Greenland to Boston. Provision was made to man a radio chain from Hull, in England, to Boston via the Orkney Islands, Iceland, Greenland, Labrador, and Nova Scotia.

All was ready for the giant step. Three planes left Brough-on-the-Humber for Kirkwall, in the Orkneys. They arrived at Scapa Flow just as a fog bank rolled in. Anchored outside the bay was the U.S.S. *Richmond*, flagship of the protective armada. Fog grounded them for several days, but on August 2, with a slight clearing, they decided to chance a takeoff. Barely 10 minutes into the flight they ran into a dense curtain of fog that extended down to the water. They flew straight into it, trying to maintain visual contact by close-formation flying, all the while pushing their planes upward, hoping to get on top of the fog.

Chicago and *Boston* cleared the fog layer at about 5,000 feet but saw no sign of Nelson in the *New Orleans*. Nelson, meanwhile, was fighting his way out of a prop-wash-induced, high-speed spiral. He finally shot through thin fog and spotted the water just in time to pull the plane up to level flight. He gained altitude and broke out of the fog. Seeing no sign of the others, he continued alone to Iceland. By now, Smith and Wade had decided to return to Kirkwall and sound the alarm. Smith swooped low over the main street and dropped the message: CONTACT RICH-MOND START SEARCH FOR NELSON. The pair landed in the harbor and waited for word. Early that evening a wireless message came through from Nelson: GOT IN PROPELLER WASH IN FOG WENT INTO SPIN PAR-TIALLY OUT OF CONTROL CAME OUT JUST ABOVE WATER CONTINUED ON LANDED AT HORNAFJORD ALL OKAY.

Smith and Wade took off the next day to catch up with Nelson. But the North Atlantic claimed the *Boston* after all. Wade's plane suddenly lost oil pressure midway between the Faroe Islands and the Orkneys. Although he landed safely, the plane went under while being hoisted aboard the *Richmond*. In describing the incident later, Wade said he stood "on the ship's deck [and] watched the crane swing over the side and drop its hook. . . . The lift signal came and the *Boston* started rising out of the water. Then all hell broke loose. Five thousand pounds of hoisting gear wrenched off its mooring and crashed down on the plane. The *Boston* was a broken mess."

With all hope of salvaging the *Boston* gone, Wade made the decision to cut the plane loose and let it sink. In doing so, he said he felt like he was giving up a part of himself. Indeed, all of the airmen on the flight felt the loss. Smith later wired General Patrick: "There is not one of the gang that did not shed a few tears over Wade's disaster."

The *New Orleans* is towed ashore after landing at Reykjavik, Iceland. (U.S. Air Force photo)

Upon learning of the loss of the *Boston*, the War Department ordered the prototype of the World Cruiser delivered to Wade and Ogden in Nova Scotia. Meanwhile, after Wade's ditching, Smith and Arnold continued to Iceland in the *Chicago*, where they joined Nelson and Harding. The four men then flew to Reykjavik. There they radically revised the flight plan. Angmagssalik, their next landing point, in Greenland, was now choked with ice. It took them more than a month to find an alternate route. The attempt took so long, in fact, that military leaders had begun to consider canceling the flight. Smith and Nelson, however, steadfastly refused to abandon the venture. They flew directly to Frederiksdal, on the southern tip of Greenland. This leg would be the most dangerous part of the trip. It meant an 835-mile flight along a route outside the steamship lanes and the naval escort. If either plane went down, they would be in trouble.

They departed from Reykjavik on August 22, accompanied by Antonio Locatelli, an Italian who was making a world-flight attempt for Italy. Locatelli sped on ahead in his faster Dornier-Wal, a twin-engine monoplane. The first 500 miles of the trip were flown in perfect weather; the

The *Boston* is prepared for a hoist aboard the USS *Richmond*. Piloted by Lieutenant Leigh Wade, it developed an engine malfunction between the Faroe Islands and the Orkneys. Wade made a forced landing in the ocean. (U.S. Navy photo)

last 300 were a flier's nightmare, with fog too high to climb over and virtually too low to fly under. The two American aviators chose to fly at wave-top level to take advantage of what little visibility existed. But cruising at 90 mph at such an altitude left little or no reaction time for dodging the icebergs that might be lurking in the fog. Somewhere along the route, the two planes became separated. Each pilot had to pick his own way through the mist. Both reached Frederiksdal safely, however, some 11 hours after leaving Reykjavik.

Locatelli was less fortunate. When he flew into the mist, he sat his plane down rather than risk flying into an iceberg. Rough water battered his plane and kept him from taking off. He drifted for three days before being rescued by the *Richmond*.

The four airmen who beat the odds against low-altitude flying in the ice-choked ocean arrived wet and exhausted but with the realization that only 560 miles now lay between them and North America.

The flight to Ivigtut (Greenland) and Icy Tickle (Labrador) was made

As the *Boston* was being lifted to the deck of the destroyer, the hoist broke and crashed down on the plane. Since it could not be repaired, Lieutenant Wade made the decision to let it sink. (U.S. Navy photo)

in even fiercer weather. A few hundred miles from the coast of Labrador, the *Chicago's* fuel pump failed, and Arnold began the muscle-wrenching task of pumping the emergency wobble pump by hand. He kept it up for two hours. "I pumped until I thought I just couldn't pump anymore," he said. "Then I'd look down at the cold water and start all over again."

The *Chicago* made it into Icy Tickle on sheer muscle power. The two planes were swamped by newsmen, movie cameras, and official greeters. Two days later, *Chicago* and *New Orleans* flew into Pictou Harbor, Nova Scotia. There Wade and Ogden waited anxiously to join the flight again in their new airplane, *Boston II*.

Although Boston was to have been the fliers' first landing point in the United States, fog, their old nemesis, forced them down in Casco Bay, off Mere Point, Maine. Once the weather cleared, the planes flew on to Boston. The next stop was Mitchell Field, in New York, then on to Bolling Field, in Washington, where President Coolidge and his cabinet had been waiting three hours in the rain to welcome the triumphant fliers.

After Washington, they hopscotched across the country, stopping at 14 cities in 9 states. Fame was assured when they reached Seattle, at 1:30 P.M. on September 28. As the aircraft circled Sand Point Airfield preparatory to landing, the pilots aligned themselves wingtip to wingtip and landed simultaneously. According to Wade, the arrangement had been agreed on earlier so historians would never have to argue about who landed first.

Lt. Leslie P. Arnold receives congratulations from President Calvin Coolidge and Secretary of War John W. Weeks at Bolling Field, Washington, D.C., September 9, 1924. Secretary of the Navy Herbert Hoover is at left. (U.S. Air Force photo)

Just as the men who made the epochal flight have been glorified, so were their machines. The *Chicago* sits at center stage in the National Air and Space Museum in Washington. The *New Orleans* rests in a place of honor at the Museum of Flying in Santa Monica, California. Because *Boston II* wasn't one of the original aircraft, it was returned to service after the flight. In 1966, the fuselage and some parts of the *Seattle* were taken to the Aviation Museum at Anchorage, Alaska, by Bob Reeve, president of Reeve Aleutian Airways, and by Lowell Thomas Jr.

Although the crews and their aircraft are today part of aviation history, one aspect of world flight continues to stir debate—the geographical starting and ending points of the flight. The three airports mentioned are Clover Field, near Los Angeles; North Field, in San Diego; and Sand Point, in Seattle. General Wade, the only living pilot of the group, gave the author

Despite the significance of the first world flight to aviation progress, Monaco is the only country to honor the feat with a stamp. A U.S. Postal Service committee turned down a commemorative stamp as not being of sufficient public interest. (*Air Line Pilot* photo)

this view of the debate: "I feel more affirmative about Clover Field since that's where the four aircraft began the attempt, on St. Patrick's Day in 1924. But the first location where we actually touched down, both going and coming, was North Field, San Diego; next was Clover Field, then Sand Point. But the Air Service, for some reason, chose to use Seattle as the official starting and terminating point of the flight."

However the debate is resolved, aviation historians agree that the first world flight was a tribute to American persistence, skill, and resourcefulness.

Those first world fliers defied great odds against success with their fragile planes and flew into parts of the world that were not yet ready for aviation. They had flown over 28 countries and colonial mandates and made 72 stops for fuel and maintenance. In addition to being the first to circumnavigate the globe by air, they were first to cross the Pacific, first to cross both the Atlantic and the Pacific, and first to cross the China Sea.

There have been many successful world flights since 1924, but no one had ever completed such an arduous flight solo in a single-engine, open-cockpit plane. One ex-military pilot from Dallas, Texas, had attempted an eastbound solo flight in 1990 but planning difficulties in Europe caused him to fly the plane back to the United States. In 1991, Carl Hayes, with a Russian navigator aboard, set out to conquer the globe in a 225-hp Stearman trainer flying east from San Diego, but he crashed in Colorado two days later. In September 1993, Frank Quigg, a Canadian businessman, departed Vancouver in a 275-hp Waco biplane and reached Bombay in only 15 days. However, he developed hepatitis there and abandoned the flight.

It was Robert Ragozzino, 42, a veteran 8,000-hour corporate pilot of Norman, Oklahoma, who was the next to try and the only one to succeed so far. He completed a global flight of more than 23,000 miles in a World War II biplane between June 1 and November 17, 2000, in five days less than the original world fliers. It was a dream that he had been nurturing since he learned about the first world flight by the Army Air Service fliers. The difference was that he wanted to be the first pilot to make the flight alone in a biplane with an open cockpit and one engine.

During the years that he was thinking about such a flight, Ragozzino found the ideal plane. It was a 1942 Navy N2S Stearman, a biplane trainer that had been used for crop dusting in Texas since the end of World War II. It was barely flyable when he bought it, but he tore it down to its skeleton, then meticulously rebuilt it during the next six and a half years. He obtained a 450-hp Pratt & Whitney engine, had an extra 350-gallon three-tank gas system installed, and attached a 150-gallon belly tank from a Navy Corsair fighter underneath the fuselage to give the plane a 1,600-mile range. Updated instruments for instrument flight, a fuel computer, and modern avionics were installed, including four ground positioning systems. The reworking was completed by recovering the framework and wings with new fabric and giving it a paint job that featured logos of his sponsors. After hundreds of hours of restoration and modification work, Ragozzino felt he knew everything there was to know about his plane. Since he would be his own mechanic, this knowledge would come in handy during the flight.

The world flight was preceded by a number of long distance "warm-up" flights. One trip was in 1996 from San Diego to New York, which he completed in 29 hours' flying time, making him the unofficial record-holder for flying a biplane solo from coast to coast. Two years later, he beat his own record with a flight of 18 hours and 30 minutes flying time. By the time he was ready for the world flight, he estimates he had flown 60,000 miles in open-cockpit aircraft, 750 hours of that time in the Stearman.

He decided to fly eastward on the world flight to take advantage of generally prevailing winds in the Northern Hemisphere instead of westward as the first world fliers had done. His route of flight was from Wiley Post Airport in Oklahoma City, Oklahoma, to New York and Bangor,

Robert Ragozzino, first since 1924 to fly around the world in an open-cockpit aircraft, is shown flying in the Stearman trainer over the mesa near Grand Junction, Colorado. The extra gas tank mounted between the wheels is from a Navy Corsair fighter plane. (Courtesy Robert Ragozzino)

Maine. One anonymous sponsor, who had made three world flights himself, accompanied him in a chase plane as far as Goose Bay, Labrador. Ragozzino then flew without an escort across the North Atlantic via Greenland and Iceland, through Scotland, France, Italy, Greece, Egypt, the Middle East, India, Southeast Asia, Taiwan, and Japan.

Unlike other world-girdling pilots, Ragozzino likes to fly at very low altitudes, usually from 50 to 500 feet above the ground or water. "This way," he says, "I get to take pictures and see the people at work and play, and get a glimpse of what life is really like in the various countries. You can't get that at high altitudes." Everywhere he landed, he said he found warm receptions from the local people.

It was in Chitose, Japan, that he had a frustrating 37-day wait while applying for permission from the Russian government to land at Petropavlovsk on the Kamchatka Peninsula. If he couldn't land in Russia, the longest and most dangerous flight lay ahead—a 1,400-mile leg from Kushiro, Japan, over the Bering Sea to Shemya in the Aleutians. The estimated range of the 1942 Stearman was 1,600 miles under no-wind condi-

Wearing a flight suit for the cold weather ahead, Ragozzino prepares to taxi out for takeoff. He flew most of his world flight at altitudes of 500 feet or less when possible to get a good view of the countryside. (Courtesy Robert Ragozzino)

tions. It would be a risky flight, and the alternate airport was at Adak over 400 miles farther.

"The forecast was right," Ragozzino said. "The weather was good, but as I got halfway, I encountered a stiff headwind and knew I couldn't make it. I radioed the Russians that I was going to have to make a 'mandatory fuel stop' at Petropavlovsk. This was an emergency that is permitted by international law."

Ragozzino admits he thought he was going to be arrested but, to his surprise, was greeted by 25 smiling Russians who just wanted to see the airplane. Instead of being jailed, he was treated to good meals and laughingly called "the Crazy Cosmonaut" by the local natives. However, no one there could give him permission to depart; it had to come from Moscow, nine time zones away.

It took 27 days before his hosts received permission to let him go. While he waited, he had an oil leak in the engine's primary oil cooler caused by the cold weather. Parts were shipped to him by air from the States. It took telephone calls from retired Air Force Brig. Gen. Tom Stafford, a former astronaut, and Oklahoma senator Jim Inhofe to persuade the Russian government to grant him permission to depart. He took off and encountered high winds, snow showers, and freezing rain. He chose to land at Attu, a few miles short of Shemya, because the high winds favored its single north-south runway. He then proceeded along the Aleutians through the worst weather he encountered on the whole trip. "There was rain and fog in the mountain valleys," he said. "The visibility was very poor and I had to trust my navigation to be sure there wasn't a mountain ahead of me."

He made subsequent landings in Alaska, Canada, and the "south 48" before arriving at Wiley Post Airport under clear, cold Oklahoma skies to a rousing welcome. In the 170 days he was gone, he had made 55 stops and was airborne for 175 hours, thus besting the elapsed and flying times of those first world fliers.

Ragozzino's flight was successful because of excellent planning and a masterful modification of the World War II Stearman. In the sophisticated world of modern aviation, he was able to receive accurate weather reports and forecasts in most instances. A Canadian flight planning organization eased his way through customs and sped up refueling by making prior handling and visa arrangements at each stop.

Ragozzino's World War II trainer is parked at one of the Aleutian Island airports awaiting favorable weather. He completed the world flight in five days less than the original Army Air Service fliers did in 1924. (Courtesy Robert Ragozzino)

First to fly around the world solo in an open-cockpit aircraft, the Norman, Okla-homa, pilot poses beside the Stearman that he had personally modified. The plane was on display for many weeks at an Oklahoma museum after the flight. (Photo by the author)

Ragozzino said his biggest problem was not the flight itself but raising the money from sponsors for the trip. He said he would make the trip again if a sponsor could be found, but he would like to have another person along and a chase plane following. He encourages a woman pilot to make the attempt, because no woman has ever made such a flight. He says, "A world flight is very doable in most of today's aircraft." But he advises those considering such a trip to "do their homework" and learn all they can before departure. His own successful flight is a tribute to aviation progress and serves to further memorialize the first world flight made by those Army Air Service fliers 76 years before.

2

JOHN HENRY MEARS: INSATIABLE GLOBE-TRAVELER

John Henry Mears, a New York theatrical producer and writer, was one of that breed of twentieth-century Magellans who have an all-consuming desire to circle the globe faster than any other human. As a youngster he had read Jules Verne's novel *The Tour of the World in Eighty Days*. "The idea of chasing at top speed around this earthly sphere fired my imagination." He followed news accounts of George Francis Train, Charles Fitzmorris, J.W.W. Sayre, Henry Frederick, and Colonel Burnley-Campbell, each of whom had gradually reduced Nellie Bly's record of just over 72 days, until Andre Jaeger-Schmidt more than halved it in 1911, making the journey in 39 days, 19 hours, 42 minutes, and 38 seconds.

Mears studied Jaeger-Schmidt's itinerary closely. Then he collected his own set of steamship and train schedules. He learned the truth of an old traveler's axiom of those days: "Nothing lies like a time table." He spent many weeks figuring out schedules in a half-dozen languages, later recalling: "Even after I thought I had these travel schedules licked, I couldn't be sure of anything. They wouldn't stay put. They were absolutely 'subject to change without notice.'"*

The itinerary Mears finally settled on included departure from the offices of the *New York Sun* on July 2, 1913, passage on the *Mauretania* to Fishguard, England, a train to London and Dover, channel steamer to Calais, then by train to Paris, Berlin, St. Petersburg, and Omsk, to Harbin,

---

* All quotes are from *Racing the Moon* by John Henry Mears. New York: Rae D. Henkle Co., 1928.

21

Manchuria; Mukden, China; and Pusan, Korea. In Pusan, he boarded a steamer for Japan, entraining at Shimonoseki for Tokyo, where he caught the *Empress of Russia* for the Pacific crossing.

As the ship approached Victoria, British Columbia, and it looked as though Mears had a record within his grasp, a heavy night fog moved in, causing the captain to stop all engines and drift until late the next morning. To try to overcome the delay of at least half a day, Mears sent a message by wireless to a friend, John Pelleter, who volunteered to pick him up on his yacht and take him to Seattle. Mears described what happened next:

> Forty miles from Seattle a hydroplane came in sight and circled over the yacht. Its pilot, Christopherson, dropped a message to the deck. It was an invitation from the Seattle *Post-Intelligencer* that I make the final lap of my journey to Seattle by air. I told Pelleter that I'd like to do it and our engines were immediately stopped. The plane, landing on the water, maneuvered alongside. With men of the yacht's crew holding off the plane's wing to avoid damage in the moderate sea . . . I climbed through wires and took my place on the wing, as indicated by the pilot, a rather precarious place as compared with the luxurious cabin of my Fairchild.*
>
> We flew over the boats on the Sound and headed for Seattle at 60-miles an hour.
>
> The plane brought me to Pier No. 2 in almost no time, and I found a great crowd awaiting me. Hands stretched down to lift me up to the dock. The most exciting lap of my trip was ended, for this was my first air hop.
>
> After [I was] interviewed, photographed and congratulated, someone told me, in order to be comforting I suppose, that the last man who had gone up with Christopherson had fallen out and was still in Puget Sound.

Mears continued his trip by train. Going by way of St. Paul, Chicago, and Cleveland, he arrived at Grand Central Station in New York City. On August 6, 1913, he raced to the offices of the *New York Sun* and recaptured the record for the United States. Mears had beaten Jaeger-Schmidt's record by 3 days, 22 hours, and 7 minutes. His reward, besides the worldwide publicity, was a congratulatory telegram from President Wilson.

Mears's record stood for 13 years, until Linton O. Wells, a news reporter, and Edward S. Evans, a New York businessman, teamed up to challenge it in the midtwenties. Wells, a world traveler continually in pursuit of stories for his news service, and who had been reported as a stowaway on the Air Service world flight the year before, was restless in the fall of 1925. During a casual conversation with Evans, he expressed a desire to do something different. The record established by Mears in 1913

---

* An aircraft Mears had acquired in 1928 for a second attempt.

entered the conversation, and the two men decided it could be beaten, especially if airplanes were used for large segments of the trip. They agreed that Wells would personally check out the overland facilities and schedules in Europe, Russia, and Asia. In the late fall of 1925, Wells set out with his son. They traveled by boat and train east from New York to Yokohama, then retraced their route. Hotel and visa arrangements were made along the way; boat, train, and airline schedules were verified.

Back in New York, Wells worked out an itinerary calling for a journey of 20,000 miles, using planes on 11 of 22 legs, trains on 7, ships on 3, and an automobile for the last dash from a New York airfield back to the World Building, their official starting place. Wells estimated an elapsed time of 27 days and 12 hours.

Wells and Evans left the World Building at 1:30 A.M., June 16, 1926, and motored to the dock, where they boarded an ocean liner. On June 22, they arrived at Cherbourg, France. Wells and Evans had originally planned to take an airliner from Cherbourg to Paris and Berlin, but no plane was available; so they drove to Paris, then took a plane to Berlin, stopping at Cologne and Magdeburg. Once again, the two men could not reach their destination by air. Instead, they were driven to Berlin but managed to catch a plane with only an hour's delay for the next leg. They flew across Germany and the Soviet Union, with stops at Danzig, Koenigsberg, Smolensk, Moscow, Krasnoufimsk, and Kurgan to Omsk, where they caught the train to Manchuria. For reasons not explained, Wells and Evans separated briefly at Harbin. While Wells continued on the train, Evans flew from Harbin to Mukden, where they rejoined and continued their journey by train to Pusan, Korea. There they caught a ship for Shimonoseki and entrained for Yokohama, where they boarded the *Empress of Russia*, landing in Victoria, British Columbia, Canada, nine days later, nearly two days off their planned schedule.

In his book, *Around the World in Twenty-eight Days,* Wells recounts his difficulties in attempting to fly on the newly founded U.S. airlines:

> Two days before we were scheduled to land at Victoria we were informed that the Sikorsky plane which we had chartered for the flight from Seattle to New York had failed us. . . . it is sad but true that . . . there were no commercial planes available for such a flight. For a considerable sum . . . Walter T. Varney, of Boise, agreed to fly us to Salt Lake City; the Western Air Express sent Captain C.C. Mosely from Los Angeles to Salt Lake City to fly us from that point to North Platte, Nebraska; . . . and Eddie Stinson left his airplane manufacturing business in Michigan to stand by. . . . Not knowing that any of these planes would be available, we called upon the Army Air Service and met with an instantaneous response.
>
> It wasn't the fault of the Army Air Service that we failed to reach New York City on schedule. . . . Lieutenants Matthews and Koenig made beauti-

ful flights between Seattle and Pasco, where Varney picked us up and carried us to Salt Lake City. We landed there after dark and Captain Mosely's
machine being unequipped to fly over the mountains at night, we laid over
there until dawn. Despite strong head winds we made a fast flight to North
Platte and there transferred to the two fast Army planes brought from Fort
Riley by Captain Boland and Lieutenant Fisher. One of these planes was
equipped for night flying; the other was not; and had it not been for continuous strong head winds we should have landed safely at Fairfield, Ohio
before dark. As it was, both planes had to land at Rantoul, Illinois for fuel.
An hour of daylight still remained, but two hours would have been necessary for the flight to Fairfield, [so] we elected to remain overnight at Rantoul, accepted the hospitality of Major McChord, and at daybreak, [were] off
again, arriving safely in New York on July 14, 1926 to establish a worthwhile
record.

Wells's careful planning had paid off. The 20,000 miles were covered
in 28 days, 14 hours, 36 minutes, and 5 seconds at an average speed of
30 mph and at a cost of $32,000.

Mears had avidly followed the progress of Evans and Wells. After they
had completed their trip, he conceived of the idea of racing the moon
around the earth. He knew that the moon requires 27 days and 7 hours
for a complete circuit, 31 hours less than the time Wells and Evans took
to set their record. To him, the notion of regaining the record took on new
meaning. Since the moon travels on a schedule that never changes, he
said, "it became incumbent upon me to get a jump on the smirking lady,
so that even a temporary setback en route would still find me in a position
to carry on. This meant that neither trains nor automobiles must be used
in Europe and Asia. The airplane alone would do."

This decision made, Mears paid $24,000 for a new Fairchild single-
engine monoplane with folding wings for easy moving from airport to
dockside and loading aboard vessels for crossing oceans. Powered by a
400-hp Pratt & Whitney Wasp engine, the Fairchild could average about
120 mph. It was christened *The City of New York* by the wife of New York
City's mayor, James Walker.

Not being a pilot, Mears chose Capt. Charles B.D. Collyer, of the U.S.
Army, a former instructor, skywriter, and airmail pilot, to take the controls. While Collyer trained in navigation at the Seaman's Institute in New
York City, Mears took care of the business and publicity aspects of the
venture. Arrangements for fuel, oil, and other supplies had to be made,
and permission to overfly and land in 12 countries had to be obtained,
the most difficult being the Soviet Union. As Mears noted, "there was no
skirting [Russia], and their good will and aid were essential."

It took a year for Mears and Collyer to complete their preparations.
As their self-imposed deadline approached, Mears wanted a mascot to

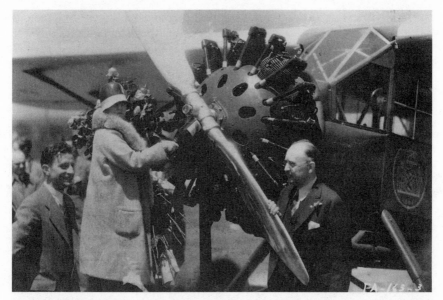

The City of New York is christened by Mrs. James J. Walker, wife of New York City's mayor, before the start of its journey around the world. Capt. Charles B. D. Collyer (left) was the pilot for John Henry Mears (right), a theatrical producer. Earlier, Mears was the first globe-girdling passenger to use an aircraft for any part of a world-circling trip. (National Air and Space Museum photo)

accompany them. Vivienne Osborne, a New York waitress, presented him with a purebred Sealyham Scotch terrier pup. The terrier was named "Tail Wind" and declared an official passenger.

The Fairchild was tested at Curtiss Field, on Long Island, in early June 1928. It was towed to the pier in New York and stowed on the deck of the liner *Olympic*. Empty, the plane weighed 2,600 pounds, including equipment and extra fuel tanks. Collyer had decided to use the recently introduced all-steel propeller and took along two extra blades. He also stowed aboard a tail-skid assembly, a landing gear strut, a complete spare engine-cylinder assembly, valves, valve springs, spark plugs, and magneto parts. Emergency equipment included "concentrated" rations, a gallon of water, a four-quart Thermos for milk and coffee, and a rubber "airaft."

Mears and Collyer arranged with Capt. Harry Rogers to be flown in his seaplane to the ship when it cleared Ambrose Light outside New York Harbor. Because their departure time would be calculated from the time they actually left the dock aboard Rogers's plane, they could save six hours. Next morning at dawn, a brief ceremony was held at Pier A. Mears and Collyer explained why they were leaving aboard Rogers's plane and not their own. On July 28, 1928, at 5:00:45 A.M., they stepped into the seaplane and took off in haze to intercept the *Olympic*. The haze soon turned to fog, and Rogers had difficulty feeling his way out of the harbor to open sea. Rogers sighted the *Mauretania*, but thought it was the *Olympic*. He landed beside the ship, but recognized it as the *Mauretania*, and they hastily took off again. At that moment, the *Olympic* loomed in the fog a few miles away and Rogers landed beside it. Mears and Collyer were hoisted aboard.

Six days later, the *Olympic*, now four hours behind schedule, entered the harbor at Cherbourg, where *The City of New York* was taken ashore by lighter and unloaded. Collyer taxied through the narrow streets of the city to the airport with the Fairchild's wings folded. While Mears and the American consul fought the local red tape to obtain a permit to depart from the port city's commandant, Collyer had the gas tank partially filled and ran up the engine. After promising not to fly over French fortifications, Mears received verbal permission to leave. At 2:00 P.M., now six hours behind schedule, Collyer took off from the short dirt strip and headed along the seacoast. He soon found the Seine, which he followed to Paris's Le Bourget Airport.

After paying a hurry-up courtesy call at the American embassy and the office of the prefect of the Seine in downtown Paris, Mears and Collyer raced back to the airport and at 6:00 P.M. were off for Berlin, 600 miles away. They were overly optimistic. At 9:00 they were only halfway. "We were both so weary after the strenuous excitement of our first day in Europe," Mears explained, "that we let the bright lights of Cologne's flying field lure us to rest." They weren't expected in Cologne. As *The City of New York* taxied up to the hangar, it was surrounded by police. It took some time for the aviators to convince the officials that the papers they carried were genuine. Their baggage was searched and a small handgun was discovered. It was agreed that if Collyer gave up the gun, they would be free to stay the night and depart early the next morning.

After two hours of fitful sleep, they roused themselves and left for the airport for a predawn takeoff. Collyer, trying to navigate by comparing his map with landmarks, realized that nothing was checking out. After nearly four hours of flight, and an hour past the time that they should have sighted Berlin, he turned to Mears and pointed downward. They landed in a pasture as the sun came up. A farmer and his children came breathlessly running up, but no one spoke English. "After much gesticulation," Mears said, "[the farmer] conveyed to us . . . that we were to stay in the hayfield while he went for assistance. He [left] through a gate. . . . Boys, girls, geese and Tail Wind went dashing after him. In spite of our anxious desire for haste, Collyer and I started laughing."

The farmer returned with a fellow German who had been a soldier and could read maps. Collyer and Mears kept saying to him, *Berlin, Berlin*. The soldier studied their map, then carefully traced with his finger the route to the capital. Collyer immediately took off. They located the city and at 9:00 A.M., July 6, landed at Tempelhof Airport. They were still behind schedule. A crowd had been waiting all night. As soon as Mears and Collyer could break away, they rushed to the American embassy to pay their respects, then drove to the Soviet embassy, where they received assurance that they would be welcome in the Soviet Union. Certain forms had to be filled out in triplicate, however, and photographs were needed. Once again, they rushed around the city, found a photographer, and complied.

At 2:00 P.M., now 12 hours behind schedule, Collyer lifted the Fairchild off the sod field and headed toward Koenigsberg, in East Prussia. There, though Mears and Collyer were impatient to refuel and keep going, they were convinced by a group of German pilots that tackling the next leg to Smolensk and landing there at night would be dangerous. The field wasn't lit, and landmarks were difficult to locate at night.

Tired and hungry, the fliers agreed to wait. They were taken to a nearby restaurant. Meanwhile, Collyer had developed a severe sore throat. A German doctor advised bed rest for the next two days, but Collyer would not hear of it. He insisted that he was well enough to continue. Dog-tired, they were driven to the field and, at 2:00 A.M., now 15 hours behind schedule, were once again in the air, headed for Moscow.

The flight was easier than expected. As Collyer and Mears approached the city, two Red Army scout planes joined them and escorted their plane to the airport, where they landed. They refused a tour of the city but acquiesced in a reception and lunch at the field. The speeches, all in Russian, were long. Mears and Collyer were fidgety with impatience. They explained as best they could to their hosts that they were now 17 hours behind schedule and had 500 miles to fly before nightfall.

Collyer's throat still bothered him. He ate chocolates and swigged cognac, which provided the only relief he could get for his aching throat. They leveled off and flew a compass course to the Volga River, landing at Kagan, the last stop in Europe, at 8:00 that night. They were 17 hours behind schedule.

"No mother worried more over an only child than I did about Collyer," Mears said. "His throat was so painful now that he could not eat solid food, and he was beginning to show the effects of the . . . days and . . . long nights without sleep. He . . . tried, in a voice as harsh as a crow's, to assure me that he felt great. Neither . . . spoke of failure, but in our minds lingered the thought that there were 17 hours to make up, and only four days [in which] to do it. We were still 6,000 miles from Yokohama. If we failed to arrive by noon on July 12th, the *Empress of Russia* would sail without us. And there would be no other way for us to cross the Pacific in time to make our record."

Violent storms had been following them eastward. After a brief stop at Kagan to refuel, they continued toward the rugged Ural Mountains. Collyer flew the tricky course through mountain passes and canyons, fighting updrafts, downdrafts, and other turbulent winds. Despite their apparent slow progress, they averaged 100 mph on this leg and landed at Kurgan, the first stop in Siberia. Three hours had been gained, but only 78 hours remained in which to complete their crossing of the world's widest continent.

While Collyer stayed at the field to supervise servicing, Mears accepted an invitation to get breakfast. He ate heartily but was eager to rejoin Collyer. Once again, however, his hosts insisted on ceremony, making long speeches and proposing grandiose toasts. When he was finally able to get to the airport, he found Collyer already in the cockpit, chafing to be off. Without a word, he started the engine, barely waiting for Mears to toss Tail Wind in the cabin and climb aboard before taxiing.

They continued east to Novosibirsk, landing at dusk after seven hours in the air. They had gained two precious hours. Collyer, still suffering from the tonsillitis that had caused his sore throat, was exhausted; all he wanted was food and sleep. But after only two hours' sleep they were in the air once more, with an estimated 4,364 miles yet to go to Yokohama. The *Empress of Russia* was docked and waiting.

At eight that morning, they landed at Krasnoyarsk to refuel for the longest leg ahead—1,068 miles to Chita. They left as soon as they could. Six uneventful hours later, as they approached the city, they were treated to a display of fireworks and a field bright with flares and torches. "In a single day," Mears said, "we had made up every one of the 12 hours lost in Europe!"

Exulting in their success, the two tired airmen accepted the 13 courses of an elaborate banquet and were treated to a reception committee whose members spoke excellent English. After only a few hours' sleep, though, they took off, this time heading for China. They crossed the Gobi Desert and the Noni and Sungari swamps, arriving at Mukden, where they were greeted by a group of Americans, including the U.S. consul, and hundreds of Chinese. They were treated to a home-cooked American meal, a hot bath, pleasant conversation, and a fair night's sleep.

It was now July 11. The flyers, accompanied by Tail Wind, had flown more than halfway around the earth. Yokohama was only 24 hours away. The day began badly, however, Mears later recalled. "It was the most perilous and exciting day of our journey." Mukden, a double-walled city at the time, was under martial law. Collyer and Mears knew nothing of the curfew, and arose at 1:00 A.M. for breakfast with their hosts. Getting to the airport would not be easy. No one was permitted beyond the inner wall between sunset and sunrise without a special permit. Although the papers they were issued upon their arrival seemed proper for entering the city, the papers weren't good enough to satisfy the night guards. As Mears and Collyer were being driven to the inner gate, they were delayed by guards who forbade them to pass. It took Mears and Collyer two hours to convince the authorities to allow them to reach the airfield.

"We had no thought of danger or disaster as we bade farewell, . . . circled the field, . . . and [headed] for Japan," Mears wrote later. As they crossed the border with Korea, though, "oil, thick and black, appeared on the instrument board, first a few drops and then a shower and then a steady fountain. . . .

> While my knowledge of aircraft enabled me to grasp the significance of this leak, I hoped that I was exaggerating the danger. Looking below I saw that there was no place to land, and studying the map hastily, I remembered noting before that there was not a place within a hundred miles where we could land the heavily laden plane without cracking up. I looked at Collyer to see what he meant to do.
>
> I saw—and my heart stood still.
>
> He signalled me to take the controls. I obeyed. I was numb with wonder. I did as I was commanded and did not stop to call his attention to the obvious fact that I had never had a stick in my hands before.
>
> While I sat there stiffly, I saw Collyer climb from the cabin half-way out of the plane. I saw him shift his body to find a better balance, and then open the cowling around the engine.
>
> I was impotent in a great crisis. For if anything happened to Collyer I should not be able to land the plane to come to his rescue. I should have to go on and on until I ran out of gas, and then drop.
>
> I saw Collyer screwing off an oil cap, and then I saw his hands relax. I watched him shift his position and crawl slowly, with cautious, minute movements, back to the cabin, He crawled in and with great calm wiped his hands and took his place at the controls, which I very happily yielded to him.
>
> It was quite a while before I dared to ask what the trouble had been, and if it was serious. After a while, my trembling fingers found a pad of paper in my pocket, and I wrote, "What was wrong?" He grinned and wrote: "Damned Chinese mechanic didn't screw the cap of the oil tank securely."
>
> I uttered a hearty sigh. Now that the danger had passed, and what I thought had been a serious leak was due to the hot oil expanding and coming through the top, I was able to enjoy the liberating sense of relief.

That wasn't the only scare Mears received on that leg of the flight, however. As the Fairchild cruised eastward, visibility lessened, and Collyer descended in an attempt to find better visibility at a lower altitude.

Suddenly, a solid wall of dark rock loomed directly ahead of us. We were headed [straight] for it. At the rate we were moving, we could not possibly avoid it. I closed my eyes to shut out the menacing darkness of the mountain, braced my feet in a vain effort to impede the progress of the plane, gripped the edges of the seat and waited for the crash. My next impression was [one] of a sharp movement in a new direction. The plane responded easily to Collyer's quick action. We zoomed upward almost perpendicularly. It was a close call. As we went over the top of that peak, I swear we trimmed the leaves off the highest trees with our landing gear.

With the near miss behind them, Collyer became concerned about the loss of oil. He landed at Pingyang, where the plane was refueled and the oil tank replenished. After takeoff, *The City of New York* flew over Seoul, down the peninsula, and out over the Sea of Japan. There, Mears and Collyer encountered head winds and cloud cover at every altitude they tried. Collyer climbed, trying to get on top; failing that, he descended as low as he dared—to within a few feet of the water—only to find no improvement in visibility. He climbed back up to 3,000 feet and flew on instruments until he thought they were over land.

Although they had planned to proceed directly to Tokyo once Collyer could establish his position, he decided to land at Osaka as soon as he had identified it. Only two hours' fuel remained in the tank. If they had not landed at Pingyang, they would have been forced down in the Sea of Japan. The stop at Osaka also proved one of Collyer's wisest decisions. After an hour on the ground, they headed for Tokyo. As they progressed, fog and mist gradually obscured their vision; daylight became twilight. Approaching Yokohama en route to Tokyo's airport, they saw heavy fog rolling in from the sea.

Fortunately, Collyer's dead reckoning was flawless. As they approached their estimated time of arrival over Yokohama, Collyer spotted the city below. He turned to the heading that would take them to their destination, Tachikawa Field, 20 miles outside Tokyo. Mears describes the harrowing situation as he sat helplessly in the rear:

Flying very low, in an effort to pick out rivers and railways, we found more than we bargained for. . . . two railways, where the map indicated only one. Not knowing which . . . to follow, Collyer took a compass course in the general direction of the Tachikawa Flying Field. We missed it in the fog and darkness.

We circled . . . and we were eventually attracted by a dull glow in the heavens, for which we headed. This proved to be Tokyo. With this city as the basis of his calculations, Collyer set out again in search of our objective, twenty miles away. Once again we failed to pick up the beacon. Back we went to Tokyo and from [there] again set forth. . . . four more times we did this, failing each time. The situation had become desperate. Our gasoline . . . was now almost completely [gone].

In any other area, with a wide field available, one might glide down to a landing. But in [the] area surrounding Tokyo, one dared not undertake this. We knew that in all directions stretching out from [Tokyo] hung a network of high-tension wires. Contact with these would mean death. I had worried my way—via Collyer's genius as a flier—through the most trying conditions, but at this hour and moment, I felt that at long last we had been beaten. And yet I didn't seem to care. The contest waged by my pilot with adversity seemed to fascinate me, so that I viewed Collyer's struggle . . . as if I were a mere onlooker safe in an arena. I was fascinated by the struggles of this master pilot. . . . [Collyer's] actions [seemed] . . . peculiarly spasmodic. In his right hand he held an ordinary pocket flashlight. For a moment he would concentrate its rays on the instrument board and I would see, with him, that our gas was almost gone, of nigh teaspoonful proportions. His quick glance would gather in the ominous signalings of the instruments on the dashboard. The next instant, he would wheel about in his seat and flash his light on the compass [which] . . . was suspended from the roof of the cabin immediately behind him.

It might have been five times that we flew back to Tokyo to start for Tachikawa anew. It might have been more. We had started with about four hours of gas and we had been aloft almost all of that time. Clearly, we [could] not be able to [return] to Tokyo [to get] our bearings again. There I sat marveling at my companion's courage and clear-headedness, feeling at the same time that the next minute might be our last. Collyer was moving back and forth . . . when suddenly he seemed to become calm. He turned to me, pointing ahead. There was the faint flash of a beacon! But by this time, I must have been reconciled to defeat. For my mind seemed slow in accepting an optimistic view of the situation. There came to me the thought: "Is this really the flying field beacon, or have we gone farther astray and run into a lighthouse beacon? Byrd was fooled that way."

But it was the beacon we sought. For as we approached it a mass of flood lights [lit] the field . . . [it was] the most welcome sight I had ever seen, [or] ever shall see. Charlie made a beautiful landing at seven forty-five. In another ten minutes we would have been out of gas! I stepped upon the field with Tail Wind in my arms and said nothing to Charlie at the time. Words are inadequate at such moments. I patted him on the back and I knew he understood. We were surrounded by a great crowd of cheering, excited Japanese. [Flashbulbs popped] and moving picture cameras ground out the picturized record of our arrival and greeting.

Mears and Collyer had been given up for lost by Japanese officials. When darkness came, it seemed certain that the Americans were doomed. Their safe arrival at Tachikawa was greeted with a rush of attention from the world press as the news was radioed around the world that the two fliers would make their departure by ship the next day.

Although all they wanted was sleep, the two tired airmen were escorted to a nearby hangar decorated with American and Japanese flags and "heavily toasted," as Mears recalled. From there, they were rushed by automobile to the Imperial Hotel for a lavish dinner and interviews. It was three in the morning before they and Tail Wind could get their much-needed rest.

Five hours later, they rose, had breakfast, and made an auto tour of Yokohama. They drove to the docks, where the Fairchild was hoisted aboard the *Empress of Russia*. They departed on schedule as Japanese crowded the dock and cheered. A.J. Hosken, the ship's captain, was well aware of the significance of his passengers and their cargo. Intrigued by the idea of racing the moon, he ordered the ship to increase speed, and they made the run of 4,848 miles to Victoria, British Columbia, arriving 12 hours ahead of schedule.

After checking the aircraft and running up the engine, Collyer supervised unloading and towing the plane to an airfield nearby. Encouraged by the thought that the record was within their grasp, Mears and Collyer took off before dawn, July 20, 1928, and headed for Seattle. Once again, fog impeded their progress. When he couldn't find the airport at Seattle, Collyer flew on to Spokane, 300 miles east, where they landed without incident.

Mears and Collyer had planned to fly to Omaha, but they changed plans while still aboard ship because of a message from the governor of Minnesota, requesting "the honor of your stopping here" in Minneapolis-St. Paul. They agreed to the stopover, and left Spokane for the 1,250-mile hop nonstop over the Rocky Mountains, arriving 12 hours later to another round of press interviews and official ceremonies. After a few hours' rest, they left for Bellefonte, Pennsylvania, a stop on the airmail route over the Alleghenies. They had scarcely left Minneapolis's Chamberlin Field when the weather changed, and it started to rain. Collyer decided to land in Chicago to refuel and assess the weather. Once again, it was a wise decision. The worsening weather was reported thickest over the Alleghenies along the route airmail pilots called the "Hell Stretch."

Collyer studied the weather reports and concluded that they could avoid the worst of the weather by flying a compass course to the southern shore of Lake Erie. They flew this course through limited visibility for about 300 miles, then decided to land at Cleveland. Checking again and finding that the weather over the Alleghenies had not improved, Collyer determined to fly on instruments and overfly Bellefonte. To Mears, this leg of the flight was as frightening as the night they searched for Tokyo in fog and darkness. "Our experience in the Alleghenies will always remain a sort of blank spot in my memory. For here we were hemmed in by such fog as I had never known before. The clouds were so thick that . . . there was no telling what was up and what was down—what was east or west, north or south. We were as lost in this area . . . as we were that dreadful night outside Tokyo. But we were trapped for two hours in the Alleghenies somewhere, and it became absolutely necessary to get our bearing accurately. . . . Collyer wheeled south, doubling partly [back over] our course. There came at last one or two quick breaks in the fog and rain and we caught glimpses of mountain tops below us, but best of all of the Susquehanna River. Here was a clue well known to my veteran pilot, and he followed it."

They landed at Middletown, Pennsylvania. After taking on gas and phoning ahead to Miller Field, on Staten Island, they headed east on the final leg. En route, Collyer got out his shaving kit and water from his canteen and shaved while holding the stick between his knees. The long journey wasn't over yet, however. As Collyer pressed eastward over familiar territory, the mist and haze turned to fog. By the time they passed over Newark, New Jersey, the ceiling had dropped to 500 feet. A wall of white hampered forward visibility; once more, it seemed as though the airmen's constant enemy—fog—might prevent a victorious homecoming.

Collyer began flying in ever-wider circles, looking for Miller Field or some usable landmark. Suddenly, in the murk he spotted the familiar hangars and buildings of the field, with a crowd encircling it. At 6:55:12 P.M., July 22, 1928, Collyer eased the faithful Fairchild out of the mist, and they touched down. Newspaper reporters and photographers rushed forward, shouting questions and commands to the pair of happy airmen and their mascot.

Still the trip wasn't over. Mears and Collyer had to return to their starting point. They were taken by automobile to St. George, on the northern tip of Staten Island, where they boarded a ferryboat and crossed to Pier A, on Manhattan. There, they were greeted by a crowd of more than a thousand. Mears and Collyer were told that they had officially broken the record set by Wells and Evans two years earlier. According to the official timer, they had traveled 19,725 miles in 23 days, 15 hours, 21 minutes, and 3 seconds at an average speed of 840 miles per day. Fifteen days were spent on steamships and eight in the air. They had covered 11,190 miles by air and 8,535 by ship.

Mears and Collyer had clipped a full five days off the Wells-Evans mark. They received many letters and telegrams, but probably the most prized was that from President Coolidge: "I wish to express my congratulations upon the splendid record you have accomplished in circling the globe. In demonstrating the practical use of aviation for communications

John Mears and Charles B.D. Collyer, pilot of *The City of New York,* pose awkwardly for photographers after completing their 1928 world flight. Three months later, Collyer, with Harry Tucker, set a coast-to-coast speed record from New York to Los Angeles of 24 hours, 51 minutes in a Lockheed Vega. (National Air and Space Museum photo)

between all countries of the world, you have done much to advance this new science."

This globe-circling effort was not only a tribute to Mears and Collyer's planning and navigation, it was also an indication of the advances made in the reliability of aircraft and engines, especially of the latter. The 400-hp Pratt & Whitney Wasp engine had performed flawlessly. Mears and Collyer also deserve recognition for their pioneering effort in a seldom-mentioned aspect of world flight. In *Man's Fight to Fly,* about his experiences as chief timer for the National Aeronautic Association, John P.V. Heinmuller describes an aviation first which deserves to be mentioned: "They were equipped with special chronometers and proved for the first time the supreme merit of chronometric time for aviators. Also, they maintained a valuable record of fuel consumption as to time. . . . For hundreds of years chronometers had been considered of importance principally to sea navigation, but these two record-breakers proved the worth of a good chronometer in air navigation. They understood how essential *exact* time knowledge [is] in wrestling with navigational problems. . . . In my opinion, Mears and Collyer were the first to experiment with and to solve problems of correct timing and position calculations. They really were the pioneers of correct time in the air."

Mears and Collyer returned in July, and Collyer was in the news four months later. On October 24–25, he set another record. Flying a Lockheed Vega, and accompanied by Harry Tucker, he flew from New York to Los Angeles nonstop in 24 hours and 51 minutes, to establish a mark for flight west across the United States. The same plane *Yankee Doodle*, piloted by Col. Arthur Goebel, had set an eastbound record of 18 hours and 58 minutes the previous August. Collyer's career ended tragically. In November 1928, caught in a blinding rainstorm in the Bradshaw Mountains of Arizona, he ducked into Crook's Canyon but couldn't get out. He crashed into the wall of the canyon and was killed.

Mears's appetite to be fastest around the globe was whetted again when, in 1929, the *Graf Zeppelin* beat his record by completing the trip in 21 days, 8 hours, and 26 minutes (see Chapter 3). Mears had followed the progress of the dirigible, and when it appeared certain that his record would be broken, he went to work on a new venture. He wanted to be fastest around in a heavier-than-air craft for the entire trip. Mears enlisted the help of Hubert Huntington, an expert navigator, and the two spent several weeks poring over maps and hydrographic charts of the Northern Hemisphere.

When they completed their work in the spring of 1930, Mears chose Henry J. Brown, an experienced airmail pilot, to do the flying. On August 1, after brief test hops, the men left Roosevelt Field and made the trip from New York to Harbour Grace, Newfoundland, in the fastest time recorded up till then. Mears never realized his dream, however. During takeoff from a poorly lit strip early the next morning, the aircraft hit some rocks and was badly damaged. Both men, slightly injured, returned to New York a few days later. Mears never tried again, and perhaps it was just as well: a one-eyed pilot from Oklahoma, named Wiley Post, and his navigator, Harold Gatty, were planning to set a record of their own.

These attempts were typical of those in the 1920s. Spurred by journalists' sensational accounts of daring flights, and by public enthusiasm, fliers from many nations were inspired to seek headlines. Lindbergh's feat of flying the Atlantic alone in 1927 had fired the public imagination as no airplane flight ever had. The honor of being first or fastest became all-important, but what was significant from a historical standpoint was that valuable lessons were learned with each attempt at the record. Even failures by the overly adventurous and the ill-prepared had lessons for those wise enough to analyze the causes of the failures.

3

TRAILBLAZERS OF OTHER NATIONS

Although the globe had been circumnavigated entirely by air in 1924, three years later it still did not seem possible to duplicate the feat without government support. The expense and the logistical problems were too formidable. Meanwhile, fliers from other countries were demonstrating the long-distance capabilities of their aircraft.

The year 1927 opened with the Italian aviator Francesco Marquis De Pinedo attempting to become the first to fly from Europe to North America and return. Departing from Rome in a Savoia-Marchetti seaplane on February 8, De Pinedo flew along the west coast of Africa and across the South Atlantic to Fernando de Naronha Island, then down the South American coast via Rio de Janeiro to Buenos Aires. Turning north, he flew over the heart of the continent to the Caribbean to the harbor at Havana. From there, he pushed on to New Orleans, then west to Roosevelt Dam, near Phoenix, Arizona. There, his plane, the *Santa Maria*, was destroyed when a careless spectator flipped a cigarette in a pool of gasoline near the plane.

Extremely disappointed but undaunted, De Pinedo immediately ordered a replacement Savoia-Marchetti sent by ship from Italy. When the aircraft arrived, he christened it *Santa Maria II* and continued on his tour. Despite running out of gasoline between Newfoundland and the Azores on the return flight, and being towed for three days, De Pinedo arrived in Rome on June 16, 1927. Although his flight had been overshadowed by Charles Lindbergh's transatlantic flight of May 20–21, De Pinedo had achieved a measure of success by crossing the Atlantic twice by air.

The hypnotic effect of these aviation successes wasn't lost on other pilots. Numerous long-distance flights were made in 1926 and 1927.

English pilots made record-setting trips to Australia, India, and Africa. Between March 2 and June 15, the Portuguese pilot Sarmiento De Beires flew in a seaplane from Lisbon to Rio de Janeiro, a distance of 8,250 miles. Shestakoff, a Russian, made a round-trip flight (August 20 to September 1) of 10,250 miles from Moscow to Tokyo. De Barros, a Brazilian flier, flew (October 1926 to April 1927) from Genoa to Fernando de Naronha Island. The Dutch recorded a round-trip flight (October 1–25, 1926) by a pilot named Koppen, from Amsterdam to Batavia, Java, a distance of 17,400 miles. The Swiss credited a pilot named Mittelholzer with an 8,300-mile flight from Zurich to Cape Town, South Africa, December 1926 and February 1927.

The French, in an effort to establish a place for themselves in the record books, wanted to send a goodwill flight of aircraft full circle around the world. Some of France's best pilots had failed to conquer the Atlantic, and several had been lost in the attempt, including Charles Nungesser and the one-eyed François Coli, popular airmen who felt they were destined to become the first to achieve Paris–New York honors. Flying an open-

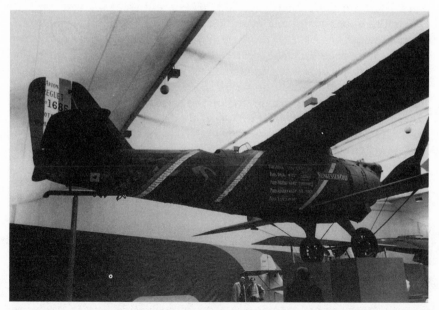

This Brequet XIX was taken around the world by French Capt. Dieudonne Costes and Lt. Cmdr. Joseph Le Brix via the South Atlantic, South America, and North America. It was then transported by ship to Tokyo and flown to Paris through Southeast Asia, India, and Greece. Named the *Nungesser-Coli* after fellow airmen who vanished on a flight from France to the United States, it hangs today in the French Air Museum at Le Bourget Airport near Paris. (Photo by the author)

cockpit, single-engine LeVasseur PL-8 christened *White Bird*, they disappeared in the mists over the Atlantic on May 8, 1927, never to be seen again. Success for France finally arrived in the persons of Capt. Dieudonne Costes, a World War I ace-turned-test-pilot, and Lt. Cmdr. Joseph Le Brix. They chose a Brequet XIX biplane manufactured by the company for which Costes was chief pilot. Powered by a single Hispano-Suiza engine, the aircraft was christened *Nungesser-Coli* in tribute to the lost airmen.

The two Frenchmen departed from Paris's Le Bourget Airport, October 10, 1927. After a remarkable nonstop flight of 2,658 miles in 26 hours and 30 minutes, they landed at St. Louis, in Senegal. There, they waited four days for good weather, then headed west across the South Atlantic. Heartened by the reliable performance of the Hispano-Suiza, they decided to bypass the minor stops that their predecessor had found so useful, and headed for Natal, Brazil. Twenty trouble-free hours later, after many radioed position reports from Le Brix, the Brequet landed at Natal. The night landing damaged the propeller slightly, but it was soon repaired.

The successful continent-to-continent crossing by Costes and Le Brix marked the first time the South Atlantic had been crossed nonstop by airplane. With no radio navigation aids to guide them, they had crossed 2,125 miles of ocean and made landfall only 25 miles from their intended destination.

When the propeller was repaired, the two fliers proceeded down the eastern coast of South America; then they crossed the southern Andes, to Santiago, Chile. In recounting this leg, Costes and Le Brix recalled encountering severe storms and fog on the coast. Costes told reporters: "I would rather cross the Atlantic again than make that trip down the coast." The weather on the western coast was far more pleasant as they flew from Chile to the 12,000-foot-high airport at La Paz, Bolivia, a route never before traversed by air.

Meanwhile, Charles Lindbergh was making a goodwill tour of Latin America. The Frenchmen turned north from La Paz, hoping to meet him. But their paths never crossed. They flew to Lima, Peru; Guayaquil, Ecuador; and Panama City, Panama. They crossed the isthmus to Colon; then went on to Caracas and Baranquilla, Venezuela, before returning to Colon, Panama; thence to Guatemala City and Mexico City. On February 4, 1928, the *Nungesser-Coli* arrived off the coast near New Orleans, and the airmen were escorted to a landing by U.S. Army and Navy planes. Pushing on after the arrival ceremonies, Costes and Le Brix flew to Washington, D.C. By the time they arrived in New York, Costes and Le Brix had logged 215 hours in flying 23,000 miles. The only mishap had been the nicked propeller at Natal.

A new engine was installed while they were in New York, and the Brequet was flown to San Francisco. Costes and Le Brix spent several weeks in San Francisco, then boarded a ship for Tokyo with their plane partially dismantled and stowed in the hold. Upon arriving in Tokyo, they reassembled the *Nungesser-Coli*, leaving the city April 8. They made long hops, first to Hanoi, then Calcutta, Karachi, Basra, Aleppo, Athens, Marseilles, and finally Paris—an itinerary that took six days. On the evening of April 14, Costes and Le Brix landed to a triumphant welcome by 100,000 people.

Costes and Le Brix, though they had not flown entirely around the world, had covered 35,944 miles in 338 hours' flying time. In doing so, they brought honor to France through their persistence and by proving that French flying machines were at least the equal of Americans', or those of any nation.

The youngest, luckiest, and certainly most inexperienced pilot ever to fly an airplane in a globe-circling attempt must be the 21-year-old F.K. Baron von Koenig-Warthausen, the son of a German count. Warthausen's mother was the first woman in Germany to make a flight on a scheduled passenger airline, and he credited her with helping him obtain the consent of his father to buy the plane in which he made his world flight.

The young baron attended schools in England and Germany. During his last year at the University of Berlin he learned of a prize—the Hindenburg Cup—to be presented each year by President von Hindenburg for significant achievements in sports flying. The cup was to be given for "either a number of short feats in aviation or one flight of enough importance to help the cause of amateur flying." In May 1928, Warthausen asked his father to buy him an airplane, which the latter did. He took ground instruction at a flying school in Magdeburg for several months, and after 12 hours of solo flying was awarded a pilot's license. The plane he bought was a Daimler-Klemm powered by a two-cylinder, 20-hp motorcycle engine, which Warthausen proudly christened *Kamerad*. Weighing only 560 pounds, the fragile, low-winged craft had a wingspan of 38 feet and could be flown as a glider when the engine was detached. According to Warthausen, "it was very stable and was furnished with a two-cylinder motor of maximum 20 horsepower [and] had a cruising speed of 70 mph. The gliding angle is [an] important [safety] feature. . . . [It] enables the flier to glide 14 feet on either side to every foot of altitude that he attains; in other words, if the flier wants to come down without using his engine, from a height of a mile, he has a diameter of 28 miles in which to make his landing."[*]

At the time he got his license, Warthausen did not intend to make a

---

[*] F.K. Baron von Koenig-Warthausen, *Wings Around the World*, New York: G.P. Putnam's Sons, 1930.

flight around the world. After a mere 17 hours of solo time, he decided to make a nonstop flight from Berlin "to some point east, in Russia, as far as my fuel would carry me and as far as Moscow, if possible." His goal was to win the Hindenburg Cup by making an exceptionally long solo flight in a sports plane that was neither military nor commercial in design.

Warthausen received no encouragement from family or friends. Even his instructor, Arndt Benzler, who accompanied him to Berlin, tried to dissuade him. "About the only preparations that I had to make for this flight were the procuring of visas from the Polish and Russian governments. . . . My equipment consisted of one altimeter, a rocket pistol, gas and oil gauges, a kick starter, a gas pump, a switch for a single magneto, a thermometer for registering the temperature of the air, a pocket compass, a small case of tools, and the necessary maps. I looked my plane over very carefully, loaded it with gasoline and oil and, as the motor seemed to be working perfectly, had only to wait for good weather."

The weather Warthausen wanted arrived on August 9, 1929. Just before midnight, he took off from Tempelhof and headed east. He took with him only his passport, a toothbrush, and a Thermos of hot tea. He estimated that, with 50 gallons of fuel on board, he could cover the 1,180 miles to Moscow with a safety margin of about 1,300 miles.

As soon as he was airborne, Warthausen picked up strong westerly winds. He quickly estimated that he was making about 90 mph instead of the 60 or 70 he had calculated. "This was my first night flight and it was thrilling . . . to see the lights of Berlin . . . disappear. . . .

> After I left the city I began to realize that I had never flown more than 40 minutes at a stretch before, this being the time requirement in sustained flight for obtaining a license in Germany. The night was clear . . . and not too cold . . . I had good luck and, after only four hours of [flight], I flew over . . . Danzig, . . . just at dawn.
>
> I waved my homeland goodbye, . . . then [flew] on over endless swamp and forest land in the direction of Lithuania. From Lithuania on, the landscape was . . . interesting, but I hated to think what might happen if I had to make a landing in the swamps. . . . Here and there I saw a tiny house with a thatched roof, but between these houses were always vast stretches of [swamp], alternated by forests and lakes. I crossed the Beresina River [and] ran into a terrible rain storm. It came down in such torrents that my vision was completely lost. My plane started to lose altitude and was gradually forced down to a little over a hundred feet. I was directly over a small forest. As soon as I cleared this, I found myself over a small Russian town and with difficulty managed to avoid the dome of the village church and a tall flour mill. The rain . . . had spent its force and I was again able to gain some altitude.
>
> I had been in the air about 14 hours. As best I could figure it, I had made

Capt. Wolfgang von Gronau, a German pilot, without the approval of his government, pioneered an air route between Germany and the United States in 1930. He
repeated the feat a year later. In 1932, he piloted the *Grönland-Wal* (*Greenland
Whale*) around the world westbound. (National Air and Space Museum photo)

about 1,100 miles. . . . Since the rain continued and I was becoming chilled, I decided to make a landing in the first place that showed itself suitable to me . . . when I found a fairly flat piece of land [near the] small village, I made my landing. I narrowly escaped a telephone pole but otherwise nego-tiated it successfully.

In spite of the rain, my descent had been observed, and in a few minutes I was surrounded by . . . peasants. . . . I [pulled] out my small pocket edition of a Russian dictionary [and] attempted to ask where I could get a tele-phone. At the time I bought this dictionary, I had not [considered] that the Russian alphabet differs so greatly from the Latin, and I soon found out that I was unable to make myself understood. But through mouth and hand gestures, I finally got across . . . that I wanted a telephone and that I wanted to get in touch with Moscow. With an escort of smiling Russians, I walked into the village and from there made communication with the German Act-ing Consul in Moscow and a few people who said they would be out very shortly to get me. They advised me that I was only ten miles from Moscow and that the distance could be covered in half hour's time.

Very shortly . . . I was picked up and driven into Moscow. I immediately telegraphed Berlin of my arrival, the distance I had made, and the time in which I had made it.

Warthausen stayed in Moscow five days. During that time, he changed his mind about returning to Germany. Instead, he decided to fly farther, "exactly where, I did not know at that time." After meeting with the Soviet minister for war, who told him that he would enjoy good flying weather in the southern part of Russia, Warthausen decided to fly to Baku and from that point make further plans. He ordered a new propeller shipped to Moscow, "because I could see that rain would probably dam-age the one I had if I went much farther."

On August 15, Warthausen took off for Baku, 2,000 miles away. En route, he had to climb to about 12,000 feet to get over a mountain range, a prodigious feat for the underpowered, frail Daimler-Klemm. He fol-lowed the railroad track for the entire distance and arrived without inci-dent. Warthausen stayed in Baku five days. After locating some spare parts he had had shipped to him, he obtained a visa for Persia. He landed at Pachlewi, where he was told that malaria was widespread. He filled his gas tank, topped off the oil supply, and quickly left for Teheran. About 30 miles from the city, Warthausen made a forced landing on a road. For reasons never given, he had run out of gas but, ever the lucky one, he did not damage the aircraft. "I had no sooner hit the ground than a Ford car stopped at my side and, in good English, a man asked me whether he could be of any assistance. I told him that I had planned to make Teheran but had been forced down on account of lack of gasoline, whereupon he drained two gallons from the tank of his car and presented it to me. I was very grateful to him and when I offered to pay . . . he absolutely refused to accept anything."

After waiting for the hot sun to drop toward the horizon and the midday heat to subside, Warthausen flew to Teheran, where he was welcomed by the German ambassador and invited to stay at his residence for as long as he wished. Warthausen intended to return to Germany by train after a week to 10 days of rest, but "my stay here was made so pleasant and my time so well-filled that . . . it was fully four weeks before I departed from Persia." During his stay, Warthausen made several flights in the area. Once he made a forced landing caused by water in the gasoline. He hadn't filtered the gas through a chamois when the tanks were filled in Teheran. "It was a good lesson," he wrote: "from that time on, I never neglected this precaution."

After a month of carefree visiting, and fully intending to return home, Warthausen found that the nearest railroad to take him and his plane back to Europe was 600 to 700 miles distant. "Since I had to fly," he reasoned, "why not fly on?" That decision made, on September 23 he flew to Bushire, on the Persian Gulf, with stops planned at Isfahan and Qum. He made another forced landing short of Isfahan when it developed that he could not transfer fuel from the reserve tank to the main tank. After three days in Isfahan, Warthausen took off for Shiraz. Once more, he made an emergency landing, this time because of high winds and turbulence over a 14,000-foot-high range of mountains. "As my plane had a low landing speed," he reported, "I had not too much difficulty in bringing her down in the soft sand right on the edge of a precipice. On getting out, I discovered that I had stopped no more than 60 feet from the edge. I think this was the luckiest landing I made on the whole trip."

While the landing may have been lucky, the takeoff proved almost disastrous. With no food or water, and the temperature well above 100 degrees Fahrenheit, Warthausen determined to fly to the village of Jasd-i-Khast, a distance of about 25 miles. He turned the plane around, but discovered that he had no runway space. The many short bushes would impede takeoff and likely tear the plane's fabric. He took out his cigarette lighter and set fire to the bushes, burning as many as he could. After some four hours of this, he started to push his plane to a likely takeoff spot, but found that it wouldn't budge. Thick sand held the wheels fast. "I started my motor, thinking I could get some help with an idling speed. This was of no assistance, so I opened the throttle a little wider and, before I knew it, the plane had started to take off. I had to scramble over the tail and jump to the rear cockpit to bring it to a standstill. After considerable maneuvering, I brought it into a position from which I thought I could take off."

Once again, however, the sand was too soft. Each time Warthausen started a takeoff run, he found himself too near the precipice. Finally real-izing that he was taking too big a chance, he secured the plane to some low shrubbery and dug holes in the sand in which to sink the wheels and tail skid. By now, it was sundown. Taking his compass and a bag of silver coins to pay for whatever assistance he could find, he set out on foot, try-ing to follow a faint road through the valley. A bright moon was up, how-ever, and he had little trouble reaching Jasd-i-Khast, though he did have to walk through sand all night.

Warthausen's arrival stirred interest among the villagers, but he found no one who could understand his pleas for assistance. He hitched a ride with a mail automobile which, coincidentally, was making its weekly trip to Shiraz, 200 miles away. Warthausen felt encouraged; he had a German friend in Shiraz who, he was sure, would help him. Twenty-four hours and 14 tire punctures later, a tired, disheveled pilot knocked on the door of his friend's house and told him his story. The friend, never identified by Warthausen, immediately got out a Ford touring car and loaded it with tins of food; the two men then set off for the plane. They drove to Jasd-i-Khast and traveled the rest of the way on horseback, along with 12 Per-sians hired to help them. They reached the plane and spent the next four days constructing a runway 300 feet long. Warthausen moved the plane into position, checked the engine carefully, and warmed it up. Then he took off for Shiraz, where he spent the next six days.

He departed for Bushire, but made an emergency landing en route—again, for lack of gasoline! Several natives met Warthausen and escorted him to the home of a local sheik. He learned that he was only 12 miles from his destination; unfortunately, there was no gasoline available to get him there. After much talk during which Warthausen employed "all the Persian I knew and added to it a quantity of French, English and Ger-man," the sheik sent two of his men on camels to Bushire to obtain fuel. When they returned two days later, he took off for Bushire, where he was the guest of a pilot for the Junkers Company.

Warthausen's next decision was to fly on to Karachi, India, where he planned to take a boat for the return to Germany. Upon leaving Bushire, he flew over seemingly endless desert to Bandar Abbas, a city in southern Persia noted for its heat and extremely high humidity. For two days he stayed with the British consul, then left for Cape Jask. The next emergency that confronted him proved once again how luck followed him:

> I had proceeded about 60 miles along the coast when a peculiar noise developed in my motor. Not knowing how serious it might be, I decided to make a landing to investigate its cause. I found a little island but hesitated to land on it because I knew that if I could not get off easily, I would be isolated from all possible help, so I continued to look for a better place.

After flying for 10 minutes . . . I spied a flat piece of ground and made my landing. I looked the motor over carefully and found that the noise was due to . . . a screw [that] had loosened between the cylinder and the crankcase. I tightened this up but, in doing so, used too much force and broke off the head of the screw. After being tightened, it had to be secured by a split pin. I knew that I could not [secure the pin] so I decided that instead of taking a chance, even though the lower part of the screw remained intact, I had better fly back to Bandar Abbas and replace it.

Warthausen crossed the Gulf of Oman to the coast of Arabia and landed at Cape Jask on a natural airstrip, which he estimated about 15 miles long and 5 miles wide. The one plane on the field had been abandoned there two years earlier by a pilot trying to fly from Karachi to England; it had been cannibalized by pilots who needed parts as they passed through the area. Warthausen found that he was expected. The British consul at Bandar Abbas had telegraphed ahead to announce his coming. There were no autos available, so Warthausen was taken by donkey to the home of a wireless telegrapher who advised his young guest to follow the telegraph lines from there to Karachi. "If you should have any trouble, and be forced down," he was told, "climb a telegraph pole and cut the lower wire. This signal will immediately be registered in the nearest town and help will be dispatched immediately."

Warthausen crossed the border dividing Persia and Baluchistan and flew along the coast to Pasni, where he was again the overnight guest of a telegraph operator. He arrived in Karachi the next day and received a warm welcome from flying officers of the Royal Air Force. He wired his parents that he would decide within the next few days whether he would return to Germany by boat or partly by boat and partly by his faithful Klemm. He did neither. After a lengthy stay in Karachi, during which time he went on several hunting trips with his British hosts, Warthausen decided to fly across India to Calcutta. Flying the route Uterlai–Jodhpur–Nasirabad–Agra–Allahbad–Gaya, he arrived in Calcutta on December 23. He was met by Baron von Plessen, the German general consul, who informed Warthausen that he had won the Hindenburg Cup.

Once again, the young flier at first thought he had completed his odyssey, then changed his mind. After two months of sight-seeing, he felt the urge to see more of the Orient to the east. After receiving spare parts ordered from Germany, and making several test flights, he headed east once more, this time intending to fly to Singapore via Akyab, Rangoon, and Bangkok. He was welcomed at each stop by natives who were "curious almost to the point of being destructive." In Rangoon, the police had to keep the crowds back. "When I stopped at smaller places, both in Persia and India, or made a forced landing, the natives crowded about and in their eagerness sometimes made holes in the wings. If this occurred in places where glue and other repair materials were unobtainable, I was forced to employ my handkerchiefs as patches and stick them on with the white of an egg."

He stayed in Rangoon five days, then flew to Bangkok, arriving at dusk after a flight of nine hours. He intended to stay there only about 10 days, but his intentions were overcome by the unusual hospitality of the Siamese. He met the king of Siam, the crown prince, and the princess. The prince had been Siam's minister in Berlin for eight years and spoke German fluently. Warthausen was presented with a "rare and valuable specimen of Siamese cat." From that point on, the cat was his constant companion. As before, Warthausen took numerous side trips. He stayed in Bangkok five weeks, finally leaving for Singapore via Prachuap Khiri Khan and Sangra. The flight from Sangra to Singapore was 750 miles, the second-longest leg of his entire journey. He detoured several times, and the flight took more than 11 hours. He had thought of boarding a ship and returning home but decided to fly north through China to Japan. "Not only had I decided to take in China and Japan," he wrote, "I had by this time made up my mind that I would make the trip around the world, flying wherever I could, and thus accomplish something with a small plane which had heretofore been considered impossible by many experts."

Warthausen's original intention had been to load *Kamerad* aboard a boat at Singapore, sail to Indochina, and from there fly up the coast and then across to Japan: but he was advised by British officials not to try this route. Instead, he booked passage to Hong Kong, where he intended to off-load and continue along the coast and cross the China Sea at a narrow point. Once again, Warthausen was advised not to try this route; he stayed aboard and continued on to Shanghai, where he off-loaded his plane. He flew to Nanking and was tempted to make the overwater flight to Japan, but eventually decided against this plan. He and *Kamerad* and the cat took a boat to Kobe, Japan, where they waited for 10 days for the weather to clear sufficiently for the trip to Tokyo. He made several abortive attempts to push through, finally succeeding despite wind, rain, and fog. Detouring extensively so as not to lose sight of the ground, he made the trip in seven hours.

After three weeks of sight-seeing, Warthausen flew the 20 miles to Yokohama and boarded the *Siberia Maru*, sailing to the United States via Honolulu. The ship arrived June 8. Before he left Japan, however, Warthausen learned of the death of Huenefeld, a pilot friend. He decided he could pay Huenefeld "no higher tribute or honor in my own small way than to name my plane after him, because he was the inspiration of whatever I have done." When Warthausen reached Alameda Airport, in California, the rechristening was held before a crowd of 15,000. At the same time, Warthausen named his cat "Tanim"; but the American press covering the event promptly dubbed the cat "Felix," for the popular cartoon character.

Warthausen enjoyed the hospitality of San Francisco for 10 days, then, on June 19, departed for Los Angeles. Once again, his fame preceded him; he was met by the German consul and by city officials and spectators. Everyone wanted to see the famous German aviator who dared to fly such a small plane on such a perilous journey. Always the sightseer, Warthausen was taken on a tour of Hollywood movie studios and flew a Ford Trimotor transport. Reluctantly, he took off for San Diego, made two short flights into Mexico, then headed for El Paso. En route, he landed at El Centro and Tucson; but on the final leg to El Paso, he battled stiff head winds, which turned what was then a four-hour flight into an eight-hour one. He arrived just ahead of a violent storm and got *Huenefeld* under cover.

At six on the morning of July 12, 1930, it appeared that Warthausen's luck was running out. As he started for the airport in a taxi, with the cat in his lap, the cab was hit broadside by another vehicle. Warthausen, badly injured and unconscious, was rushed to a hospital, where his condition was classified as very serious. After a few days, though, he was out of danger and his injuries had begun to heal. Word of the accident quickly reached Warthausen's parents. Now an international celebrity, he was the center of attention. Many aviation personalities visited him, among them Capt. Leigh Wade, one of the round-the-world fliers on the 1924 flight.

Warthausen was concerned about Felix, or Tanim, who had escaped in the excitement of the accident. The newspapers, always eager for human-interest stories, publicized the cat's disappearance, and Felix/Tanim was finally located unharmed, sitting in a tree. He was taken in by some people who attempted to straighten out the crook in his tail by massaging it, thinking the tail had been injured in the accident.

Warthausen recuperated for two months. The *Graf Zeppelin*, which was on its famous globe-circling journey, had announced that its eastward route over the United States would take it over El Paso. He later wrote: "Can you imagine the inner excitement of a young German as he stood on the roof of the tallest building in El Paso and saw the giant Zeppelin slowly move into sight on the western horizon? If I had only been well enough to fly, I would have taken my little plane and gone out to greet it. I had to content myself with wiring Dr. [Hugo von] Eckener and he replied with a . . . telegram, in which he compared my plane to the little brother of *Zeppelin*. I was pretty proud of my countrymen as I watched that ship pass over the city."

While recuperating further at a hotel, Warthausen got word that if he could arrive in New York by October 31, he would win the Hindenburg

Cup for the second time. The date was important: it was the deadline for nominations. He was told that it would be awarded "for having circled the globe in a light plane with no accidents and no thorough overhauling." After pestering the doctors, Warthausen was released. He left El Paso on September 15 and landed at Big Spring, Texas, six hours later. He stayed overnight, then flew to Sweetwater, where he landed after dark on a muddy field. As he taxied to the hangar, the plane's left wheel sank, and the left wing crumpled. A group of people helped him drag the plane into a hangar where he assessed the damage. He immediately called the Aero Marine Klemm Corporation in New York, the American firm that had built his plane in the United States. The company's president told Warthausen that he would send a left wing and wheel assembly immediately, but only to Dallas; the express company wouldn't ship them to Sweetwater. Thus the problem became one of getting the aircraft to Dallas. The continuously lucky Warthausen found a truck driver who volunteered to drive plane and pilot. With the help of local mechanics, he got the landing gear repaired sufficiently to allow rolling the plane, and the tail was lifted into the bed of the truck. "It was a sight worth seeing," Warthausen commented "and created quite a stir as we passed through the different localities. My plane has a wingspread of 38 feet, and you can just imagine the difficulty we sometimes had in negotiating passage in the road. At last, to avoid congestion and inconvenience, we took the wings off the fuselage and, in this manner, proceeded to Dallas."

While the plane was being repaired, Warthausen was called back to El Paso to appear as a witness in a trial concerning the accident. He was awarded $1,500 compensation, which went a long way toward paying his expenses thus far in the United States. Returning to Dallas, he flight-tested *Huenefeld*, then flew to Oklahoma City. "I stayed here overnight," he wrote, "but in that short time I experienced another typical American trait (besides helping others in trouble). No sooner does my ship touch the ground and I have it housed in a hangar, than people approach it, take lead pencils from pockets, borrow them from friends, or ask them from me, and proceed to write their names and addresses on it. I have encountered this in every American airport that I have visited. Americans wish to write their names on airplanes, carve their initials on trees, and register their telephone numbers in every conceivable place. In Oklahoma City, I counted at least 50 new names on my plane after a one-night stay."

The flight from Oklahoma City to St. Louis and Chicago went without incident. In both cities Warthausen was given dinners by aviation enthusiasts; although he wanted to stay longer, he was worried about meeting the October 31 deadline. From Chicago, he wired ahead to book passage on the liner *Bremen* and on October 17 left Chicago for Detroit. Warthausen encountered a windstorm along the southern end of Lake Michigan so severe that a ferryboat was sunk at about the time he was struggling to get through overhead. He weathered the storm and sailed ahead smoothly until he was about 20 miles out of Detroit. Although it was now dark, Warthausen used the beacon of Ford Airport to guide himself in, and landed on the stubble field. "I hopped out, a little stiff from the cold, examined my motor, and found that I had a broken valve," he reported. "This was the first engine trouble I had had since I left Germany. I got out my tools and a light, took off one of the cylinders, removed my cat from the back of the plane, and proceeded to the road where I was picked up by a man in a car and taken into Detroit."

Warthausen wired the manufacturer's representative in New York for a valve, which arrived the next day and was installed. The weather front delayed his departure for four days, however. To shorten the distance to New York, he planned to fly over Canada. He obtained a Canadian permit and took off but had to land at London, Ontario, because of water in the gasoline. While Warthausen was clearing up this difficulty, a snowstorm enveloped the area. He waited for two days. When it cleared somewhat, he took off. "Scarcely had I reached a thousand feet of altitude when I encountered a headwind that permitted me to make only thirty miles an hour. Sometimes the wind was so terrific that I seemed to be standing still, and freight trains that were below me and going in the same direction seemed to be running away from me. . . . many times I would drop as much as two hundred feet. This was a terrible battle because it started to snow again and, in order to keep my bearings and follow my map, I had to fly reasonably low. At the end of four hours I gave it up and decided to . . . land. Below me, I could see what looked like an airport. I was correct in this guess, and made a landing in Hamilton [New York] on a field which is maintained by the Hamilton Flying Club."

Warthausen left Hamilton late the next day for Buffalo, where a reception was planned. Also awaiting him were Captains Wade and Smith. Again, weather delayed his departure; but when it cleared briefly, he took off. Encountering heavy rain, he made landings at Syracuse, Little Falls, and Albany, always soaked to the skin. Time was now critical. Warthausen checked the weather that lay ahead and against his better judgment took off from Albany in fog and drizzling rain. He described this important leg, one that threatened to be his undoing:

> I set my course along the Hudson River and, in order to see my way, I had to fly as low as a hundred feet directly over the river, because the mountains on either side were enveloped in fog. This was the worst part of the . . . trip in the United States. I . . . was a little worried about ever reaching New York. I had heard about a bridge that spans the Hudson and anticipated no difficulty in flying over it, but before I had expected it, the bridge

loomed suddenly into view, so suddenly . . . that . . . I did not know whether to fly over or under it. I negotiated a turn, flew back a short way, gained a higher altitude, and passed successfully over it. . . . After that, I continued my course directly over the river. The fog was getting thicker and the boats on the river more numerous. I proceeded at the one-hundred-foot altitude until I passed over what appeared to be a break in the river which resembled a lake. I knew I must be . . . close to New York so I took a little more altitude, looked at my map, . . . and [turned] southeast, flying diagonally over Long Island.

Here I had to take a big chance. I could not see very much below me, but it did not appear as though I might hit any tall buildings and, in some places, there seemed to be no buildings at all. The fog had lifted a little, so I was able to discern a wide strip of land on which I might land. I made a perfect three-point landing. . . . [Among] the people [who] came running . . . to meet me . . . [were members of] the welcoming committee, I had been fortunate on the entire trip, but it was just the sheerest luck that brought me down on Roosevelt Field that day.

Over the next three days, Warthausen was interviewed by newspaper and radio reporters. He was given an official dinner where he received the bad news that he probably could not qualify for the Hindenburg Cup since he would arrive two days past the deadline even if he caught the next ship to Germany. Warthausen made a quick trip to Washington by train to see the German ambassador. On November 15, he sailed from New York, with *Huenefeld* lashed on the deck of the *Bremen*. He arrived in Bremerhaven November 22 and was met by a delegation of German pilots. His plane was unloaded and readied for the flight to Berlin. The next day, he left but was forced down near Hanover by fog. Although Warthausen wanted to make the final leg to Berlin by air, he decided against it despite news that spectators and friends were awaiting his arrival at Tempelhof Airport and a large reception was planned. His only recourse, he felt, was to leave his plane in Hanover and take a train to Berlin.

Warthausen caught the next train for Berlin, but it was barely out of the city when the engine broke down and the passengers had to return to the station. He then hired an automobile and driver, but the fog that had grounded him also threatened to stop road travel as well. The driver persisted, however, and about midnight they reached Potsdam, on the outskirts of Berlin. Then a tire blew out. When Warthausen had not arrived by 10:30 P.M., a number of his friends set out by car to look for him. "Consequently," he reported, "I received official welcome on a roadside in the suburbs of Berlin by the glare of automobile headlights." He was rushed into the city, arriving at the Opera House at 2:30 that morning, "wet, cold and dirty." He was welcomed by officials of the German government and by his parents, who hadn't seen their son for 15 months. President von Hindenburg presented Warthausen with the cup he had won the year before—"a very beautiful loving cup which is the aspiration of all German aviators since it is solely a sports award entirely free from any commercial complications."

The plucky airman, a pure amateur and a flying novice, had accomplished a feat never repeated since. Warthausen had flown an estimated 20,000 miles in 450 flying hours and had used less than 1,000 gallons of gasoline, which cost about $300. He spent $70 for oil but figured taxicabs to and from airports had cost about $700. What was more noteworthy was the fact that he had flown over some of the most desolate areas on earth in a single-engine, open-cockpit aircraft. Although he made several forced landings, none were directly attributable to engine failure, and he survived them without injury. Warthausen set no records, and he sought none, but he must go down in aviation history as the most consistently lucky pilot ever to circle the globe. Inexperienced but resourceful, he managed to solve problems of logistics that would have discouraged many others under similar circumstances, especially when not driven to make a mark for themselves. His success was also a tribute to the Daimler-Klemm aircraft and its superbly reliable engine.

The defeat of the German Air Service in World War I did not hamper Germans interested in aeronautics. Forbidden to revive the air service by the Treaty of Versailles, signed in 1919, German aeronautical engineers and designers concentrated on passenger-carrying aircraft. The Dornier works at Friedrichshafen, on Lake Constance, were by 1922 turning out a seaworthy freight and passenger flying boat, the first in a series of aircraft that were continuously improved and which were used in making several pioneering flights. Nicknamed *Wals* ("Whales"), the seaplanes were destined for the aviation history books.

In 1922, two Whales owned by the Condor Syndikat, the *Atlantico* and the *Pacifico*, explored Central America, looking for a commercial air route. In 1925, Roald Amundsen used two Whales in a vain attempt to fly over the North Pole. And in 1930, Wolfgang von Gronau, with a crew of three, made his first successful round-trip flight from Germany to New York. Von Gronau had foreseen the possibility of flying via Iceland and Greenland so that each hop would be only 600 miles. Fearing failure, however, the German government withheld approval of the venture. Therefore, von Gronau, at his own expense, made preparations in great secrecy. After 47 hours of flying and five stops, he landed in New York harbor.

Now convinced that a commercial air route between Germany and the United States was feasible, von Gronau, upon his return, held numerous conferences with German air officials in an unsuccessful effort to induce

The *Grönland-Wal* rides at anchor in the harbor at List, on the island of Sylt in the North Frisian Islands before beginning its world flight. The flight was completed in four months. (Lufthansa Airlines photo)

them to establish regular passenger service. But von Gronau was not to be denied. In 1931, he made another round-trip flight over the route he had flown the year before. This time, when he returned, he told representatives of the Air Ministry: "I have made this journey to the United States twice without a single accident or delay of any kind. You should now be convinced of the feasibility of this path for mail and passenger service between Germany and America. I have every confidence in it myself. It is the shortest route between the two continents. It is also the safest."

German officials still were not convinced. "Just because you have made such a flight twice," they told him, "does not mean you can do it successfully a third time!" "Then I'll do it a third time," von Gronau retorted. "I'll prove once more that it can be done safely."

On the morning of July 22, 1932, a Dornier christened *Grönland-Wal* *(Greenland Whale)* was readied for flight at List, in the Island of Sylt in the North Frisian Islands. Aboard with von Gronau were Gerth von Roth, copilot; Franzl Hack, mechanic; and Fritz Albrecht, radio operator. Their announced destination was Chicago. The sea was calm for takeoff. Because the plane was heavily loaded, von Gronau asked that another flying boat taxi across the harbor to make waves. This would help the Dornier break the surface friction of the water and thus get airborne. Von

Gronau taxied out, lined up into the wind, and, after a short run, easily lifted off.

The weather was fair. After an uneventful 1,000-mile flight, they landed at Seydisfjördur, on the northern coast of Iceland early in the evening. The next day, they departed for Reykjavik and reached the city that night. On the morning of July 24, after receiving reports of favorable weather from a station at Julianehab, they flew the 700 miles to Ivigtut, on the southwest coast of Greenland, in six hours. "If we were crossing the Atlantic now on the great Circle Route we would probably be fighting fog and storm with our hearts in our mouths and our knees quaking," von Gronau reportedly told his flight mates. "That route is all right for a stunt and sensation, or for committing suicide when you are tired of life; but this is the real route for pleasure and business!"

At Ivigtut, the fliers were welcomed by villagers. The next day, they flew to Cartwright, Labrador, where, once again, they were welcomed as old friends. Keeping to their schedule, von Gronau and his crew left on the morning of the twenty-sixth, following the St. Lawrence valley past Quebec. They landed at Montreal that evening, hardly fatigued. They had covered 4,000 miles in relative leisure and had slept normal nights at three stops.

Von Gronau discussed inaugurating regular air service with Canadian officials. Afterward, he told reporters that after landing at Chicago, he would not return to Germany over the route he had come, but would continue west until he had circled the earth. He and his crew then flew to Ottawa and on July 30, left for Chicago. En route, the cooling system of one Dornier engine failed. Von Gronau landed on Lake Saint Clair and had the plane towed to Detroit for repair. He and the *Grönland-Wal* reached Chicago on August 2, after a visit in Detroit with Henry Ford and a tour of Ford's River Rouge plant.

From Chicago, the Dornier was flown to Milwaukee and Minneapolis, followed by stops in Canada. On August 22, en route to Cordova, Alaska, von Gronau changed course and flew to Juneau. Subsequent stops were made at Yakutat and Cordova, both on the mainland, then Dutch Harbor, Kanaga Island, and Attu, in the Aleutians. By September 4, the four airmen were in Tokyo. After leisurely stops in Nagoya and Kagoshima, they flew to Shanghai, Hong Kong, and Manila; to Borneo, Java, India, and Persia; then Athens, Rome, and Genoa—touching down at Lake Constance, November 9, 1932.

Though flattered by the attention he and his crew received, von Gronau expressed a desire to circle the globe completely and reminded his hosts that he and his crew had not yet returned to their starting point. On November 23, he flew from Friedrichshafen to List.

Von Gronau's world-girdling flight in a seaplane was the forerunner of other ocean-spanning flights by seaplanes, most notably by Pan American World Airways in the Pacific shortly thereafter. His success was duly noted by many who were now convinced that intercontinental travel by flying boat was safer and more efficient than by ship.

4

THE LIGHTER-
THAN-AIR WAY

The first practical balloon was the invention of the brothers Jacques Etienne and Joseph Michel Montgolfier. Its first passengers, on September 19, 1783, were a sheep, a rooster, and a duck. The first humans to break the bonds of earth did so by ascending in a tethered Montgolfier balloon a month later. On November 21, 1783, Pilatre de Rozier and the Marquis François-Laurend d'Arlandes made the first free flight.

Others improved the balloon by giving it power and maneuverability. On August 9, 1884, there occurred one of the great moments in air history when two French army officers, Charles Renaud and Arthur C. Krebs, ascended in an electric-powered dirigible. They gave the first demonstration of a lighter-than-air vehicle capable of taking off, steering a course, and landing at the point of departure.

Gottlieb Daimler's invention and development of the gasoline engine in the 1880s not only revolutionized ground travel by making the automobile possible but made dirigibles practical and capable of exceptionally long flights. At the turn of the century, many countries saw the potential in mating the gasoline engine with lighter-than-air craft, especially semi-rigid dirigibles. The man who brought this combination to its peak was Count Ferdinand von Zeppelin, whose name became synonymous with giant dirigibles.

The serious-minded son of a German count, Zeppelin graduated from the Tubingen School and became a lieutenant in the German Army Corps of Engineers. In 1863, he went to the United States and offered his services to President Lincoln. He served in a cavalry unit and made several balloon ascents to reconnoiter Confederate positions. Zeppelin returned to Germany and was commissioned a captain, later fighting in the Austro-

Prussian War. He resigned from the army at the age of 56. In 1892, he began a second career by making his first free-balloon ascent. Zeppelin experimented with rigid airships in which the shape of a gas-inflated bag was maintained by using a rigid, fabric-covered frame. Power for the propellers was supplied by Daimler engines, which used benzine as fuel. Zeppelin's dirigible, the LZ-1, first consisted of a row of 17 balloons confined in a cylindrical shell 416 feet long and 38 feet in diameter. Steering was accomplished by two rudders.

Zeppelin made his first trial flight in the LZ-1 in July 1900, over Lake Constance. Despite technical problems and difficulty obtaining financial backing, subsequent LZ models became more efficient, and in 1910, Zeppelin built *Deutschland*, his first passenger-carrying airship, which made numerous successful trips in Europe. Zeppelin's success was followed by improved dirigibles with greater capacity and range. One, the ZR-3, left Friedrichshafen in November 1924, crossed France and Spain, and proceeded toward New York. Because of a storm that forced the craft north to Newfoundland, it landed on Long Island 70 hours after takeoff.

The flight of the ZR-3 wasn't the first across the Atlantic. The British-made R-34, under the command of Maj. G.H. Scott, made the crossing in July 1919 in 108 hours. In May 1926, Italy attempted a record-setting flight by backing Umberto Nobile in a race to be the first to cross the North Pole. Nobile lost that race to Cmdr. Richard E. Byrd but succeeded in flying the airship *Norge* nonstop from Spitzbergen, off Norway, over the North Pole to Teller, Alaska—a distance of 2,700 miles.

Not to be outdone, the Germans announced that they would inaugurate regularly scheduled transatlantic passenger service between Friedrichshafen and Lakehurst, New Jersey, using their newest airship, *Graf Zeppelin*, built under the direction of Dr. Hugo von Eckener, a protégé of Count Zeppelin. Designed as a luxury airship, it was 776 feet long, 100 feet high, and carried more than 3.5 million cubic feet of hydrogen in its massive ellipsoid shape. Power was supplied by five 500-hp Maybach engines. It had a crew of 40 to run the ship and care for its 20 passengers.

On *Graf Zeppelin*'s first westward voyage, begun October 11, 1928, with a full passenger load, strong head winds forced it to alter course and head south toward Africa before turning west again. The cover of a tail fin was damaged while the airship battled turbulence, and it became necessary to stop the engines for 12 hours while emergency, in-flight repairs were made. Upon arrival at Lakehurst 111.5 hours after departure, it was discovered that the huge craft had flown nearly 6,000 miles; but it was reported that it had enough fuel aboard for another 55 hours of flight if that had been necessary. On October 25, *Graf Zeppelin* departed from Lakehurst with a full complement of passengers and crew. Seventy-one

The *Graf Zeppelin* was the first, and thus far only, airship to circumnavigate the world. Departing from Lakehurst, New Jersey, she made the 21,000-mile flight in slightly over 21 days. (National Air and Space Museum photo)

hours and 12 minutes, and 3,967 miles later, it was moored safely at Friedrichshafen.

The glory year was 1929, a year in which the Atlantic Ocean was spanned four times. New York and Los Angeles were brought closer together by record nonstop flights. Alaska was linked with the East Coast (38 hours elapsed time); 169 passengers were carried aloft in one aircraft; and the South Pole was reached by airplane. Included were lengthy flights by *Graf*, climaxed by its globe-circling, record-setting flight in August 1929.

The newest pride of Germany began the year with a 5,040-mile flight from Friedrichshafen to the Near East, completing the trip in 81 hours and 20 minutes. It left its hangar March 25 and flew via Marseilles, Genoa, Rome, Naples, and Constantinople, returning to Germany on March 28. Next was a nonstop, 57-hour flight around the Mediterranean. *Graf Zeppelin* flew over France, Portugal, Spain, North Africa, and returned via the Rhone valley. Now confident that his ship was up to any task, Hugo von Eckener attempted to cross the Atlantic. Departing May 16, he went by way of Lyons, Barcelona, and the Mediterranean but was forced to return to Germany when an engine failed. Battered by high winds, the crippled *Graf* barely made it to home port. The airship had to remain aloft for two days before mooring safely for repairs. Von Eckener's next flight began on July 31, when he guided his airship to Lakehurst via Switzerland, Lyons, Nimes, Gibraltar, and the Azores. This flight of 5,000 miles was completed in 95 hours and 23 minutes.

To further prove the superiority of his lighter-than-air Zeppelins, Dr. Eckener announced that he would make a flight around the globe, carrying passengers. The flight would be financed largely by William Randolph Hearst in exchange for exclusive rights to publish the story in Hearst's newspapers. Two reporters were chosen: Lady Grace Drummond-Hay, the only woman passenger, and Karl H. Wiegand, both of whom had been on the first eastbound transatlantic voyage of the airship. Also aboard were the Arctic explorer Sir Hubert Wilkins; Cmdr. Charles E. Rosendahl, the U.S. Navy's expert on lighter-than-air craft; and naval and scientific representatives of the Soviet and Japanese governments.

With paying passengers aboard, and anticipating long flights, German planners knew they had to provide superior creature comforts, such as sleeping accommodations, meals, and facilities for social gatherings. These were duly provided in a setting comparable to those on the best ocean liners of the day.

At dusk on August 8, 1929, *Graf Zeppelin* was eased out of its hangar at Lakehurst and readied for flight. An estimated 10,000 spectators had been waiting all day behind guarded barriers. Floodlights lit up the area, playing along the silvery outline of the cigar-shaped airship. A few minutes before midnight, the restraining ropes were released and *Graf Zeppelin*, its engines purring in unison, nosed up and rose into the darkness, heading for the Statue of Liberty, the official starting point. Karl Wiegand described the moment:

> It was 12:40 o'clock, eastern standard time, when New York's millions of gleaming lights spread out below us. . . . the passengers were fascinated by the roar of whistles and sirens by which the . . . city bade Godspeed to the . . . airliner. . . . Dr. Eckener, his face wreathed in smiles, . . . [came] up to me from the bridge, slapping a strong, firm hand on my shoulder, and [said]: "Isn't that great?"
>
> We passed the starting line, the Statue of Liberty . . . at 12:45, and entered upon that epic of the air, the round-the–world cruise. Dr. Eckener was visibly in an intense emotional mood. . . . In almost a whisper, he confided: "At 12:45 we made our curtsy to the guardian goddess. We are off around the world—off on our greatest trip!"

The airship flew along the coast, following the Great Circle Route to Europe. Most of the passengers went to their cabins to rest until dawn.

Next morning, all were up early. They breakfasted in the luxurious dining area and enjoyed the view from the spacious windows. Since *Graf Zeppelin* seldom flew more than 3,000 feet above the surface, at a speed never exceeding about 75 mph, details on the ground were clearly visible during most of the trip.

The service was superb, and the passengers enjoyed each other's company, especially at mealtime. As Lady Hay commented: "It is like going to a party three times a day in a small town—we meet the same people all the time and chat over delicacies that no home kitchen provides for work-a-day occasions." The ship reached Friedrichshafen 55 hours and 22 minutes after leaving Lakehurst.

Four days later, *Graf* headed east for the 6,800-mile voyage nonstop to Tokyo. It would be the longest leg of the entire flight. The great airship sailed through mists over Prussia; the visibility improved in the Soviet Union. Wiegand wrote in his diary: "Rapidly the mists and [fog] melted

All meals during the *Graf Zeppelin's* 1929 world flight were served in the salon. Ernst Fischbach serves (left to right) Sir Hubert Wilkins; Dr. Jeronimo Megias, personal physician to the king of Spain; Dr. Hugo Eckener; and Lady Grace Drummond-Hay, reporter for Hearst newspapers and the only woman passenger on the flight. It was the longest dirigible flight in history and the first aerial craft to carry passengers around the world. (History of Aviation Collection, University of Texas, Dallas)

away from the earth and the sphere became clear . . . as a vast relief map. Medieval towns . . . stood out picturesquely against the green background." Flying low over the ground, the passengers could almost see the change of cultures below. Wiegand wrote that after crossing the Urals, they could see that the giant craft "began to panic the ignorant peasants below us. . . . Many of the peasants, who have never [even] seen a train, evidently mistake the Zeppelin . . . for a celestial monster."

As *Graf Zeppelin* passed into sparsely settled Siberia, the temperature inside the cabin dropped to near the freezing point, and the passengers were advised to dress warmly. Wilkens noted in his diary that he had observed "some trails, a few teepee tents, shaggy people, shaggy horses and wolf-like dogs, a few birds." Moving easterly and deviating only to take advantage of tailwinds, the slow-moving Zeppelin finally reached Tokyo and the harbor of Yokohama. With the help of several hundred sailors, the huge airship moored at the naval base at Kasumigaura. This 6,980-mile leg had been covered in 101 hours and 53 minutes, with enough fuel left to fly another 3,000 miles.

The crew and passengers were almost overwhelmed by the surging crowd as they stepped down from the gondola of the airship. Over the next four days, they were entertained and feted. The officers were decorated by emissaries from the emperor, and the crew and passengers received numerous tokens of welcome.

Von Eckener was eager to proceed, however, The Pacific Ocean lay ahead. It had never been crossed by a lighter-than-air craft. He set departure for the morning of August 23. At dawn, however, Tokyo was struck by a severe thunderstorm—rain punctuated by lightning flashes. The hydrogen-filled *Graf* was in a dangerous situation. By noon, the storm had passed out to sea, and von Eckener ordered the ship readied for flight. After much handshaking by the Germans and bowing by the Japanese, the ropes were cast off and *Graf Zeppelin* rose in the air.

As they headed toward the ocean, von Eckener was concerned that he might catch up with the storm front. Shortly after midnight, about 700 miles into the flight, they encountered towering thunderheads. Lightning flashes showed not far ahead. Von Eckener ordered the immediate release of hydrogen so the ship could descend to more stable air, about 1,000 feet above the ocean. Even at that altitude, though, the air did not long remain stable. *Graf Zeppelin* began to rock and plunge violently as it entered the storm proper. Wiegand wrote:

> We were caught in an uprushing current of tremendous force, and the *Graf* was carried up more than 300 feet in a few seconds. Then it plunged downward like a rock. [It] buckled like a bronco jumping stiff-legged. . . . It all came quickly. [But] half of the passengers had no idea what was going

on, and two of them slept through it all. [Some] were hanging out of the windows watching the play of the elements, it being the first time that the big German airship [had] encountered real lightning.

Cruising over the fog-swept islands of the Aleutians, *Graf Zeppelin* flew in and out of clouds. The hours seemed to drag for the passengers, who for the next few days had only rare glimpses of ocean or land. Finally, on the evening of August 25, *Graf* slipped out of the mists north of San Francisco. Von Eckener steered low over the Golden Gate Bridge as hundreds of ships and automobiles saluted the airship. Military and private planes flew formation.

San Francisco wasn't their destination, however, and von Eckener continued south, landing at Mines Field, near Los Angeles, at 5:30 A.M., August 26, *Graf Zeppelin* had flown 5,500 miles in 78 hours and 58 minutes. Despite plans by the city for luncheons, dinners, and parades, von Eckener was eager to continue. He permitted one dinner, after which he ordered crew and passengers back to the airport. The hurried takeoff almost proved disastrous. It was now dusk, and the hydrogen in the airship had cooled, causing it to respond slowly during takeoff. With all five engines at full throttle, von Eckener ordered the water ballast released. Then he pulled back on the elevator wheel. There was now cause for concern: The slow-moving airship was headed straight for high-tension wires at the edge of the field. The watching crowd gasped as *Graf Zeppelin* seemed to slide *through* the wires. But at what seemed the last possible moment, the ponderous craft inched upward. Its gondola barely missed the wires. As though spurning such minor hurdles, the airship quietly ascended and began the last leg of the journey to New York. It followed a circuitous route via northern Mexico, through the southwestern United States, then north to Chicago and Wisconsin and just into Canada, east to Detroit, Cleveland, and, finally, New York. All along the way, spectators by the hundreds and then the thousands, following the *Graf's* progress by radio, waved a welcome. Aircraft of practically every type flew up to greet the airship and escort it as far as they could.

On August 29, 1929, 21 days, 7 hours, and 34 minutes after crossing the starting point, *Graf Zeppelin* cruised over the Statue of Liberty. It had flown 19,500 miles; the final leg of 2,940 miles had been covered in 51 hours and 13 minutes. Of the total elapsed time, *Graf Zeppelin* had been aloft 9 days, 20 hours, and 23 minutes—a tribute to the Daimler engines, superior navigation, and superb airmanship.

The *Graf's* successful round-the-world flight confirmed predictions by enthusiasts of lighter-than-air flight that the future of passenger transportation over great distances lay with gas-filled dirigibles. In the next six years, *Graf Zeppelin* made more than 50 ocean crossings and flew 12 million passengers without mishap.

On March 27, 1930, Dr. Hugo von Eckener accepted the Special Gold Medal of the National Geographic Society, given in recognition of his being the first to navigate an airship around the world. In his acceptance speech, von Eckener said:

> If someone were to ask me what the purpose of the *Graf Zeppelin's* world cruise was, I should answer, frankly, that no definite plan existed when first the thought of the trip occurred. President Hoover once mentioned in a telegram to us that the period of great adventure was apparently not over. Something similar to what Magellan or Captain Ross, or later on, Peary, or Nansen [had] must also have been in our blood when the idea of flying around the world in our airship occurred to us. We knew we had a good . . . airship. We had proved it on various trips . . . and the desire to explore spurred us on. So we conceived the . . . idea of a world cruise. . . . There was the desire, above all, to learn what the capabilities of an airship are, how to make the utmost use of them, so that regular air traffic may be possible in various zones and climates. A trip around the world . . . seemed likely to increase our knowledge of the airship's reaction under various circumstances; and so, [from] the very beginning, it was . . . a flight into uncertainty to gain . . . experience in air navigation.

In presenting the medal to von Eckener, Dr. Gilbert Grosvenor, president of the National Geographic Society, said: "We honor Dr. Eckener tonight for the years of experiment, inventive genius, and patient research which culminated in his astounding achievement. The whole world literally held its breath till his flight was finished. . . . His remarkable voyage illustrates his unusual organizing and executive ability as well as his mastery of aeronautics, acquired by hard laboratory study and by more than 3,000 journeys."

The successful conclusion of the *Graf Zeppelin's* epic voyage was the dirigible's finest hour. Considering the vagaries of the weather on both sides of the equator, the vast distances flown over uninhabited and forbidding areas and over the oceans far from regular sea-lanes, the feat was, indeed, extraordinary. It has not been repeated, nor have any other attempts by dirigible been made.

In 1934, an airship larger than *Graf Zeppelin* was being built: the LZ-129. It would be the largest in the world—815 feet long and 137 feet at its greatest diameter. It was to be filled with 7 million cubic feet of hydrogen. Later christened *Hindenburg,* the LZ-129 carried 50 passengers, but within its body rather than in a gondola. Its four diesel engines produced 4,400 hp. Giving the airship an airspeed of 80 mph and a range of 8,000 miles. The end of an era came on May 6, 1937, when the *Hindenburg* exploded and burned at Lakehurst, as it approached for mooring. What had taken three decades to perfect took only 30 seconds to destroy. No Zeppelin flew again.

5

HE DARED THE WORLD'S OCEANS

He had a hyphenated last name, but those who knew him never used it, nor did they call him by his first name. He was simply "Smithy." Charles Kingsford-Smith was born and grew up in Australia. In 1915, on his eighteenth birthday, he enlisted in Australia's Signal Engineers and served in Egypt and Gallipoli. Smithy transferred to France in 1916 as a motorcycle courier, then signed up with the Royal Flying Corps for pilot training. Upon graduation, he was assigned to fly Spads. He was credited with shooting down three German aircraft before himself being shot down and wounded. Smithy was awarded the Military Cross for his victories but paid a penalty; he lost three toes and for the rest of his life walked with a slight limp.

At the end of the war, Smithy left the service and briefly flew surplus deHavilland DH-6 two-seat trainers on air taxi and mail flights in England. He then went to the United States and spent some time in Hollywood as a stunt pilot and wing walker. A few harrowing experiences convinced him that there was no future in stunt flying, and he returned to Australia.

Smithy's experience in aviation led to a job as pilot for Western Australian Airways. After two years, however, Smithy quit. Straight-and-level flying was boring. In 1927, he met Charles T.P. Ulm, another pilot, and the two men became close friends. Each ardently wished to make a name for himself in aviation. In pursuit of that goal, they hatched the project of becoming the first to fly around the rim of the Australian continent, and for that purpose bought an aging Bristol fighter. They announced to the press that they intended to make the flight in 10 days. As it turned out, they made the flight in just five hours over 10 days—a feat that deserved recognition in those days because of the almost total lack of landing fields in Australia and the otherwise primitive conditions under which they flew.

The two aviators had an ulterior motive in making the flight. What they really wanted to do was fly the Pacific Ocean from the United States to Australia, but felt they needed the experience and publicity of a record-setting flight to obtain the necessary financial backing for the much more ambitious attempt at flying the Pacific. They succeeded. The government of New South Wales approved the idea and promised aid; so did the *Sun*, a prominent newspaper in Sydney.

Thus encouraged, Smithy and Ulm sailed to the United States, landing at San Francisco, August 5, 1927. They shopped for an aircraft with long-range-flight capability and found what they thought fit the bill: a trimotor Fokker F-7, which they bought from Sir Hubert Wilkins, the Australian explorer of the Arctic and a reporter for the Hearst newspaper chain on the round-the-world flight of *Graf Zeppelin* in 1929. Unfortunately, the plane had no engines, and spare ones were hard to come by. When engines were found, Smithy and Ulm, now almost broke, discovered that they couldn't buy the engines and still have enough money to purchase the spare parts and pay for installation of the extra gas tanks that would be needed. They bought the engines anyway.

To raise money, Smithy and Ulm decided to try to beat the record for flight duration for an unrefueled flight (52 hours and 22 minutes), then held by German fliers. They failed, by 2 hours and 18 minutes. The failure nearly ended their dream. They had accumulated further debts in making the attempt at the record; now they couldn't even buy a meal. The New South Wales government responded by sending word for them to sell the Fokker and return.

News of their predicament had spread in the United States, however. G. Allan Hancock, a wealthy Californian, invited them for a cruise on his yacht. During the cruise, Hancock and the fliers talked at length about their attempt to make the flight over the Pacific. As they were returning to port, Hancock told them that he would buy the Fokker, lend it to them to fly to Australia, and advance them the money to pay their debts and order necessary supplies. With renewed enthusiasm for the venture, Smithy and Ulm went to work. The Fokker was shipped to the Douglas factory in Santa Monica and there overhauled. While Ulm oversaw the work, Smithy pored over charts and atlases. He recruited two Americans for the flight—Harry W. Lyons, an experienced Navy navigator, and James Warner, a veteran ship's radio operator.

On the morning of May 31, 1928, the Fokker, newly christened *Southern Cross*, took off from Oakland Airport and headed out to sea. On June 1, after an uneventful flight of 2,408 miles, Smithy made a pass over Honolulu and the crew of four landed at Wheeler Field, the major Hawaiian base of the U.S. Army Air Corps—27 hours after takeoff. The next day, they flew to Barking Sands Beach, at Kauai, so named because of the sound made by the coarse sand when anything moved on it. Smithy had chosen this spot as his departure point for the next leg because it offered a longer strip for the heavily loaded Fokker than did Wheeler Field.

At 5:30 A.M., June 3, Smithy guided *Southern Cross* down the beach and lifted into the air. It would be the longest stage of the journey—3,138 miles from Kauai to Suva, in the Fiji Islands. Fully fueled, the Fokker had a range of about 3,645 miles, which left a margin of 500 miles—not much when one degree off in heading meant missing their destination by

Australian Charles Kingsford-Smith, World War I pilot, and Charles T. P. Ulm, were first to fly around the rim of Australia. In 1928, the quartet shown here flew from the United States to Australia across the Pacific in a Fokker named the *Southern Cross* in 1928. Smith and Ulm, joined by J. W. Stannage, radio operator, and J. P. Saul, navigator, after many mishaps, completed the trip around the world in 1930, 2 years, 1 month, and 4 days after the original departure. Shown are, left to right, Harry W. Lyons, navigator; Ulm; Kingsford-Smith; and James Warner, radio operator on the 1928 flight. (National Air and Space Museum photo)

several miles. The first hundred miles or so weren't difficult; Smithy could fly outbound on Wheeler Field's radio beacon. As the Fokker proceeded under overcast skies, the signal faded, and so did the sun. Because Lyons could no longer determine their position by celestial navigation, he asked Smithy to try to keep a southwesterly heading.

They encountered tropical thunderstorms that night, which obliterated the stars they had hoped to navigate by. Smithy fought to get out of the storm. He swerved, climbed, and dived; but each time he did so, it became more difficult for Lyons to plot their position. The violent, turbulent weather worried them not only because of its effect on navigation, but also because of its effect on their fuel supply. Daylight brought no relief. Although Lyons calculated that Suva, in the Fiji Islands, lay 690 nautical miles ahead, he couldn't be sure of that until he had gotten a sighting on the sun. At midafternoon, however, the clouds cleared, and he was able to give Smithy a course correction. Soon afterward, Suva was sighted.

The *Southern Cross* landed at 3:50 P.M. It was the longest transoceanic flight up to that time. The Fokker was also the first trimotor aircraft to land in Fiji. Crossing the international date line, however, changed their landing date from June 4 to June 5.

The Fokker had made the landing without difficulty, but Smithy realized that he couldn't get the plane off the ground with a full load of fuel. Therefore, he flew the plane to the beach at Naselai, where the tanks were filled by Fijians from drums brought to the beach by surf boats. That afternoon, while the tide was out, Smithy and his crew climbed aboard and took off. About an hour into the flight, Lyons passed a note to Smithy: EARTH INDUCTOR COMPASS NOT WORKING. In the excitement of landing at Fiji and refueling at Naselai, he had forgotten to oil the instrument. All they now had to give them a course was the free-swinging magnetic compass. As darkness came on, they ran into another tropical storm, this one more violent than the storm they had encountered on the flight to Suva. The turbulence was so severe that each man had to hold on to his seat rigidly to keep from straining at the seat belt and from banging his head against the plane's superstructure. With the magnetic compass varying so much that it was virtually useless, it was all Smithy could do to keep the plane right side up and headed more or less southwest.

At dawn, after some four hours of this, the storm finally ended, and Lyons got his first sun sighting. He found that they were far off their route and headed southeast; he gave Smithy a westerly course. When they made landfall, Lyons estimated that they were 110 miles south of where they should have been. Smithy therefore changed course, heading north. Shortly after 10:00 A.M., they landed at Brisbane. When they flew on to Sydney the next day, there were surprised to see a huge crowd at the airport. About 300,000 people were on hand to greet the first aviators to fly the Pacific.

Honors were heaped on them. Each was awarded the Air Force Cross by the government of Australia, along with a check for £5,000 (about $20,000). Private awards totaled another £15,000, and they received the trophy of the Federation Aeronautique Internationale. Though he welcomed the honors and the money, Smithy wasn't through. To maintain public interest, he decided to make long-distance flights around Australia. Lyons and Warner returned to the United States and were replaced by H.A. Litchfield, an Australian, and T.H. McWilliams, a New Zealander, as navigator and radio operator, respectively. The four airmen flew *Southern Cross* nonstop from Melbourne to Perth, then to Adelaide and Sydney, for a total of 4,390 miles.

Next came a flight from Sydney to Christchurch, New Zealand, 1,625 miles across the Tasman Sea, generally recognized as one of the world's roughest bodies of water. They made it, but only after a nighttime flight through a severe thunderstorm in which *Southern Cross* iced up and was nearly forced down, out of control. Ice on the pitot tube caused the airspeed indicator needle to drop to zero, forcing Smithy to fly by altimeter and engine rpms and to stay near the water. Smithy eventually landed the Fokker safely, but, as he later admitted, he had panicked and nearly lost control of both himself and the aircraft. Nevertheless, he had managed another first when he landed at Christchurch's Wigram Aerodrome, September 11, 1928.

After a month of celebrating and waiting for new propellers to arrive and be installed on the Fokker, Smithy and his crew returned to Sydney. Not content to rest on their laurels, Smithy and Ulm decided to start an airline—Australian National Airways Limited. First, they would fly *Southern Cross* to England and shop for aircraft.

En route from Sydney to Wyndham, an aerial broke off. This meant *Southern Cross* could transmit messages but not receive them. Their radioman at Wyndham, who had earlier sent them a report of favorable weather, now found the weather worsening. He cabled Sydney to have *Southern Cross* delay its start. The radio station at Sydney tried to contact the plane in flight, to no avail. Without this warning, the unsuspecting crew flew into a storm front, cursing their weather information all the while. The 2,000-mile flight across Australia proved as difficult as the one across the Pacific. *Southern Cross* was due at Wyndham at 10:30 A.M., April 1, 1929; but they couldn't find the town. When they reached the coast, they turned north and flew to a village they identified as Drysdale Mission. Ulm dropped a message asking for directions to Wyndham. Smithy and Ulm didn't know it, but the villagers on the ground never found the message. As Smithy flew low over the village, they appeared to point southwest. Smithy dutifully headed in that direction; but as they droned on, they saw nothing but jungle, rocky cliffs, and a forbidding sea. There wasn't even a beach long enough to use as a landing strip.

Smithy and Ulm spotted another village, and again Ulm dropped a message asking the way to Wyndham. This time the villagers were prepared. They laid out strips of cloth which read: EAST 250. Smithy looked at Ulm and both looked at the fuel gauge. *Southern Cross* did not have 250 miles of fuel left. Smithy flew east for an hour. The gauge now read nearly empty. Pointing to a mud flat below, he cut the throttle and landed. As their speed dropped, the plane's wheels sank into the mud and they stopped. They were safe but down in the middle of nowhere.

News of the disappearance of *Southern Cross* was flashed around the world and aircraft were dispatched to look for it. Meanwhile, Smithy and his crew, not knowing where they were, took stock of their food supply. Someone had stolen their emergency rations. All they had was some baby food they were delivering to Wyndham, a little coffee, and some brandy. Fortunately, potable water was available. The situation soon became critical. They were constantly tormented by flies and mosquitoes. As their frustration grew, their strength ebbed. Checking the radio, they found they could receive messages but not transmit them. They tried to rig a transmitter by using a wheel of the plane as a generator but couldn't turn it fast enough or long enough to get adequate power. After some 12 days, a search plane found them. It roared low overhead and dropped food and supplies, returning the next day to make another drop. On April 15, a small plane landed on the now sunbaked surface, and the next day, two planes landed with fuel. Finally, on April 18, *Southern Cross* took off and flew to Wyndham.

The story wasn't without controversy or tragedy, however. A search plane had gone down in the desert and its two occupants had died of thirst and heat. A court of inquiry investigating their deaths, while absolving Smithy and his crew of staging a forced landing as a publicity stunt, did find them guilty of inadequate planning. The court concluded that *Southern Cross* and all its navigation equipment was sound; therefore, they should not have become lost, and the death of their would-be rescuers could have been avoided.

On June 25, 1929, with the inquiry over, Smithy and his crew left Sydney. They made the first nonstop flight to Singapore from Australia, then flew on to India, Persia, Greece, and Rome, arriving at London's Croydon Airport in the record time of 12 days and 18 hours. When officials of the Fokker Company learned of their arrival, the company offered to overhaul *Southern Cross* free of charge. This would enable Smithy to continue his round-the-world flight if he wished. The offer was gladly accepted. While the plane was being overhauled, Smithy contracted to buy four

Avro Ten aircraft, actually Fokker planes with British engines, built under license to the British.

While Ulm returned to Australia, Smithy took a boat to the United States, seeking funds to cover the expenses of a flight across the Atlantic and on to California. There he met Anthony Fokker, who donated £1,000 to the effort, telling Smithy that it had been his exploits that had made the name Fokker better known after World War I than it had been during the war. Smithy traveled across the United States, then went to Vancouver, where he took a ship for Australia. The Avro Tens were delivered later that year, and on January 1, 1930, the new airline began operations with an inaugural flight by Smithy from Sydney to Brisbane.

With the airline started, Smithy decided to continue his globe-circling flight. He asked his board of directors for a leave of absence for himself and Ulm, but the board didn't want both gone at the same time for so long. Ulm decided to trade his share in *Southern Cross* to Smithy for stock in the airline, and dropped out of the world flight. Smithy went alone to the Fokker plant in Amsterdam, where he found *Southern Cross* completely reconditioned. He recruited Evert Van Dyk, a Royal Dutch Airline pilot, as his copilot and hired J.W. Stannage as his radio operator. Stannage was the flier who had found *Southern Cross* in Australia. J.P. Saul, as navigator, rounded out the crew.

At 4:25 A.M., after several test flights of the refurbished Fokker, Smithy pushed the throttles forward and they lifted off the strip of Port Marnock Beach, in Ireland, heading for Cape Race, Newfoundland, 1,900 miles away. Flying at altitudes rarely exceeding 1,000 feet, to avoid high head winds, he had to fly mostly in fog and mist throughout that day and night. More than once, Saul passed notes forward to Smithy and Van Dyk, asking why they weren't following the course he had given them. When they checked, the pilots and Saul found that their compasses did not agree. Saul's even had a third reading that differed from that of the other two. It was still daylight, and Smithy decided to climb above the overcast and fog so Saul could take a sun shot with his sextant. Suddenly, as the plane leveled off in bright sunlight, all three compasses read the same. They never learned the cause—whether it was ice particles in the compass bearings or electricity in the fog. Whatever it was, the sun sighting gave them a firm position.

As they neared the coast of North America, Stannage got a bearing from radio stations at Cape Race and Belle Isle. Although they now knew approximately where they were, Smithy had to descend through thickening overcast to find Harbour Grace. It wasn't easy. At ground level, heavy fog forced Smithy back up on top for a better fix from the two radio stations. After several attempts, an anxious Smithy spotted the field, and they landed. The flight had taken 31.5 hours.

After a night's rest, Smithy and his crew flew on to New York. The *New York Times* headline read: "10,000 Rush Plane, 150 Patrolmen Bowled Over in Rush to Acclaim Flyers. Spectators Perched on Every Vantage Point. Hear Reports Through Horse Amplifiers." In a dizzying whirl of events, the four airmen were presented the city's Medal of Honor and were invited to the White House for lunch with President Hoover. But Smithy hadn't fulfilled his other dream—circling the earth completely by air. He had yet to return to his takeoff point in California. As they left Roosevelt Field, another aircraft took off and briefly flew formation. In it was Anthony Fokker.

Southern Cross landed at Chicago, July 2, then flew on to Salt Lake City. On July 4, 1930, Smithy landed at Oakland Airport, his starting point. He had circumnavigated the globe in 2 years, 1 month, and 4 days. He was the only member of the original crew who had flown the entire distance, making him the first man to circle the earth by air over the equator.

Smithy was given full title to *Southern Cross*. He returned to Australia to resume flying for his airline. The venture wasn't successful, however, and in 1931 he began a barnstorming tour of Australian cities, giving rides to passengers. He still had the urge to make epochal flights, though. His recent exploit had generated keen competition to make the flight between England and Australia. The feat was accomplished, first by C.W.A. Scott and then by James Mollison. By mid-1931 Smithy was ready to add his name to the list. Mollison's time from Australia to England was 8 days and 21 hours.

On September 24, 1931, Smithy left Wyndham in a Percival Gull but was forced down by bad weather on a beach 80 miles south of Victoria Point. He dried out his ignition harness and the next day continued the flight. While over the Bay of Bengal, however, he suffered carbon monoxide poisoning and had to make an emergency landing in Turkey, where the Turks confiscated his plane. Unable to persuade them to let him continue the flight, Smithy had to return to Australia by ship.

More barnstorming and an abortive attempt to run another airline followed. In 1934, Smithy entered the MacPherson-Robertson Air Race, from Mildenhall, England, to Melbourne, Australia, but because of damage to the Lockheed Altair he had bought with funds provided by backers, he didn't reach England in time to start the race. Undaunted, from October 20 to November 4, 1934, he and P.G. Taylor flew from Australia to the United States in the single-engine, two-seat Lockheed. It was the first transpacific flight in that direction. The airplane, christened *Lady Southern Cross*, was put up for sale, and Smithy returned by ship to Australia. In an attempt to remain solvent, he once more took up barnstorming.

Smithy hadn't given up dreaming. He was determined to establish air service between Australia and New Zealand. His main asset now was the aging but reliable Fokker, *Southern Cross*. He obtained permission from the governments of Australia and New Zealand to fly mail between the two countries. On May 15, 1935, Smithy, with Taylor and Stannage as crew members, took off from Sydney. Halfway across the Tasman Sea, a piece of exhaust pipe flew off the center engine and struck the propeller of a wing engine. The aircraft shuddered violently as the prop spun around in an unbalanced orbit. To maintain flying speed, Smithy cut back the center engine and increased power on the other two engines. He turned back to Australia, 500 miles away; but the heavily loaded Fokker struggled, losing airspeed and altitude. Smithy nursed the two good engines, one of which was overheating from loss of oil. Taylor volunteered to climb out on the right wheel strut. Hanging in the slipstream, and with a Thermos bottle in hand, he drained oil from the starboard engine—a feat demanded by the urgency of the situation, since the Fokker could not fly on one engine. Taylor then poured the hot oil into the oil tank of the port engine. Somehow, Taylor performed this task six times as *Southern Cross* limped home. Meanwhile, Stannage sent radio messages describing their struggle to save the aircraft. To reduce weight, Smithy dumped as much fuel as he dared, then ordered the freight thrown overboard, followed by the mail. Finally, to everyone's relief, *Southern Cross* landed at Sydney. It marked the end of Smithy's attempts to start another airline.

Taylor, the hero of the flight, was awarded the George Cross. Later, he was knighted for pioneering the route from Australia to South Africa via the Cocos Islands. Smithy, who felt that *Southern Cross*, now suffering from age, deserved to be remembered, offered it to the government of Australia to be preserved for posterity. His offer was accepted and he received £3,000 when he formally turned over ownership of the aircraft on July 18, 1935.

Despite setbacks, Smithy still yearned for fame. His Lockheed Altair, left in the United States to be sold, had not found a buyer; so he decided to try again to beat the England–Australia record of 71 hours, set by C.W.A. Scott and T. Campbell Black in the MacPherson-Robertson Race of 1934. With J.T. Pethybridge as copilot, he departed from London in October 1935, only to return two days later because of damage by hail suffered near Brindisi, Italy. Smithy and Pethybridge started again on November 7 and were well ahead of Scott and Black's time when they reached Allahabad two days later. The next day, Smithy, now Sir Charles Kingsford-Smith, vanished while crossing the Bay of Bengal. Neither the aircraft nor the two crewmen were ever found. A year later, the tail wheel of *Lady Southern Cross* was found washed up on a beach on the coast of Burma, 1,400 miles from Allahabad.

The man who had always feared a watery grave, yet had dared the world's oceans, had finally lost the dare.

6

WILEY POST:
THE ONE-EYED WONDER

Wiley Hardeman Post was born in a farmhouse near Grand Saline, Texas, November 22, 1898, the fourth of seven children. As the family moved from one hardscrabble farm to another in Texas and Oklahoma, it was plain to Wiley's parents that he had not taken to farming; nor did he like school. He had developed such an intense dislike for it that he quit at the age of 14 after completing the eighth grade. At this time, and throughout Wiley's life, his only evident interest was in repairing mechanical devices.

According to Post, the turning point in his life came in 1913. He and his brother, James, went to the Oklahoma state fair and there saw a Curtiss Pusher, piloted by Art Smith, put on an exhibition of aerobatics. Post was entranced. Smith's exhibition included attaching roman candles to the aircraft and setting them off while flying night aerobatics. It may have been the first time the stunt was performed. Post later acknowledged that from that time on, he felt destined to be part of aviation. He even began to dream of a "Wiley Post Institute for Aeronautical Research."

Determined to pursue his goal, Post started by taking a seven-month automobile mechanics course at the Sweeney Auto School, in Kansas City. He couldn't afford to continue, though, and returned to the family farm. When World War I began, he enlisted in the army's radio operator school at Norman, Oklahoma; but the war ended before he could complete the course. Not wanting to return to the farm, Post went to work in the Oklahoma oil fields as a roughneck. The pay was good, but he couldn't get the thought of flying out of his mind. In the summer of 1918, he paid a barnstorming pilot $25 for a flight in an open-cockpit airplane. To Post's disappointment, the flight wasn't as exciting as he had expected even though the pilot had performed every aerobatic maneuver he knew. Post later recalled that he was disillusioned because he suddenly realized that pilots did not possess supernatural powers.

The next five years were restless ones for Post. He went back to the family farm and stayed there a short while; then he returned to the oil fields. In 1924, he heard that a flying circus was coming to Wewoka. He felt compelled to see it. Arriving early, he struck up a conversation with some members of Burrell Tibbs's "Texas Topnotch Fliers" and learned that the team's parachute jumper had been injured and couldn't jump that day. Post suddenly announced: "Hell, I'll jump for you. Show me what to do."

A few minutes later he had the parachute harness on and was airborne in a Curtiss JN-4 "Jenny." The parachute canopy was tied to the strut of the right wing. At 2,000 feet, the pilot gave the signal, and Post climbed onto the right wing and buckled his harness to the rings of the chute. He jumped as though he had been doing it all his life. The jump gave Post "one of the biggest thrills" of his life. It also gave him a start toward his dream of learning to fly, of being a part of aviation. He was hired by the flying circus as a jumper and picked up some pilot instruction as the troupe traveled. Over the next two years, Post made 99 jumps. He was now firmly convinced that his future lay in aviation. "I was studying crowd psychology," he later wrote; "my desire to thwart the spectators' hope of witnessing my untimely end was so strong that I grew so reckless as to scare myself."

Post received more pilot instruction, and in 1926, made his first solo flight in a Canuck, the Canadian version of the Curtiss JN-4. He had caught the fever and wanted a plane of his own. He returned to the oil fields for the third time to earn the money. On October 1, 1926, while working on a drilling rig near Seminole, Oklahoma, Post was standing near another worker. The worker was using a sledgehammer to drive a bolt in place. As the sledge came down, a chip flew off the bolt and struck Post in the left eye, lodging there. When the eye became infected and the infection appeared to be spreading to the other eye, the left eye was removed.

To the aspiring pilot, the loss of an eye was a severe blow. Here he was, 28 years old, with only an eighth-grade education and experience as a laborer and sometime parachute jumper. The future seemed bleak, but Post refused to be deterred. While recuperating at the home of an uncle, he practiced estimating distances to such objects as a tree or a fence post, then paced off the distance to check his accuracy. Like other one-eyed people, he trained the vision of his good eye so that eventually he became nearly as competent with one eye as normal people are with two.

What fate took through the loss of an eye, it restored through an award of $1,800 in workmen's compensation. Post used part of the money to buy a secondhand Canuck. Because he didn't need a pilot's license (at that time, the Department of Commerce had no licensing requirements), Post was free to give flight instruction and to fly passengers, both for a fee. With a friend who also owned a Canuck, he started a barnstorming operation.

During a trip to Sweetwater, Texas, in 1927, Post met, eloped with, and married Mae Laine, then 17. The next few months were difficult ones for them. Post wrecked his Canuck, and he couldn't afford to have it repaired. He got what money he could for the plane and eked out a living putting the plane back in flying shape and giving lessons to the man who bought it.

In late 1927, Post again found himself out of work. While hunting for a job, he met Powell Briscoe and F. C. Hall. As partners in the oil business, these men knew the value of speed in being the first to get to prospective oil-lease sites. Briscoe and Hall were exploring the possibility of using an airplane to beat their competitors to sites and were planning to buy a new, three-place open-cockpit Travel Air when Post appeared, asking for a job. Despite the lack of an eye, Briscoe and Hall liked Post and hired him. By now, pilots were required to be licensed. Fortunately for Post, the regulations provided for granting waivers of the physical exam by the Secretary of Commerce for physical defects when the pilot's experience compensated for the deficiency. Post passed the written examination but was required to fly on probation for about 700 hours before being granted a license. He passed that mark in eight months and on September 16, 1928, was granted a license.

As Post was proving the value of airplanes in the oil industry, a new plane appeared on the aviation scene. Called the Lockheed Vega, it featured a closed cabin, a powerful engine, and considerable speed, especially compared to that of the Travel Air. The Vega, in short, represented a significant advance in aircraft design. Wiley flew the Travel Air to the West Coast and, on behalf of Hall, traded it in for a Vega. Hall christened the plane *Winnie Mae*, for his daughter. It was the first of three planes that Hall owned, each carrying the same name.

Hall and Briscoe made several trips in the Vega. With the stock market crash and the onset of the Great Depression, however, they had to sell the plane. Post flew it back to the Lockheed plant in California, knowing all the time that he was out of a job. When he landed, he asked for, and got, a job with Lockheed as a salesman and test pilot. In the ensuing months, he accrued flying time while acquiring invaluable knowledge of aircraft design and test-flight procedures. He ferried Lockheed Vegas to various cities and even flew them for an airline that operated in Texas and Mexico. It was during this period that Post heard about recent developments in techniques of blind flying, pioneered by Jimmy Doolittle, using gyroscopic instruments.

In June 1930, Post received a call from Hall, asking him to be his pilot again and to supervise construction of the new Lockheed 5B that Hall had ordered. Powered by a 420-hp Pratt & Whitney Wasp engine, the 5B had a seven-place cabin. It, too, was christened *Winnie Mae*. Now experienced as a pilot and eager to see what the new Vega could do, Post asked Hall for permission to enter a nonstop race between Los Angeles and Chicago, a special event of the 1930 National Air Races. Post wanted not only to enter the race but also to continue to New York and attempt to break the coast-to-coast speed record. He asked Harold Gatty, an Australian-born navigator then living in California, to lay out a course.

Post had modified the Vega by adding gas tanks and a special supercharger to the engine (for better performance at high altitudes). When all was ready and approved for flight, Post felt confident he could not only win the race but capture the ocean-to-ocean record as well. A few minutes after takeoff, however, the magnetic compass of the *Winnie Mae* stuck and Post lost 40 minutes when he got off course before discovering the malfunction. He continued the flight by pilotage (visual reference to the ground) and landed at Chicago, 1,760 miles from Los Angeles in 9 hours, 9 minutes, and 4 seconds, to capture the prize of $7,500. The faulty compass had ruled out any chance of setting the coast-to-coast record, however. Arthur Goebel, flying the first *Winnie Mae*, placed second.

The success of this flight set Post and Hall to thinking of other record-setting ventures. They first considered going after the coast-to-coast record but decided on a more ambitious attempt: an around-the-world speed flight. As Post wrote in his book, *Around the World in Eight Days*, he felt that "aviation needed something original to stimulate passenger business."* With Hall's flying requirements diminished as the Depression deepened, he approved the attempt and authorized Post to take the plane to California for "long-range modifications." While there, Post visited Gatty and enlisted his help in planning the flight. He also asked Gatty to go with him. Gatty had a wealth of navigational experience, having graduated from the Royal Australian Naval College. He had also served as a navigator on merchant vessels before coming to the United States in 1927, where he opened a school for navigators and trained fliers.

Post and Gatty calculated that it would take 10 days to circle the globe. They agreed that Gatty would work on the route and logistical problems, and Post would concentrate on preparing the Lockheed 5B Vega. Gatty had invented a drift and ground-speed indicator, which he made mostly from gears and clock parts. They would use it on the flight. The device

---

* Post and Gatty, New York: Rand McNally & Co., 1931.

Wiley Post (left) and Harold Gatty, navigator, pose beside the *Winnie Mae* before their 1931 world flight. Post flew it solo around the world in 1933 to become the first pilot in history to fly a plane around twice. The Lockheed Vega is enshrined in the National Air and Space Museum in Washington, D.C. (National Air and Space Museum photo)

worked so well that it was later adopted by the Army and the Navy. On the advice of Doolittle, Post grouped the bank-and-turn indicator, rate-of-climb, and artificial-horizon instruments so they could be scanned more easily during solo flights. Duplicate instruments were installed for Gatty in the rear, in addition to a drift meter and a "master" aperiodic compass, located on the floor. A bulky continuous-wave transmitter and receiver was installed for emergency communications.

Post was also concerned about his own conditioning, both physical and mental. He realized that fatigue would be as great a threat as the weather. He spent hours training himself to keep his mind blank, on the theory that self-induced relaxation would enable him to counter the inevitable slowed reactions during the long flight.

In the weeks immediately preceding the flight, Post slept at different times each day, to accustom himself to an interrupted schedule. As he wrote in his book, "I knew that the variance in time as we progressed would bring on acute fatigue if I were used to regular hours." (As far as can be determined, Post was the first to tackle the problem of "jet lag," or human adjustment to crossing time zones on long airplane flights.)

Post and Gatty left the Lockheed plant in early May 1931 and headed east. They stopped at Chickasha, Oklahoma, to see Hall, then went on to Washington, D.C., to get permission to land in or fly over Great Britain, the Netherlands, Germany, Poland, the Soviet Union, China, and Japan. Although the last two countries weren't included in their flight plan, Post wanted approval in case they were forced off course or had to detour because of bad weather. Permission to fly over Soviet territory was as difficult to obtain then as it was later in the century, but Hall enlisted the aid of Secretary of War Patrick J. Hurley. Because the United States did not have diplomatic relations with the Soviet Union at that time, permission was obtained through the Amtorg Trading Corporation, which functioned as the unofficial embassy in the United States.

Post and Gatty arrived at Roosevelt Field in late May and prepared the *Winnie Mae*. They were eager to depart, but the weather over the Atlantic was unfavorable. Over the next four weeks, they taxied out several times but returned each time after receiving reports of fog, icing conditions, or thunderstorms from ships at sea. Finally, on June 23, Post decided to go. He waited for the soggy field to dry, then, at 4:55 A.M., guided the *Winnie Mae* into the air and set a course for Harbour Grace, Newfoundland. There they had the gas tanks filled, then headed into 1,900 miles of uncertain weather. The visibility was so poor that Post had to fly blind for hours, relying on his instruments. Sixteen hours into the flight, they entered an area of broken clouds and could see land below. It had been boring for Gatty in the rear, with nothing to look at but his instruments. He dozed fitfully. Suddenly he was wide awake. The engine had quit for a moment, then started again. This was caused by Post's habit of letting one gas tank run completely dry before switching to another. "That way, I know exactly how much gas I've got in each tank," he explained. "You can't always trust the gas gauges when the tanks get down low."

Post had intended to fly nonstop from Newfoundland to Berlin, but 16 hours and 17 minutes after takeoff, and unsure of their position, they landed at the British Royal Air Force's Sealand Aerodrome, near Chester, England. "Is this England, Scotland, or Wales?" he asked a mechanic. "England, mate." When Post was later asked whether he was lost on this leg, he said: "I don't think we can honestly say we were lost . . . we just didn't know where we were."

After refueling, Post and Gatty headed for Berlin. Over the continent, the weather worsened, and Post again flew on instruments. When he estimated that the time was right, he eased the plane down through the clouds. Post was so tired that he decided to land at the first airport he could find. They circled a large city, found a landing strip, and landed. The city was Hanover, Germany. They took off once more, heading for Berlin. But their judgment had been impaired by fatigue. They were so tired and so preoccupied with reaching Berlin that they had forgotten to check their fuel supply. When Post realized this, he returned to Hanover, and refueled. A hollow-eyed pair finally landed at Tempelhof Airport before a crowd that had been waiting for hours. Post and Gatty, numb from lack of sleep, eventually broke away from the well-wishers to bathe, eat a hearty dinner, and get a good night's sleep.

At 2:38 A.M. the next morning, June 25, they were airborne for the 994-mile leg to Moscow. Flying through weather that Post later described as "the dirtiest experienced on this or any other flight. The ceiling simply closed down on us and forced us right down on the tree tops. We had to fight wind and rain as well as fog. Landmarks slipped by us so fast that we had trouble checking the course. The drift indicator held out, though, and we hit our mark on the nose through dead reckoning." The flight from Berlin to Moscow's October Field had taken 8 hours and 52 minutes. Post and Gatty were grateful for the small crowd that met them. All they wanted was sleep: Siberia lay ahead.

What the Russians lacked in numbers in the greeting party at the airport, they made up for with a gala banquet at the Grand Hotel. To the numerous speeches and toasts, Post and Gatty responded by lifting their glasses of water. Post ate lightly; he knew that a heavy meal would make him tired and sleepy that much sooner. To the fliers' chagrin, the banquet dragged on so long that they got only about two hours' sleep before having to get up again. Taking off into a murky sky, Post followed the Trans-Siberian Railroad to Novosibirsk, a distance of 1,200 miles. There they had breakfast and refueled the plane. Then they took off for Irkutsk. It was June 27.

Blagoveshchensk was next, and this leg proved to be one of the roughest. "For hours we flew a bare 25 feet above the trees, and in a strange country, which was wholly unknown to us, strange apparitions loomed up in the mist ahead. Two or three times we thought the end had come and pulled the ship up sharply until the angle of climb became dangerous." Post never said what the apparitions were.

When they arrived at Blagoveshchensk, they found the field a sea of mud and water. Post set the *Winnie Mae* down gingerly, but it immediately became bogged down; he couldn't taxi. As Post later told it: "Our sleep at Blagoveshchensk on the hardest of Soviet beds was somewhat spoiled by [worrying] whether a tractor would arrive [in] time to pull the *Winnie Mae* to firmer ground, and if it did, whether the Russians could do it without breaking the already taxed landing gear."

With the help of Russian soldiers, the plane was eventually pulled free of the mud, and the weary airmen took off for Khabarovsk, their last stop in the Soviet Union. They landed there at 1:30 in the morning, June 28. They planned to leave after a few hours' rest, but the weather deteriorated and the *Winnie Mae* developed engine trouble. Post and Gatty spent the day tuning the engine, then got 12 hours' sleep. On the twenty-ninth they were off again on the 2,400-mile flight to North America. Describing this leg of the trip as "the really dangerous section of the journey," Post had this to say:

> We flew first across the Sea of Okhotsk. It was just getting dark as we started out, and it began to rain. We soon found ourselves enclosed in a fog so thick that we did not see a thing outside . . . for four hours.
>
> When it began to get light—the nights are short there . . . we pulled up between two large layers of clouds and stayed there. We knew there were mountains ahead on the Kamchatka Peninsula, but we managed all right. We saw a mountain loom up between the layers and we followed that down to the water. . . . [We] flew along, skipping over the waves at about 25 feet.
>
> So there we were, over the Bering Sea, and it was more fog. We simply had to fight our way through it. We didn't know just how we were going to get down to land once we got to Alaska, for the fog hid everything below us; but we figured that it would be better to crack up in Alaska if we were going to crack up than to go down in the sea. It was one of the crucial spots of the trip. We might have played it safer and waited at Khabarovsk for better weather, but we [could] have waited [there] six months.

After a grueling 16 hours and 45 minutes, Post and Gatty made landfall at Solomon's Beach, about 25 miles east of Nome. The gas tanks were nearly empty. The landing was fast, and the sand was soft. Post nearly nosed the Vega over, catching it just in time. They took on about 100 gallons of gas, intending to push on to Fairbanks to spend the night. As Post tried to get airborne from the sand, however, he nosed over and bent the tips of the propeller. Though concerned that the engine had been damaged internally, Post gambled that it had not. With a hammer, wrench, and rock, he straightened out the tips and prepared to take off. When he ran up the engine to check for vibration, the engine backfired, and Gatty, who was standing near the nose, was struck in the shoulder by the prop. Fortunately, he received only a bad bruise and a sprained back. Two hours and 45 minutes after landing on the beach, they took off, in a hurry to get to Fairbanks. Gatty's back was bothering him so much that they rested there while Gatty saw a doctor and was bandaged up. Meanwhile, Post bought a new propeller and had it installed. After that, they got some three hours of much-needed sleep.

Post described the next leg, to Edmonton, Alberta, Canada, this way:

> Leaving Fairbanks, it seemed as if the rain would never stop. We were hardly off the ground before we started running into it. As we came along the side of Mount McKinley the weather began to thicken, so we barged upstairs. We figured that it was better to be high coming down along the shelf of the Canadian Rockies and, anyhow, the sky was lighter at higher altitudes, even if it wasn't clear.
>
> As we came down further, and our load lightened, we climbed still higher, where we got a sight and checked our position. We found that we were pretty nearly on course and needed only a slight change to get us to Edmonton. As we slid downhill through the murk the rain got heavier and so flooded the windshield and windows that we had to poke little pieces of rag and whatever we had handy into all of the little crevices to keep it from splashing in.
>
> The visibility near the ground was better than we expected, but when we looked at the field at the municipal airport at Edmonton we were almost afraid to try to land on it. It looked like a swamp.

Post managed a safe landing by keeping the nose high with the power on. But after seeing how soft the field was, he realized he would have great difficulty getting off. A Canadian airmail pilot suggested to Post that he try the main street of Edmonton, which was paved. The city authorities who greeted them were eager to cooperate. They authorized the removal of power and telephone lines, which was done while Post and Gatty slept.

Post didn't like the delay, but neither did he worry; the hardest part of the flight was behind them. As he rationalized, "We still had three days in which to make good our word that we would be back at Roosevelt Field in ten days. That's where the hurrying we did on the early part of the trip stood us in good stead and relieved our minds of worry."

While work crews removed the obstacles to takeoff, volunteers towed the *Winnie Mae* from the airport and washed it. The next morning, Post and Gatty raced down Edmonton's Portage Avenue in a sparkling white-and-purple Vega to cheers from everyone. Their next stop was Cleveland, Ohio.

This leg proved the fastest of the entire flight because of tailwinds, but it was over some of the most forbidding terrain for navigation. They had to fly over seemingly endless second-growth forests with no landmarks to guide by. The *Winnie Mae* crossed into the United States southeast of Winnipeg, then flew over a corner of Lake Superior and crossed Lake Michigan to a point north of Detroit. They landed in Cleveland, where the plane was refueled for the final leg. Thirty minutes after touching down, they were airborne again. "Then came the most impatient part of the trip," Post recalled. "That last hour before we got to New York just dragged along. We never knew before that the Jersey marshes were so wide. Presently, though, the ground haze that [often] covers New York City came up over the nose. . . . it was the most welcome sight you can imagine." Post circled Roosevelt Field twice and sideslipped in for a landing. "We could hear the automobile horns and the police sirens," Post said, "even though we were almost deaf from the . . . roar of our own [engines]."

The flight was completed July 1, 1931. Post and Gatty had beaten the *Graf Zeppelin's* mark by more than 12 days. An official timer from the National Aeronautic Association clocked the flight at 8 days, 15 hours, and 51 minutes, covering 15,474 miles. Out of this total, the *Winnie Mae* had logged 107 hours and 2 minutes in the air.

All Post and Gatty wanted at this point was a good night's sleep, but they didn't get it, not right away. There were radio and press interviews, a ticker tape parade down Broadway, a meeting with President Hoover, and luncheons and dinners, where they were given awards and citations. The praise did not impress Post. He was pleased that he had done what he set out to do, but he didn't believe the flight had made a particular contribution to aviation progress. "Our flight didn't prove a thing," he said. "No stunt flying ever does. It is silly to say that such flights are made to develop aviation. We didn't advance the mechanics of aviation one inch."

Despite this evaluation, Post's feat received worldwide praise. Although it may not have advanced aviation "one inch," it did highlight the technical advances made in aviation up to that time. The *Daily Oklahoman* predicted: "Such feats as that of Post and Gatty are destined to become commonplace before the world is very much older. [Soon] the world will pay no more attention to the feat cheered so insanely . . . Wednesday than it will to a morning flight from New York to Philadelphia. The future of the human race is in the air."

The flight of Wiley Post and Harold Gatty was a test of men as much as it was a display of technological progress in aviation. Physical and mental fatigue can cause great damage to the human nervous system. Lack of sleep is the aviator's worst enemy; the desire for it can overcome willpower and dull the senses. The sound of a smoothly operating engine acts like a sedative, lulling an already dulled mind. The lone flier who succumbs to the combination of fatigue from sleeplessness and the drone of an airplane engine rarely lives to tell about the experience.

7

PANGBORN AND HERNDON

The urge to set new speed and distance marks spread like wildfire in the later 1920s and early '30s. For every success, however, there were many failures. Rare was the individual who turned failure into success. Two airmen who did were Clyde E. Pangborn and Hugh Herndon Jr. Pangborn was a gypsy pilot who had barnstormed his way from coast to coast for more than a decade; Herndon, scion of a wealthy eastern family, had teamed up with Pangborn to form "The Flying Fleet," a traveling air circus.

In the late '20s, Pangborn and Herndon got nearly a hundred bookings in 36 states and carried 121,000 passengers. But in 1931, they and their entourage found themselves in Palo Alto, California, with three New Standard planes and no bookings. They had to sell the planes to pay the hangar rent. For all practical purposes, barnstorming in open-cockpit planes was at an end. Not only was the Great Depression raging but other barnstormers were selling rides in such closed-cabin planes as the Ford Trimotor and the Fokker.

The decline of barnstorming often meant the end of friendships, but the breakup of The Flying Fleet did not end the friendship of Pangborn and Herndon. Herndon's family had helped finance the air circus. Pangborn felt sure they would help again if they could be convinced that another flying venture was feasible. Pangborn is credited with being among the first to wonder about trying to beat the round-the-world record of 21 days, 7 hours, and 34 minutes set by the *Graf Zeppelin* in 1929. Herndon was enthusiastic about the idea, and the two men set up the RTW (Round The World) Corporation, with headquarters in New York

City to handle the financial end of the project. Herndon, at his family's insistence, was made president of the company.

Pangborn selected a Bellanca Skyrocket monoplane as the aircraft for the flight. Herndon's mother gave them a check for $100,000, which, after paying for the plane, left them with enough to buy special long-range equipment, fuel, and other supplies. In the spring of 1931, Herndon told the press of his and Pangborn's intention to beat the *Graf's* mark, but under three conditions: "We will take no subscriptions from anybody. We will pay cash for the things we have to get, including gas and oil. . . . we will make the most careful preparations that have ever been made for a long-distance flight."

Pangborn planned the flight somewhat differently from those of other round-the-world fliers. The route he projected would take them over the shipping lanes east of New York (their point of departure), then northeast to England. They would thus avoid the fog and uncertain weather of the Great Circle Route via Newfoundland. Then they would proceed as others had—across Europe, the Soviet Union, the Aleutians, Alaska, and across Canada, returning to New York City. There was an air of urgency about Pangborn and Herndon's plans. Several other pilots were at that moment planning long-distance flights. Among them were Bernt Balchen, Roger Q. Williams, Wiley Post and Harold Gatty, Ruth Nichols, John Mears, and Russell Boardman and John Polando. Post and Gatty started their flight on June 21, 1931, but Pangborn and Herndon were undaunted. On June 30, as Post and Gatty neared the end of their journey, Pangborn and Herndon bumped down the rough grass strip of Roosevelt Field in *Miss Veedol.* Their avowed purpose was to top the speed of their rivals, whatever that speed turned out to be. John Heinmuller describes what happened next:

> It was well known to all experienced fliers acquainted with Roosevelt Field that unless a plane could be lifted from the rough space within 2,000 feet, it would meet disaster at the end of the field, where holes and earth craters marked the border lines.
>
> Since the Lindbergh takeoff, one of the largest embankments at the southern end was known as a hoodoo to all fliers, but Pangborn figured that he would have his plane well up before reaching the end of the line, despite its heavy load.
>
> Russell Boardman and I (he was studying takeoffs by means of the $^{1}/_{10}$th-second chronograph and stopwatch to gain knowledge for his subsequent long-distance flight) were posted within 50 yards of the takeoff point; and after giving the signal and looking at the timepiece to record the actual moment of departure, we turned again to the speeding ship to record the time the wheels actually lifted into the air. The critical moment arrived, and

to our surprise the wheels never left the ground. At the end of the 2,000 feet the plane disappeared. . . . we rushed to Boardman's nearby automobile and drove at top speed to the scene of the supposed crash.

Arriving at the end of the field we jumped out . . . but instead of wreckage we saw the plane circling above us at a dangerously low altitude.

And at that moment a general baptism took place. Pangborn, seeing that it was impossible to gain a safe altitude, nodded to Herndon who was waiting with hand on the emergency valve, and they dumped between four and five hundred gallons of gasoline. . . .

Through skillful handling of the lightened plane, he then managed to get slowly into the air, but, of course he could not continue the flight and in a few minutes the *Miss Veedol* came in to a landing.*

The near accident was soon forgotten, but Pangborn moved the Bellanca to nearby Floyd Bennett Field to take advantage of its newly completed concrete runway. Four weeks went by, however, before *Miss Veedol* was ready to fly again. Meanwhile, Post and Gatty had returned to a rousing tribute, which seemed to diminish the enthusiasm of the group of well-wishers who came to see Pangborn and Herndon off.

At 6:16 A.M., July 28, *Miss Veedol* lifted into the brightening dawn just 17 minutes behind Boardman and Polando, also in a Bellanca. Although it wasn't forecast, they encountered fog only a few minutes offshore. For the next 30 hours, without sighting land or water, Pangborn fought boredom and fatigue while trying to stay on course. He seldom gave Herndon the controls, because he didn't trust Herndon's ability to fly on instruments. At the end of the 30 hours, as dusk of the second day enveloped them, Pangborn knew they had to be over land; he spiraled down through a break in the clouds. Spotting a field below that looked fairly level, he landed and bumped across the furrows. The farmer who rushed out told them this was Moylegrove, in Pembrokeshire, Wales, near Cardiff. He took them to an inn where the weary pilots had dinner and got some sleep.

The next morning, Pangborn and Herndon took off for Croydon Airport, outside London. There, Herndon was met by relatives who whisked him away, much to Pangborn's chagrin. Pangborn wanted to refuel and push on. Herndon did not return for six hours. When he did show up, Pangborn was fuming with frustration. He had the engine started and was about to taxi out alone when Herndon arrived in a limousine and cheerfully bade his hosts good-bye.

As they headed over the Urals toward Novosibirsk, Pangborn estimated that they were 10 hours and 57 minutes behind Post and Gatty's time. En route, they lost more time as they flew under endless overcast,

---

* Heinmuller, *Man's Fight to Fly*, New York: Funk & Wagnalls, 1944.

parallel to the mountains, looking for a pass to slip through. Pausing briefly at Novosibirsk for fuel, they continued east, this time with Herndon at the controls; Pangborn slept. Once again, Herndon got off course; when Pangborn awoke, he could identify nothing on the ground. In desperation, he landed at a small village and, after a frustrating attempt to find someone who could speak English, was told, through signs and a few English words, that they were in Mongolia, not far from Chita. They took off again and landed at Chita, to find that they were now nearly a day behind Post's time. Heavy rain and fog made the nighttime flight to Khabarovsk difficult. At dawn they sighted a village and landed on a muddy airfield that was much too short. Unable to stop in time, the Bellanca plunged off the end into the mud and sank to the fuselage. It was a day before the rain stopped and the plane could be hauled to a hangar for cleaning.

Pangborn and Herndon were now more than 27 hours behind; they knew they couldn't overtake Post and Gatty. As they agonized over what to do, Pangborn recalled that a prize of $25,000 had been offered by the Japanese newspaper *Asahi Shimbun* to the first person or persons to fly nonstop from Japan to the United States. Another $25,000 had been offered by the city of Seattle for the first Japan–Seattle flight. Since they were so close to Japan, and were out of the running for a new world-circling record, they decided to see if they could turn defeat into victory of another kind.

Pangborn telegraphed the editor of the *Japanese Times*, an English-language newspaper in Tokyo, and asked that the American embassy be notified so permission could be obtained from the Japanese Aviation Bureau to overfly and land in Japan. Because he had no maps of Japan, Pangborn also asked for directions from the center of Tokyo to Tachikawa Field. When no reply was received, Pangborn, fearing more bad weather, decided to take off. En route to Japan, Herndon took still and motion pictures. Pangborn sighted Tokyo Bay and flew around its rim to Haneda Airport, a new field between Tokyo and Yokohama not yet open to air traffic. He landed and taxied to the parking ramp, where he was ordered to take off and fly to Tachikawa Field. Sensing that he was in trouble, but confident that the American embassy would straighten things out, Pangborn landed at Tachikawa a few minutes later. As he taxied *Miss Veedol* to the ramp, police and vehicles surrounded the plane. He shut the engine down, and Japanese authorities climbed aboard, demanding evidence of permission to land in Japan. Pangborn and Herndon, of course, had no permission. The cameras only made matters worse. When the authorities spotted them, they hustled the fliers out of the plane and placed them under house arrest at the Imperial Hotel. Pangborn and Herndon were questioned at length. They were accused of flying over restricted territory without a permit and of taking photographs of military installations.

At a press interview later, Pangborn admitted that he had left Khabarovsk without a permit but denied seeing any military installations. "We were just tourists taking what we thought were pretty landscape shots," he said disarmingly. It was widely reported that the two airmen had been put in a Tokyo prison, but Herndon denied this, complaining bitterly to the press:

> We weren't jailed, but we were restricted in our movements. We had to be escorted everywhere and were subjected to endless questioning. . . . in searching the plane, the police found a few pounds of rice. They couldn't understand why we carried it. It was impossible to make clear that this was part of our emergency food supply in case we should have been forced down in a remote area.
>
> It was likewise impossible to get [across] to them that it would have been very stupid to fly more than halfway around the world, get lost, bog down in mud, take pictures of restricted areas, and then land in the very country allegedly being spied on.
>
> And we couldn't get through to the American ambassador. Every time we tried to contact him, we were told he was out playing golf. If he had been on the job we would have been released in no time. It was only when my mother got Senator Borah to again intercede for us, this time direct with the Japanese ambassador in Washington, D.C., that we were released.

The frustration and unreasonable attitude of the Japanese authorities only made Pangborn more determined to compete for the prize money. In the meantime, he had learned of still another prize—$25,000 for the first one-stop Japan-to-Texas flight, offered by W.E. Easterwood, a Texas businessman. After days of frustrating talks, Pangborn finally convinced Japanese officials that they were serious, and they were given a permit to depart, but with the stipulation that they would be allowed only one take-off. If they failed, they would have to go home by ship, with their airplane in a crate. In the hindsight of history, the Japanese may have had good reason to make such a proviso. It is possible that they were already preparing for war, and wanted no outsiders, especially Americans, spying on their military installations. It is also possible that the prize was offered to stimulate the development of aviation in Japan to the point where Japanese aircraft could eventually reach American shores for military purposes.

Pangborn and Herndon weren't the first to attempt the Japan–United States flight in pursuit of the prize money and the fame. On September 15, 1931, while Pangborn and Herndon were battling the Japanese bureaucracy, Harold Bromley and Harold Gatty departed in a Lockheed

Sirius from Sabishiro Beach, about 200 miles north of Tokyo. They chose Sabishiro because it was relatively hard and had an 8,000-foot stretch that would enable a heavily loaded plane to take off. Nearly 24 hours into the flight, though, the Lockheed's engine malfunctioned, and they were forced to return.

On June 1, 1931, Thomas Ash attempted a takeoff from the same point, but cracked up during takeoff. Then, on September 8, Don Moyle and Cecil Allen got off successfully but were forced down on the Kamchatka Peninsula. They took off but were forced down again on an uninhabited island in the Aleutians, where they stayed for seven days without food or shelter. Improving weather enabled them to reach Nome and Fairbanks, Alaska, on October 5, 1931. They flew to Seattle, arriving October 9.

Although they did not know of these attempts, Pangborn and Herndon were determined to try their luck from Sabishiro Beach, feeling that it offered the best chance for a successful takeoff. On September 2, their Bellanca was released to them. After a few days of delays trying to get permission to fly to Sabishiro and take off there, they were granted clearance. A new stipulation was added, however. To make the flight from Tokyo to Sabishiro, they would have to fly 50 miles offshore; otherwise, their take-off permit would be revoked.

During the weeks of their involuntary stay, Pangborn had studied the best charts he could obtain. He also designed an extra gas tank, concluding that they would have to take off with the heaviest load the Bellanca had ever lifted. "Even then, it was marginal," he told the press later; "we would have enough fuel to take us the approximately 4,500 miles to the U.S. west coast. Studying the problem I calculated that we could increase our speed approximately 15 mph if we could rid ourselves of the drag of the fixed landing gear. On a 40-hour flight that would be the equivalent of adding 600 miles to our range, and that might make the difference between success and failure."

Pangborn was correct. He had been trained as a civil engineer, and now he applied his know-how to the technical modifications needed to enable them to drop the landing gear after takeoff and make a safe belly landing at, they hoped, the Seattle airport. Pangborn designed a release-pin mechanism that he could operate from the cockpit. The work on the Bellanca was done mostly by Pangborn himself in a hangar guarded by Japanese soldiers, but some machine-shop assistance was given secretly by Americans living in Tokyo, who wanted Pangborn and Herndon to succeed.

On September 16, *Miss Veedol* landed at Sabishiro; again, with the help of Americans, it was readied for flight. Fearing that the Japanese would discover the secret modification and revoke their permit, they busied themselves with the rest of the plane, deliberately avoiding a check of the gear mechanism. Pangborn, walking every inch of the beach, found a wood ramp built for other attempts, to help aircraft gain speed before they reached the soft sand. The ramp was modified to accommodate the Bellanca's landing gear.

Finally, at dawn on the morning of October 1, 1931, *Miss Veedol's* engine was warmed up and the gas tanks were topped off. Then, just before they were to walk out to the plane, they discovered that the charts Pangborn had prepared so carefully had been stolen. "Everyone who had anything to do with us in Japan had threatening letters from the Black Dragon Society," Pangborn said later; "so we place the blame for the missing maps on that organization."

Thoroughly frustrated, they decided to take off anyway. At the top of the ramp, Pangborn revved up the engine and released the brakes. The heavily laden Bellanca plunged down the boards to the beach and slowly gathered speed on the soft sand. At the halfway point of the 8,000-foot stretch, it still had not gained enough speed to lift the tail. At 6,000 feet the tail slowly lifted. As the logs at the end of the beach loomed, Pangborn pulled back on the elevator controls and *Miss Veedol* lifted off with agonizing slowness. "Since I had permission for only one takeoff," Pangborn said later, "I was going to get it off the ground or pile into those logs. We had seen enough of Japan!"

In a story that appeared in the *New York Times,* Herndon described the flight:

It climbed steadily, going southward. After two or three miles, we turned slowly, circled back over the beach at 1,000 feet, and headed on course for America.

We had figured it out previously that if we could hold a compass course of 72 degrees we would eventually arrive over Queen Charlotte Island on the Canadian [coast] and fly from there to the United States. We checked our compass over Hokkaido Island and other islands in the Kuriles. About 300 miles from Sabishiro we dropped our wheels. First one, then the other.

After proceeding for about 500 miles up the Kurile Islands, we headed out to sea with a handful of . . . weather reports and plenty of fog ahead. We dropped the rest of the landing gear . . . by pulling the cables . . . thereby pulling the steel pins out that [held] the gear in place. The air speed increased about 15 mph with the landing gear removed.

The first serious trouble we met was due to ice forming on our wings just as night fell. With our still heavy load we were trying to climb above the clouds and having a tough time at that.

It was bitterly cold. Even the drinking water in our canteens froze, to say nothing about our hands and feet.

The first encouraging sign we saw . . . was a volcano. Before leaving Japan we had hoped that we might see it at a distance, as it was on our course. . . . it loomed directly under us in the fog, showing us that we were exactly . . . on . . . course. . . .

After passing the volcano we came to a high bank of clouds which we could not fly over, so we had to go through and took on a . . . load of ice. We had to fly with wide-open throttle at 17,000 feet for four hours, thereby using up our precious supply of gasoline rapidly.

Pangborn here climbed out on the wing struts and unscrewed the remaining two landing gear struts. . . . We were both suffering from the terrific cold in spite of . . . wearing heavy flying suits and . . . warm blankets. . . . We had figured on reaching Charlotte Island at 10 o'clock on the night of October 2. We finally reached the north part of Vancouver Island at midnight. . . . We kept looking for lighthouses blinking on the coast, but for a long time we saw nothing but winking stars, which we mistook for lighthouses.

The first sight of America was the flashing beacon on Vancouver Island. We changed our course for Seattle. Soon, flying at 16,000 feet, with the clouds just under us, we thought we were over Seattle. We could see the . . . lights reflected on the clouds, but we weren't sure it was Seattle. A high cloud bank ahead proved to be Mount Rainier, so we established our position definitely.

We then had to plan a landing in a big field from which we might have to take a heavily loaded ship on a non-stop flight to Dallas . . . we still believed that we had been accepted as entrants [in] Colonel Easterwood's Japan-to-Dallas one-stop flight. . . .

We changed our course for Spokane, where we knew there was a big field; but on arriving there we found it fog-bound, so we headed for Wenatchee, which . . . was always clear, [we had] visited that city several times. . . . Had we not been planning on flying on to Dallas, we would have continued on until our gas was exhausted, not caring where we landed, so long as we established a long-distance record.

We gave up the long-distance idea in the hope of capturing the Easterwood prize.*

For Pangborn, the moment of decision meant that he had to try to land the Bellanca on its belly with a minimum of damage so new gear could be attached and the plane flown to Dallas. But the flight wasn't over yet. Where was Wenatchee? Pangborn's mother and his brother, Percy, who lived there, were waiting to hear from him. The earth below was covered with fog; only the high points of the terrain showed. Finally, Pangborn got his bearings, dipped below the fog layer, and hedgehopped among familiar landmarks toward his destination.

Although their ultimate destination wasn't Wenatchee, Pangborn's mother and a few family friends thought they might land there. Word

---

* *New York Times*, Oct. 6, 1931.

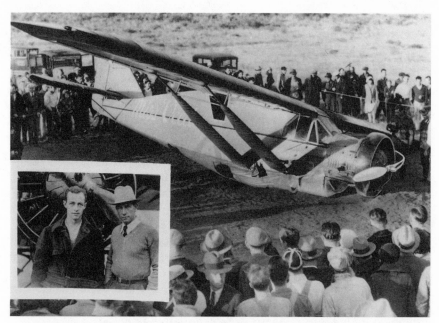

Hugh Herndon (left) and Clyde Pangborn were upstaged by Wiley Post's record-setting 1931 flight but were the first to fly the Pacific from Japan to the contiguous 48 states. They released their landing gear after takeoff to reduce weight and drag. The crash landing was made at Wenatchee, Washington, Pangborn's hometown. (National Air and Space Museum photo)

had been flashed across the Pacific that the fliers had left Sabishiro. A ham operator at Dutch Harbor had radioed that he heard a plane overhead at approximately the time the Bellanca was due if it was on course. When he finally located the field, Pangborn made a low pass to look for obstructions and then pulled up to dump most of the remaining fuel before attempting the belly landing. When he was satisfied, he lined up with the runway and told Herndon to get as far back in the rear cabin as possible, so as to hold the tail down and prevent a noseup when they skidded on the plane's underbelly.

Pangborn kept the power on slightly, established a glide, and eased back on the throttle, keeping the plane just above stall speed. As he crossed the fence at the end of the runway, he cut the switch, hoping to stop the prop in a horizontal position. He didn't; the prop was vertical and touched the ground first. The wheelless plane skidded forward, sending up a cloud of dust. As it slowed, it rolled onto the left wing. Finally, they stopped.

Alerted by radio news reports, about a hundred people were gathered, including Opal Pangborn. By the time the haggard fliers had slowly crawled from the plane, a much larger crowd had gathered. Herndon dabbed at blood on his forehead. He had been cut as the plane slid to a stop. Both men were shaky, red-eyed, weak from the flight. They asked to be taken somewhere to rest. Later that day, Seattle broke loose in the greatest demonstration in its history. When the two heroes awoke, they were treated to a parade, a formal welcome by the state's lieutenant governor and by representatives of *Asahi Shimbun*, who presented Pangborn and Herndon with a check for $25,000. Congratulatory messages poured in, but there was one message with bad news. Colonel Easterwood telegraphed from Dallas that the two pilots were not eligible for his prize because he had reserved the right to select who would try for it, and he had chosen someone else.

This was a huge disappointment. Instead of being flown to Dallas, *Miss Veedol* was trucked to Seattle and there put on display for a few days. After a round of dinners, parades, and personal appearances, Pangborn and Herndon had a new landing gear installed and flew to New York. The plane, which Herndon owned, was later sold and rechristened *The American Nurse*. Subsequently, it was lost at sea when its new owner attempted to fly the Atlantic from New York to Rome.

Pangborn and Herndon parted company when it was discovered that what Pangborn assumed was a 50–50 partnership was in actuality more like 90–10, in favor of Herndon. Pangborn's total income for the flight was about $2,500 after all the bills had been paid. As the principal pilot on the flight, however, he was awarded the prestigious Harmon International Trophy for 1931. Although it had not been given for a round-the-world flight, it was well deserved as recognition of the first nonstop air crossing of the Pacific (it took 41 hours and 13 minutes). What began as an effort to beat Post and Gatty ended in a spectacular aviation first.

Miss Veedol did not survive to be placed in a museum, but its flight and pilots are memorialized. A wood shaft stands today at Sabishiro Beach, and a granite shaft—in reality, a memorial to Pangborn—can be seen on a hilltop overlooking the Columbia River at Wenatchee, Washington, where it was erected in 1968.

8

POST DOES IT AGAIN!

Shortly after his flight in 1931, Wiley Post and F.C. Hall, his principal backer and the owner of the *Winnie Mae,* had strong differences of opinion concerning the use of the plane for personal appearances. Post resolved the dispute by purchasing the Vega from Hall for $21,000. Hall immediately bought another Vega, which he christened *Winnie Mae of Oklahoma,* and hired a pilot named Frank Hoover. Hall announced that he would sponsor Hoover's assault on the Post-Gatty record in the new plane.

Wiley Post wasn't disturbed by this threat to his record. In August 1931, he talked about trying to make a nonstop flight from Tokyo to Seattle but was upstaged by the success of Pangborn and Herndon's flight. The Great Depression was also having an adverse effect on aviation. The demand for personal appearances by Post and Gatty dropped off. Gatty returned to his business in San Diego and, in general, thoughts of setting flight records receded. The popular *Literary Digest* editorialized that ocean fliers could not "raise the price of gasoline to fill the tanks let alone make any profit on the trip."

The year 1932 was one of the low points in aviation history. Only five transatlantic flights were made. Hoover's flight never materialized. Although Post managed to keep the *Winnie Mae* in the air, and made some personal appearances, he was scraping bottom. He was preoccupied by thoughts of making another world-girdling flight. There was no longer an F.C. Hall to back the effort, however. Still Post envisioned not only beating his own record but doing it alone. It wouldn't be easy; his greatest enemy would again be fatigue. Meanwhile, the rumor was circulating that Post would use a robot pilot to fly the plane while he slept.

Various aspirants surfaced from time to time, and then disappeared. A few were serious and found backers. Two of the latter were Bennett

Griffin and James J. Mattern. In the summer of 1932, Griffin and Mattern announced an attempt to beat Post and Gatty's record. They left on July 5 but were forced down in the Soviet Union when the cabin hatch fell off and damaged the vertical stabilizer, causing them to crash land. They had to abandon the flight for that year. They planned another flight for the next year. When they heard that Post was going to fly solo, they decided to do the same and flipped a coin to see who would go. Mattern won and immediately purchased a used Vega.

In the meantime, Post had installed his "robot" pilot in the *Winnie Mae*—a Sperry automatic pilot. Refusing to say what his plans were, he made a flight from Oklahoma City to Mexico City to test the device. He was pleased with his "autopilot." Because he would be flying alone, more room would be available in the rear cabin of the Vega for installing extra gas tanks. This he did.

But now fate intervened. After his flight to Mexico City, Post wanted to demonstrate the autopilot to his friend, L.E. ("Red") Gray, a pilot for Braniff. When Gray climbed in the cockpit, he noticed that the fuel gauges read empty. Post assured Gray that he had personally put some gas in the tanks the night before, enough for a hop around the Chickasha airport. Gray shrugged and started the engine. Accompanied by Post and two passengers in the rear cabin, Gray took off. At an altitude of only 50 feet, the engine suddenly quit and the *Winnie Mae* plunged into a peach orchard at the end of the field. The plywood fuselage was shattered. It seemed impossible that anyone had survived. But the occupants of the plane were lucky: Gray and one of the passengers were unhurt; Post cut a finger, and the other passenger had two cracked ribs. Later it was discovered that teenagers had siphoned the gas for their car.

Although the *Winnie Mae* seemed a jumbled mess, its airframe had survived. With the help of George Brauer, a master woodworker and a mechanic for Braniff, Post restored the plane and even made some changes in the cockpit that he had wanted made for some time. Larger gas tanks were installed in the wings, and the entire rear cabin was filled with fuel tanks. The aircraft could now carry a total of 645 gallons. To compensate for the shifting weight as gasoline was consumed, a transfer system was installed that enabled Post to shift fuel between the fore and aft tanks.

The Wasp engine was improved by installing cylinders of higher compression, and a new type of carburetor, magnetos, and an ignition harness replaced the old equipment. A controllable-pitch propeller was added to improve fuel consumption. As a result, the *Winnie Mae* rolled out of the Braniff shop a much improved airplane; it could now climb better and cruise faster and more efficiently.

Post still had not formally announced his plans, but aviation writers in the know were guessing that he was serious about a solo attempt to break his own record. Actually, Post had been mentally preparing himself for a long time. Scheduling only five refueling stops—Berlin, Novosibirsk, Khabarovsk, Fairbanks, and Edmonton—he was confident that the modifications to the Vega would enable him to fly the longer legs without difficulty.

There remained a major obstacle, however: money. Post had had to borrow to pay for the repairs on the plane, and he was now broke. Knowing this, a group of Oklahoma City businessmen came to his rescue; 41 people and business firms contributed to financing Post's venture. The Pratt & Whitney Company not only furnished parts for the revitalized Wasp engine but loaned Post a technician as well. The Sperry Gyroscope Company donated the autopilot and provided technical assistance. The Socony-Vacuum Company (now Mobil) agreed to furnish gas, oil, and grease at the company's facilities en route. The effort almost foundered, however, when the Amtorg Company, remembering its experience with the Griffin-Mattern flight the year before, demanded $1,000 as an advance to cover emergencies. The matter was resolved when the head of the Texas Company (now Texaco) persuaded the Russians to agree to a letter of credit of $1,500.

At the end of May 1933, the *Winnie Mae* was nearly ready. Post put it through a series of test flights. Meanwhile, Mattern was pushing ahead, readying his Vega, *Century of Progress*. The newspapers tried to build up a rivalry between the two fliers, but Post would not be pushed; he had no intention of taking off before July 1, and he said so.

Mattern, on the other hand, had made all the preparations he thought necessary and departed from Floyd Bennett Field on June 3. Twenty-three hours and fifty-five minutes later he landed at Jomfruland, Norway. Until he found someone to tell him where he was, he thought he had landed in Scotland. Undisturbed by this navigational error, Mattern refueled, and took off, heading for Oslo, Moscow, Omsk, and Chita. At this point, he was far ahead of the Post-Gatty schedule; but from Moscow on, the flight became more difficult. Mattern experienced engine trouble and was eventually forced down in a remote part of Siberia. His survival and eventual rescue became legend.

Post, who was following Mattern's flight in the papers, told reporters that even if Mattern was successful, he would stick to his plans and make the flight. Post arrived at Floyd Bennett Field about mid-June. As had happened before, he waited for days for reports of favorable weather over the North Atlantic. Post and other fliers of the period had a problem in obtaining reliable weather information. There was no systematic reporting of weather over the ocean or around its rim. The only source of weather information was ships at sea, which did not always report along the routes of flights. As before, however, James K. Kimball, meteorologist in New York for the U.S. Weather Bureau, helped considerably. Despite the meager information coming into his office in downtown Manhattan, Kimball had been correct about the weather on Post's first flight, and Post respected his forecasts this time. He would not take off until Kimball told him the weather out over the Atlantic was favorable.

Post postponed his flight several times, and there were some false starts. Finally, just after midnight, July 15, Kimball's report was for improving flight conditions. Post decided to go. Dressed in a double-breasted business suit (Post never adopted the cavalry boots, riding breeches, helmet, and goggles of the time), he lowered himself through the hatch of the cockpit. At 5:10 A.M. he released the brakes, and the *Winnie Mae* was soon airborne.

Shortly after taking off, Post flew into fog and clouds and immediately turned on the autopilot. He cruised northeast over the coast of Nova Scotia and tuned in the station at St. John's, Newfoundland, to get a fix on his position. He was pleased with the station's weather report. As Dr. Kimball had predicted, the weather was clear about halfway to England. There, however, he caught up with the front that had kept him grounded for so long at Floyd Bennett Field. Clouds, rain, and fog engulfed him. He switched to instrument flight, keeping his radio tuned for weather information. Sometime later, out of the static came the welcome words "a special broadcast for Wiley Post." It was station G2L0, in Manchester, England, broadcasting a message for him. Post turned his radio compass needle to get a fix on the station. As he crossed the British Isles, he picked up others. Now confident of his position, he crossed the Irish Sea and sped across the Continent, heading for Berlin. The weather was gradually improving, and Post could now see the ground. He passed over the Elbe and soon saw the skyline of Berlin ahead.

Twenty-five hours and forty-five minutes after takeoff, he landed at Tempelhof. Among the cheering thousands was the chief of the German Air Ministry, Hermann Goering. Although others had tried, Post was the first actually to fly nonstop the 3,942 miles from New York to Berlin. It was the greatest distance anyone had flown from the United States to a point in Europe.

When Post climbed down from the cockpit, eager welcomers offered him food and beer. But he was too fatigued by the strain of the trip to eat. "I don't want to eat," he said. "I don't want to shave. I don't want to bathe. I just want to clear out of here. I flew here on tomato juice and chewing gum, and that's enough for me."

Post was in Berlin only two hours and fifteen minutes. Then he headed for Novosibirsk. Near the Soviet border he discovered that his maps for the route ahead were missing. He searched frantically in the cockpit but couldn't find them. Forced to turn back, he landed at Koenigsberg, in East Prussia. Not only were his maps missing, but the oil supply line for the autopilot had sprung a leak and could not be used to fly the Vega hands off. Fortunately, its directional gyro and artificial horizon were functioning and could be used when flying blind. The delay seemed like a terrible waste of time to Post, but, in retrospect, it was fortuitous. After landing, he learned that the weather ahead had worsened. Now grounded for the night anyway, he got six hours of sound sleep.

When Post awoke, he faced a difficult decision: stop in Moscow and have the autopilot repaired, or push on to Novosibirsk as originally planned? Deciding on the former, he left Koenigsberg in such a hurry that he forgot his luggage. He landed without incident at October Field. There, Soviet mechanics repaired the oil line to the autopilot's servo units as best they could, but the autopilot did not work as well as it had. Two hours and fifteen minutes later, Post was en route to Novosibirsk, flying beneath a lowering, overcast sky. While flying on instruments, he had a near miss with a hilltop, and the incident frightened him. He climbed to 21,000 feet to try and get on top of the weather, but was unsuccessful. He descended, knowing that even if he had broken into the clear, lack of oxygen at that altitude would have soon dulled his senses.

This leg of the flight took 13 hours and 15 minutes, 7 hours of which were on instruments. At Novosibirsk, Post was met by Fay Gillis. Miss Gillis's father was an American engineer who had gone to the Soviet Union in 1930 as an advisor in the construction of two electrolytic zinc plants, part of the Soviets' first five-year plan. She had learned to fly when she was 19 and had the dubious distinction of being forced to bail out during a training flight with her instructor when the tail surfaces of their plane disintegrated. She thus became the first female member of the Caterpillar Club. At Post's request before he left New York, she had gone to Novosibirsk from Moscow, where she was living, to supervise refueling arrangements and to act as Post's interpreter. His cable to her read: LIKE YOU ARRIVE NOVOSIBIRSK BY JULY FIRST ARRANGE GAS PLANE IN TWO HOURS WHILE I SLEEP THEN FLY WITH ME TO KHABAROVSK TO DIRECT SERVICE THERE GET ME BEST MAPS NOVOSIBIRSK-KHABAROVSK WILL PAY YOUR EXPENSES REGARDS WILEY POST.

Fay flew to Novosibirsk, as requested, and met the *Winnie Mae*. She did not fly on to Khabarovsk, however, because, as was later explained, that would have negated any claim of Post's to having made a solo flight. Two hours after landing, Post was on his way again, this time with the proper maps. More trouble with the autopilot developed during this leg, and Post made an unscheduled stop at Irkutsk. His flight time for the 1,055 miles was 6 hours and 33 minutes, the fastest leg of the entire flight. At this stop, the Russians reported heavy thunderstorms over the Baikal

Mountains to the east; Post delayed his departure for a few hours. The enforced delay gave him a chance to get some sleep and allowed mechanics to repair the autopilot.

Post ran into rain soon after taking off. It and darkness made flight by ground reference points almost impossible. He was following the tracks of the Trans-Siberian Railroad to Khabarovsk but lost sight of them and wandered off course. After a flight of seven and a half hours, he sighted the town of Skovorodino and landed. Dismayed to find that his ground speed was less than 100 mph, Post decided to push on to Khabarovsk. Comparing his time with the 1931 flight, he found that he was only an hour behind schedule.

What happened next is detailed in a monograph published by the Smithsonian's National Air and Space Museum, "Wiley Post, His *Winnie Mae*, and the World's First Pressure Suit," by Mohler and Johnson:

> Upon landing at Skovorodino, Wiley was thirsty, but the Russians were unable to understand him when he asked for a drink of water. They thought he wanted liquor. Finally, . . . the Russians brought forth a samovar of tea. . . . After a few hours, Post took off for Khabarovsk; the headwinds over this leg were negligible; he was able to make a ground speed of 150 miles per hour, and touched down at Khabarovsk after a flight of four and one-half hours.
>
> Two hours were spent refueling the *Winnie Mae* at Khabarovsk, and Post studied the Russians' weather reports carefully. Jimmy Mattern, who was still at Anadyr, assisted the Russians in preparing the weather reports of the Bering Sea area for Post. When Post took off for Khabarovsk, he faced a 3,100-mile flight to Fairbanks, . . . but by this stage of the flight he was by no means as fresh. And between Khabarovsk and his Alaskan landfall at Nome stretched the Sea of Okhotsk, the Kamchatka Peninsula, which had mountains that reached up to 15,000 feet, and then the . . . Bering Sea. It was an arduous flight, even for a pilot who was well rested and who enjoyed good weather over the route, but Wiley teetered on the edge of fatigue, and the weather he met was bad.
>
> Thick clouds stood . . . across the Sea of Okhotsk, but Post plunged into them and for the next seven hours he flew by instruments and autopilot. Post was unequivocal in his praise of the autopilot during these hours and credited it for his success between Khabarovsk and Fairbanks. When the *Winnie Mae* finally flew out of the murk, Post found himself flying at 14,000 feet above a great cloud layer above the Gulf of Anadyr; he was able to recognize the Gulf by the smoothness of the clouds, where they covered the sea. Somewhere below. . . . in the village of Anadyr, Jimmy Mattern sat by a radio, sweating out Post's passage. . . . [Two hours went by] . . . then a purple fringe took shape across the monotonous horizon ahead, . . . —the mountains of the Seward Peninsula. With the coast of Alaska in sight, Post began a gradual letdown to about 3,000 feet and a few minutes later, the

Winnie Mae's shadow crossed the Alaskan shoreline at Cape Prince of Wales. From the Cape, Wiley swung . . . southeast and followed the desolate coastline to Nome; he circled the Nome radio station to announce his arrival, and then sped off . . . east for the Yukon and Fairbanks.

Now Wiley began to have troubles with his radio and ADF set; he could not pick up the Fairbanks radio station. About halfway between Nome and Fairbanks, Noel and Ada Wien, pioneer Alaskan bush pilots . . . were in the air . . . and spotted the *Winnie Mae*. She was circling over the Yukon River, as if lost. They flew toward the *Winnie Mae*, hoping to get Post's attention. But he never saw them, and flew off toward the southeast. The Wiens attempted to follow, but . . . the *Winnie Mae* was soon lost to sight.

Post was flying southeast toward McGrath, which was considerably off course from the correct heading for Fairbanks. As the *Winnie Mae* flew over McGrath, Oscar Winchell, a radio operator for McGee Airways of Anchorage, tried to get radio contact with Post, but with no results. The *Winnie Mae* flew off into the southwest, and on a heading which was exactly the opposite from a course for Fairbanks.

Having troubles with his radio, being unfamiliar with the terrain, afflicted by poor visibility, and being crowded by fatigue, Post was wandering around Alaska's skies, looking for a landmark that would correspond to something on his charts and that would provide a bearing for a course to Fairbanks. Meanwhile, he also had to take care to dodge the 20,000-foot summit of Mount McKinley and its satellite peaks. . . .

Post finally looked out his windshield and saw the small mining settlement of Flat below him. . . . The radio operator at Flat called Winchell at McGrath and notified him that the *Winnie Mae* was circling overhead. At this point . . . Post was 31 hours and 29 minutes ahead of the 1931 record. . . . But [he] was tired; he knew he was lost, and in no condition to continue; he throttled back his Wasp and trimmed out the *Winnie Mae* for a landing at Flat.

The airfield at Flat was no more than a crude landing strip; it was 700 feet long and had a ditch across its end. Post brought the *Winnie Mae* in lightly, touched down easily, and rolled out nicely—but was unable to brake in time to avoid running into the ditch. As the *Winnie Mae's* wheels skidded into the ditch, she lurched over on her right wing, and the right leg of her landing gear crumpled; her tail came up, driving her nose into the earth, bending the complex Smith propeller; and she finally came to a stop with her engine cowl in the dirt. As Post studied the damage, he ruefully recalled that the accident was similar to the one he and Gatty had experienced at Solomon Beach in 1931. However, the two accidents probably had less to do with Solomon, Flat, or Alaska's primitive airfields, than it did with Post's state of fatigue in this final stage of his flights.

Once again, luck was on Post's side, as the damage turned out to be minor. Fellow aviators in Alaska, listening closely for news of Post, responded to his call for help. Joe Crosson, then a pilot with Pacific

Alaska Airways, was reached by radio in Fairbanks and volunteered to fly a new propeller to Flat. While Crosson was en route, also with a mechanic, Post got some much-needed sleep. Employees of the Flat Mining Company erected a tripod derrick of timbers from a nearby mine and hoisted the plane out of the ditch, then blocked it up so the gear could be repaired. When Crosson arrived, Post was awakened; he showed the mechanic what was needed and went back to sleep.

At dawn the next day, Post was awakened to find the *Winnie Mae* repaired and ready to go. He took off, followed by Crosson. They flew formation to Fairbanks, where the Vega was quickly refueled. Post was eager to push on to Edmonton, but the weather reports were ominous. For the next eight hours he waited, and eventually his judgment proved correct. Knowing the condition of the field at Edmonton, Post did not want to land there after dark. When he finally decided to go, he found that the weather ahead was as bad as had been predicted earlier during the 1,450 miles to Edmonton. He flew four of the nine hours on instruments, sometimes climbing to 20,000 feet to avoid the 15,000-foot peaks and the thunderheads they helped create.

Post landed at Edmonton, this time on a dry field. He refueled, had the autopilot serviced, and took off, not down the main street as before but from the airport, heading for New York. Post let "Mechanical Mike," as he had dubbed the autopilot, do much of the work. He dozed from time to time. To make sure he would do no more than that, he tied a wrench to a finger and held the wrench in one hand. Whenever he dozed off, the wrench would fall and jerk his finger, waking him.

Between naps, Post checked his position, with the direction finder tuned to a growing number of commercial radio stations en route. He sensed the excitement building as news commentators reported his progress and forecast his arrival time at Floyd Bennett Field. It was getting dark as Post neared his destination. By this time, some 50,000 spectators had jammed the airport and roads nearby. As he neared New York City, Post flicked on his landing lights. The pinpoints of light grew larger. He touched down to cheers, whistles, sirens, and horns. He taxied slowly to the terminal, bewildered by the uproar of the crowd engulfing the *Winnie Mae*. The 600 policemen called out to handle them weren't enough. Weak and shaky, Post crawled out of the cockpit but could not descend for fear of being crushed. With the help of police and a detail of sailors, he slipped off the wing's trailing edge and into a waiting car where friends, including Harold Gatty and his wife, waited to greet him.

Now that the flight was over, official timers of the National Aeronautic Association reported that Post had circled the globe in a record-setting 186 hours and 49.5 minutes, of which 115 hours and 36.5 minutes were in the air. He had beaten his previous mark by more than 21 hours. Beside the honor of establishing a new speed record, Post went into the record book as the first to circumnavigate the earth twice by airplane and the first to do it alone. It would be 14 years before another pilot surpassed the solo speed record; but no one could ever take away Post's two firsts. It was only five years, however, until Howard Hughes and a crew of four smashed Post's time.

9

HOWARD HUGHES:
RECORD-BREAKER

He was tall, skinny, and rich—just the opposite of Wiley Post. Both had been associated with the oil business, Post as a roughneck making the minimum wage and Hughes as the son of the inventor of a conical drill bit that helped open the oil fields to exploitation.

Orphaned at 19, Hughes inherited $500,000 and control of the Hughes Tool Company, a legacy he parlayed into a multimillion-dollar empire. Having no desire to be just another white-collar businessman, however, the young Hughes went to Hollywood and plunged into moviemaking. After a couple of flops from which he learned much about the industry, Hughes turned out the hits *Hell's Angels; Scarface;* and *The Outlaw.* As his fortune grew, so did his fame, but before long he became bored with Hollywood.

Hughes turned to aviation. After learning to fly, he was briefly, in 1932, a copilot for American Airlines. By 1935, Hughes, now a millionaire, had demonstrated a flair for aircraft design and engineering, though he had no formal training. That same year, he introduced a sleek racing plane, called the Hughes Special, or H-1. It was the first plane that incorporated flush riveting to reduce drag. In it, Hughes set an official speed record of 352.388 mph. For this achievement, President Roosevelt presented him with the Harmon International Trophy.

On January 19, 1937, after refitting the H-1 with a larger wing and a new engine, Hughes flew the plane from Los Angeles to Newark, setting a new transcontinental speed record of 7 hours and 28 minutes and beating his own record of 9 hours, 27 minutes, and 10 seconds, set in 1936. Other records followed, but the record Hughes wanted most was the round-the-world mark held by Wiley Post. Without announcing his intentions, Hughes, in 1935, quietly began planning an attempt on Post's record. His intra-United States marks were mere practice runs. Meanwhile, he looked for the ideal plane. He thought of using Douglas's new DC-2 twin-engine transport, which was fast becoming the workhorse of the world's airlines. Instead, he chose the smaller Lockheed 14, modified according to his specifications, which included two 1,100-hp Wright Cyclone engines. He insisted on the latest navigation and radio equipment, plus an autopilot and blind-flying instruments. He gathered experts to plan for the frequent transmission of weather reports to him in flight and to procure accurate maps. Six stops were planned, and arrangements were made to have fuel, oil, and spare parts stocked at each stop.

In the late spring of 1938, when all seemed ready, it was decided that the Lockheed must have a name. Hughes had been named aeronautic director for the World's Fair of 1939; so, to publicize the fair and focus world attention on his flight, he christened the plane *New York World's Fair, 1939*.

The equipment aboard the Lockheed was unprecedented. Much new instrumentation was installed that had been under development for several years and which was described in the press as "revolutionary." Special radios would give the crew two-way communication throughout the flight. The plane was equipped with three transmitters, two standard airline receivers, a radio compass, a remote directional control for the automatic pilot (which permitted the navigator to turn the aircraft the exact number of degrees required to stay on course), a vertical face compass, a line-of-position indicator, a Sperry gyropilot, Kollsman and Pioneer gyrocompasses, a Sperry artificial horizon, and special timing devices made by Longines. In addition, Hughes insisted on a shirtsleeves environment for the crew, so adequate cabin heat was provided. Also, oxygen would be available for legs of the flight that would be flown above 10,000 feet. So much new equipment was aboard, in fact, that the newspapers took to calling the plane "The Flying Laboratory."

While it was obvious that Hughes was out to break Post's record, he insisted that the flight was primarily to test the equipment in the various environments that would be encountered in a globe-circling flight. He chose an Army Air Corps lieutenant, Thomas L. Thurlow, as copilot and navigator; Henry P.M. Conner, on leave from the Department of Commerce, as assistant navigator; Eddie Lund as flight engineer; and Richard Stoddart as radio operator. "Nothing will be left to chance," Hughes told his crew.

In the weeks before takeoff, a number of ideas about survival equipment were discussed and accepted if they were within the weight limitations of the aircraft. Twenty gallons of New York City drinking water were loaded aboard so no water would be needed from other sources en route.

Howard Hughes parks his Lockheed 14, *New York World's Fair, 1939,* at the Floyd Bennett air terminal upon completion of his 1938 world flight. With four crewmen, he established a new record for global flight of 3 days, 19 hours, 17 minutes. (National Air and Space Museum photo)

Also included was special food that had been scientifically prepared and protected against decomposition so it could be opened and eaten in the rain or in a lifeboat, if necessary. Careful arrangements were made for additional food to be placed at various stops. A special radio was designed and built for automatic broadcasting of the crew's position from a lifeboat in case they had to ditch. Some 250 orange balloons were stowed aboard; they could be released from the life raft at intervals so search planes could spot them and follow a trail to the craft. Parachutes for all the crew were provided at the main door of the plane, and the door itself could be released from its hinges by removing only one rod.

A major innovation was the weather-reporting system organized by Hughes at his World's Fair headquarters. Two weeks before the flight, meteorologists charted the weather in the Northern Hemisphere, based on radio reports from ground stations and ships at sea. Collection of the data required about six hours of continuous operation by four radio receivers tuned to different stations. In addition, Ralph Thomas, an amateur radio operator on Long Island, tuned in broadcast wavelengths that could not be received at Hughes's headquarters. As the broadcasts were received, the information was interpreted and entered on weather maps. The purpose of gathering weather reports two weeks in advance was to enable Hughes to determine the ideal time to take off. The foremost consideration was favorable winds and flying conditions over the Atlantic. At the same time, Hughes and his crew would have to keep in mind the long-range outlook, particularly over Siberia and Alaska. At least one forecast would be provided for each leg of the flight; the forecast would be radioed to the next stop before the plane's scheduled arrival time.

By early July 1938, the Lockheed had been thoroughly tested. Hughes and his crew flew from California to New York on July 4. En route, they noted fuel consumption and engine readings and carefully recorded the data. When they arrived at Floyd Bennett Field, Hughes asked Lund to disassemble both engines, to determine their condition. It was a wise decision. The cylinder walls of the engines were scored and pitted, the result of using gasoline of too-high octane. Hughes ordered that new cylinders be installed. On July 9, Hughes was advised that the best weather conditions he could expect were developing over the route. Hughes was ready, but Lund, his flight engineer, wasn't; Lund needed another day to complete installation of the cylinders. Hughes used the delay to assess the takeoff runway. It was only 3,600 feet long; at the end was a perimeter fence. "Tear it down!" Hughes demanded; "I'll pay for it."

Hughes went to sleep in the hangar, intending to take off at daybreak. At dawn, however, Lund still wasn't ready. The engines needed running up to break in the new cylinders. Finally, at sunset, Lund was satisfied; and the crew boarded for takeoff. At 7:20, as spectators and observers from the National Aeronautic Association (NAA) watched, Hughes taxied out and revved the engines with the brakes set. When the Cyclone engines had reached their highest rpm, he released the brakes and the plane slowly moved forward. But it didn't seem to be responding. At midpoint on the runway, the tail still had not come up. The Lockheed roared forward and reached the point where the perimeter fence had been. It ran off the tarmac into the dirt, throwing up a cloud of dust. The spectators were convinced the plane had crashed. (Hughes later said that the takeoff was "the most dangerous part of the trip.") A gray form lifted out of the slowly settling dust, and *New York World's Fair, 1939* could be seen climbing over Jamaica Bay. Hughes turned east and was soon out of sight. They landed at Le Bourget Airport 16 hours and 35 minutes later. The flight had taken half the time of Lindbergh's flight 11 years earlier. En route, Hughes and his crew kept in contact with all three major radio networks, plus 30 separate broadcast channels made available for emergencies. Fifteen ships at sea were alerted to provide radio bearings on request.

There was a slight delay at Le Bourget to repair the tail wheel, which had been bent during takeoff from Floyd Bennett. Hughes was aware on takeoff that something had happened; the NAA timers informed him by radio that they had seen the strut bend dangerously. Much to his dismay, the delay stretched to eight and a half hours. Finally, they took off. With a tailwind still favoring them, the flight to Moscow, of 1,675 miles, was made in 7 hours and 51 minutes. En route, Hughes radioed New York that he had sighted the ground only two or three times and had flown mostly in rain, fog, and clouds. He had also had a serious problem with icing of the wing and prop surfaces. In Moscow, the fliers were invited to the usual round of parties, but Hughes said no, and just over two hours later had the Lockheed back in the air headed for Omsk. The Lockheed droned on into the dawn. Stoddart used the radio compass to find radio stations. By prearrangement, Soviet radio stations played five minutes of organ music every half hour for station identification and because the sustained notes of the organ provided a constant signal. Seven and a half hours later, Hughes eased the plane down at Omsk. He wasted no time, however, but pushed on to Yakutsk. They were within a few minutes of their schedule and well ahead of Post's time at this point. After less than three hours on the ground, Hughes and his crew, now showing signs of fatigue, headed for Fairbanks.

From Fairbanks, they pushed on to Minneapolis, then, finally, Floyd Bennett Field and a record of 3 days, 19 hours, and 17 minutes, at an average speed of 208 mph for the 14,284 miles flown. Exhausted and short of temper despite their success, Hughes and his crew emerged from the plane and posed reluctantly before photographers and reporters. Hughes didn't want to face them but finally agreed to answer questions. Among the official greeters were New York City mayor Fiorello La Guardia and Governor Grover Whalen. Whalen tried to make a speech over the din: "Seven million New Yorkers offer congratulations. . . . Welcome home!" "I am ever so much honored," Hughes replied. "Thank you very much." Hughes and his crew were half-led and half-dragged to a crowded press tent where they were confronted by more reporters. The reporters fired questions and heard some answers, but the pushing and shouting spectators prevented anything like a press conference. Before departing, Hughes declared to a questioner that he would "never again" attempt another flight around the world, that this trip hadn't been all that exciting.

Later, at the governor's New York residence, Hughes disclosed that he had meticulously kept a log of the flight, "about thirty to forty pages," and that the second most dangerous part of the flight had been on the Yakutsk–Fairbanks leg. "It's a damn good thing I didn't try to fly out of Yakutsk at night," he said. The maps of Siberia given him by the U.S. Hydrographic Survey were "all wrong. . . . I had to draw my own maps."

Hughes reported that the flight had taken them across mountains that the maps showed as 6,500 feet but which were actually more than 9,000. The plane had accumulated ice during climbs, and at times it was touch and go.

In a speech the next day, acknowledging the welcome given him by New Yorkers, Hughes said:

> I . . . have consented to make this [speech] only because there is one thing about this flight that I would like everyone to know. It was in no way a stunt. It was the carrying out of a careful plan and it functioned because it was carefully planned.
>
> We who did it are entitled to no particular credit. We are no supermen. . . . Any one of the airline pilots of this nation, with . . . navigators and competent radio engineers in any one of our modern passenger transports,

Howard Hughes waves to a New York crowd during a motorcade down Broadway in New York City after his record-setting flight. Left to right: Grover Whalen, New York's official greeter (hidden behind Hughes's hand), Hughes, and Albert Lodwick, Curtiss Wright Co. executive, maker of the plane's engines, who handled flight clearances, landing rights, and refueling arrangements. (National Air and Space Museum photo)

could have done the same thing. The airline pilots of this country, who . . . are the finest fliers in the world, face much worse conditions . . . during every winter of scheduled operations in this country.

If credit is due anyone, it is due the men who designed and perfected . . . the modern American flying machine and its equipment. If we made a fast flight, it is because many young men . . . went to engineering schools . . . and designed a fast airplane and navigation and radio equipment which would keep this plane on its course. All we did was to operate the equipment and the plane according to the instruction book. . . .

There is one thing about the flight which pleases me more than the actual time which elapsed. . . . We made no unscheduled stops. We arrived at every destination within a few minutes of the time we set as our arrival time. . . .

Like many fliers of the period, Hughes had become concerned that American aviation supremacy was fading and that Europe was replacing the United States as the leader in aviation. "The speed record for seaplanes is held by Italy," he said. "The speed record for land planes by Germany, the altitude record is held by England, and Russia, with its magnificent flight of last year [from Russia to California over the North Pole] will probably hold the distance record for a long time to come. If this flight [has] demonstrated to Europe . . . that American engineers and American workmen can build just as fine and just as efficient an airplane and its equipment as any other country in the world, then I . . . feel it has been well worth while."

An event that had been arranged for Hughes upon his return was the laying of a wreath on a concrete star embedded in the ground where Wiley Post ended his solo flight in 1933. The star is inscribed: "On this site Wiley Post landed the *Winnie Mae* completing his first solo flight around the world in 7 days, 18 hours, 49 1/2 minutes. Started July 15, 1933. Returned July 22, 1933." Hughes, who never got to lay the wreath, later expressed regret that he had not done so. "Post's flight was the most impossible bit of flying ever accomplished," he said; "as far as I'm concerned, his flight was the greatest of all time."

More honors came to Hughes for his newest aeronautical achievement, among them the Harmon International Trophy (the second time) and the Collier Trophy. At the White House, President Roosevelt presented him with a citation that read: "To Howard Hughes and his associates for their epoch-making round-the-world flight in 91 hours and 17 minutes. This flight involved notable advances in aerial navigation, communications and engineering; demonstrated the value of organization and planning in long-range aircraft operation and afforded a world-wide demonstration of the superiority of American aviation products and techniques."

John Heinmuller, the official NAA timer for the flight, said that it was a triumph of celestial air navigation, proving that navigation with time-pieces, sextant, compass, and stars was now an accurate science. "Fifteen thousand miles in 91 hours, mostly blind flying, and at the exact speeds necessary to conserve the fuel supply, was possible because Hughes and his men knew where they were in time and space at every instant of the flight. They were never more than a few miles off the course, and never off the planned schedule for landings by more than a few minutes."*

* Heinmuller, *Man's Fight to Fly*, New York: Funk & Wagnalls, 1944.

10

AROUND THE WAR,
AROUND THE WORLD

It was 5:54 A.M., January 6, 1942, and bitterly cold. Inside the control tower of New York's La Guardia Field the operator on duty picked up a startling message: PACIFIC CLIPPER INBOUND FROM AUCKLAND NEW ZEALAND   CAPTAIN FORD REPORTING   DUE ARRIVE PAN AMERICAN MARINE TERMINAL LA GUARDIA SEVEN MINUTES. There had been no flight plan for a Pan Am flying boat arriving at that time, and certainly not one from the western Pacific. After all, there was a war on. Was it a hoax? A coded message of some kind? Or the real thing—an arrival announcement? It was still dark, and no night landings were permitted in Bowery Bay. After circling for more than an hour waiting for sunrise, Robert Ford, captain of the Clipper, landed and thus completed one of the most unusual flights of World War II.

During the hour or so that Ford circled New York, Pan Am officials in the city were roused from bed and rushed to Pan Am's Marine Terminal. When the Boeing 314 flying boat was moored, the 10-man crew and 3 passengers, all wearing summer clothes and clutching blankets against the cold, filed hurriedly into the terminal. Two hours later, after each crew member had been interviewed by military intelligence officers, newspaper reporters were given the bare facts: Forced to deviate from its flight plan by the attack on Pearl Harbor, December 7, 1941, the *Pacific Clipper* had completed a world-girdling flight of 31,000 miles, nearly circumnavigating the globe from San Francisco across the Pacific to the Far East and Middle East war zones, across Africa and the South Atlantic, along the northern coast of South America to New York. In doing this, the Clipper also made the first flight between New Caledonia and Australia, the first world flight by a commercial aircraft, the longest continuous flight by a

110

commercial airplane, and the first round-the-world flight by a plane following a route near the equator.

The trip had been routine for the crew until they were two hours out from Noumea, New Caledonia, en route to Auckland, New Zealand, on December 8 (it was still December 7 in Hawaii). John Poindexter, the Clipper's radio operator, who was listening to reports via Morse code, heard the first reports of the Japanese attack. Captain Ford received a two-word message on the company frequency: Code A. This prearranged signal meant that all U.S. commercial aircraft in flight were to land at their next destination and await instructions. "It seemed incredible that the news could be true," Homans Rothe, the first engineering officer, recalled. "It might have been a mistake or maybe only a test. Nevertheless, the big flying boat was . . . on a wartime basis less than a minute after receiving . . . word."

Throughout the next week, the crew awaited instructions at Auckland. The instructions came on December 15. "We had begun a camouflage job on the Clipper," John Steers, then fourth officer on the plane, recalled; "[we] had only half the American flag removed when the urgent message was received to disassemble two engines and load them aboard. We were to return to Noumea, pick up 22 employees, women and children and take them to Gladstone, Australia . . . then proceed . . . to New York."

And so the saga of the *Pacific Clipper* began. The flight was made via Noumea and Gladstone, then to Darwin. At this point, it was still routine; but no one knew how far south the Japanese had pushed. Therefore, strict radio silence was required. The Clipper landed at Surabaja, in the Netherlands East Indies, intending to stop only long enough to refuel. As Captain Steers recalled, Java was "definitely war zone. The American Consul in Port Darwin was to have notified Surabaja of our coming. We had arranged to answer challenges from Surabaja on CW [continuous wave] frequencies. Our challenge was B-E-A-M, our answer, H-O-R-N. The Dutch [at Port Darwin] never got the message."

Steers was right. No word had been received that an American flying boat was inbound to Java, using British call letters furnished at the suggestion of BOAC, the British airline. A patrolling Curtiss Brewster fighter with Dutch insignia intercepted the Clipper as it approached Surabaja. The Clipper's crew later found out—in English—that the following conversation had taken place between the pilot and a controller on the ground:

CONTROLLER: "What is she?"

PILOT: "I don't know, but she's a big one. Might be German or Japanese. Wait. There's part of an American flag on her side."

CONTROLLER: "That doesn't mean a thing. Anyone can paint on an American flag."

PILOT: "Then you'd better send up some help."

Three more Brewsters scrambled and moved into position, apparently with the intent of blasting the unarmed, slow-moving flying boat out of the sky. "We were told later that one of them remarked they'd better call the ground before they opened fire." Steers recalled. "One of them peeled off and drew up on our tail. He asked: 'Shall I let them have it?' Then the ground station asked if we had some marks of identification. They hesitated and one of them came over the top. It was then that they spotted what remained of the U.S. flag on the topside wing. They were still suspicious and followed us right on to the bay. When we hit the water, they sailed over . . . us and on to their airport. As we slowed down, a speedboat zigzagged out to our position. Captain Ford put the Clipper into a tight turn to stop our forward progress. The boat approached and we were instructed by bullhorn to follow close behind to our mooring. Then the voice told us why: 'The harbor is mined!'"

The Clipper arrived in Java on December 18 and was detained while the Dutch sought approval from Ceylon to release the plane. Meanwhile, the crew were immunized against typhus and cholera. On December 21, they departed for Trincomali, Ceylon. An hour after takeoff from Trincomali, on December 24, the studs of the cylinder head on the number-three engine snapped and the propeller had to be feathered. The Clipper returned, and with help from the RAF machine shop at Trincomali, made repairs. On December 26, they tried again, flying to Karachi, in northwest India. Two days later they went on to Bahrain and Khartoum, landing on the Nile.

Captain Ford did not intend to remain at Khartoum, but he received a message instructing him to wait for three unidentified VIPs who would arrive on a BOAC flight. "We waited two days. . . . The VIPs were the publisher of a Chicago newspaper, his wife and [his] sister-in-law. The aircraft flying them from Cairo had a forced landing because of engine trouble. When Captain Ford accepted them, the British released us for the next leg."

Upon takeoff from Khartoum, bound for Leopoldville, the Clipper blew off part of an engine exhaust stack; this made the engine not only noisy but a fire hazard as well. At Leopoldville the Clipper took on fuel, bringing its total load to 5,100 gallons, necessary for the long flight across the South Atlantic to Natal, Brazil. The takeoff run from the Congo River took 91 seconds, with Ford keeping the power on full for more than three minutes—a severe strain on the engines.

The 3,583-mile flight to Natal was completed in 23.5 hours. "Rod

Brown, [the navigator], constructed a Mercator projection of ten degrees latitude on a strip of paper," Steers said. "This served as our chart from Leopoldville to Natal. At night over water, we dropped flares and with our drift sight checked wind drift and ground speed. During daylight we dropped smoke bombs. We stayed in Natal about four hours, gassing and putting the exhaust stack that had blown off . . . back together. . . . we put part of a PBY twin-engine Navy flying boat on it, wrapped a tin can around it, and wired up the whole business with baling wire. So, on January 3, we left Natal and headed for Port-of-Spain, Trinidad. The exhaust stack blew off on takeoff from Natal, [and] the engine hammered all the way to Trinidad."

The flight of the *Pacific Clipper* had taken a month and four days. The plane touched down on 5 continents, crossed 3 oceans, made 18 stops under the flags of 12 nations, spent 209.5 hours aloft (including the longest nonstop flight in Pan Am's history), crossed the equator 6 times, and flew 6,026 miles over desert and jungle, where a forced landing would have been disastrous for a flying boat. Understandably proud, Pan Am publicized the flight heavily. "As a test of ingenuity, self-reliance and resourcefulness, the flight had no equal in aviation's history," boasted the company in its magazine *New Horizons* for January 1942. "It proved . . . that Pan American's multiple crews, operating techniques, and technicians could meet any possible situation that might arise in long-distance flying."

As soon as the aircraft had tied up at the marine terminal at La Guardia, Edward McNitty, a company engineer, went aboard to check its condition. The only evidence he could find of the Clipper's world cruise was the following, which appeared in his report.:

1. A sign in the washroom telling crew members to conserve water.
2. One dirty white shirt hanging in the tail compartment.
3. A ship's bucket.
4. English-made foods in the galley.
5. One bottle of a white liquid labeled "On Sudan Government Service—one tablespoon every four hours."

Although the flight of the Pan Am Clipper received considerable publicity, another world flight, this one top secret, had been mounted a few weeks before the United States declared war. In the fall of 1941, England was struggling for its survival. France, the Netherlands, Belgium, Denmark, and Norway had fallen, and the Wehrmacht was approaching Moscow. To bolster the Russian war effort, President Roosevelt sent Averell Harriman to Moscow at the head of a mission. The U.S. Army Air Corps was ordered to ferry additional staff to Moscow to work out the details of American aid.

Fortunately for the pilots involved, Great Britain and the United States had been developing closer ties as the president took measures to make the United States an "arsenal of democracy." With traffic between the two countries increasing, the need for rapid movement of supplies by some means other than ship became urgent. One way to do this was to set up an air service across the Atlantic to ferry supplies and communications to England more efficiently. Therefore, in May 1941, the Ferrying Command was established by the War Department. On July 1, 1941, Lt. Col. Caleb V. Haynes flew a Consolidated B-24 bomber to England from Washington, D.C., via Montreal and Newfoundland. Between that date and mid-October, when the onset of winter made flying too risky, 22 round-trip flights were made. Two of the flights were in support of the Harriman mission, and one circled the globe.

The B-24s used by the Ferrying Command had been modified to carry passengers. In September 1941, pilots Alva L. Harvey and Louis T. Reichers were specially briefed and ordered to fly several American experts of the president's Special War Supply Mission to Moscow via Great Britain. After crossing the Atlantic and landing in Scotland, Major Harvey and Lieutenant Reichers were instructed to fly their planes to Moscow on a route north of the Scandinavian peninsula. Harvey, who was a mechanic on the Air Service world flight in 1924, and who had crashed in the Aleutians with Maj. Frederick L. Martin, told of his experiences after taking off from Prestwick, Scotland:

> After a three-day delay at Prestwick, we proceeded on to Moscow, a flight made at night. A direct flight from Prestwick to Moscow would have been of rather short duration; however, the intensity of the war in Russia, Norway and Sweden made the prospect of a direct flight far too hazardous. I instructed Hutchins [the navigator] to plot our course over a route keeping us to the west of Norway, onward to an area over the Arctic Ocean to pass the northern tip of Norway, Lapland and Finland; thence to enter the Soviet Union from the Arctic Ocean by way of Arkhangelsk (Arkangel). It was a long, cold night and military planes, such as the B-24, were not built with comfort in mind. The route took us over the Arctic Ocean to within 900 miles of the North Pole, a total distance to Moscow of 3,150 miles, reaching the maximum range for the B-24.
>
> We reached Moscow later the next morning, cold, hungry and out of gasoline. On my approach to land at the main terminal, a Russian fighter landed across my path, forcing me to go around. While [we were] climbing out, Sergeant Moran, one of my crew, yelled, 'You better get this crate down fast . . . my fuel gauges have been reading empty for twenty minutes.' A

landing was made on the second attempt without incident; just how much fuel remained in the tanks was never determined, but it was low.*

Harvey and his crew remained in Moscow 12 days, virtually under house arrest. Every time they ventured out of their hotel and strolled more than a block or two, they were rounded up and escorted back by the Soviet secret police. Some nights, while the Germans bombed the city, were spent in air-raid shelters. Before their departure from Washington, Harvey had been ordered to return from Moscow by a route which, if possible, would take him over the South Pacific. The aim of this plan was to pioneer a land route for land-based planes. It would be risky, since there was little information on landing fields and facilities. If Harvey could obtain enough information from the Royal Air Force to conduct the flight safely, he was to make the attempt.

Harvey got some information on the eastward route but found that it had no navigational aids, no air-to-ground communications, and no systematic weather reporting; also, some landing fields might not safely accommodate a B-24. Harvey decided to make the attempt anyway, fully expecting to do some "adventurous pioneering." He and his crew left Moscow, October 11, 1941. Their next stop was Baghdad. Harvey's projected route would take him to Karachi, Rangoon, Singapore, Darwin, Port Moresby (Papua, New Guinea), Wake Island, and on to Washington, D.C., via Riverside, California, and Fort Worth, Texas. Harvey describes the rest of the flight:

> We attempted to gather information at each stop regarding conditions at the next landing site. The base of Karachi was found to be about as we expected, just usable. Some of the RAF fellows at Karachi advised that we would find a very good field at Calcutta, and it was, but only for small light aircraft, most undesirable for the heavy B-24, we learned upon arrival. While circling the field, we observed a hard surface runway I estimated to be about 3,800 feet in length, it being 1,200 to 1,500 feet shorter than a desired minimum. It was either the short runway or the swamps . . . The approach was over tall palm trees, which was not to my advantage, but I managed somehow to get down on the runway. All appeared to be going smoothly until we rolled to a stop; then the wheels began to break through the thin macadam surface; it would not support the weight of our . . . B-24. I continued to taxi around (while moving, the wheels did not break through). I finally spotted a concrete block used [to orient] compasses; I made a run and parked there. . . . When we were ready to leave Calcutta we warmed up engines . . . and made our take-off from a running start. If I had been aware of the size and condition of the Calcutta field prior to starting,

---

* Excerpted, with permission, from a monograph prepared for the Air Force Historical Foundation.

I'm confident the attempt never would have been made. We squeezed through a close one.

After the Calcutta experience, we found the remainder of the landing sites acceptable, though not always totally desirable. Rangoon had a hard-surface landing strip, limited in length [but] otherwise very acceptable. Our flight to Singapore was made along the Malay Peninsula, . . . The landing site at Singapore was a large sod field, sufficient in size but slippery and treacherous from constant rain.

Our flight from Singapore to Port Darwin, Australia, was a night flight, [it] took us over many of the small islands of the Dutch East Indies, but we saw little due to darkness. The Australians received us royally and we enjoyed a one-day layover. A day flight was made on the leg to Port Moresby, crossing the Arafura Sea in nearly four hours, taking us to . . . New Guinea. A three-day delay was necessary at Port Moresby while a Pacific typhoon churned its way from the general area of Wake Island, my next stop. We were able to receive weather reports from the Hawaii-based Air Corps, a luxury not enjoyed since leaving Prestwick, Scotland.

Fully rested and anxious, [we made an] overnight flight to Wake, a distance of 2,300 miles, [in] twelve hours. Wake Island was so small we couldn't believe we had reached the correct place . . . Our first leg of the . . . crossing [of the South Pacific] was back of us. . . . On to Honolulu the following night, and I had the pleasure of again meeting and visiting with my old flying partner of the 1924 World Flight, Major Fred Martin . . . Time to move on, [we covered] the last leg of our Pacific Ocean crossing . . . in nine hours. On the flight from Riverside to Fort Worth we encountered some of the worst weather of the entire trip; I found it necessary to fly on instruments the greater part of the distance, arrived at Fort Worth to find a moderately heavy rain falling and with a ceiling of less than 200 feet, visibility less than a mile. With the use of some navigational aids, no serious problem was encountered in the approach and [the landing]. More instrument flying took place the following day, October 30, when en route to Bolling Field, Washington, D.C. The final landing was made at mid-afternoon completing a flight around the world.

Harvey's flight had covered 27,238 miles at an average ground speed of 233 mph. It was the first flight by a military land-based aircraft across the South Pacific.

Louis Reichers had returned in another B-24 by way of Cairo, across central Africa, the South Atlantic, and north through Brazil to the United States. Both exploratory flights, made before the United States entered the war, involved hazardous landings at undeveloped fields barely able to accommodate large aircraft. Each leg was made in all kinds of weather, without pre-takeoff briefings, weather information, or up-to-date maps. Harvey and Reichers's experiences provided valuable information to the Army Air Corps in its planning for the development of the two major overseas air routes to combat zones—the Pacific and the South Atlantic. Five weeks after Major Harvey completed his flight, America entered the war, a war in which long-range flights became routine. But the routes had been pioneered by Harvey and Reichers.

The experiences and information gathered by Harvey, Reichers, and the Pan Am crew were recorded by military intelligence and disseminated. The success of the two B-24 flights proved the potential of land-based airplanes—especially large four-engine bombers—for globe-circling flights. Sturdy, capable of withstanding the punishment of long-distance bombing missions, the plane envisioned was a cargo version of the B-24. Designated the C-87, this version resembled a boxcar with wings. Outfitted with seats, it could carry both passengers and freight.

In August 1942, a C-87 christened *Gulliver* entered the history books when it carried Wendell Willkie on a mission that has never been explained adequately. An idealist who espoused a one-world theory, Willkie, at the invitation of President Roosevelt, was ostensibly a goodwill ambassador to the Soviet Union and China. It fell to Army Air Corps pilots Richard Kight and Alexis Klotz to fly Willkie and his aides "for the purpose of carrying out a special mission for the Air Transport Command."

In August 1942, Kight and Klotz flew Willkie and his party to West Palm Beach, Florida, for special weather and route briefings. The passengers and crew were outfitted with survival kits for jungle, ocean, and desert; K rations, guns, winter and summer flying clothes, and rubber rafts were provided. The *Gulliver* left the United States on August 27 and flew to Puerto Rico, Belem, Natal, and Ascension Island. Klotz describes what it was like to land on that British-owned point of land halfway across the Atlantic:

> This was a small, mountainous, volcanic island, with a main peak near the middle. There was one poor harbor where the British maintained a cable station, otherwise the island had been unoccupied until the U.S. decided to use it as a mid-ocean base for ferrying aircraft across the South Atlantic. The engineers had had to bulldoze and blast a corridor through the smaller mountain for a runway. As you approached for a landing you had to come in over the surf breaking on a 300-foot cliff where the runway began and started uphill. You could only see the first 400 feet of runway where it was imperative that you get your wheels on and start using your brakes while you were still going uphill. Then you hit the brow of the runway as you went screeching through the cut in the hill which reached out for each wingtip. As you hit the high spot, you could see the runway begin again and fall away fast, ending in a rock pile covered with wide-awake birds.

The *China Clipper*, a Boeing 314, berths at Manila on its initial crossing of the Pacific in 1935. An identical plane, the *Pacific Clipper*, was ordered to fly around the world to escape the Japanese following the bombing of Pearl Harbor on December 7, 1941. The unprecedented flight took one month and four days, marking the first time a commercial fixed-wing aircraft circled the world with passengers. (Pan American World Airways photo)

This was reminiscent of a scenic railway with both the scenes and the railway removed. This airport certainly put the romance back into flying.

Gulliver flew on—Acera, Kano, Khartoum, Cairo, Baghdad, Teheran, Kuobyshev—arriving in Moscow September 20. Willkie played his role to perfection at every stop. The crew enjoyed the attention and took advantage of the importance of Willkie's mission to make side trips and see the local sights. In Moscow, they met Premier Stalin and, despite the war, were treated to a lavish dinner. They left Moscow September 27 and returned to the United States, making nine stops in Siberia and China before landing at Fairbanks in mid-October. From there, they flew to Edmonton and Minneapolis, then returned to Washington.

Although it is difficult to assess Willkie's mission to Moscow, the fact that the flight was completed without accident or mechanical failure demonstrated that America's aircraft could stretch their legs literally around the world.

11

EVANS AND TRUMAN: THE FLIVVER FLIERS

The idea came to them in 1946. Clifford Evans, aged 26, and George Truman, 39, were having an idle conversation at an airport near Washington, D.C. Both had been pilots during World War II and were now flight instructors at the Brinckerhoff Flying Service, in College Park, Maryland, training student pilots under the GI Bill.

One day, as Evans watched idly, a student pilot taxied a Piper Cub Super Cruiser trainer to a stop in front of the hangar and switched off the engine. As the aircraft coughed to a stop, Evans said to Truman, who was standing nearby: "You know, I'll bet one of those Cubs could be fitted out to fly around the world." Joining Evans at the window, Truman nodded. "If you put a tank in that back seat," he mused, "and the stops were close enough together, maybe you *could* do it."

Significant achievements sometimes have such small beginnings. Within 24 hours, Evans and Truman were pouring over world aeronautical charts and plotting a route around the world that included hops of 850 to 1,000 miles each. The more they talked, the more such a flight seemed possible. As the weeks went by and the men quietly carried out their calculations, they became obsessed with the idea. At first, their wives encouraged them only reluctantly, then eagerly. They got no encouragement, however, from the aircraft manufacturers they contacted about financial backing. An offer might be made, they were told, but only "after you've completed the flight."

Evans and Truman did not give up, though. After studying the capabilities of several light aircraft, including some government-surplus planes, they settled on the Piper Super Cruiser that had sparked the idea originally. A three-passenger craft with a 100-hp engine and plenty of space

119

in the cabin for an extra tank for carrying about 100 gallons of fuel, it could cruise at about 120 mph. Two planes would be needed, one for each pilot.

Evans and Truman were convinced that technically the flight was feasible; they were also convinced that secrecy was essential if they were to avoid being upstaged by someone with better financial backing. Therefore, between flight lessons, they huddled furtively in a corner of the main hangar, discussing plans and assessing the latest developments. During this time, Evans, who was studying mechanical engineering at the University of Maryland while also serving as a flight instructor, averaged less than six hours' sleep a night. Trying to amass enough flying time to become an inspector for the Civil Aeronautics Authority, Truman, who had no other income and who had to make ends meet, spent as much time instructing as he could. Meanwhile, their families were growing; both men added children to their families during this time.

What was significant about the proposed flight of two light planes wasn't setting a speed record (they did not plan to attempt to beat Howard Hughes's record). If the flight was successful, it would be the first around the world by an aircraft with less than 575 hp. What they hoped to prove was that the globe could be circled by small planes, and thereby demonstrate the capabilities, efficiency, and dependability of American-built airplanes.

Once the details of the flight were established, financing it and modifying the planes became the major—almost the insurmountable—obstacle. Evans and Truman, thinking the publicity would help sell planes worldwide, approached officials of the Piper Aircraft Company. All they wanted Piper to do was "give or lend us two planes and enough cash to cover our expenses, plus something for ourselves [afterward]." Piper's reply, while not entirely negative, wasn't hopeful either. "See what the Lycoming people say about furnishing the engines," Piper officials told them. Lycoming, on the other hand, while not very hopeful, wasn't altogether negative. All in all, it looked as though Piper and Lycoming might support the flight. Meanwhile, Evans and Truman scraped together what cash they could. Evans sold his prewar car, borrowed from relatives, and cleaned out his savings account. Truman sold the defense bonds he had accumulated during the war and mortgaged his mobile home.

Then, with it looking as though Piper and Lycoming would support the flight, they reneged. Postwar cutbacks and other economic factors had severely affected the aircraft industry, and predicted sales of light planes did not materialize. "We were tempted to quit," Evans and Truman said later. "We made a list of every company that made parts for the Cub, and besieged them with letters, telegrams, phone calls and personal visits, appealing for funds in return for publicity for their products."

Piper's management eventually gave in and agreed to let the fliers have two secondhand but nearly new Piper PA-12 Super Cruisers. William T. Piper, the company's founder and its president, had his engineers design and install extra tanks in the rear-seat area. Lycoming, warming to the project, sold Evans and Truman two new engines for a dollar apiece. It now appeared as though they could start by the early summer of 1947.

Truman took his plane to Dayton, Ohio, for load and pitch tests on the plane's aluminum propeller. During the last test flight, the engine failed on final approach to a landing and Truman had to set the Cub down in a wheat field. It nosed over on its back, knocking Truman out for a moment; otherwise, he was unhurt. It was later found that the cause of the failure was water in the fuel line and the carburetor, not an engine or propeller defect.

Repairs weren't difficult to make, and Truman and Evans flew the planes to Washington National Airport, where public relations people for Piper and Lycoming had arranged a welcome, including embassy representatives of countries in which Evans and Truman planned to touch down. The fliers were given a party and the planes were christened. Evans gave his the name *City of Washington,* for his hometown, and had water from the Atlantic Ocean splashed on the nose of the plane; Truman christened his plane *The City of the Angels,* for his adopted hometown, Los Angeles. With the ceremonies over, they flew to Teterboro, New Jersey. It was now August, later than they had planned to start. They would have to fly the route under winter conditions. With no deicing equipment, flying at northern latitudes would be dangerous and could even be fatal.

The threat of winter, though, wasn't as worrisome as that of running out of money. Until just before the flight, they did not know how they would pay for fuel en route or cover such expenses as spare parts, landing fees, meals, and lodging; and no oil company would underwrite these expenses.

Evans managed to persuade a relative to put up some security, thus enabling them to get international charge cards and obtain $850 in traveler's checks. With this money in hand, they kissed their wives and daughters good-bye, posed for newsreel photographers "until we felt like puppets," and were off. On August 9, 1947, weary from preflight checks, they lifted into the haze above Teterboro and headed northeast. Within minutes, however, they lost sight of each other and the horizon and had to fly mostly by instruments. They had filed a flight plan for Presque Isle, Maine, but in the confusion of the takeoff, Truman had gotten mixed up and headed for Bangor. "We weren't too familiar with our radios yet and we couldn't raise each other," he said. "An exchange of messages between Bangor and Presque Isle got us back together, and we were never

George Truman (left) and Clifford Evans pose before the Piper Super Cruiser, *The City of the Angels*. They proved that the earth could be circled by small single-engine aircraft of less than 200 hp without mishap. (Don Downie photo)

separated again for more than a few minutes." But that first tense day conjured up nightmarish visions of disaster.

Weather was to be a constant worry, one that plagued them throughout the world flight. Arriving at Presque Isle, they rested and on August 10 flew to Goose Bay, Labrador, where they were delayed for three days by a report of rain and fog over the next leg of the flight. On the thirteenth, they flew the 750 miles to Bluie West One, a U.S. Air Force refueling stop on a fjord in Greenland. Due to head winds, the flight took nearly nine hours.

A delay occurred that they had not counted on: influenza. The fliers were in the base hospital for several days, which delayed their departure until August 24. On that day they took off in marginally good weather and flew east above the overcast to Meeks Field, at Reykjavik, 950 miles away. Flying by dead reckoning, they overshot the field but realized their error in time to turn back. An hour after they landed, clouds closed in and the field was closed.

On August 28, Evans and Truman climbed into their Cubs and took a heading for Prestwick, Scotland. They found it fogbound and landed instead at Newton Ards, Ireland, for refueling. Two hours later, they took off for Croydon Airport, where they found themselves acclaimed as pilots of the smallest planes ever to fly the Atlantic. They had flown the 3,602 miles from New York to London in 42 flying hours. Two days later, they flew to Ypenburg, the Netherlands, by way of Brussels. This detour was made so Evans could visit the Van der Bogaerts family, who lived on the outskirts of Hedel. Evans and his family had been sending food and clothing to the family since the end of the war.

On September 3, Evans and Truman arrived at Orly Field, near Paris. From there, they flew to Marseilles but were grounded by severe rainstorms. On September 7, they reached Ciampino Air Field, near Rome. The next leg, 1,350 miles, included a thousand miles over water to Cairo and Baghdad. Then they headed southeast to Dhahran, Saudi Arabia, where they were detained for six days by Saudi officials, who took their time checking the fliers' visas and flight permits. Early on the morning of September 19, Evans and Truman took off for Karachi, Pakistan, covering the 1,100 miles in 9.5 hours. The next day they flew to Jodhpur, India, where they were guests of the maharaja. Impressed by their palace, Evans, in a letter to his wife, described it as an "amazing place to be stuck out here in the middle of the desert."

On September 22, they continued, flying across India and Burma and landing at Rangoon. By the twenty-seventh, seven weeks after departing from the United States, they were halfway around the globe. Two days later, after a stop at Hanoi, they landed in Hong Kong. Here bad weather grounded them. A typhoon off the coast of southern China raged for six days. Finally, on October 6, they left Kai Tak Airport and headed north to Shanghai. Three hundred miles into the flight, however, they encountered 80-mph head winds and had to land at Amoy, in China. When they did not arrive at Shanghai on schedule, radio messages went out, asking for information about them. The winds held for four days; when they subsided, Evans and Truman still had to contend with 40-mph head winds all the way to Shanghai, where they stayed for five days.

The next leg was to Fukuoka, Japan, on Kyushu Island. There, a ham operator in New Jersey patched through a call from the pilots to their wives. It was the first conversation they had had since leaving the United States. Subsequent landings were made at Nagoya, Tokyo, and Chitose, as well as a small airfield at the northern tip of Kokkaido Island. On October 27, unable to obtain permission from the Soviets to land in the Kuriles, the airmen climbed into their Cubs for the 1,500-mile flight across the northern Pacific to the U.S. Air Force base at Shemya, in the Aleutians.

"Flivver Flier" George Truman (left) looks on as Clifford Evans points out the signature of Pope Pius XII to Mayor Fletcher Brown on arrival at Los Angeles after their 1947 world flight in two Piper Super Cubs. They covered 25,162 miles in 122 days, 23 hours, 4 minutes. This plane, flown by Evans, is on display at the National Air and Space Museum, Washington, D.C. (Don Downie photo)

The fliers considered this leg the most dangerous of the entire world flight.

On the afternoon of October 28, 13 hours and 35 minutes after leaving Japan, Evans and Truman landed at Shemya. Their safe arrival marked the first time small aircraft had crossed both the Atlantic and the Pacific. The going had not been easy, however; because of the almost constant poor visibility and high winds, the Aleutians were rightly considered "the home of the worst weather in the world." The U.S. Air Force helped by providing a B-17 Flying Fortress from the 3rd Air Rescue Squadron as an escort, to "mother" them during the flight to Shemya. On October 31, accompanied by the B-17 and a Navy PBY flying boat, Evans and Truman left Shemya, arriving at Adak Island, in the Aleutians, 3 hours and 30 minutes later.

The weather showed no improvement as Evans and Truman progressed up the Aleutian chain to the mainland, though the islands were now closer together. On November 2, they flew to Cold Bay, then toward Naknek, turning back when visibility deteriorated and icing developed. Two days later, they made it to Elmendorf Air Force Base, near Anchorage, where, grounded by snowstorms and zero cold, they spent a week.

They made several stops in Canada, then hopped off from Lethbridge and flew 1,275 miles nonstop to Los Angeles, their first landing in the United States. After receiving plaudits from the city for which Truman had named his airplane, they proceeded east, making stops at Phoenix, El Paso, Amarillo, Oklahoma City, Dayton, and Harrisburg before setting down at Teterboro, December 8, 1947. They had covered 25,162 miles in 122 days, 23 hours, and 4 minutes. Broke when they started and still broke when they landed, they were satisfied that they had accomplished what they set out to do. "There must be somebody who was the first . . . to circumnavigate the U.S.A. in the flivver," Evans said afterward, referring to the ancient Model A Ford of bygone years. "He knows how we feel." Truman added: "There are probably [a hundred thousand] pilots in the

The two "flivver fliers" make a flyby at Teterboro Airport, New Jersey, on December 8, 1947. (Don Downie photo)

country who could do what we have done if they were careful. That's about all we were trying to prove."

Although Evans and Truman set no record for speed, they achieved something no one can take away: They flew two small, single-engine aircraft around the world without mishap and were the first to do so. In tribute to this feat, the Super Cruiser flown by Evans is on display at the National Air and Space Museum in Washington, D.C.

12

THE SAGA OF THE A-26S

The end of World War II prompted others to attempt globe-circling records. Col. Joseph R. Holzapple, commander of the 319th Bombardment Group, wanted to establish a mark before the dissolution of the wartime Army Air Forces. The Pentagon gave him permission, and he chose a Douglas A-26 Invader, a twin-engine, medium attack bomber used late in the war. It normally carried two pilots or a pilot and a radar operator/gunner or mechanic. Holzapple chose Lt. Col. C.R. Meyers as his copilot and Lt. Otto H. Schumacher as navigator. They somehow found room in the cockpit for a radio operator as well, Cpl. Howard J. Walden.

On November 23, 1945, they left Savannah, Georgia, with the announced purpose of proving "that the Douglas A-26 [is] so fast and mobile that squadrons of these light bombers [can] be dispatched quickly from the U.S. to any point in the world." Heading west against the prevailing winds, Holzapple flew to Sacramento, a distance of 2,750 miles, in 12 hours, then to Hawaii in 10 hours and 10 minutes. From there, they flew the Pacific via Johnston, Majuro, and Eniwetok atolls, Saipan, Okinawa, and Manila—6,472 miles in 23 hours and 50 minutes.

Neither the crew nor the aircraft experienced difficulties. All stops were at Air Force bases, where maintenance and weather-reporting facilities were still available. Proceeding west, Holzapple and his crew flew via Calcutta, Agra, Karachi, Abadan, Baghdad, Cairo, Tunis, Casablanca, the Azores, and Bermuda. Instead of returning to Savannah, however, Holzapple flew to Washington, landing on November 29 at National Airport. He claimed a record for the 24,859-mile flight of 96 hours and 50 minutes actual flying time, for an average of 256.7 mph, as well as three records en route: Honolulu to Johnston Atoll, 880 miles in 3 hours and 10 minutes; Manila to Calcutta, 2,215 miles in 9 hours and 10 minutes; and the Azores to Bermuda, 2,285 miles in 9 hours and 15 minutes. The long overwater flights were nothing new for Holzapple. In May 1945, three months before the war ended, he had led a flight of 96 A-26s of the 319th Bombardment Group to Okinawa to join the Far Eastern Air Forces for the anticipated assault on Japan. "My airplane . . . flew as far as Saipan ahead for the other 95 planes, [where I] made arrangements for the group to arrive. . . . [Then I] flew back to Honolulu and . . . led the group . . . to Saipan. During all this time the airplane performed perfectly. All I ever did . . . was put gas and oil in it. I was amazed that any airplane could fly continuously and not even need a spark plug change."

The reliability and speed of the A-26 also impressed Milton Reynolds, a millionaire pen manufacturer. Reynolds bought a surplus A-26 from the government for use as an executive plane, dubbing it the *Reynolds Bombshell*. A pilot himself and a fervent advocate of aviation, Reynolds wanted his A-26 to break Howard Hughes's record set in 1938 and, not surprisingly, to promote Reynolds's pen worldwide. He had the plane modified by removing all nonessential gear such as gun turrets and armor plate. Extra fuel tanks were installed, which brought the fuel capacity to 2,400 U.S. gallons. In March 1947, he hired William P. Odom, a former Air Force captain, as pilot. Odom had more than 6,000 hours' flying time, including flying the India–China route as a commercial pilot before the war and ferrying bombers across the Atlantic to England during the war. Reynolds also hired as flight engineer, T. Carroll Sallee, an experienced crew chief, then decided to go along himself as navigator. When asked why he wanted to make such a trip, Reynolds said, "I want to set a new round-the-world record . . . other people collect stamps and some collect buttons."

Critics of the flamboyant millionaire did not believe the preparations for the flight were thorough enough, certainly not as thorough as Hughes's preparations for his flight in 1938. Preflight calculations by Odom showed that the flight could be made in 55 hours; but it was not to be. "It is quite likely," a reporter wrote afterward, "that the hastiness of the preparations, in addition to bad weather encountered en route, was to blame for the fact that the flight was not completed in the 55 hours. . . . In Paris [they were] held up by radio trouble and refueling difficulties; in Cairo, repairs had to be carried out on a faulty nose wheel and again on the wireless equipment; the oxygen supply ran short on parts of the way, and on the last leg of the trip, one of the engines gave some trouble."

Nevertheless, Odom and his crew did set a record for the 20,020-mile course from LaGuardia Airport, with landings at Gander, Paris, Cairo, Karachi, Calcutta, Shanghai, Tokyo, Adak, and Edmonton. The plan had been to fly the same route Hughes followed—New York to Paris, Moscow,

Omsk, Yakutsk, Fairbanks, and Minneapolis, a distance of only 14,824 miles—but the Soviet Union would not grant Odom permission to land.

Just before Odom's scheduled takeoff from La Guardia, April 12, 1947, federal authorities refused him permission to take off, saying the runway was too short for a plane with that much fuel aboard. The *Bombshell* had to be defueled and a refueling stop hurriedly scheduled for Gander, Newfoundland. Minor mechanical difficulties were overcome en route. Because of a lack of accurate weather information, the leg across the Himalayas from Calcutta to Shanghai was extremely hazardous. Most of it was at altitudes ranging from 19,000 to 23,000 feet, with the crew on oxygen nearly the entire time.

Odom had intended to fly from Tokyo to Anchorage, then New York; over the Pacific, however, he encountered rough weather and had to land at the U.S. Naval Air Station on Adak Island, in the Aleutians, for refueling and an update of the weather. Armed with new but ominous informa-

Reynolds Bombshell crew relaxes at Yakota Air Base, Japan, while their Douglas A-26 is being serviced. Left to right: Col. H. Saderhill, Yakota base commander; Milton J. Reynolds; T. Carroll "Tex" Sallee, copilot; Capt. William P. "Bill" Odom, pilot; Lt. Col. C. Crocker, 3rd Bomb Group commander. (U.S. Air Force photo)

tion, he flew to Edmonton. It was the third deviation from the flight plan. At each stop, Reynolds made the most of their ground time by handing out his pens to spectators and granting interviews to reporters. On April 14, while Reynolds was en route, a judge presiding over a breach-of-contract case in Toronto, in which Reynolds was a defendant, asked the defense attorney where his client was. "He left Calcutta at 4:30 A.M. today on his way to Shanghai, Tokyo and Alaska, your Honor." "Will he be back tomorrow?" the judge asked. "I don't know," the attorney replied.

Reynolds almost made it; Odom landed the A-26 at La Guardia at six minutes past midnight, April 16. The fliers had covered 20,020 miles in 3 days, 6 hours, 55 minutes, and 56 seconds. Although they had beat Hughes's time, their mark was declared unofficial; Odom had disobeyed

An Air Force ground crew assists the *Reynolds Bombshell* crew during the stop at the Yakota Air Base. The flight of 20,020 miles was completed in 3 days, 6 hours, 55 minutes, 56 seconds. It was not considered a world record because Odom had not applied for sanction from the National Aeronautic Association and Federation Aeronautique Internationale. He tried again solo and made the 19,645-mile flight in 73 hours, 5 minutes, 11 seconds, beating his previous time by nearly 6 hours. (U.S. Air Force photo)

the rules by not applying to the Federation Aeronautique Internationale, the only international organization that keeps official records.

The day after their return, Odom, Reynolds, and Sallee flew to Washington and Chicago, then returned to New York. By April 18, they were back in Washington, where they were congratulated by President Truman.

Odom, dissatisfied with the unofficial mark, wanted to try again. Now that he had the experience of the first flight behind him, he was convinced that the A-26 could make the trip in less time. Also, he was determined to try it solo and thus become the second man in history to fly around the world without a navigator or a mechanic. Reynolds endorsed Odom's plan. Reynolds, who had made the earlier flight riding backward in the converted bomber's cramped cockpit, told newsmen that he "wouldn't make the trip again for a hundred million dollars."

This time, Odom's preparation was better, especially for refueling stops, and four months later, he was ready. On August 7, 1947, he took off from Chicago. The flight was not an easy one, however. Odom made a false start three days earlier, returning when several minor instruments malfunctioned. When he finally got under way, he said later, he felt the first few legs "were a pleasure." For about half the flight he used an automatic pilot dubbed "Little Willie," claiming that no one could make a solo round-the-world flight without such a device.

Although the early legs were a "pleasure," Odom was plagued by bad weather throughout his world flight. At Gander, he made a ground-controlled radar approach, and over the North Atlantic, en route to Paris, picked up a heavy load of ice, which slowed him down.

"At Karachi (after refueling at Cairo), the clouds were in the palm trees," he recalled. It was the monsoon season, and the rain was continuous. Odom was forced to spend a half hour making an approach by automatic direction finder. After leaving Karachi for Calcutta, he was in solid cloud cover and "didn't see any of India."

Over Burma, Odom lost the autopilot when severe turbulence threw his seat back suddenly and cut the electric control cable, forcing him to fly the A-26 manually the rest of the way. He flew the 1,500 miles to Shanghai in solid clouds and turbulence that constantly threw the plane from side to side. Without landing at Shanghai, he pressed on to Tokyo, where he refueled. He flew along the Aleutian chain to Anchorage, picking up severe icing along the way. When he reached the city, 62 hours and 54 minutes had elapsed, and fatigue was beginning to get the best of him. "Going out of Anchorage had a special procedure," he later told reporters. "You fly so many minutes on one course, turn and fly another to miss the mountains. [Physically], I guess this was just about the end for me. I'd had no sleep on the ground and none in the air since Calcutta. I got straightened out on course, pulled up the collar of my jacket and settled back in my seat. That did it. I went right to sleep. I [heard] the signal of a radio station in a pass as I did this." Odom awakened an hour and forty minutes later to find that he had almost reversed course. He looked up and saw snow-capped mountain peaks glinting in the moonlight. "First thing I saw on the instrument panel was the compass, he recalled. "It read due north. When I fell asleep I was heading on a course of 107 degrees, or southeast. Then I saw my altitude was 16,000 feet, when I should have been at 21,000. I turned back on course and started to climb. I turned on the cockpit lights, which blinded me from outside vision, and dug out a couple of charts. When I turned them off I looked up and saw I was headed straight for a huge cloud."

But it wasn't a cloud; it was the top of a 19,000-foot-high mountain. "It made me sick at my stomach," Odom said. "There I'd been milling around, circling down at 16,000 feet for who knows how long, and that thing was [waiting] to be hit. I pulled back on the wheel and spiralled right up to the stars, on top of clouds and mountains before I straightened out for home."

His "milling around" over Canada had, of course, used up gasoline. Odom decided that the best thing to do was head for Fargo, North Dakota, and refuel. "I could have come straight in to Chicago," he said; "but I'd have stretched the fuel too thin." He made the final leg at 378 mph and landed at Chicago's Douglas Airport.

Odom had beaten his own record by nearly 6 hours in posting a time of 73 hours, 5 minutes, and 11 seconds for the 19,645-mile course, at an average speed of 310.6 mph. This flight of the *Reynolds Bombshell* was a grueling test of plane, structure, engines, and pilot. As one editorial writer noted, "No better demonstration of plane and pilot performance could be devised than a dash around the globe—over all kinds of terrain and in all kinds of weather."

13

THE LUCKY LADIES

July 1948. The Cold War had begun in earnest. In June, the Soviets had closed off all roads and rail lines into Berlin. Stating that the action was necessary because of "technical difficulties," the Russian military authorities seemed intent on driving the other three Allied powers out of the city. In the view of the Allies, such an overt, calculated act could not be tolerated.

The Soviets underestimated the resolve of the Western powers. Although highways and railroads were closed, the three air corridors linking Berlin to the three Western zones were not. Within hours, an airlift such as the world had never seen began, with Douglas C-47s hauling medical supplies and food to the beleagured city. As the days and weeks wore on, and the Russians showed no sign of relenting, the Western Allies formed the Berlin Airlift in an attempt to prevent the Soviets from starving the city into submission. For a while, war seemed possible, even probable. With U.S. military forces greatly diminished by postwar reductions, it became clear that only through a rejuvenated air force could Soviet expansion be countered. In 1947, the U.S. military was overhauled, and the three services were organized under the Department of Defense, with a separate Air Force now on a par with the Army and the Navy. By the time of the Berlin Airlift, major Air Force commands had been established. The threat of another world conflict spurred authorization of funds for new aircraft and to rebuild air bases at strategic points around the globe.

A major type of aircraft in use at this time was the Boeing B-29, the same airplane that had carried the war to Japan and that had dropped two atomic bombs on Japanese cities. B-29 bombardment units stationed in the United States were strengthened and readied for deployment, and practice missions were flown to sharpen crew skills. Although many

133

missions were intended merely to show the flag around the world, others were conducted in great secrecy.

In July 1948, top secret orders were flashed to the bomb group at Davis-Monthan Air Force Base, in Tucson, Arizona: Prepare three B-29s for a round-the-world flight under simulated war conditions. Fifteen days after takeoff, two of the three bombers returned to Davis-Monthan; the third had crashed in the Arabian Sea. No records were set, nor were any intended; the flight isn't even mentioned in the official Air Force chronology of significant aerospace events. The flight, covering some 20,000 miles, was made in 103 hours and 50 minutes' flying time. One of the B-29s was christened *Lucky Lady*, the other *Gas Gobbler*, Lt. Arthur M. Neal, pilot of the former, was later transferred to the newer Boeing B-50s; he liked the name "Lucky Lady" so much that he named the airplane assigned to his crew *Lucky Lady II*.

In the fall of 1948, the Pentagon again ordered the Strategic Air Com-

Secretary of the Air Force W. Stuart Symington (in civilian clothes) and Gen. Hoyt S. Vandenberg, Air Force chief of staff (officer with decorations), welcome crew of Boeing B-50 "Lucky Lady II" after record-setting nonstop flight on March 2, 1949. (U.S. Air Force photo)

mand (SAC) to prepare for a nonstop, round-the-world flight, this time using
B-50s. Refueling would be accomplished in flight by B-29 tankers at four rendezvous. The flight was to be to and from Carswell AFB (Air Force Base), in Fort Worth, Texas, via the Azores, Saudi Arabia, the Philippines, and Hawaii. The order was not for a do-or-die mission. Air refueling was already a proven technique. In 1948, exhaustive engineering and experimentation was done. Crews for B-29s and B-50s trained, ate, and slept refueling missions. They "hangar flew" day and night, discussing the best altitudes, right speeds, perfect timing for contact, and time for fuel flow; day after day, they practiced and improved their techniques.

Planners in the Pentagon and at SAC headquarters, near Omaha, Nebraska, eager to accomplish a significant aviation first for the United States, calculated that it would take about four days for the global trip if flown to take advantage of the prevailing westerly winds. Five periods of darkness and daylight would be encountered. Because refueling would be easiest during daylight, four U.S. air bases were chosen as departure points for the tankers at approximately equidistant intervals. Five aircraft were modified, but only one plane would actually make the attempt. It would fly with its normal complement of 12 machine guns but would carry no ammunition or bombs. Extra fuel tanks were installed, which would enable the planes to carry two tanker loads of fuel, or 12,000 gallons. Auxiliary oil tanks and a pumping system were also installed to ensure an adequate supply for the Pratt & Whitney engines.

By early February 1949, modification of the five bombers was complete, and they were flown to Tucson. Meanwhile, tankers were flown to their assigned positions. The bomber crews practiced air-to-air hookups and made shakedown flights and final flight plans. On February 22, the five B-50s were flown to Carswell AFB, where two were chosen for the world flight—*Global Queen* and *Lucky Lady II*. On February 25, *Global Queen* taxied out for takeoff, closely followed by *Lucky Lady II*. If *Global Queen* developed problems within one hour of takeoff, *Lucky Lady II* would take over. An hour after departure, all was going well, and *Lucky Lady II* returned to Carswell. But late that night, *Global Queen,* over the Atlantic for its first refueling, developed engine trouble and had to land at Lages Field, in the Azores. It was now *Lucky Lady II's* turn. At 11:21 A.M., Saturday, February 26, 1949, Capt. James G. Gallagher and his crew of 13, including Lieutenant Neal as backup pilot, took off on their secret mission under the code name "Scordo."

Throughout the flight, secrecy was maintained by a prearranged number-shuffling plan. *Lucky Lady II* was assigned a special tail number for the flight to the Azores; then it assumed the tail number of one of the tankers that filed a flight plan to Saudi Arabia from the Azores. After the refueling, the tanker announced the B-50's tail number to the tower at the field in the Azores and landed. Over Saudi Arabia, and at the third and fourth refueling rendezvous, the same scheme was repeated. Over the Philippines, however, the plan almost backfired. Of the five tankers sent aloft for the rendezvous, one had filed a flight plan for Hawaii, as arranged. Unaware of the secret flight, an alert operations officer made a quick calculation and, knowing the normal range of a B-50, realized that it could not possibly reach Hawaii. The operations officer was finally talked out of recalling the tanker by the SAC officer in charge of refueling in the Philippines.

Although the other refuelings were successful, one KB-29, after refueling *Lucky Lady II*, hit a mountain in the Philippines and exploded, killing all aboard. By today's standards, the methods and equipment used were primitive. To ensure an adequate fuel supply, five tankers were dispatched over each rendezvous. Both the tankers and the B-50 had reels in the rear of the aircraft. The tanker approached the plane to be fueled from above and to the rear. The B-50 then let out a cable with a drogue, which held the line behind the plane. The tanker used another cable to grab the B-50's line and pull it in. Fuel was transferred by gravity feed. A refueling took two hours.

On March 2, *Lucky Lady II* landed at Carswell, having flown 23,452 miles around the earth in 94 hours and 1 minute. When it seemed certain that the plane would make it, news of the flight was made public. As the happy but weary crew emerged from the B-50, they were met by Stuart Symington, secretary of the Air Force; Gen. Hoyt S. Vandenberg, Air Force chief of staff; Gen. Curtis E. LeMay, SAC commander; and by reporters and photographers. All 14 crew members were decorated with the Distinguished Flying Cross (DFC). Their citations read, in part: "The successful execution of this historic flight demonstrated the feasibility of aerial refueling to extend the operating range of military aircraft and contributed other data of inestimable value to the future of military aviation." The crew were later awarded the Mackay Trophy for the most meritorious flight of 1949. Secretary Symington called the flight "an epochal step in the development of air power. What it actually does is turn our medium bombers into intercontinental bombers."

When *Lucky Lady II* had touched down, it ended a flight two hours short of four days and two minutes ahead of the time estimated before the flight. Captain Gallagher later re-created a diary of the trip for *Boeing Magazine*, an in-house publication of the plane's manufacturer, in which he recounts the odd nature of a flight in which takeoff was on a Saturday and which consisted of five nights and mornings, but which should have ended on Thursday but didn't:

> *Saturday Night:* I am sitting up here thinking how . . . Columbus might have liked this vantage point to check his theory that the world is round.

Families, photographers, and reporters crowd the crew of a B-52 Stratofortress at March Air Force Base, California. This was one of three B-52 bombers that made a nonstop world flight, January 16–18, 1957. (U.S. Air Force photo)

My assignment is to stay up here and hold a course so that while the world goes around four times, I'll be going around it once and we'll both come out even at Fort Worth where I started my sit just before lunch today.

All's dark below. My navigator says we're at a point over the Atlantic Ocean, but I can't tell by looking down. Neither can he. He keeps in line with the stars. We're more with the stars than with the earth.

Daybreak Sunday: It's pretty much the same up here [where] we're sitting. It's the globe and things below that are changing. While it was dark the . . . globe was turning around so now we can see the sun beyond the water's edge. Until now we've been alone up here. . . . a B-29 is rising up to meet us. . . . He's going to give us his gas so we can stay up here.

Sunday Night: Here with the stars again. Bright, diamond street lights above, but no street below. My navigator says it's the Sahara that's been passing under. . . . Without a moon it's absolutely black.

Monday Morning: Still sitting comfortably. But something has surely gone wrong with the day-and-night situation up here. It's getting light at 10:00 P.M. I know I could have corrected it by setting the ship's clock up one hour every four hours, but I can't do that because I plan to land at Forth Worth.

That's central standard time. If I keep setting the clock up it will be Thursday when I land, but the fellows at Carswell Field will insist it's only Wednesday.

There is an endless sea of white clouds below us, and out of it rises a pair of B-29s. More fuel so we can sit some more.

Monday Night: That globe below is mostly water. . . . Maybe that's why it seems we're the one that's standing still while it slowly twists around. All day it was mostly water—the Indian Ocean, the Bay of Bengal—soon it will be the Pacific. India passed beneath us this afternoon.

Tuesday Morning: The Philippines are under. We could see jungle occasionally through holes in the undercast, and caught one glimpse of Clark Field. We are circling now while two tankers come up from Clark. . . .

Tuesday Night: . . . water below all day and all night. My navigator says we got a position check over Wake Island while I was napping. . . .

Wednesday: The crew's weary. Things are very much the same up here. Doesn't seem as though we've been doing much except for the refueling session each morning, which puts us on our toes. This morning it was between Johnston [Atoll] and Hawaii.

Wednesday Night: Darkness overtook us over more open water east of Hawaii. The nights are the same.

Thursday Morning: Just as I thought, now there's something wrong with the day-of-the-week situation. I haven't reset my watch but my diary accounts for every day from Saturday to Thursday. Now we're due to land at Fort Worth on Wednesday.

10 O'clock Wednesday Morning: We're on the ground at Fort Worth. Everybody's been congratulating us. They say we travelled 23,452 miles nonstop. I think that may be wrong. It seems more like we were sitting up there while Fort Worth travelled 23,452 miles, and came around to meet us. No, my navigator corrects me. Fort Worth travelled 6,295,019 miles along a somewhat uneven path, while we were detached from it. It followed the earth's orbit and at the same time made four revolutions around the earth's axis. . . . We set a slightly different course through the heavens than Fort Worth, and travelled 6,318,471 miles. He calculated our course exactly with the aid of the other stars, so that when we finished 6,318,471, Fort Worth had finished its 6,295,019 miles, and here we are. Now that I think of it, I'm rather glad he figured that out right. I wonder where we would be if we had travelled 6,318,471 miles in some other direction.

In the 1950s, the prop-driven B-29 and B-50 passed into history and were replaced by the jet-propelled B-47 and, later, by the B-52, both equipped for aerial refueling. It was probably inevitable that SAC crews would attempt another nonstop, globe-circling flight when crews were trained. In "Operation Power Flite," planned during the fall of 1956, five B-52s would leave Castle AFB, near Merced, California, and head east. Over Morocco, two of them would be diverted to England for their initial exhibition to the public. The other would continue east via Ceylon, the Philippines, Guam, and Hawaii, returning to Castle AFB. Air refueling over those points would be by SAC KC-97 tankers.

The purpose of the flight was to demonstrate once more the long-range strike capability of the U.S. Air Force. Maj. Gen. Archie J. Old, commander of the 15th Air Force and the senior officer for the flight, was also assigned to monitor preparations. As before, the mission was classified secret, and the many technicians, supply specialists, and others who helped ready the aircraft were not told of its significance until success was assured. For Lt. Col. James H. Morris, commander of the lead aircraft, this trip was a repeat performance. The copilot of *Lucky Lady II*, he now christened his B-52 *Lucky Lady III*. The second bomber was *La Victoria*, named for Magellan's ship, the first to circumnavigate the globe. The third was christened *Lonesome George*, for the comedian George Gobel, who had flown B-25 bombers during World War II.

A B-52 usually carries a crew of two pilots, navigator, bombardier,

Col. Robert R. Schaeffer, a Strategic Air Command operations officer, briefs B-52 crew members prior to takeoff for their 1957 world flight from Castle AFB, California. One of the B-52s was christened *Lucky Lady III*, by Lt. Col. James H. Morris, who had been copilot on *Lucky Lady II*. (U.S. Air Force photo)

One of the three world-circling Boeing B-52 bombers is refueled in flight by a Boeing KC-97 tanker somewhere over the Pacific. The mission began at Castle AFB, California, and terminated at March AFB, California, after covering 24,325 miles in 45 hours, 19 minutes. (U.S. Air Force photo)

electronic-countermeasures operator, and tail gunner. For this mission, four to five times the length of a normal SAC training flight, each bomber would carry three or four extra men. Although space was at a premium, the extra crew would provide relief for pilots and navigators, who were scheduled to be on duty eight hours and off four hours. Food for the crews was carefully prepared ahead of time. The most popular items were fruit juice, soup, and candy bars. Bite-size steaks, later chosen as a standard food for SAC bomber crews on long flights, were also a favorite. Each aircraft was equipped with a small electric oven. Early in the flight of *Lucky Lady III*, the oven shorted out. The crew chief thought the electrical system of the plane might malfunction if he tried to repair it in flight, so the crew heated their food over hot-air ducts. During the first six hours of flight, between the takeoff point, Castle Air Force Base, in California, and Labrador, the crews were alert and active. They made full use of the equipment placed aboard to record the flight, including cameras, wire recorders, and notepads. Much of the data was later used in studies of crew fatigue.

The formation proceeded without incident toward Labrador. There, however, the crew aboard *La Victoria* found that the refueling boom would not engage the bomber's receptacle, and the plane had to turn back to Goose Bay. Ice, the archenemy of flying, had caused the problem. About two pounds of it formed over the refueling receptacle, thus preventing insertion of the tanker's boom. The other bombers, now refueled, reached North Africa on schedule. Over Morocco, General Old ordered only one bomber to proceed to England, thus providing a spare for the main group.

Fatigue began to take its toll as they reached the halfway point, 20 hours into the flight. Only a few crew members had been on missions longer than 15 hours. One was Capt. Rene M. Woog, a navigator, who had stayed aloft 28 hours in a B-36 and 31 hours on polar flights. Mattresses and hammocks were available, but the crews reported that they got little sleep, catching catnaps instead.

The bombers flew over the Arabian Sea to a point south of Ceylon, about 350 miles north of the equator, where they turned northeast to the Malay Peninsula, the target of a simulated bombing. Cameras recorded the points of impact. The formation refueled as scheduled over the Philippines and over Hawaii. As the planes approached the California coast, the pilots were informed that fog had closed Castle AFB and that they should land at March AFB, near Riverside, California. Originally, only the lead B-52, the one carrying General Old, was to land there.

It was January 18, 1957. On hand to greet the crews was General LeMay, who decorated each crew member with the DFC. It was another first for the U.S. Air Force: 24,325 miles in 45 hours and 19 minutes, according to the official timer. After decorating the crews, General LeMay revealed that "intercontinental bombers many times have flown separate legs similar to today's flight. This is the first time, however, that we have put them all together. Many other crews of the Strategic Air Command could fly the same mission."

The successful flight received worldwide publicity. Nor did it go unnoticed by the Soviets, who had their own, quite different globe-circling plans. On October 5, 1957, the U.S. Naval Research Laboratory announced that it had recorded four crossings of the United States the day before by a Soviet earth satellite traveling at more than 18,000 mph. The United States had been planning to launch a 21.5-pound satellite before the end of the year; but the Soviet Union surprised the world by launching an orbiting satellite eight times as heavy and much earlier than Western scientists had thought possible. The Space Age, with its race to the moon, had begun.

The record set by the B-52s in 1957 went unchallenged until 1980, when the U.S. Air Force decided once more to test the capability of its bomber strike force. On March 12, 1980, two B-52s of the 410th Bomb Wing left K.I. Sawyer Air Force Base, in Michigan, to "locate and photograph elements of the Soviet navy operating in the Arabian Gulf." The bombers and their crews landed at their base 42.5 hours later and reported "mission completed." They had flown the 19,353-nautical-mile mission "with only minor equipment and communications problems." The planes refueled in flight nine times.

For their record flight, the 14 airmen were awarded the Mackay Trophy, "for the most meritorious flight of the year by an Air Force person, persons or organization." While this was the third time such a flight had been undertaken, it marked the first time a mission had been flown with an operational objective; it was also the fourth time the Mackay Trophy had been awarded for a round-the-world flight by U.S. Air Force aircraft and crews.

14

THE FLYING GRANDFATHER

Max Conrad was one of a kind. They called him the "Flying Grandfather," and for good reason. He and his wife Betty had 10 children and 37 grandchildren, and when Conrad died in 1979 at the age of 76, he was among the flyingest humans who had ever lived, with more than 53,000 hours' flying time.

Conrad made his first solo flight in 1928. In subsequent years, his flying career touched just about every facet of aviation. He attended Notre Dame University but, after earning his pilot's license, quit to start his own flying school, in Winona, Minnesota. When his first student soloed, Conrad himself had only 34 hours in his log book. Among the more than 3,000 pilots he trained, at least 40 became airline pilots.

In the spring of 1930, Conrad launched an airline that linked Winona, Rochester, Minneapolis-St. Paul, Duluth, and Virginia—all in Minnesota. When the airline went out of business, Conrad put his two six-passenger Ryan Broughams to use, conducting air tours between Minnesota and Los Angeles. The 80 round-trips he made were his first cross-country flights. Throughout the 1930s, Conrad remained active as a flight instructor. During World War II, he operated six flight schools under the Civilian Pilot Training (CPT) program, which gave future military pilots their first flying experience. When a fire in 1943 destroyed 28 of his training planes, he was out of business. He got a job for a while flying in the Canadian bush for Northwest Airlines.

Conrad became known nationally in 1950 when, lonesome for his family, then living in Switzerland, he flew the Atlantic alone in a standard 150-hp Piper Pacer to visit them. His route took him from Minneapolis via Labrador, Greenland, and Iceland. A month later, he returned by the

A pilot with over 53,000 hours when he died in 1979, Max Conrad set numerous long-distance records in Piper aircraft. He failed in two attempts to fly around the world over both poles in 1968 and 1969. The aircraft was damaged beyond repair at McMurdo Sound, Antarctica, during the second attempt. (Piper Aircraft Co. photo)

same route. In 1951, flying the same plane, Conrad began a series of good-will flights to promote light-plane aviation. He flew nonstop from Winona to Miami, enhancing his reputation for great distances. In May 1952, he set an official world and U.S. record for Class 2 aircraft from Los Angeles to New York, a mark that was not bettered until 1959. In 1953, Conrad made a 17,000-mile, 14-day trip in which he visited each of the 48 capitals to help commemorate the fiftieth anniversary of powered flight. Returning to New York from San Francisco, he set another record—this one unofficial because the required recording barographs weren't set before takeoff. It was "the toughest [trip] I ever tackled," he said in recalling all the stops he made, the dinners he attended, and the speeches he had to listen to.

About this time, Conrad began to ferry airplanes for the Piper Aircraft Company, flying planes from factory to purchaser. He made an increasing number of transatlantic flights. His list of records also began to expand as he became known for endurance flights that tested both flier and machine. He gained a reputation for doing the impossible with a light plane, particularly with the type of plane Piper produced. His formula for success was: Start with the best equipment you can lay your hands on, then put it to tests no one else had dared make.

Conrad had been a track star in his school days and was in superb physical condition. His self-discipline later came in handy during the hundreds of long solo flights that he made. He prepared for sleepless periods by going without sleep; he steeled himself to hunger pangs by eating nothing for considerable periods. While flying, he denied himself creature comforts yet found during those flights "the only real rest I ever get." To keep his mind alert, he composed poems and songs, played the harmonica, and wrote down the words and music as they occurred to him. Over the years, he recorded several albums of music and was a bona fide member of the American Society of Composers, Authors and Publishers.

As he gathered valuable long-distance experience, Conrad applied the same discipline to the care of aircraft that he applied to himself. He would take a standard, assembly-line Piper, tune it (doing most of the maintenance himself), then take off every knob, dial, control, and door handle that could be dispensed with and that would otherwise add weight that could be better used for fuel. By 1959, he had set three world records for Class 3 and Class 4 aircraft within 13 months. On June 4, 1959, he landed his Piper Comanche at Los Angeles International Airport, 58 hours and 38 minutes after taking off from Casablanca. His officially measured, nonstop distance of 7,668 miles exceeded by 812 miles the previous record for Class 4 aircraft set by Pat Boling.

Still on the record books in 1959 was the Class 3 record (aircraft not exceeding 3,858 pounds) set in 1949 by Bill Odom. On November 24, 1959, Conrad took off again from Casablanca, this time with a lighter engine and less fuel, to qualify for a Class 3 record. Fifty-six hours and twenty-six minutes later he landed at El Paso International Airport, having covered 6,967 miles, some 2,000 miles more than was covered in the previous Class 3 record. Having kept fuel consumption to an average 5.8 gallons per hour, Conrad had enough for 10 more hours of flight when he landed.

The third record Conrad set was for a closed-circuit distance. He left Minneapolis on July 4, 1960, and returned two days later, having flown from Minneapolis to Chicago to Des Moines and back eight times, for a total 6,921 miles nonstop in 60 hours and 10 minutes. Conrad had more than doubled the previous record of 3,084 miles set in September 1959 by the Czech pilot Jire Kunc. With these successes behind him, perhaps it was inevitable that Conrad would tackle a round-the-world flight for record. The world mark for light planes had been set by Peter K. Gluckman, who had since died. On February 27, 1961, with Richard Jennings as the official NAA (National Aeronautic Association) observer, Conrad left Miami, intending to beat Gluckman's record. On March 8, 8 days, 18 hours, 35 minutes, and 57 seconds later, he and Jennings returned to Miami, and Conrad had three records. Of the total elapsed time, 160 hours and 34 minutes were spent in flight and only 50 hours and 2 minutes were on the ground. Later, to honor Conrad for this and his earlier flights, the municipal airport of Winona, Minnesota, was named Max Conrad Field.

The flight was not an easy one. At takeoff, the green-and-white Piper Aztec, christened *New Frontiers*, weighed 6,160 pounds, with 432 gallons of fuel in standard wing tanks and two extra cabin tanks. Thirteen stops were made to rest and refuel. Flying west, Conrad and Jennings landed at Long Beach, Honolulu, Wake Island, Guam, Manila, Singapore, Bombay, Nairobi (Kenya), Lagos (Nigeria), Dakar, Amapa (Brazil), Atkinson (Guiana), and the island of Trinidad. The longest leg was the 2,821 miles from Bombay to Nairobi. The most difficult part of the flight was Conrad's hallucinations. But Miami's lights were no hallucination. "The glow of Miami Beach lights as I came in over the Atlantic was one of the most welcome sights in my whole life," he told reporters. The Amazon was an even more welcome sight. Conrad had been having difficulty with two of his seven radios and was unsure of his position. "When I saw those muddy waters," he said, "I knew the coastline of Brazil was close at hand."

Typically, Conrad's record-setting did not end with this flight. Conrad, who was 61 at the time, observed the Christmas 1964 weekend by flying a Piper Twin Comanche nonstop from Cape Town, South Africa, to St. Petersburg, Florida, officially a distance of 7,878 miles. This remarkable flight brought him the coveted Harmon International Trophy in 1964, for the outstanding feat of individual piloting skill of the year, and made him the first winner in the FAI (Federation Aeronautique Internationale) Class 5 record category (for piston-powered planes weighing 6,614 to 13,227 pounds at takeoff).

In 1966, Conrad was persuaded to make a combined world flight-goodwill tour to call attention to Canada's centenary Expo 67 scheduled for the next year. Accompanied by David N. Shefler, a former Royal Canadian Air Force pilot, Conrad, in his Twin Comanche, *Rendezvous Expo 67*, flew east around the world, carrying greetings and an invitation to the Canadian celebration to 34 nations and covering 34,000 miles. Later that year, Conrad announced his intention to attempt another first: flying solo around the world in a light plane over both poles. Although he did not achieve this goal, it certainly wasn't for lack of trying. He was thwarted by bureaucracy, by the inadequacy of aviation facilities in the Antarctic, and by the reluctance of financial backers. He made his first attempt in 1968. After conquering the Arctic, he was stopped at Adelaide Island, a

Max Conrad, the "flying grandfather," flies the Piper Twin Comanche *Let's Fly* on one of the overwater legs of his many record-setting flights. Fuel capacity was increased eight times the plane's normal capacity of 90 gallons to 720 gallons. (Piper Aircraft Co. photo)

British station halfway down the Antarctic Peninsula. For nearly a month, he waited for decent weather, but it was not to be. If he pressed on despite the weather, he would be risking not only his own life but the lives of those who would search for him if he went down in the frozen wasteland of Antarctica. Besides, he had damaged the propeller slightly when he taxied across the *sastrugi* (hard ridges in the snow of the runway).

Conrad returned home, despondent, wondering whether he should try again. The dream wouldn't go away, though. He had to try again, if only because he, better than anyone else, knew the risks involved. This time, his route would include a landing at the 11,000-foot strip maintained by the U.S. Navy at the South Pole. That would lessen the distance he had to fly nonstop over Antarctica and consequently the risk. The Navy, while dubious about Conrad's attempt, acquiesced in his request but advised him that "Navy personnel experienced in aviation and polar operations consider your flight potentially extremely hazardous." The commander of the U.S. Naval Support Force, Antarctic, asked that Conrad provide "legal evidence" that he fully understood the hazards and would release the U.S. government "from all responsibility for any accident that may occur." In addition, Conrad was asked to pay in advance for all services to be rendered, including supplies, repairs, escort flights, and search-and-rescue activities—a total of about $86,000.

With assistance from Senator Barry Goldwater, himself a pilot, Conrad succeeded in having these conditions dropped, and, on November 30, 1969, he took off from Winona. En route to Tarawa from Hawaii, he lost power in an engine and had to coax the overloaded plane 600 miles to Espiritu Santo, in the New Hebrides, on the remaining engine. He repaired the engine, then pushed on to Christchurch, New Zealand, by way of Australia. There, he waited a week. Eight hours after takeoff from Christchurch, he had to shut down the same engine, with no choice but to return to Christchurch and have the engine replaced.

Another week had been lost, but Conrad refused to give up. He flew without incident to Invercargill, New Zealand, then on to McMurdo Sound, where he encountered more Navy red tape. The commander now wanted written confirmation from the Piper Aircraft Company that the Aztec could make the proposed flight in view of the fact that it weighed 6,600 pounds. While Conrad awaited the company's reply, the weather held good; by the time the answer arrived, and approval was granted, it had deteriorated. Despite poor visibility, high winds and low clouds, Conrad easily reached the South Pole station. He landed at the station's airstrip, 9,500 feet above sea level, and stepped out into air so cold "I found it hard to breathe." He stayed at the station for days, waiting for improved weather conditions that would allow him to proceed to Punta Arenas, Chile. He kept busy by stamping the thousands of postcards he carried with him (for later sale), working on his plane, and making short

Vice President Hubert Humphrey presents the Harmon International Trophy to Max Conrad for setting a nonstop record of 7,878 miles from South Africa to St. Petersburg, Florida, in a twin-engine Piper Comanche in 1965. (Piper Aircraft Co. photo)

test hops with greater and greater fuel loads, to be sure he could take off when the weather cleared.

The weather did finally clear; the Navy predicted good conditions all the way to Punta Arenas. Though weary from working on his plane, Conrad began loading the plane. Then the Navy insisted that he get a radio briefing from a meteorologist at McMurdo Sound. By the time this had been done, ice fog was forming around the airstrip. It was a classic white-out, nothing was visible—no horizon, no ground references, nothing. But Conrad was eager to be off. He started the engines. He could still see the black runway markers at thousand-foot intervals, as well as the oil barrels at the end of the runway; so he decided to go. As he moved down the runway, trying to pick up speed, visibility suddenly worsened, and he drifted off to one side of the runway, where the snow wasn't packed as hard. The plane's left wheel broke through the crust several times, slowing it down. Conrad was tempted to cut power and abort the takeoff but feared that if he did, the left wheel would dig in and he would ground-loop, thus damaging the plane. Using more power on the left engine and by touching the right brake lightly, he got back on the center of the runway and the plane gathered speed. He lifted off, all the while keeping an eye on the oil barrels—the only objects he could make out in the whiteness. At 10,000 feet above sea level and with the plane's weight a factor, it was hard to gain speed. Preoccupied with climbing and achieving a safe flying speed while following climb-out instruction from the Navy radar operator and setting his polar path compass, Conrad failed to see that he was headed toward a mound of snow. He hit it; the left prop grazed the mound. But the plane kept going. Damage had been done, however, for moments later, the engine began to vibrate violently and the left prop started to throw oil on the windshield. Airspeed fell off sharply; the heavily loaded plane was nearing stall speed.

Conrad gingerly tried to turn back to the runway, now invisible. As he gradually lost altitude, he looked desperately for the markers and the oil barrels. When he finally spotted them, it was too late. The plane smashed into the *sastrugi*. Conrad survived the crash, but the plane was damaged virtually beyond repair.

Conrad never realized his dream of flying around the world over the poles. After an 11-year absence, he returned to the Piper Company's plant in Lock Haven, Pennsylvania, and resumed ferrying aircraft to purchasers. There was, however, still one more long-distance flight he felt he had to make: duplicating Lindbergh's flight of 1927. "I want to fly the very same route Lindbergh did," he said, "on the same dates, and land at the very same airport." Conrad rechristened his Piper Comanche, *Spirit of Chicagoland*, and did what he set out to do.

The book jacket of Sally Buegeleisen's biography of Conrad, written after his death, reads in part:

> Max Conrad lived at the extremes of human experience. His life is a chronicle of personal courage, survival against the elements, loneliness and bitter defeat, triumphs, tragedies, and most of all, the will to keep trying. His life became a series of undertakings in which part of him always remained aware of the constant possibility of sudden violent death. Spurning conventional enterprise where other men had succeeded, he has triumphed where most men would not even dare.[*]

* Buegeleisen, *Into the Wind*, New York: Random House, 1973.

15

WOMEN CAN DO IT, TOO!

"Women must try to do things as men have tried," Amelia Earhart once wrote. "When they fail, their failure must be but a challenge to others." Many women fliers have followed this advice. Madame Therese Peltier, a French sculptress, is thought to be the first woman to pilot a heavier-than-air machine, making her first flight from Turin, Italy, July 8, 1908. Although Peltier never qualified for a license, she is considered the first woman to fly solo. The honor of being the first woman to qualify for a license goes to another Frenchwoman, Madame Elise De Laroche. De Laroche, who won the Women's Cup for a four-hour flight of 160 miles in 1913, was killed during a flight in 1919. She was one of the first women pilots to die in a plane crash. Actually, the first woman to die in a crash was Denise Moore, an American taking lessons at the Henry Farman School, in France, in July 1911. Another Frenchwoman, Helene Dutrieux, a barnstorming trick cyclist, was the second woman to win a pilot's license. In September 1910, she became the first to win the Women's Cup and the 2,000-franc prize that went with it, for a 28-mile flight from Ostend to Bruges, Belgium. At the same time, Dutrieux set a women's altitude record of 1,300 feet. A month later, she flew 157 miles nonstop in an unprecedented 2 hours and 58 minutes. In addition to these records, she was the first woman to stay aloft for an hour and the first to take up a passenger.

The first *American* woman to earn a pilot's license was Harriet Quimby, who also went into the record book as the first woman to fly the English Channel solo. Blanche Scott, the first American woman to fly an aircraft alone (September 1910), was a student of the German instructor Gustav Hamel. In subsequent years, other American women sought the limelight in flying: Ruth Law, Katharine and Marjorie Stinson, Jeanie Macpherson, Mathile Moisant, Phoebe Omlie, and Ethel Dare. In the United States, only a few women invaded what until then had been considered a male domain, and it wasn't until the 1930s that women took to the air as pilots in significant numbers. In 1929, seven held Department of Commerce transport licenses. Only two years later, 50 held a transport license, and 450 received limited commercial and private licenses. Twelve women held glider licenses that year.

One of those who held a transport license was Elinor Smith—not exactly a household name today, but in 1929 Smith made aviation headlines when she and five other women participated in the transcontinental race that year. Having flown as a passenger with her father since she was eight, Smith received many hours of instruction as a teenager but could not solo legally until she turned 18. She first attracted notoriety by flying under all the bridges along New York City's East River one Sunday afternoon. This cost her a brief license suspension; three months later, however, she made her first attempt at a solo endurance record. Although she was unsuccessful, six months later she set a record of 28 hours aloft. A few months after this accomplishment, she set an altitude mark of 27,418 feet.

One of the most active female pilots during the 1930s was Ruth Nichols, whose trademark was a purple leather flying suit and a purple helmet. A graduate of Wellesley, she soloed in a seaplane. With her instructor, Harry Rogers, she made the first nonstop flight from New York to Miami, in 12 hours. A devotee of aviation, Nichols helped organize the Aviation Country Clubs, for promoting country clubs for sports pilots. In 1928, she made a 12,000-mile solo flight to 96 cities in 48 states. After competing in the 1929 transcontinental derby, she went on a record-setting fling. In a Lockheed Vega, she broke Elinor Smith's altitude record with a women's mark of 28,743 feet, set in March 1931. The next month, she set a speed record of 210.63 mph, and in October, on a flight from California to Kentucky, set a long-distance record for women of 1,977.6 miles nonstop. Later, Nichols set an east–west transcontinental record for men and women, of 16 hours and 59.5 minutes, as well as a women's west–east record of 13 hours and 21 minutes.

Ruth Nichols achieved many firsts during her flying career. Although she was a contemporary and a friend of Amelia Earhart, she received less attention from the press; consequently, today, she is less well remembered. Among Nichols's achievements, however, are:

The first woman to be licensed as a seaplane pilot.
The first woman airline pilot in the United States (New York and New England Airways, 1932).
The first woman to attempt a solo flight of the Atlantic Ocean.
The first woman pilot to fly to Honolulu (1925).

The first—and only—woman to hold maximum speed, distance, and
altitude records simultaneously.
The first woman in the United States to pilot an executive jet.

Nichols was also the first woman executive of a million-dollar aviation
corporation (Fairchild Aviation) and the first woman officer of an aviation
magazine *(The Sportsman Pilot)*. There was one distinction she wanted
more than any other, though, and that was to do what Earhart had failed
to do—become the first woman pilot to circumnavigate the globe by air.
She eventually claimed the title, and thereby hangs a tale.

She had become interested in the use of the airplane for mercy flying,
for example, in disaster relief and as an aerial ambulance. Toward that
end, in 1940, she founded Relief Wings, enlisting as many private planes
and existing facilities as she could for emergency and disaster-relief work.
Her idea met with nationwide acceptance and received substantial backing from industry and private business. She built a disaster-oriented organization of volunteer directors, coordinators, and volunteer aircraft
owners, pilots, surgeons, nurses, and radio stations that covered 36 states.
When the United States entered World War II, she turned over the organization's assets to the Civil Air Patrol, a government agency equipped not
only to perform the same service as Relief Wings but that was also
engaged in patrolling the coasts of the United States and serving as a courier for the armed forces. During the war, Nichols served as a volunteer
Red Cross nurse's aide and gave flying instruction. She obtained a multiengine pilot rating and became proficient in instrument flying. After the
war, her dream of flying around the world became closer to realization.
In the winter of 1948, she joined the president of a nonprofit youth group
who was planning a globe-circling flight to inaugurate a series of youth
tours for promoting international unity among young people. This organization became UNICEF.

The idea of being a special volunteer correspondent appealed to Nichols as "work into which I could put my heart as well as my hands, and
for which I could finally unite an adventurer's heart with a Quaker
spirit." Thus, shortly after midnight, July 9, 1949, a DC-4 lifted off from
Bradley Field, in Connecticut, and headed west, with Nichols in the cockpit as a spare pilot. The DC-4 flew to San Francisco, then Tokyo, Hong
Kong, and Bangkok, across India to New Delhi, then Teheran, Athens,
and Rome. At each stop, she interviewed UNICEF officials, visited children's homes, and saw the suffering and tragedy that war had inflicted
on the world's young.

She had intended all along to leave the plane at Rome, together with
the youngsters aboard who would be returning by ship. She hoped to
make arrangements to continue the flight by air, however, preferably as

the copilot of a DC-4 airliner returning to the United States. Eventually, though, she had to settle for replacing a stewardess on the crew of a nonscheduled airliner leaving Rome for the United States.

The first, and only, stop would be Shannon, Ireland. After takeoff from Rome, she was invited to the cockpit and briefly took the controls. Tiring of this, she returned to the passenger cabin and fell asleep. When she work up sometime later and looked at her watch, she realized that the plane was overdue at Shannon. She went to the cockpit, where she learned that not only had they overshot Shannon, but they had lost contact with all ground stations. The captain had turned back, but the big question was, would the fuel last until they determined where they were, now presumably somewhere between Ireland and Iceland. In her memoirs, *Wings for Life*, Nichols describes the terror and near panic of that night:

> I returned to my seat and tried to relax. The passengers apparently were unaware that anything was amiss. Most of them were asleep, a few were reading or conversing in low tones. Forty-five minutes passed, which seemed an eternity. I now could for the first—and, I hope, only—time feel the second-by-second agony of "sweating it out," with no one to talk to and nothing to do. I could only wait and in not one of all my fifty-five narrow escapes, during over thirty years of flying, did I ever have such inner tension. A pilot's ear is tuned to the rhythm of the engines, and my heart jumped as I heard an engine sputter. This great airliner, so swift and powerful in the sky, would sink like a stone in the icy waters of the North Sea.
>
> The First Pilot, poker-faced and brisk, came into the passenger cabin and snapped out: "Prepare to ditch!"

The command wasn't fully understood. Some of the sleeping passengers, awakened by the urgency of the man's voice, were frightened. They could not understand English, but a stewardess who spoke Italian calmly told them to don life preservers as though that's what passengers always did when preparing to land. Nichols knew, however, that a night ditching in such cold waters could mean instant death as the plane smashed into the sea or a lingering one from exposure. One by one, the four engines ran out of fuel and sputtered. The propellers began to windmill. The plane descended, first slowly and then faster.

Suddenly an engine roared and came to life, followed by the other three. The flight crew had discovered an emergency tank with 80 gallons of gasoline, enough for about 15 minutes of flight.

"The reprieve was more torture than the preceding hour of suspense," Nichols says in her book. When the fuel reserve was exhausted, the airliner again started its fatal descent. As the plane hit the water, first came a swishing sound from the windmilling props cutting the wave tops; then there was a hard smack and a sudden stop. As water surged into the cabin, the passengers began to scream. Nichols and two other Americans found a gaping hole in the fuselage and leaped out into the water. They tried to inflate a life raft they found but lost it in the darkness. Finding herself alone, Nichols swam away from the sinking plane, telling herself not to panic.

> I looked about for other survivors and saw, far ahead, a crowded raft. But no matter how I struggled to reach it, the distance between us grew steadily greater. The raft was drifting away from me faster than I could swim . . . I felt the sudden desolation of being completely alone in the vast darkness of [the] impersonal sea.
>
> With all my efforts directed toward reaching the receding life raft, I had not looked behind me. Now, to my amazement, I saw the raft we had pushed overboard. It had inflated automatically on hitting the water, and others were clinging to it. Weak with relief I turned and made for it. Some distance to the right I saw a man floating on his back, arms folded, making no apparent effort to save himself. I shouted at him and motioned toward the raft. But he only lifted one arm in an apparent gesture of farewell, and made no further move. He was too far away for me to reach him and fight my way back to the raft. I began to realize that I was badly out of condition; my strength was almost gone. If I could reach the raft, perhaps we could paddle it in his direction and save him. I made a final desperate effort, lost sight of the raft in the trough of a giant wave, then was tossed high on its crest—and the raft was within reach. With my last ounce of strength I reached out and touched the slippery rubber side—but there were no ropes to grasp. The raft had inflated upside down, with the ropes underneath. A number of people had managed to clamber on top of it and were trying to hold on to others, still in the water.

Nichols and the others turned the raft over and slowly lifted and pulled each other onto the raft. Fourteen survivors had crowded onto a raft built for ten. Top-heavy from the extra weight, the raft bucked and plunged. "None of us could see. With each lurch of the raft, the weight of bodies shifted, the moans and prayers rose in volume, cramped muscles protested more fiercely."

Lights loomed in the darkness. It was a fishing trawler, but no one aboard saw the raft or heard the shouts of its occupants, and the trawler veered away. Nichols lapsed into an exhausted sleep. She was aroused when she heard a shout, which she recognized as coming from the aircraft's captain. He told her to let herself over the side and work her way around to his side of the raft where he was shielding the head of the radio operator, who was unconscious.

In the first light of dawn, the survivors took stock. The radio operator had regained consciousness and sent an SOS message. The captain was optimistic that planes would be out searching for them. The first plane passed overhead without seeing them. Then a second and a third plane flew on. Each time, hope sprang anew, only to die as the 14 people aboard the raft realized they had not been sighted. "How often can hope come back to life?" Nichols wondered. "I can tell you. Twelve times. Twelve times a plane passed over us. Twelve times it flew away. Then the thirteenth—no, it was the twelfth, flying low, coming back, wagging its wings, then flying on." As the last plane disappeared, they spotted a fishing trawler coming toward them. Before long, the cold, wet survivors were hauled aboard. Their battle for survival had been won.

Nine were lost. The 49 survivors, all safely aboard the trawler *Stalberg*, were given food and clothing and taken to Galway, Ireland. Their rescue was the result of a coordinated search by the British Air-Sea Rescue Service. Just before the DC-4 ditched, the pilots had made radio contact with another airliner, a TWA DC-4 en route to New York from Shannon. Its captain was trying to guide the other plane back to Shannon when the latter's fuel ran out. The radio operator had sent out a series of Mayday calls, which had been heard by the *Stalberg*. The trawler's crew actually saw the aircraft go down but couldn't find the life rafts in the darkness.

The raft carrying Nichols and the others was first sighted by Allen D. Reedy, a Pan Am pilot. Reedy landed at Shannon, unloaded his passengers, refueled, and, despite the fact that he had been flying all day, joined the search. Low on fuel, he was about to return to Shannon when he spotted the raft and radioed a shore station, which directed the trawler to the location of the survivors.

Nichols later survived several plane crashes, but in this one, she was not injured. After a few hours' rest in the hospital, she met with survivors and an airline president, who promised that she could return on his airline the next day, "with the same courtesy-pilot arrangements for me as before." She landed at Bradley Field on August 18, where she was greeted by a crowd of reporters. As she recalls in her book, "an old dream had at last been realized, and with it the direction and purpose of my life."

Although Ruth Nichols claimed to have been the first woman pilot to circle the globe, it cannot be claimed—and should not be inferred—that she *piloted* an airplane around the world. Furthermore, she had a rival claimant whom she beat by only one day. Mrs. Richard Morrow-Tait, a British housewife, had been attempting a west–east flight from England. She and her navigator had reached Chicago the day Nichols departed westbound on the DC-4. Mrs. Morrow-Tait crashed in Marseilles and in Alaska, which, of course, delayed her. In Chicago, failure to get financial backing kept her from continuing. The day after Nichols returned to Bradley Field, Morrow-Tait successfully completed her globe-circling flight, though part of it had been by boat. Thus, to Ruth Nichols should go the honor of being the first woman pilot actually to fly *in* a fixed-wing aircraft entirely around the world.

Another British housewife also deserves mention. Like several male pilots before her, Mrs. Victor Bruce, a novice, learned to fly, then set out in a British-built, single-engine, open-cockpit Bluebird to conquer the world. She had spotted the plane in London in 1930 and on the spur of the moment had decided to buy it. She would learn to fly this plane, advertised as "Ready to Go Anywhere," and fly it around the world via the United States. In September 1930, she passed the test for a British pilot's license. When she taxied the Bluebird out for takeoff, she had a mere 40 hours in her logbook. She flew from England to Syria without mishap but was forced down in the desert by lack of fuel. She caught a ride on an Arab's horse to the nearest village, where she found gas. At the mouth of the Persian Gulf, she landed in quicksand and had to be pulled out.

Mrs. Bruce flew to Bangkok, Hanoi, and Japan, where she boarded an ocean liner for Canada, then took the Bluebird across the United States. In a symbolic gesture, she dropped a flag weighted with spark plugs near her mother's former home in New Albany, New York. She boarded an ocean liner for Le Havre, then flew to Croydon, England, where she was welcomed by hundreds of well-wishers, including a fleet of Bluebirds gathered to honor her achievement. Mrs. Bruce had traveled more than 20,000 miles in slightly less than five months. On her Bluebird were thousands of signatures, including that of Al Capone, the Chicago racketeer. To her, certainly, goes much credit for persistence and courage for piloting a light aircraft successfully over a great distance.

The flights of Nichols, Morrow-Tait, and Bruce were significant, in that they proved piloting an airplane on long flights could also be accomplished by women. They foreshadowed the day when a female pilot would fly alone completely around the world. A diminutive housewife from Columbus, Ohio, became the first to do this. Geraldine ("Jerrie") L. Mock flew 23,103 miles in 29 days, 11 hours, 59 minutes, and 38 seconds, setting a record for women. In addition, Mock became the first woman to fly the Pacific alone from west to east, and the first to fly solo either way in a single-engine plane.

Mock also set a round-the-world speed record for aircraft weighing less than 3,858 pounds. Christened *Spirit of Columbus*, the Cessna 180 she flew was not a new plane. Manufactured in 1953, it had been owned by several others when she bought it in 1964. Typically, it had to be modified before the world flight could be attempted. Extra fuel tanks were installed in the cabin; other available space was devoted to survival equipment. The extra tanks gave the plane 178 gallons of fuel in the cabin and 65 in the wings, enough for 25 hours' flying time. Two ADF radios, a VHF radio, and HF radio were installed, along with a vertical reading compass and a drum altimeter. In the spring of 1964, Mock decided that she was ready.

Although she had only about 750 hours of flying time, Mock had been thinking about this flight for years. As a schoolgirl, she had watched planes flying out of Newark Airport and wished that someday she could learn to fly. In pursuit of her dream, she studied aeronautical engineering at Ohio State University. When she graduated, though, the dream was still far from reality. Despite her engineering background, she went into newspaper advertising, then produced a five-year series of educational television shows, radio shows, and a preschool TV series, as well as the first transoceanic telecast. The urge to fly remained, however. She took flying lessons. Before earning her private pilot's license, she bought a single-engine, all-metal Luscombe with earnings from network newsreel photography. After receiving her license, she became manager of an airport in Lincoln, Illinois, and later at Price Field, in Columbus, Ohio.

Mock's world flight originated one evening when she was feeling restless and told her husband Russell that she wanted to go somewhere. Thinking he would put an end to the matter quickly, Russell suggested that she "get in that airplane and fly around the world." But this facetious suggestion had the opposite effect of setting his wife to thinking about a mission that would eventually put her in the record books. Within minutes, she had rounded up several navigation charts and had spread them out on the floor downstairs, doing calculations and making notes. Fired by the idea, Jerrie Mock wrote to the National Aeronautic Association, asking for advice about flying a Cessna 180 around the world. She was pleased to learn that only a few men had done it successfully and that no woman had yet made the flight.

The children got caught up in the project, and planning began in earnest. Russell set out to raise money while Jerrie planned the details of the flight. With only 500 hours of flying time and no instrument rating, she would need more instruction and experience. As she accumulated hours, she learned of Joan Merriam Smith's plans to make an attempt. Mock, however, refused to be hurried into taking off before she was ready. She left nothing to chance, and on March 19, 1964, the aircraft, its equipment, and its pilot were ready. Mock kept an in-flight diary of her trip, which was later filed with the NAA. It not only shows how her careful planning paid off but provides insight into what such a flight is like. It is reproduced here verbatim:

N1538C Departed Columbus on March 19, 1964 at approximately 9:25 Eastern. Tried to get official time . . . everyone was too busy. Flight to

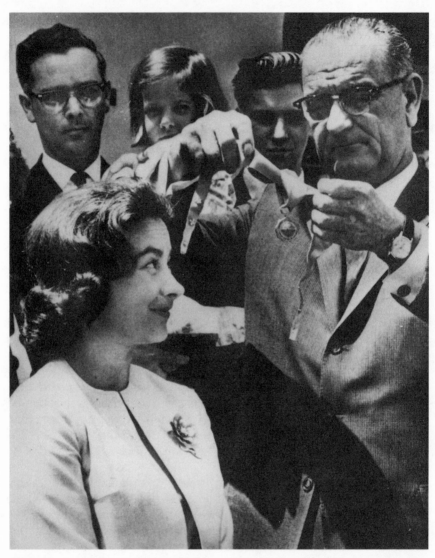

Jerrie Mock receives a specially struck gold medal from President Lyndon Johnson for her feat as the first woman pilot to circle the earth solo as her husband Russel, son Gary, and daughter Valerie look on. (National Air and Space Museum photo)

Bermuda smooth. HF radio disconnected by someone installing something else, so unable to contact Kindley for wind information. So had to estimate. . . . Picked up Kindley on ADF 300 miles out. Sighted land at 3:45 Eastern. On ground at 4:05. Very strong surface wind. Had to taxi for several miles crosswind. Hard on brakes.

Bermuda to Santa Maria, Azores. March 25–26.

March 25, one week after landing at Kindley Air Force Base, Bermuda, N1538C took off for Santa Maria in the Azores. Climbed to FL 90. Heading 097°. Left Kindley at 20:16Z, reached Weather Ship Echo at 0205. Slightly north, of course, so tuned in Lugo Consulan. Corrected course 10°. It's hard to write because every time I start someone calls on the radio. A real party line. Heard Santa Maria 200 miles from Kindley. Past Echo in clouds at 9000'. Picked up an inch of ice. Cleared to 11,000'. No additional ice, but didn't melt until the sun came out.

Still north of course in spite of 10° correction. Sighted a western island and found my position and proceeded to Santa Maria. ADF approach. After landing I was told they had a 100 ft. ceiling.

Santa Maria, Azores–Casablanca, Morocco. March 28.

Departed Santa Maria at 1122Z. Crossed 20° W at 1308Z. Should be going through a front between here and 15° W but so far nothing has materialized. No front to speak of. Decided I was north of course again. Must be compass. Picked up Casablanca VOR much earlier than I expected. Approached over the city. It's quite pretty from the air. Bounced on landing as usual.

March 30. Casablanca to Bone, Algeria.

That direct route from Casablanca to Tunis had very low ceiling over the mountains. Thunderstorms were all around so I decided to go up to Tangier and down the Mediterranean coast. By the time we got everything straightened out it was too late to get to Tunis before dark so I needed to stop at Bone. . . . Weather was good for halfway, then storms began. The mountain tops along the shore were hidden by low clouds. I flew out over the sea until I came to Bone. Storms all around but the airport was fine. [An] official stamped my FAI form. I don't know what his title was because no one there spoke English.

March 31. Bone, Algeria to Tripoli.

Filed flight plan to Cairo, but they insisted I put Tripoli down as first landing. Got very concerned when I said I would carry 15 hours fuel. "Oh no, we'll put down 10 hours," I finally realized (they were all talking in French) that the reason Tripoli was in the flight plan was . . . they had no weather information beyond that place. Of course, they knew Cairo was good. Then as I was ready to start the engine, someone ran out and said that past Tripoli were bad sandstorms and I must land. I said "OK, I will land at Tripoli." When I arrived Tripoli had no record of me, but confirmed the sandstorms and I stayed on the ground. Oil change. Need my brakes repaired but no one has parts. They all say the next place. It is like manana. A man in ATC signed NAA forms.

April 1. Tripoli to Cairo.

Delayed at Customs by 150 Pilgrims going to Jedda. Then starter solenoid broken. Fortunately, I had a spare, so it only cost an hour delay. Tripoli is expensive but the mechanics and oil change were free.

Arrived at Cairo and landed. As I turned off the runway the tower controller called, "Where are you, 38C?" "On the ground," I answered. "You are fading, 38C. Give me your position." About this time 3 trucks full of soldiers drove out to see who I was. They took me to their mess hall which [had been] a palace of King Farouk's, showed me the garden, fed me cider and made phone calls. An hour later I was permitted to take off from the air force base for Cairo. There I was met again. This time it was by dozens of newspaper and radio people.

April 3. Cairo to Dhahran.

It can be very confusing in a foreign airport. Everyone was very friendly but communication was difficult, and I ended up in a parking area by the terminal that was soon to be occupied by a Convair. I had gone there for a 15 min. refueling and 45 minutes later finally had the fuel, but was still unparked. I had removed my bags because the pump was leaking, so everyone got excited and began to shout about what I should do . . . I ended up taxiing the plane through the crowd with a life raft on my shoulders.

The flight over the desert was uneventful. No comm. for some time because I accidentally burned out motor of HF reel. I relayed through other planes.

Dhahran airport was filled with hundreds of people to see the lady pilot. I learned later that many of them kept watching for the man pilot to climb out. In Arabia a woman is not allowed to drive a car. They never heard of one flying an airplane.

Customs in Dhahran was very easy. They walked me through and everyone waved.

TWA took care of the plane. I need my brakes fixed but no one has the parts. Oil was all over the plane and I had it checked; however, it was as I suspected. They had filled it too full at Cairo. It was still too full in Dhahran.

April 4. Dhahran to Karachi.

Writing is unusually bad because of bumpy air. Just ate an orange that began to taste like gasoline. When they fueled the plane at Cairo my things were sitting on the ground and got dripped upon. The orange was in cellophane, but it must have leaked.

Light rain over the Persian Gulf and low clouds over the mountains of Sarkjah. Must fly out over the Gulf of Oman because flying over Iran is prohibited.

I am getting used to an ADF. It works quite well now that I have determined my compass correction card is off 10°. I have been trying to have the compass swung since Santa Maria but always some reason why not. I finally checked runway headings and marked my compass card that way.

April 5. Karachi–Delhi.

The flying of the airplane is very easy, but the foreign rules and regulations are difficult. Back home this would be easy. There is more red tape. Each country has something new added. They keep giving me papers to sign and to not lose and it gets confusing. When I considered a crew member I must declare my wedding ring. Of course, the next day no one checks to see if I still have it. The farther east I go the more complicated it gets. I don't think I'll mind the Pacific as much as this. I'll be glad when I get to Manila. Met by members of the Aero Club of India who are going to look after me during my stay.

April 6. Delhi to Calcutta.

Just crossed the Ganges River. I have been flying along it for 150 or so miles. There are many villages below. I think all of India must be full of people. India has more private flying than the other countries, but still very little. I haven't seen a cloud since Cairo. There should be some near Calcutta and from there east. Any day the monsoons will arrive and disrupt flying, but I should be past before they arrive.

April 7. Calcutta to Bangkok.

Now I am in the Far East. I had trouble getting clearance to overfly Burma. It came through after I left Columbus. Burma refused to grant landing permission, and I was a little hesitant about what might happen; however, when I filed my flight plan last night it went through right away, and when I passed over Rangoon the control tower men were friendly and wished me good luck on the rest of my trip. Saw a few pagodas from the air but since flying over the cities is forbidden, I didn't get a good look, just shiny carved gold roofs in the distance. I did VFR but Bangkok control had me IFR. Somehow I lost a day.

April 8. Bangkok to Manila.

Over Vietnam. Just talked to Saigon Radio and they asked me if I had a man aboard. I said. "No." On my way to Karachi, approach control wanted my occupation. I was relaying through an airliner and they were all amazed when I said "housewife."

Every other sentence I must stop to answer someone on the radio. This far away I am beginning to find some inaccuracies in the maps. Not all the fault of the mapmakers. In one case they were to change the airways, but after the new charts came out changed their minds. I had the new charts.

Starting out over the South China Sea. 750 miles of water to Manila. Picked up Rosario beacon 650 miles out!

It was dark when I reached Manila. Came in over Lubang VOR, then to Rosario. ADF approach. Weather VFR. The requirement to fly airways rather than direct to the strong stations makes navigation more difficult. I don't have radar, Doppler and celestial like air force and airlines. Just ADF and VOR.

Manila–Guam. April 10th or 11th, depending on which side of the date-line you are.

I find the times confusing. I talk to my husband in Columbus. He is on one day and I on another.

Out over the Pacific.

Getting away from the airports is such a problem. I had to file two flight plans. One international, one domestic, in different buildings. I find their weather forecasts very confusing too. I go to the weather office and come out with a map with pretty colored lines and everything in meters, kilometers and millibars. I was fortunate today in getting a weather report in plain English from Clark Air Force Base. I went to the meteorology building just to be polite and not upset the local people. They tried to make things easy by bringing the customs people to me. Only trouble was they were very busy and I had to wait a long time while they chased around.

Weather here is fine but Guam is not as good as I would like. 1000 broken 3 miles in rain showers and winds. But I will be with people I can understand and they have good radar.

The clouds over the oceans are fabulous. I amuse myself watching them. One ahead looks like George Washington. Some have rainbows in them. Almost time to report over 137° 30′ E. It seems rather silly because I don't know where I am at all. They should put some markers down below. I have been tuned to Agana beacon for some time. Seemed to be on course, but I'll never really know.

Several hours of night flying. Radar approach. This is my first chance to make a precision radar approach. The controller did a very good job.

April 12. Guam–Wake.

Takeoff at 2031Z. Now 2311. Just passed a small plane headed for Guam. Altitude 9000. Clouds below scattered to broken. Nothing else to look at. I have had headwinds since Bangkok. Wake has a strong radio beacon. Too bumpy to write for awhile. The ceiling at Wake was 3000 scattered. ADF approach. For some reason as I started the approach the radio reception became very garbled. They could hear me and I continued the approach. After landing, the audio became clear again.

April 13 to 13. Wake to Honolulu.

The dates are getting confused with the date lines. Took off at 10:30 Wake time. I had planned to leave in the afternoon, but there was a front to go through which the weather bureau suggested I hit after daylight. Dawn and no front! Weather forecasting is the same all around the world. The front was only four hours ahead. Flying instruments on and off for about an hour. Scattered storms around the islands. As I approached Honolulu Airport the mountain tops were in the clouds but the airport was clear. 16 hours 30 minutes. A long flight, but easy. Some radar men complained I was 12 miles south of course. I'd like to see him do better with small plane equipment.

April 14–15. Honolulu to Oakland.

Thunderstorms all around at takeoff, but airport OK. Flight level 90. Should have had slight tailwind, but someone made a mistake. More than 30 minutes late over Weather Ship November. Many clouds. This dawn was different because of flying between layers. 300 miles from Honolulu could talk to San Francisco as if they were underneath the plane. Got Honolulu a good 2 hours out of Oakland. Engine smoother than ever. Flight took 13 hours, 1.5 hours longer than estimate. More than 5 hours fuel remaining. Beautiful weather in Oakland.

April 16. Oakland–Tucson.

Had a late start today. Needed sleep. Everyone kept asking, "What is your departure time?" and I kept answering "When I am ready!" Very unsympathetic. Both of us. Reached Tucson after dark.

April 17. Tucson–El Paso.

Up before dawn. Takeoff at sunrise. Short trip to El Paso for breakfast, which was coffee. Became an honorary citizen of El Paso, but didn't have time to stay for the big breakfast they had planned. Bad weather ahead to beat.

April 17. El Paso–Bowling Green, Ky.

Some of the worst weather of the whole trip. There's a long violent weather front across my course. It's nice to have VORs again. Started out VFR on top, but this became between layers which closed up. I'm curious where the weather bureau gets some of its information. Hoped to go nonstop to Columbus, but had not filled the tanks and decided to land for fuel.

Bowling Green–Columbus. April 17, 1964.

A quick 2-hour flight. Takeoff at sunset. Arrival in Columbus, the end of the line, at 9:35 P.M. Columbus time or 2235Z. People all around to see me. It was a nice easy trip. I'm glad to be home.

The flight was over, but the fame Jerrie Mock had won would turn her life into a whirlwind of activity. She was besieged for interviews by newspapers, magazines, and radio and television networks but turned down most such requests. A major magazine offered her one of its highest fees ever for an exclusive interview. She refused the offer, saying that such a story would not advance the cause of general aviation. She felt that if the flight were made to look extremely dangerous, that cause would not be well served.

Jerrie never flew *Spirit of Columbus* again. The Cessna Company gave her a later model in exchange for the plane she flew around the world. The record-setting plane was displayed at the Cessna factory in Wichita until 1975, when it was given to the National Air and Space Museum. Today, it hangs in the museum's General Aviation Gallery.

As if to prove further that age and gender are no hindrance to long-distance flying, one of the most recent world girdlers was Polly Vacher, 57, the mother of three grown sons and an instrument-rated commercial pilot from Abingdon, England. Her stated objective was to be the first woman to fly the smallest single-engine aircraft around the world solo via Australia and the Pacific. She departed Birmingham, England, alone in a Piper Dakota on January 12, 2001, and returned from the 29,000-mile flight on May 17. She spent two years preparing for the trip, including survival training. The two rear seats of the Dakota had been removed to make room for an extra gas tank, and she had a life raft fitted into the right seat beside her. Her route took her over 20 countries by way of Cyprus, Jordan, India, Indonesia, Australia, Fiji, Samoa, Hawaii, and across the United States to Washington, D.C., for an award ceremony by the British ambassador to the United States. She then flew home to England via the North Atlantic. As she approached the Birmingham Airport, she was escorted by two British Royal Air Force Harrier jump jets.

The longest time she spent in the air was 19 hours, much of it at night, when en route from Hawaii to California. Her scariest moment was when she miscalculated the amount of gas in one tank and the engine quit. She quickly switched tanks and proceeded without further difficulty. Her most difficult leg, as far as control of the aircraft was concerned, occurred later over the Rocky Mountains between Big Bear, California, and Colorado Springs, Colorado, where she encountered severe turbulence.

Polly Vacher was backed by contributions from 32 sponsors and more than 1,400 contributors who signed the wings of her Dakota. Her efforts raised $230,000 for the Royal International Air Tattoo Flying Scholarship for the Disabled.

16

THE COMPETITORS

Jerrie Mock—quiet, unassuming, noncompetitive—didn't seem to mind that another woman was preparing to span the globe in what the press was calling a race. The other woman was Joan Merriam Smith, the wife of a Navy commander. Joan Smith announced that she would follow the route planned but not completed by Amelia Earhart. Earhart, trying to become the first woman to fly her own plane around the world, vanished in the South Pacific in 1937, along with her navigator, Fred Noonan.

According to Smith, she had been eager to make the flight for a long time. She started taking flight lessons when she was 15. She soloed at 16, received her private license at 17, her commercial license at the minimum age of 23, and soon thereafter added instrument, instructor, and air-transport ratings. Several years of instruction followed flying charter and company planes and saving money for *the* plane, the one that would be suitable for a round-the-world flight.

In November 1963, Smith deposited her life's savings—$10,000—as a down payment on a six-year-old twin-engine Piper Apache. Over the next few months she spent more than $21,000 borrowed from friends on the plane. Modifications to the Apache were extensive, with consequent problems that plagued her throughout the world flight.

Unable to get approval of a world-girdling flight from the NAA (Jerrie Mock had filed first), Smith decided not to try for the speed record, neither in the next higher weight category above Mock's Cessna nor in an effort to beat Mock's record for a female pilot. Smith's route, following Earhart's, would be 4,000 miles longer than Earhart's and would cross the equator four times. Disappointed because she couldn't get NAA approval, Smith resented the press calling the two separate flights a race. "About five weeks before I was a ready for takeoff, and after working on this project for over a year," she said, "I found out about Mrs. Mock. I

Joan Merriam Smith circled the globe soon after Jerrie Mock and was awarded the Harmon International Trophy in 1965 for her round-the-world flight at the equator, the longest solo flight ever made by a woman. She flew 27,750 miles in 56 days with 34 stops. (National Air and Space Museum photo)

had been planning this flight in my mind for 10 years and had muffed the chance twice because of lack of funds and shortage of equipment. It is not a race as far as I'm concerned."

On March 17, 1964, two days before Jerrie Mock took off, and 27 years since Amelia Earhart had left on her ill-fated flight, Joan Merriam Smith left Oakland, California, Earhart's departure point in *The City of Long Beach*. She had amassed 9,000 hours of flight time, far more than Mock's experience. Even though she didn't think of it as a race, the press considered her chances of coming in first better than Mock's primarily because Smith was so much more experienced and because she would be flying a twin-engine plane, which substantially lowered the risks.

Smith flew to Tucson and then New Orleans without incident. After a night's rest, she went on to Miami, where she spent two days preparing for her first overseas hop. Then it was on to San Juan, Puerto Rico; and Paramaribo, Surinam. On this leg, "for the first time I saw the wilds and jungles of South America, an unpleasant sight at any altitude." It was at Paramaribo that problems growing out of the modifications began. The welded seam of a cabin fuel tank sprang a leak, and both tanks had to be removed and rewelded, a job that took seven days. The tanks were finally repaired. Now Smith faced the formidable 1,500-mile leg to Natal, Brazil. Not only would she be flying over seemingly endless jungle, but she would be in the equatorial frontal zone, with its rain squalls and turbulence. She encountered the zone in the form of fog, then gradually building clouds that she could not top. Ducking underneath them, she got radio clearance to land at Belem just minutes before a torrential downpour closed the field.

On March 31, Smith landed at Natal. She found herself among a fleet of bombers, fighters, and trainers. She had landed the night before a revolution; all communications to the outside world were cut, and no flights were permitted inside Brazil. Nor was any weather information available for the 1,900-mile leg across the Atlantic to Dakar, Senegal. Two days later, she was cleared to leave; but she still had no weather reports. She took off anyway, and a few minutes out went on instruments. For the next six hours, she flew with no outside reference. Unable to raise anyone on the HF radio, she doggedly flew on, hour after hour, on a heading of 55 degrees at altitudes ranging from 500 feet to 17,000. She ran into the equatorial front again but couldn't get over it. After 16 hours on this course, she picked up the radio beacon at Dakar and found she was only 40 miles north of her course.

After a brief layover at Dakar, she took off for Mali, Chad, and the Sudan, enjoying fair weather but strong head winds and some turbulence during daylight hours. Following Earhart's flight plan, she flew to Massawa/Assab, both in Ethiopia, then to Aden for refueling. "Following the coast of Saudi Arabia for over 1,300 miles [to] Karachi brought hours of sheer boredom," she said. Landing at Karachi, she found she had to land at Ahmadabad, India, to clear customs before pushing on to Calcutta. "This landing presented the biggest jumble of red tape and frustration I have ever experienced." She sat in the heat for four hours while Indian officials argued among themselves. Once cleared, she flew to Bangkok, where she had to pay $150 in fees before being allowed to proceed.

Smith made her third equatorial crossing on the leg to Singapore, 900 miles south of Bangkok. She was delayed in Singapore for a day, awaiting clearance, then left for Djakarta, Surabaja, Darwin (Australia), and Kupang (Timor). She described the next leg of the journey in an article that appeared in *AOPA Pilot,* the journal of the Aircraft Owners and Pilots Association:

> Darwin is 1,500 miles from Lae, New Guinea, and much of the terrain is uncharted. The north coast of Australia is shown as "Relief data incom-

plete" on WAC charts, and no airways are plotted in IFR charts. The route crosses the Gulf of Carpenteria, [the] Coral Sea, and the Gulf of Papua into New Guinea. I had thought that one of my biggest problems on this flight would be fuel and refueling the plane if facilities were as antiquated as in 1937. I brought along a funnel and three chamois, but even in out-of-the-way places I found Shell Oil Company facilities with modern filtering systems.

The flight from Darwin to Lae was undoubtedly the most harrowing of all. On April 20th, with decent weather forecast for the trip, I found myself fighting the most unusual, violent weather I have ever experienced. After nine hours of combating the elements—on instruments most of the time—I managed to get into Horn Island, Australia after circling for three hours waiting for a storm to move out of the airport area.

Another pilot, flying to Port Moresby, New Guinea, also landed there. He said it was the worst storm he had experienced in 18 years of charter flying in that territory. Later, we learned we had flown partially through the formation of a cyclone.

The next afternoon, with marginal weather, we both took off and skirted around storms into Port Moresby. The Owen-Stanley Mountain range between Lae and Port Moresby extends up to 15,000 feet with heavy storms building up to 50,000 feet daily after 11 A.M., so an afternoon crossing was out. Annual rainfall can exceed 500 inches per year, and New Guinea is undoubtedly the most primitive and remote region [of] the world.

I was met at Lae by hundreds of people, including the last six to see A.E. [Amelia Earhart] and Noonan in 1937. I had followed the 1937 A.E. flight precisely and was now anxious to make the Pacific crossing to Oakland.

Flying the Pacific should have been the easiest part of my trip, with accurate weather forecasts, heavy aircraft traffic, powerful radio aids, search-and-rescue stations, and the smooth sailing one finds flying on top of an overcast at 8,000 to 10,000 feet. I still would have the headwinds, as a new high had developed east of Hawaii.

The simplicity of the Pacific crossing was marred, however, by mechanical problems from Guam on, including hydraulic failure out of Guam. After seven days of overhauling the Hydraulic Power-Pak and checking out the entire system, I was off to Wake Island. Now the gear kept slipping down in flight and had to be hand retracted regularly. Headwinds kept me three days at Wake. Later, I had to detour into Midway, due to strong headwinds. A good, reliable, strong ADF receiver paid off at this point in my ability to get a cross-bearing out of Midway, 700 miles to the north, which told me I was an hour behind schedule. Without this knowledge and the assistance of sun line shots from the sextant, I would have run short of fuel.

I met [thousands of] gooney birds at Midway during my brief landing and then had to sit it out again at Honolulu for better winds. With 20 hours of fuel, I took off on May 11, and, after 18:04 flying time, landed at Oakland on May 12, at 9:12 A.M.

The total flight took 170 hours of which 47 were on instruments. The equator was crossed four times and headwinds ranging from 10 to 40 knots plagued me for 25,000 miles.

Amelia's dream to be the first woman to circle the globe at the equator and to establish a new long-distance record had been my accomplishment, but I must thank her for the inspiration that obsessed me to try it.

Although Smith did not mention it in her article, fuel leaks were a persistent (and potentially dangerous) nuisance, as were malfunctions in the plane's electrical system. Between Wake Island and Honolulu, insects and debris clogged the oil cooler on the starboard engine, the gear would not stay in the "up" position properly, and the autopilot was unreliable. Fourteen hours out of Honolulu on the leg to Oakland, she had to feather the propeller of the starboard engine because of engine overheating.

Despite the fact that she had lost the race—if, indeed, there had ever been one—Joan Smith deserves credit for courage and persistence. She flew 27,750 miles in about 56 days, with 34 stops—not a speed record, but she did achieve five aviation firsts and one "longest":

The first to fly solo around the world at the equator.
The first woman to fly a twin-engine plane around the world.
The first woman to fly solo from Africa to Australia.
The first woman to fly from Wake Island to the Midway Islands.
The longest solo flight in the history of aviation up to that time.

The successful flight of Joan Merriam Smith inspired other women to think seriously about the exhilarating experience of flying around the world. One of them was Ann Holtgren Pellegreno, who says she got the idea in 1962, when Lee Koepke, an airline mechanic, mentioned that he was rebuilding a Lockheed 10, a model similar to the one Earhart had used in 1937. As they talked about Earhart, her dream, and the Lockheed Koepke was restoring, Pellegreno asked him what he planned to do with it. Smiling, he said: "Well, Ann, I thought you'd like to fly it around the world—and do what Amelia didn't."

She had only about 100 hours' flying time then, but she was fascinated with the thought. Restoration of the Lockheed 10 took four years. By the time it was ready to fly, Pellegreno had a commercial license, with instrument and multiengine ratings. After reading Fred Goerner's *The Search for Amelia Earhart,* she was motivated to duplicate the flight and, as a tribute, drop a wreath on tiny, now unoccupied Howland Island, Earhart's destination when she disappeared. Pellegreno enlisted the support of Koepke and her husband and was soon deeply involved in planning the flight. Typically, preparations included installation of extra fuel tanks, acquisition of maps, weather analysis, selection of airports within range of the

Lockheed 10, and obtaining visas and landing or overflight permission. Financial backing was also needed; therefore, letters were written to oil and equipment companies and to the Lockheed Aircraft Company. No one wanted to back the flight of an airplane more than 30 years old, however. Finally, persistence paid off; help arrived in the form of a loan of a radio and navigation and other equipment. Contact with Bill Polhemus, president of a navigation research engineering firm, opened up contacts who were persuaded to help in one way or another: Collins Radio; Kollsman Instruments; Air Canada; Champion Spark Plug; Goodyear Tire and Rubber; and Jeppesen, maker of aeronautical charts. Some products of these companies were experimental. The flight would give the companies a chance to test their products under realistic conditions and at little cost.

As planning progressed, Pellegreno and Koepke acquired two crew members: Polhemus and William R. Payne, an Air Force pilot friend of his who, with Polhemus as navigator, had set a speed record from Washington to Paris in 1961 in a B-58.

Ann Holtgren Pellegreno, during her flight to duplicate the world flight intended by Amelia Earhart, poses with her crew at Honolulu International Airport. Left to right: Bill Polhemus, navigator; Lee Koepke, mechanic; Pellegreno; and Col. William R. Payne, copilot. (Wide World photo)

On June 9, 1967, 30 years after Earhart and Noonan's departure, Pellegreno, Koepke, and Payne (Polhemus was to join them in Miami) took off from Oakland with Ann at the controls. They flew to Tucson, Fort Worth, New Orleans, and Miami, where Polhemus climbed aboard for the first of the eastbound, overwater legs. Stops were made at San Juan, Caracas, Trinidad, Belem, and Natal without incident except for an unscheduled stop in Trinidad instead of Paramaribo because the bubble lights in the two sextants were out and Polhemus couldn't take a star fix during the night part of the flight to Belem. Facing a head wind of 40 knots, they made a 180-degree turn and landed at Trinidad.

Out of Natal, over the South Atlantic, they flew through several severe thunderstorms as Payne and Pellegreno traded stints at the controls. When the clouds parted briefly, Polhemus got a sextant shot, and they found they were only 50 miles off course. A strong wind shift developed, however. By the time they made landfall on the west coast of Africa, they had drifted 90 miles off course. Fortunately, radio reception improved and a landing was made at Dakar.

Polhemus left the crew at Dakar and jetted back to Ann Arbor to attend to business, planning to rejoin the group in Singapore a week later. The others pushed on to Las Palmas, in the Canary Islands, then Lisbon, Rome, Ankara, Teheran, Karachi, New Delhi, Calcutta, Bangkok, and Singapore, where Polhemus was waiting. Then it was on to Djakarta, Kupang, and Darwin. Besides the usual aggravation of clearing customs, arranging for servicing, and dealing with reporters, the only problem for Pellegreno, Koepke, and Payne was a medical one: dysentery. Polhemus had escaped this affliction by returning home during the crucial week.

On July 1, they pressed on, flying to Port Moresby and Lae, New Guinea, Earhart's last stop, then to Nauru Island, a dot in the Pacific only 12 miles in circumference. The next leg, to Canton Island via Howland, is described by Pellegreno in her book, *World Flight: The Earhart Trail:*

> By now we knew the Lockheed well: the fuel transfer, the power settings and cruise altitudes. We knew the sound of converters whirring when we transmitted on the HF, the high whine of the inverter when we needed 110-volt AC, the two-minute intervals when we held the plane level for astro shots. And always the throb of the engines was there, conveying the feeling that the plane was alive beneath our feet. I looked out the window through the shining propeller arc to the dark ocean below. . . . the pilot flying over this ocean hour after hour sees only limitless water. Even the "island constellations" do not shatter this illusion, for often only one island in them is visible at a time, so distant are these pinpoints, so often cloud shrouded.
>
> One of the pinpoints is Howland Island. Its nearest neighbor, Baker Island, is approximately 50 miles south and [is] slightly larger. However, one could not call the two islands a constellation in any sense. Their nearest

Ann Pellegreno's Lockheed 10A is shown on display at the National Museum of Canada, Ottawa. It was restored by Lee Koepke, an airline mechanic, who participated in the world flight as crew chief. Restoration took four years. (Photo courtesy National Museums of Canada)

neighbors (except for a sand bar about 100 miles southeast) are the Phoenix Islands, slightly over 400 miles southeast. Six hundred miles to the west are the Gilbert Islands and 800 miles to the northwest lie the Marshall Islands.

We were putting our faith in the chart makers. Before World War II, accurate maps of the Pacific were unavailable. Later mapping put more pinpoints nearer their correct positions. But even on the charts we used, none dated earlier than 1966. . . . This vast ocean is broken only by the bits of coral, atolls, and islands, and even these are not charted accurately.

Polhemus took frequent star fixes while Pellegreno held the Lockheed on course; shortly after noon, he estimated their position as approximately 700 miles west of Howland. As time passed, they flew on through scattered showers. At dawn, they crossed the international date line and began to watch for the tiny island that had been Earhart and Noonan's destination years before. The U.S. Coast Guard cutter *Blackhaw* was supposed to be positioned offshore, listening for their call. When Polhemus's shots showed they were about 60 miles from Howland, Pellegreno began trying to raise *Blackhaw*, with no success. Rain squalls had developed and were coming closer together. As the ceiling lowered, Pellegreno, afraid they would miss the island in the poor visibility, took the plane down to 300 feet. She asked *Blackhaw*, now 37 nautical miles southwest of Howland, for radio direction. Concerned, Polhemus gave several heading changes. Everyone strained to see the island. The Lockheed flew between showers, but only the sea was visible. "We have about 20 minutes more to search," Polhemus warned; "then we'll have to go on."

It was Koepke who spotted Howland first. There, to their left, was the tiny island—only a half-mile wide and two miles long—with a red-and-white tower housing the Earhart Beacon. Nearby was the foundation of a building. Pellegreno describes her feelings as she banked the Lockheed and they looked down:

> As we circled Howland, lying jewellike in a dark blue ocean, I felt a sense of history—an exciting feeling—and also one of extreme relief that we had found the island. This is where another Lockheed 10 should have landed thirty years ago. No trace of the three runways prepared for the other plane [was] visible, the scrub brush having obscured them. It was easy to imagine that high above us the ghostly silver wings of another Lockheed 10 were casting a shadow on the island. . . .
>
> When the second circle around the island was completed, Payne took the controls and I went back to where Lee had strapped himself in his seat. I held the wreath and Lee's arms encircled me in a bearlike grip, for opening the door would create a suction toward the outside. The reds, greens, and yellows of the leaves were as bright as they had been in Port Moresby. Payne flew north of the island and then turned back, descending to 50 feet above the sea and flying slowly. Polhemus waited near the window to tell us when to drop the wreath.
>
> "Get ready," he said. "We're over the island."
>
> Lee rammed his foot harder against the door and wedged it open with his boot. Leaning forward, I pushed the wreath through the opening, feeling it torn from my hands. It landed on the island, hopefully where another pair of Lockheed 10 wheels [should have] touched thirty years ago.

They headed southeast toward Canton Island, 421 miles away, arriving cramped and stiff. They had been in the plane for nearly 24 of the last 28 hours. After relaxing in the warmth of the tropical island for three days, the adventurers took off, with Honolulu as their destination, 1,972 miles to the northeast. It was July 4, the day Earhart had planned to return to the United States. After 14.5 hours, they landed triumphantly at Honolulu International Airport, leaving two days later on the longest leg of the world flight—2,461 miles to Oakland. Eighteen hours and 25 minutes later, they landed and were met by friends, admirers, and the press. Vivian Maata, Earhart's secretary at the time of the final flight, met them. "Amelia was a marvelous person, and I admired her greatly," she said to Ann Pellegreno. "I would have been only too glad to welcome her back to this airport thirty years ago. Your plane, coming in today, could have been hers, and I feel a little sad. But I congratulate you for completing the flight. It was a wonderful tribute."

There was another woman pilot who wanted to retrace Amelia Earhart's last great flying adventure. It was Linda Duerler Finch (now Mrs. Laird Doctor), a San Antonio businesswoman and aviation history buff who

Ann Pellegreno is interviewed after landing at Oakland, California, upon completion of her world-circling flight on July 7, 1967. She conceived the idea of following the flight path planned by Amelia Earhart after seeing the Lockheed 10A being restored. Her flight is documented in her excellent book entitled *World Flight: The Earhart Trail,* published by Iowa State University Press in 1971. (Photo courtesy Port of Oakland, California)

had spent more than 21 years acquiring, restoring, maintaining, and flying historic aircraft. A mother of three, she was an accomplished 8,000-
hour pilot who had helped restore and fly war birds such as a Republic
P-47 Thunderbolt fighter and the North American AT-6 Texan, a WWII
trainer that she flew at the national air races in Reno, Nevada.

She decided that her world flight would be made in 1997 on the sixtieth
anniversary of Earhart's last flight and the one hundredth anniversary of
her birth. And it was to be made in the Lockheed Electra 10E, the same
type of aircraft used by Amelia on her ill-fated flight in 1937 and by Ann
H. Pellegreno on the thirtieth anniversary of Amelia's departure from
Oakland.

Finch found that there were only two Electra 10Es known to exist by
the beginning of the 1990s, and she launched a three-year campaign to
buy one of them from its reluctant owners John O. Magoffin Jr., and Frederick W. Patterson. A deal was finally made in 1995. The plane, dismantled and in sad shape at the airport in Amery, Wisconsin, was trucked to
San Antonio. She persuaded Pratt & Whitney, the company that furnished the original Wasp engines used on Earhart's plane, to be the chief

Linda Finch waves good-bye before her departure from Oakland in the Lockheed
10. The 45-year-old mother of three had over 8,000 hours of flying time and had
participated in air races at Reno, Nevada, in T-6 trainers. She was accompanied
by experienced ocean fliers as copilots on various legs. (Courtesy Reid W. Dennis)

Linda Finch and Reid W. Dennis, pilot of the Grumman Albatross that accompanied the Lockheed Electra as chase plane, shake hands and wish each other luck before takeoff from Oakland. (Courtesy Reid W. Dennis)

sponsor of the flight; other organizations added their support, such as the Ninety-Nines, an organization of women pilots founded by Earhart.

The painstaking work to restore the Lockheed to flyable condition began in March 1995. The modifications included a more powerful engine with original parts, new exhaust and intake systems built to factory standards, and addition of six gas tanks in the fuselage. Based on original drawings and photographs, and with replacement parts made to order for those that were unavailable, the 1935 aircraft was restored externally to look as much like Earhart's as possible. However, Finch's Electra was equipped in the cockpit with advanced electronic navigation and communications equipment, whereas Earhart had a comparatively primitive radio and only basic gyro instruments.

Meanwhile, it was decided that an amphibious chase plane with two pilots and a mechanic would accompany the Electra with spare parts and rescue capability if it went down in the ocean. Several photographers and a journalist would be taken along to obtain video footage and photographs for future showing and publication. A Grumman Albatross, a 1955 twin-engine amphibian, was chosen with its owner Reid W. Dennis

Howland Island, about two miles long and a mile wide, the intended next stop for Amelia Earhart in 1937, as seen from the air. The short airstrip is now overgrown. (Courtesy Reid W. Dennis)

of Woodside, California, as pilot-in-command. Bob Bell flew as copilot for most of the flight; Andy MacFie was the chief mechanic. Several other pilots were selected to accompany Finch in the Electra on different flight segments to assist in navigation. Peter Cousins, a veteran pilot of many ocean crossings, flew with her about sixty percent of the time. A third pilot was on board the Electra on several flight segments.

Finch wanted the flight to inspire schoolchildren, especially those in grades five through eight, to learn about Earhart's life and realize that they, too, should find a dream and follow it. She formed a nonprofit organization called "World Flight 1997" and established a free multimedia educational program called "You Can Soar." Backed by Pratt & Whitney, 40,000 packages of instructional materials about the flight were sent to middle schools in the United States; they contained a poster, a documentary film entitled *Heroines of the Sky*, and a teacher's guide. An interactive web site was established on the Internet so that children could follow Finch's progress on a day-to-day basis.

The original Earhart plan was to fly westward from Oakland, California, approximating the equator as nearly as possible. She departed March

In-flight photo of the Grumman Albatross, piloted by Reid W. Dennis, that accompanied Finch's world flight. It is the first amphibious aircraft to complete a world flight. It would have been available to rescue the Electra crew at sea if a ditching had been necessary. (Courtesy Reid W. Dennis)

17, 1937, and got to Luke Field, an Army Air Corps base near Honolulu. But on the takeoff for Howland Island, she lost control and the heavy-loaded plane ground-looped. It was damaged severely and returned by ship to the States for repairs that took two months. She decided to reverse the route in her second attempt by flying eastward from Oakland to Miami, still planning to fly around the world as much as possible at its greatest span—the equator—leaving the Pacific stretch until last. Accompanied by Frederick J. Noonan, navigator, she left Oakland on May 21, 1937, and was last heard from on July 2, 1937, as she neared the end of the longest and most dangerous leg of the flight from Lae, New Guinea, to Howland Island. The island was an uninhabited sandbar atoll in the Pacific only one and a half miles long and a half-mile wide with a maximum elevation of 25 feet.

Linda Finch's planned route, prepared by Jeppesen Data Plan Company, was to follow the same itinerary as Amelia had taken as nearly as possible. On March 17, 1997, the sixtieth anniversary of the Earhart takeoff, Linda, with Peter Cousins aboard as copilot and navigator, departed California's Oakland Airport, accompanied by the Grumman chase

The Lockheed 10 Electra flies south off the California coast. The flight was sponsored chiefly by Pratt & Whitney, the company that manufactured the original Wasp engines used on Amelia Earhart's plane. (Courtesy Reid W. Dennis)

plane. The two planes flew over the Golden Gate Bridge and headed southeast. Their route of flight took them to New Orleans, Miami, Brazil, west Africa, Morocco, Spain, Greece, Egypt, India, Indonesia, and Australia. Finch landed at Nadzab, New Guinea, instead of Lae, New Guinea, which had been Amelia's final takeoff point, because the Lae airport was suitable only for helicopters and light planes. Finch made several low passes over the airstrip as a tribute and for photographic purposes.

The Lockheed continued via stops at the tiny islands of Nauru and Tarawa to Howland Island, all made much easier to locate because of the Electra's sophisticated satellite navigation system. The plane was videotaped and photographed from the Albatross as it circled several times over the tiny atoll, Earhart's intended fuel stop, where overgrowth now obscures the abandoned runway. A memorial wreath was dropped, and the two planes continued to Canton Island (population 60), 421 miles southeast of Howland for refueling before going to Kiritimati Atoll (formerly Christmas Island) and then the 1,500 miles to Hawaii. Fueling the two aircraft at the small island stops required detailed arranging ahead of time by the flight planning company because fuel for piston aircraft engines is becoming scarce in isolated parts of the world as world aviation transfers to jet fuel. The high octane aviation gas had to be shipped to the islands by boat in advance.

When Finch landed before a large crowd at Oakland on May 28, 1997, 73 days after her departure, she completed the longest leg of the trip— 2,118 nautical miles. The Albatross had mechanical difficulty in Hawaii and followed the next day.

Finch and the escorting Albatross had flown 26,347 nautical miles and stopped in 18 countries. An estimated one million schoolchildren had followed the flight daily on the interactive web site and about 150 million "hits" on the web site were recorded.

Although Linda was not the first to complete Amelia Earhart's round-the-world journey in a Lockheed 10, she was the latest. She did not set any point-to-point world speed records that were recognized by the NAA or the FAI (Federation Aeronautique Internationale).

It is doubtful that anyone else will try a commemorative world flight again in the same type of aircraft. The plane sat at the Denton, Texas, airport for some time after the flight and was reportedly sold to an anonymous buyer in August 2001.

What makes this world flight especially significant, however, is that it was the accompanying Albatross that established an aviation "first." No one had ever flown an amphibious aircraft around the world before Reid W. Dennis and his crew followed Finch's Lockheed so faithfully and without publicity or intention of seeking a record of their own. Although the original world fliers had used wheels and pontoons interchangeably during their 1924 flight, their World Cruisers were not considered true amphibious aircraft.

17

SHEILA SCOTT AND BROOKE KNAPP: SUPER RECORD-SETTERS

When an aviation first is achieved, the record becomes either official if approved by the National Aeronautic Association and/or the Federation Aeronautique Internationale, or unofficial if no sanction has been obtained or no category exists. Since the records set by Mock and Smith went into the record books, it remains for other women to better those records or seek other precedents.

The British aviatrix Sheila Scott, aspiring actress and the holder of more than 50 trophies from racing events and 100 world-class records, decided to try to add a round-the-world title to the list of her achievements in flying. Scott started flying in 1959. Her first plane was a Tiger Moth biplane christened *Myth,* in which she toured and raced throughout Europe. She won or placed in everything she entered. Next, she acquired a Piper Comanche, which she christened *Myth Sunpip.* She accumulated flying experience by ferrying aircraft for manufacturers and buyers, and obtained both a British and an American commercial pilot's license, with multiengine, instrument, seaplane, glider, and helicopter ratings.

Her earliest records came in 1965 when, within 36 hours, she set or beat 15 European intercapital records with a new Piper Comanche christened *Myth Too.* In May 1966, she decided to try to become the first European pilot, man or woman, to fly around the world in a single-engine light plane. At the same time, she would attempt a women's world speed record. What she didn't realize is that she is the only person in the world to fly around the world barefoot. In her book, *Barefoot in the Sky,* she describes her thoughts and emotions during the first of three solo trips:

I shopped around for some flat shoes, and ordered a size too large. The store assistant refused to sell me such "boats," and I tried to explain. This only made matters worse, and I heard her whisper to her colleague, "We have a crazy woman . . . who thinks she's going to fly around the world solo." It was then that I found it easier to fly barefoot. . . .

On such a . . . flight so much happens in a short . . . time, yet each place and each incident is . . . remembered better than if you stayed there for weeks as a tourist. You see the whole again just as you see the mass of a . . . galaxy, yet you are aware of the individual atoms . . . that make it something visible . . .

Memories like Damascus, where the Syrians had heard I used cologne to refresh myself; they filled the cockpit with . . . jasmine—a special flower for Syrian women. . . . Memories of the Syrian desert whose dust storms confused me, where, like Lindbergh, I made friends with a little fly trapped in my cockpit, followed by the loss of my little fly friend when the immigration men debugged me and the aircraft at Karachi! Karachi at midnight, and the scene under a night of stars of my first big welcome. The movie cameras had caught up and I was at first blinded by the arc lamps but became aware of . . . feminine voices. As my eyes cleared, I saw dozens of . . . women dressed in beautiful Pakistani costumes of loose pants covered by . . . silk tunics, each woman holding garlands of flowers . . . to welcome me with. In contrast, the moonlight in Calcutta emphasizing the shocking scene of hundreds of living bodies, each lying on a rug on the street—the rug their only possession. . . . My own forced landing in . . . forbidden Burma owing to an electrical failure in monsoon conditions—and the Buddha in Shwe Dagon, the largest pagoda in the world, working overtime for me that day! The luxury of being given dozens of orchids at Singapore—the snake charmer outside the Raffles Hotel contrasting with the very English RAF rest house at Changi. The RAF warning me to take a certain airway, otherwise someone might take a pot shot at me. . . .

A sunny, golden morning over the Timor Sea, made me forget its sharks. My first . . . glimpse of the coast of Australia when I . . . [talked] to the women of the outback over HF radio, looking down and seeing their homesteads hundreds of miles from anywhere but complete with small aircraft and landing strips. . . . Lonely and afraid over the storm-tossed Tasman Sea, and a woman's voice in my ear saying "Look behind you, Sheila." A flock of light aircraft had crept up on me under secret radar surveillance to give me the full VIP lead into New Zealand. . . . the coral reefs and sandy beaches of the South Pacific isles . . . the old Fijian chiefs who garlanded me with necklaces of shells to bring me happiness. . . .

Canton . . . once [an] atoll [for space-tracking] where the whole population came out to greet me—all fifty-one of them—and I found I was the only woman that night on a Pacific [island] with fifty-one . . . men! Then on to mainland America. . . . Newfoundland and the Royal Canadian Air Force's youngest cadet with huge yellow umbrella in one hand and Union Jack in the other, who when I laughed, said, "There you are—I knew she'd choose the flag."

The last leg home and a message from the Channel [Islands] to return . . . for a . . . free holiday after the flight, and the welcome-home words of yet another airline captain as we touched down together on parallel runways at London airport. I had completed the longest solo flight around the world.

TScott completed her flight June 22, 1966, at an average speed of 36.68 mph, beating Jerrie Mock's record by 12 percent and exceeding Mock's distance by 25 percent. Scott had flown the six-passenger, single-engine Comanche 29,055 miles in 33 days, about half of the time on instruments. En route, she set 12 intercity records and a world-flight record.

Buoyed by her success, over the next four years, Scott set other speed records, from London to Cape Town, South Africa, and in the classic London-to-Australia race (which she extended into another world flight, in 1969–70). Her obsession with flying and setting records led her to enter the London–Australia race, which came close to being her last race. Not only was the weather exceptionally bad, but she had communications difficulties and lost her navigational radios en route. Sixty-eight multipilot crews were in the race, but only two other pilots were flying solo. She saw no chance of winning: "A solo pilot has to overcome the physical endurance factor as well as spending more time on chores, while with a crew one pilot can eat, drink and sleep a little while the other flies. The important thing was not the winning but being part of this great race; yet I began to feel that luck had deserted me entirely as I . . . struggled on."

Scott flew from London to Athens, Karachi, Calcutta, and Singapore. After leaving Singapore, however, she found that she could not communicate or navigate precisely in adverse weather conditions; she had to fly south by dead reckoning. Before reaching Australia, she had to clear the mountains of Indonesia. As she flew over the lifting hills, towering clouds forced her lower and lower. She got around the mountains and out over the open sea, but cloud cover kept her almost at wave-top level for hours. She was unsure of her position, and her attempts to contact someone— anyone—went unanswered. Hour after hour, she flew on, dodging rain squalls and, occasionally, islands that loomed in the mists. At one point, she considered ditching the plane beside an island. She dropped the idea when she saw no sign of life other than a large school of sharks cruising just beneath the surface of the water.

The only thing she had in abundance was fuel; though lost, she could stay airborne for hours. She flew on, steering a course southeast. She could hear Morse code messages and occasionally a voice, but could get no one to answer her radio transmissions. She thought she detected her name in some of the messages, expressing the belief that she was down somewhere and was probably dead. Other voices indicated that a search for her was on, which was reassuring, because she was near panic.

Eventually, Scott reached a coast and with it, rice fields. Civilization. As she was savoring this thought, directly ahead she saw "the most comforting, beautiful, long piece of ordinary concrete runway that I have ever seen." Gratefully, she touched down, and the plane rolled the length of the runway. Her legs were so weak that she couldn't use the brakes. She simply let the plane roll off the runway on the grass. She shut off the engine and opened the window—to total silence. Where on earth am I? she thought. She was alone on an abandoned airstrip—but where and in what country?

As she sat there, confused but grateful to be alive, a truck with uniformed men came roaring down the runway. The cabin door was jerked open and a gruff voice said in broken English, "Get out! Come with me immediately!"

After numerous questions in distorted English, which she answered as best she could, Scott realized that she had landed on a military airfield near Makassar, the principal city on the Indonesian island of Celebes—a full eight hours' flying time from Darwin, her destination. After several days of frustrating delay, during which she tried to communicate with the outside world through an antiquated radio system, an American missionary and some other people tried to persuade her not to continue her flight. But she refused; all she wanted was help getting her radios fixed. Word gradually spread that she needed help, and Indonesian Air Force personnel repaired her VHF radio. She was ready to go. Meanwhile, the crew of *Air Race 34*—a Marchetti being flown as an unofficial entry by two British pilots, accompanied by a television film man—heard about Scott's plight and volunteered to change course and escort her to Darwin and Sydney.

She promptly accepted the offer. *Myth Too* and the Marchetti took off, heading south. Scott lost the other plane when storm clouds and rain reduced visibility to about 50 feet, forcing her down to wave-top level. She grazed a coconut tree on an island, but the plane was undamaged. After an agonizingly long time during which she did not see the Marchetti, she found a deserted airstrip near a small Indonesian village, and landed. The village turned out to be Sumbawa. There were no telephones, however; the only means of communication was by Morse code over a static-ridden high-frequency set. Now desperate, and thinking the Marchetti—faster than the Piper but with less fuel aboard—had crashed, Scott tried to tell the villagers about the other plane. But they spoke only pidgin

Champion record-setter Sheila Scott debarks from her Piper Comanche at London after a 29,005-mile global flight in 1966 for which she was awarded the Harmon International Trophy. In her flying career, she set over 100 speed and distance records for women. (Photo courtesy The Clifford B. Harmon Trust)

English. She tried to get the radioman to contact someone to start a search for the crew of the Marchetti.

The Marchetti had landed safely in Australia. When contact was finally established, Scott learned that the Indonesian Air Force had offered to fly fuel to Sumbawa, an offer she gladly accepted. Airborne once again, Scott flew to Bali, where she luxuriated briefly at the Bali Continental Hotel and where she had her first bath in 10 days. She flew to Darwin, then Alice Springs (a compulsory stop), and finally to Adelaide, the race's destination. But there was still another race: Adelaide to Sydney. Scott entered *Myth Too*. En route to Sydney, she was delayed at Griffith by poor weather conditions. She pushed on anyway, coming in fourth in her class. "Not bad for such a battle-weary pair," she wrote.

After a few days' rest and celebration with others who had made it safely to Sydney, Scott made plans to continue around the world, across the Pacific, the United States, then the Atlantic. She flew to Brisbane, then New Caledonia and to Fiji, where she spent several weeks exploring and photographing. She completed the flight in the spring of 1970.

Still obsessed with achieving another first, Scott decided to tackle what was possibly the most dangerous challenge of all—over the North Pole from equator to equator, which would make her the first woman to fly over the top of the world and the first person to do it in a light plane. "There were also some other standing records I wanted to capture," she said. "With a little luck I could gain my hundredth record since 1965." This time she would be flying most of the trip against prevailing winds, an undertaking that would require precise navigation, a reliable and fuel-efficient airplane, well-placed refueling stops, and perhaps most important of all, continuing good luck.

Scott plunged into planning this new venture with characteristic enthusiasm and vigor. She spent nearly every waking hour studying maps, weather analyses, and equipment brochures and writing hundreds of letters seeking information and support, both in the form of finances and equipment. Her London apartment was filled with "an avalanche of paper." She needed numerous visas and permissions, as well as consultations with various governing bodies involved in aviation. Modification of her new Piper Aztec, christened *Mythre*, became a special problem. Its fuel system, designed to give the plane a range of 1,100 miles, had to be expanded to provide a 3,000-mile range. When the mathematics of fuel load and consumption rate were worked out, however, it was found that, if an engine failed in flight, the Aztec's performance would be 700 feet below sea level! In other words, both engines had to function in order for the plane to make the flight.

Special help came from NASA, which was experimenting with a small interrogation recording and locating system (IRLS), an electronic "black box" that could be used to plot position at any time during a flight in the high latitudes. Battery-operated and weighing only 10 pounds, the device could be installed in the plane for transmitting data to the polar satellite Nimbus, which, in turn, would transmit the data to NASA's Goddard Space Center in Maryland, as well as to a facility in Fairbanks, Alaska. If it worked, the IRLS would transmit not only Scott's position above the earth but also data on the earth's environment and the well-being of the pilot. Her mental acuity could also be tested. Preparations included tests of arctic survival gear and clothing, a session in an Air Force pressure chamber, and a search for an astrocompass (for polar navigation) and a catalytic heater (to protect the pilot from the polar air).

After tests of the Aztec, Scott took off for Nairobi, Kenya, on the equator, her starting point. En route, she battled thunderstorms and the dreaded *haboob*, a violent storm of wind and sand. She stopped at Bengazi, Khartoum, Malaki, Juba, and Entebbe. When she reached Nairobi, the temperature stood at 100 degrees Fahrenheit.

The four days of fighting storms and the red tape at strange airports took their toll. Scott rested for three days while *Mythre* was serviced and NASA officials stationed at Nairobi tested the plane's equipment. The flight to London, on June 11, 1971, was uneventful. There, *Mythre* was winterized for the leg over the North Pole to Alaska, with two stops planned for Norway, at Bodo and Andoya. These legs were relatively easy. Scott, however, was delayed when the autopilot she was depending on to ease the workload failed and could not be repaired. It was on the leg over the pole to Barrow, Alaska, that she nearly met her end. En route to the pole, *Mythre* would not pick up cruising speed. Scott discovered that the plane's landing gear would not stay fully retracted, which caused drag, resulting in excessive fuel consumption and lower air speed. Scott's ADF needles would not pick up the necessary stations. Conflicting signals were received from the Soviet Union and elsewhere. She got lost but finally made contact with a weather station at Nord, Greenland, where she landed.

The station had ample aviation fuel. In addition to refueling, Scott sent messages to her colleagues at NASA and to others concerned about her and her flight. The U.S. Air Base at Thule, on the west coast of Greenland, volunteered to send a transport to Nord if she needed spare parts or assistance. After a stay of three days, Scott left Nord.

It was another leg plagued by difficulties and uncertainty. The landing gear again slipped out of its retracted position, and the best air speed *Mythre* could muster was only 130 mph. Scott now had fuel to spare, however—provided head winds weren't unusually strong. She entered the Arctic blackout area, where static reigns and communication becomes impossible. Foremost among her problems was ice formation. Slowly, ice was spreading to the rear from the nose and leading edges of the wings. The plane was becoming heavier, and consequently, its speed was dropping. Eventually, the aircraft would stall. The situation was made worse when the loose nosewheel door opened, allowing the wheel to dangle and ice to form inside the wheel well. Then, as the Piper Aztec cruised into warmer air, hail followed by freezing rain bombarded the plane. In the cabin, Scott was stiff from cold and physical inactivity. To distract herself, she took sun shots with the astrocompass and bearings with the radio compass when the clouds parted, both calculations to make sure she did not drift off course.

When Scott calculated that she was indeed over the pole, she unfurled a Union Jack and a paper "Snoopy" given her by her American friends at NASA and dropped them through the cockpit's storm window. Elated that she had achieved this goal, she broadcast a message to anyone who might be listening: "I'm on top of the world! Operations normal. Tango Oscar is at ninety north."

But operations were not normal. The nosewheel, which had remained in its well during the approach to the North Pole, now fell out again. Time after time, Scott cranked it back up, but each time, after about five minutes, it slipped out. Then, with a desperate attempt to get it to lock in position, the handle broke and the wheel fell down for good. With this drag added, what should have been a flight of 13 hours would now be one of 17. Fuel conservation had suddenly become Scott's most critical problem.

She banked *Mythre* and flew toward Alaska but before long entered clouds, which caused another serious buildup of ice. She was again unsure of her position. To her other problems was now added the fear of being lost. She worried about ditching in the Arctic Ocean or landing on an ice floe, never to be found alive. Her concern grew when she could not get a sun shot or a radio bearing.

About three hours from the North Pole, Scott got a firm radio bearing using the radio compass. Just as she did this, a voice came in loud and clear over the VHF radio, directing her to change course to Barter Island. Flight conditions there were better than at her destination, Barrow, Alaska. As Scott banked left, the clouds parted and she could see a coastline. The weather suddenly closed in on her, however, and the radio operator at Barter Island told her that the weather was deteriorating rapidly; he advised her to change course and go back to Barrow. She was now flying through a raging snowstorm. Soon, though, she raised Barrow, and a cheerful voice confirmed that the storm had passed. She flew out of it into warm sunshine and landed at the northernmost town in the United States, weary and glad to be on the ground again.

Scott, who had been airborne for 17 hours, learned that the NASA team at Goddard had tracked her directly over the North Pole at the exact moment she had been radioing to anyone listening. It was an exhilarating feeling that she shared with personnel of the Naval Arctic Laboratory and with the Eskimos who greeted her upon her arrival. Exhausted, she stayed at Barrow for two days. Meanwhile, the landing gear on *Mythre* was checked and repaired. The problem had been caused by loss of hydraulic fluid when aileron wires rubbed a hole in a hydraulic line.

From Barrow, now with a light load of fuel, Scott flew to Fairbanks and then Anchorage. Her next stop was San Francisco, where she quickly prepared for the transpacific hop to the equator. On this leg, she again encountered poor flight conditions as she struggled to cross the equator en route to Canton Island, some 2,000 miles south of Hawaii. Once on the ground, with her goal achieved, Scott spent some time exploring the island and meeting the military men stationed there. When she was rested, she flew to Fiji, one of her favorite landing spots, this time arriving from the opposite direction. She spent several days on Fiji, awaiting spare parts ordered from Australia. Scott made several landings on the way to Darwin. She was considering using the city as a jumping-off point in an attempt to beat the Australia-to-London record of five and a half days, set in 1937 by Jean Batten of New Zealand. By making only five landings and by sleeping as little as possible, she hoped to lop two days off Batten's mark. Scott left Darwin, July 31, 1971, and arrived in London August 4, as planned, thus setting her one-hundredth speed record for women. She was "unutterably tired" on this flight and "longed to land and just sleep and not bother with a record." The urge to follow her obsession was overwhelming, however, and she kept on despite clearance snarls, customs red tape, tropical heat, and mind-numbing fatigue. Grateful to be alive, she had completed what many had claimed was an "impossible" flight.

Why did Sheila Scott drive herself nearly to the breaking point? Why did she have to fly to find true happiness and personal satisfaction? She replies:

> I think it is because in the sky I am able to stretch my brain rather than my legs, and find motivation to satisfy my insatiable curiosity to experience things myself, to be able to understand them, and to find meaning and a sense of man's superconscious. . . .
>
> Flying also gives me a spirit of adventure—which I believe is a necessary thing for future progress, both individually and internationally. Soon computers will [provide much] . . . knowledge . . . in a very short . . . time . . . unless man [demonstrates] individuality and [has] some responsibility for his . . . actions, he will become as a computer himself. Now . . . satellites can help the whole Earth eat, learn more quickly and extensively, and above all, promote earthly peace as people learn more about each other. But all of

these advantages would be useless if [we] lost [our] . . . quest for . . . knowledge.

After a series of television, radio, and speaking engagements, Scott began planning still another flight, this one over the South Pole. But in June 1972, *Mythre* was badly damaged by a flood at the Piper factory in Lock Haven, Pennsylvania. After months of repair work, it flew again; but Scott could not afford the expense of getting the plane ready for assault on Antarctica, and she never realized her dream. She died in 1987.

Brooke Knapp, president and chairman of the board of Jet Airways, an aviation management company she founded in 1979, wanted to be a woman of accomplishment and to be respected in an industry dominated by men. She had a strong business background, beginning with the management of a large citrus grove in Florida. She later went into real estate investment in New York and became involved with many financial arrangements, which often put her in the air as a reluctant passenger on executive charter flights. She decided to start her own executive charter company in California because of the complaints of many executives that they wasted too much valuable time in airports trying to make connections on commercial flights.

Although surrounded by pilots and aviation enthusiasts in her new enterprise, Brooke had a problem: she was terrified of flying. Nevertheless, highly competitive, she felt compelled to win the respect of her peers and make a contribution to aviation. She decided to solve her phobia by making a list of her fears and "prioritizing" them—then taking on the most unpleasant one first.

"I would go to the hangar and everyone would take off for the day's flying," she said, "and I would be left alone with my dog Beaufort. I didn't like that, because I'm a person who likes to participate. I began to take flying lessons."

But overcoming the phobia wasn't easy. She enrolled in ground school and spent extra time in the classroom, thus putting off the inevitable flying lessons. When scheduled for a flight, she often found excuses not to go. She eventually overcame her fear and then couldn't be kept out of the air. After earning private and commercial licenses, she embarked on a campaign of record-setting in small jet aircraft that rivaled what Sheila Scott had accomplished in propeller-driven planes.

On February 16, 1983, Knapp, accompanied by copilots Paul Broyles and Jim Topalian, and crew chief Jim Magill, departed San Francisco International Airport in *The American Dream*, a Lear Jet 35A, to attempt to break the existing world speed record in her weight class of aircraft—65 hours, 38 minutes, 49 seconds, set in 1966 by Henry Beaird Jr. in a Lear 24.

Eleven stops were planned: Wisconsin, Newfoundland, England, Corfu, Bahrain, Sri Lanka, Singapore, Manila, Guam, the Caroline Islands, the Marshall Islands, and Hawaii. The flight was well-planned and uneventful with an average of 19-minute turn-arounds at each stop. There was an unscheduled twelfth landing, however, at Ponape, in the Caroline Islands.

"We'd been in the air about 30 hours and were between Guam and the Marshall Islands when we developed a standby fuel problem in the left wing," she said. "This meant we had a lot of fuel in our right wing but very little in the left. I don't want to take unnecessary chances, so we made an emergency landing at Ponape. Fortunately, we were able to fix the problem in about an hour and were on our way."

When The American Dream landed at San Francisco after 50 hours, 22 minutes, 42 seconds of elapsed time, it had shaved more than 15 hours off the previous record for small jets weighing between 13,277 and 17,636 pounds. She had also beaten the record of 57 hours, 24 minutes set by famous golfer Arnold Palmer in 1976, in a Lear 36. (Palmer's record stood, however, because his jet was in a different weight category.) Knapp set a number of point-to-point records during the flight.

Now established as a "name" in aviation, Knapp wanted to shoot for another record in a higher aircraft weight category. In November 1983, she undertook the next world-girdling flight—a circumnavigation of both poles. Piloting The American Dream II, a Gulfstream III, with copilots Curt Olds, Paul Broyles, and Bob Smyth; crew chief C. B. Allen; and Bella English, a newspaper reporter, the route of the flight was from Los Angeles to Hawaii, Pago Pago, Christchurch, McMurdo Sound, Punta Arenas, Recife, Tenerife, Trondheim, and Fairbanks. Although she wanted to break the polar circumnavigation record set by a Pan American 747SP in 1978, bad luck intervened. The aircraft had landing gear problems and spent 20 hours on the ground at Tenerife. Although it took 85 hours, 1 minute, 44 seconds to make the trip and could not beat the Pan Am record, the flight did set a speed record for the aircraft class and established two "firsts." The Gulfstream III was the first business jet to land at McMurdo Sound in the Antarctic on a round-the-world flight and the first business jet to make the flight over both poles.

In February 1984, Knapp piloted The American Dream III, another Gulfstream III, around the world, besting the record set in 1976 by a Boeing 747SP Pan American jumbojet. Her route of flight was eastbound from Washington National Airport via the Soviet Union, the first time that the Soviets had allowed an American plane to cross their country in 40 years. This time the Gulfstream carried three copilots, a crew chief, and three reporters. Her flight time of 45 hours, 32 minutes, and 53 seconds bested the Pan Am record by a half hour and set 43 point-to-point records to give

Brooke Knapp, pilot of a Gulfstream III business jet, poses with her crew after a record-setting world flight in *The American Dream III* in 1984. Shown, left to right: Jim Magill, Paul Broyles, Knapp, Bob Smyth, and Curt Olds. Knapp set over 100 point-to-point national and world speed records in jet aircraft, including a circum-navigation over both poles. (Photo courtesy Brooke Knapp)

her a lifetime total of 103. In addition, she had raised nearly a half million dollars for charity through her appeals for donations and pledges to the United Nations Children's Fund (UNICEF).

Between them, Sheila Scott and Brooke Knapp had put more than 200 speed records on the books. When asked if women can speed up their progress in aviation, Knapp replied: "They will progress the same way men have: through discipline and determination and tenacity and survival skills. We just don't come from the background where we have been taught to take risks and to keep on. We're not talking about basic employment any more. We're talking about the pursuit of excellence; we're talking about getting into jobs that are coveted. That's going to take a lot more determination."

18

THE DIFFICULT
BECOMES EASIER

With the development of sporting codes for speed, distance, and altitude records, all competitors must adhere to the codes for their marks to be official. The Federation Aeronautique Internationale (FAI) determines whether a world record is in strict accordance with the codes. The National Aeronautic Association (NAA) is the U.S. equivalent of the FAI; most countries of the free world have similar organizations.

When Wiley Post and Harold Gatty flew around the world in 1931, their route was entirely in the upper portion of the Northern Hemisphere. Because they flew only 15,500 miles, they would not qualify for a record today. In 1959, the FAI established a requirement that the minimum distance acceptable for "Speed Around the World" record flights must be greater than the length of the tropic of Cancer—22,859.44 statute miles (36,787.599 kilometers). To better an existing speed record, a contestant must exceed that mark by at least 1 percent.

After the record-setting heyday of active and converted military aircraft following World War II, light planes became more prominent. The latter had improved performance, greater range, more reliable engines, and upgraded radio navigation equipment. The urge to try for ever greater distance became an obsession among pilots of light planes. Representative Peter F. Mack Jr. (D-Illinois), however, had a different motive than attempting to set a speed record. Elected to Congress in 1948 and again in 1950, the former Navy pilot was motivated to try to counter the anti-American propaganda that coincided with the Korean War by flying around the world in a Beechcraft Bonanza, formerly owned by William Odom, which had set a Honolulu–New Jersey record in 1948 and was then loaned to the National Air and Space Museum for display. Mack

Congressman Peter F. Mack Jr. (D.-Illinois), waves from *Friendship Flame*, a Beechcraft Bonanza at Beech Field, Wichita, Kansas, on April 19, 1952. The plane was formerly owned by William Odom, who had set a nonstop Hawaii–New Jersey record in it in 1948. (Beech Aircraft Co. photo)

changed the name from *Waikiki Beach* to *Friendship Flame* and departed on October 7, 1951, from Springfield, Missouri. He returned 111 days later on a flight that had taken him from Newfoundland to the Azores, then on to Portugal, Spain, Holland, Norway, Finland, Sweden, Germany, and other European countries. He continued eastward through the Middle East, India, the Philippines, Taiwan, Japan, and across the Pacific via Wake Island, Midway, and Hawaii to San Francisco. Returning home he noted that he had visited 30 countries in three and a half months, and covered 33,789 miles during the 223 hours he was airborne.

While Congressman Mack was not obsessed with record setting, Peter K. Gluckman was. From August to September of 1959, he set a world record of 29 days, 6 hours, and 9 minutes flying a single-engine Meyers 200A weighing 5,099 pounds. Gluckman's log of the flight, filed with the NAA upon his return, is the only record of a magnificent flight:

8-22-59. Departed San Francisco at 7:20 A.M. Pacific Daylight Time. Good weather all the way. Landed in Mazatlan (Mexico) at 4:20 P.M. Found out that Mazatlan was not an airport of entry. Had lots of trouble.

8-23-59. Departed Mazatlan at 10 A.M. Landed after 9½ hours in San Jose, Guatemala. The last two hours of the flight made after dark were most unpleasant. I wanted to land at Tapachula, Mexico, but neither the runway lights nor the radio beacon were turned on. I wasn't sure if San Jose had runway lights, and nearby thunderstorms made radio communications almost impossible. I had no chart other than an Aeronautical Planning Chart with a 1/5,000,000 scale. Not exactly detailed. I made it all right, thanks to the cooperation and help of Guatemala City and San Jose tower.

8-24-59. Left San Jose at 8:40 for Puerto Barrios on the other side of the mountains, a 1½ hour flight. After refueling at Puerto Barrios, we took off for Kingston, Jamaica.

8-25-59. Flight to Kingston took 7 hours. 22 knot headwind all the way. Took off at 9:15 for San Juan (Puerto Rico), my official checkpoint. Again have 20 knot headwinds. Expected flight to take about 6 hours.

8-26-59. Took off at 7:45 A.M. on long flight to Santa Maria in the Azores, 2800 miles away, ETE 22 hours. Landed at Santa Maria 0600Z after 18 hours.

8-27-59. Departed for Lisbon at 0105Z. Landed at Lisbon at 0705Z.

Left Lisbon at 1030Z for Cairo. Landed at 1030 at Benina Airport, Bengasi.

8-29-59. Left at 8 A.M. for Cairo. Arrived Cairo at 1 P.M..

8-30. Left at 3 A.M. for 15 hour flight to Karachi. Arrived Karachi after 14½ hours.

9-1-59. Took off this morning for New Delhi. Eye injury prevented flying yesterday. Weather not good. Landed at New Delhi after 6 hour flight. FAI timer was on hand.

9-2-59. Took off for Calcutta at 1545Z. Arrived Calcutta after 7 hour flight.

9-3-59. Took off for Manila at 2315Z this morning but doubt [that] I'm going to make it all the way. Weather very bad. Landed at Bangkok at 0625Z.

Took off at 8:15 local, 0115Z, for Manila. Autopilot quit working yesterday. Hope to get spare amplifier in Tokyo. Took 10 hours to Manila.

9-6-59. Took off at 8:15 A.M. for Hong Kong. Cannot go to Tokyo direct because of Typhoon Louise. Also wanted to give amplifier time to reach Tokyo.

9-7-59. Left Hong Kong for Tokyo at 9 A.M. ETE 12 hours.

Landed at Tokyo International Airport at 10:08 P.M. after an instrument letdown.

9-10-59. Departed for Wake Island but had to return to Tokyo because of rough engine. Flew total 3½ hours.

Installed new spark plugs and changed oil filter and everything checked out OK. Departed again for Wake 9-11-59 at 8:25 A.M. ETE 13 hours.

After 3 hours out, again had to return to Tokyo. Flew total of just over 6 hours. Something is very much the matter with the plane but I have no idea what it might be. All engine instruments check out perfect, but at 4,000–5,000 feet, plane starts buffeting and engine doesn't sound right. Slowing airplane to climbing speed seems to improve the situation.

9-15-59. Again left Tokyo for Wake. We went over the airplane with a fine-tooth comb but found nothing wrong; now, 9 hours out, everything OK.

9-18-59. Had to replace battery and voltage regulator at Wake. The old voltage regulator apparently stuck and I burned up the battery. Had to send to Honolulu for new battery. 2-day delay.

Departed at 5 A.M. this morning for estimated 18 hour flight to Honolulu. Crossed International Date Line at 1230Z so now it's yesterday, the 17th. Landed after 18 hours and 15 minutes.

Departed 5 P.M. Honolulu time, 0300Z, for San Francisco. ETE 17^1/$_2$ hours.

9-29-59. Arrived San Francisco at 1:30 PDST, 17^1/$_2$ hours out of Honolulu.

Gluckman's record flight, made in only a few hours shy of 30 days elapsed time, set the stage for other flights. He had flown 23,765.27 miles, establishing a solo record. In 1961, Max Conrad beat Gluckman's mark, but Gluckman did not live to learn of it. In late 1959, he disappeared after taking off from Tokyo attempting to set a maximum distance record for a light plane.

On October 17, 1962, Gunther Balz and his wife Alice set out from their home in Kalamazoo, Michigan, intending to make a leisurely, 265-day flight around the world. Flying a 1957 Beech D-50 Twin Bonanza, they would fly 48,000 miles.

Balz, then 32, was a graduate of MIT and had served on a destroyer in the U.S. Navy for four years. He was now the president of two companies. Balz checked out the aircraft thoroughly, sparing no expense. A complete narrative of the Balzes' trip would take many pages, but an excerpt from the *AOPA Pilot* gives a sample of their experiences. After takeoff from Honolulu, westbound for the privately owned island of Palmyra, Gunther and Alice begin the tale:

Cleared to Palmyra Island, via direct. South Honolulu intersection, flight plan route. Maintain 8000'.

We acknowledged the clearance, shifted to tower on 118.1 and took off at 0132 local. We were 1,200 pounds over gross with 12 hours of fuel on board. We climbed, banking gently left, into the peaceful moonless night. Our eyes adjusted rapidly.

We reported South Honolulu intersection and took up a magnetic heading of 192°. Using my old hotel-top friends Rigel, Canopus and Sirius, I took a star fix which checked when DR'd to our last VOR position. 8845.5 would be our control frequency on HF, but we were too close in to use it. We relayed our first and second position reports on 131.9 via Nandi-bound Pan Am Clipper Flight 811.

After an hour and a half we were flying in and out of the tops at 8,000. Nothing to worry about but unexpected. We were unable to raise Honolulu or anyone else for our next position report. Briefly we heard Bombay and then nothing but static. We were flying through light to moderate rain by then, continuously in the clouds. Nothing serious, I thought. Local disturbance. Alice was getting nervous. The staccato of the rain increased. I was so busy flying that I forgot about position reports even though our last contact had been one and a half hours before. The turbulence gave us some concern because of the cabin fuel—we thought we smelled gas.

"What's that?"

I looked up from the instruments. The airplane appeared to be on fire. Green glowed off every rivet. The propeller arcs were pinwheels of eerie flame.

"St. Elmo's fire," I said, my voice a mixture of raw fear and curiosity.

We banged along for another 10 minutes. Lightning flashes detonated ahead. I put the plane in a left bank, flying with both hands to keep control.

"We're going back," I said. Alice's teeth chattered a reply.

After 45 minutes on a reverse course we could see the stars occasionally. I DR'd our last known position and tried to HF. No contact. I tried "any station" on 121.5. No contact. It was getting light in the east. We looked at the backlighted towering Cu's [cumulus clouds] behind us. The Intertropical Front had moved north.

Ninety minutes out we got Honolulu on 121.5 and reported our position. We received a new clearance, and after 7^1/$_2$ hours, we touched down at Honolulu on 4R, glad to be alive and not the least bit sheepish about the log book entry—N4371D, 7^1/$_2$ hours local.

On November 1, they left Honolulu for Christmas Island via Palmyra, then to Tahiti, Bora Bora, Rarotonga, Aitutaki, Pago Pago, Samoa, Fiji, Nandi, and New Caledonia, landing at Auckland (New Zealand) on December 7. They had encountered extremely heavy rain and turbulence between Nandi and New Caledonia. The Balzes next flew to Australia, then New Guinea, Taipei, Manila, Borneo, Brunei, Singapore, Thailand, Burma, and India. On March 8, 1963, they left Karachi, Pakistan, making a fuel stop at Sharja, Oman, and visiting Bahrain Island. Balz picks up the narrative:

Shortly after takeoff the forward visibility reduced to one mile at flight level 85. We were bucking a 40-knot headwind and would all day. As we headed out over the Gulf of Oman, our sun lines showed a ground speed of 109 knots. After six hours, turbulence signaled our approach to the unseen 7,000-foot mountains of Oman. We were in contact with a reassuringly crisp British approach controller at Sharja as we crossed the mountains (at 10,000 feet for insurance), who informed us local conditions were sky obscured, visibility one-half mile and blowing sand. A military [aircraft] was making an approach as we started our letdown. He radioed back that field was in sight, visibility two miles. Not knowing what to expect, we continued through the thick yellow haze, fairly certain our gas would get us to Bahrain in a pinch. The visibility was at least 10 miles when we touched down. . . .

Gunther and Alice continued to Bahrain, Baghdad, and Damascus. At Damascus, they were ordered to land by military authorities trying to quell a revolution. But they were soon cleared to depart and proceeded to Beirut. Concerned that the blowing sand would damage the engines, Gunther took a precaution: "The large polyethylene bags which we had used throughout the Pacific to keep our charts and books from mildewing served in Bahrain as engine covers to keep out the sand. Masking tape held them in place. . . . I cleaned the filters and changed the oil every 8 to 10 hours throughout the desert flying." The flight continued: Alexandria, Luxor, Khartoum, Entebbe, Gunther describes his reactions at this point: "The . . . transition from the barren expanses of sand in Egypt and Sudan to the green rolling highlands of central Africa are [amazing: central Africa is] endowed with some of the most beautiful country in the world—vast plains, snow-capped mountains, countless animals, [and there were] friendly people and plenty of facilities for private flying."

Leaving Uganda, the Balzes flew to the east coast of Zanzibar, then to Mozambique, and inland again to Johannesburg. The flight continued northward, with stops in Angola, Morocco, Spain, Italy, Switzerland, West Germany, France, and England. They decided to fly the North Atlantic instead of flying by way of the Azores. "All things considered," Gunther said later, "this decision was a mistake. North Atlantic weather, even in summer, is unpredictable. Icing conditions and cold-water temperatures prevail, so that survival at sea would be doubtful even if a successful ditching were accomplished."

Alice and Gunther flew to Keflavik, Iceland, without difficulty but became lost after passing Greenland while on instruments. Near Cartwright, Newfoundland, they encountered snow and rain; visibility dropped to less than two miles. Unable to raise a station on HF radio, they made a blind call on the emergency VHF channel. Immediately, an Air France airliner answered and relayed their call to Goose Bay, Labrador, their destination. The Air France captain gave them the weather at Goose Bay (bad) and at Gander (good). Gunther established their probable position, and they hugged the coastline south all the way to Gander. The flight had taken 11 hours and 20 minutes.

The Balzes returned to Kalamazoo unannounced on July 3, 1963.

Would they do it again? "With a few exceptions, we would enthusiastically revisit every place on our itinerary, and add several hundred more as well," Balz replies. "But having done it, the prospect of hour after hour of overwater flying looms more as work than pleasure. In the meantime, we lay claim to eight and a half months of travel at its best. [That] should last us a lifetime."

In 1966, while Sheila Scott was on the first of her three solo world flights, Robert L. Wallick, a pilot for an aircraft-ferrying company in Newton, Kansas, and his wife Joan, also a pilot, decided to try for a record. During a delivery flight from Kansas to Manila in late 1964, Mike Campos, the Beechcraft distributor for the Philippines, Borneo, and Hong Kong, had suggested the flight to Wallick as a way of demonstrating the reliability of the Beech Baron C-55. Wallick did some figuring; it seemed fairly easy to break the existing round-the-world record for this class of aircraft: 8 days, 18 hours, 35 minutes, and 57 seconds, set by Max Conrad in 1961. The Wallicks estimated they could beat the mark by 3.5 days.

After doing the paperwork required by the NAA to qualify for a record attempt, Robert and Joan ferried the Baron from Wichita to Manila, their starting point (because of the backing of Campos). If successful, the flight would bring a record to the Philippines. In Manila, the Baron was modified with extra tanks—giving it a range of 3,540 miles, or 19.9 hours in the air under zero wind conditions—and christened *Philippine Baron*. On June 2, 1966, the Wallicks taxied into takeoff position; they checked the magnetos on both engines, then lifted off.

They flew to Tokyo, then Wake Island and Honolulu, and on to Seattle. In Tokyo, they were held up about 30 minutes by reporters and photographers. "We knew that would not be possible if we were to make our schedule, so we ruled out talking and posing from then on," Wallick said. In Seattle, they encountered the only serious weather trouble during the entire flight. A deep low-pressure area had developed east of the city. The best route seemed to be south along the coast, then east to Texas and north to Boston; but there was a chance they would slip down to Boise, then east, if they dared risk it.

"I didn't want to go to Texas," Robert Wallick said, "so we decided to try Boise. We ran into solid ice." The decision nearly proved their undoing. Joan Wallick recalled later that this leg of the trip was the only time she actually felt worried. A chunk of ice the size of a grapefruit had built up around the outside temperature gauge and three to four inches accumulated on the wings. The plane's speed was reduced by 35 knots. Although it was a close call, the ice wasn't bad enough to force the plane down.

After passing Boise, Robert and Joan headed for Rapid City, South

Joan and Robert Wallick pose casually beside their twin-engine Beech Baron C-55 in which they set a round-the-world record for light aircraft in 1966. Their departure-arrival point was Manila International Airport. (Photo courtesy National Aeronautic Association)

Dakota. More bad weather forced them north, almost to the Canadian border. They finally landed at Boston 12 hours and 27 minutes after take-off from Seattle. While Robert slept, Joan flew the leg from Boston to Santa Maria, in the Azores. The Jet Commander carrying Arthur Godfrey on his round-the-world record flight was flying the same route, and she chatted with the crew. Godfrey had just taken off when she landed at Santa Maria. She flew from the Azores to the coast of Portugal. Then Bob took over flying to Athens and then Damascus; it was the shortest leg of the trip—837 miles. Out of Damascus, lack of sleep finally caught up with him. "I told Joan—'Just head east. Don't bother me.'" He fell asleep and didn't awaken until the next morning. Joan recalled this leg, 2,185 miles to Bombay, as the loneliest she ever experienced. "The Arabian Desert was a vast void. Either the radio beacons were all out, or I missed them. It was so lonely out there that everyone in the air at the time was talking. That's all there was to do."

The stop at Bombay was an hour and a half, whereas it usually took all day to refuel and get through the red tape. But the customs officials were now somewhat familiar with world fliers. Godfrey's jet and Sheila Scott's Comanche had come through just a few hours earlier. Despite the time they made up on the ground at Bombay, they were still about three hours behind schedule. They really picked up lost time on the Bombay-to-Singapore hop, however. Afraid they would collide with the monsoon season, they ended up beating the rains by a week. And instead of the 14 hours and 10 minutes they had estimated for the 2,265-mile trip, they made it in 12 hours and 32 minutes. "They weren't expecting us," Robert Wallick said. Joan went to look for fuel trucks while her husband searched for the official timer to verify their arrival and departure. The timer didn't show up until they were climbing into the plane for takeoff.

They had good weather throughout the leg to Manila. Head winds developed, however; they wanted very much to arrive as near as possible to their predeparture flight plan. It was Joan's leg, and she was egging the plane on, trying to make up time. "Joan had the throttles to the firewall," Wallick recalled. "Every time I looked around she was dumping fuel overboard to get more speed out of the plane."

They arrived only six minutes late, beating Max Conrad's record by making the world flight in 5 days, 6 hours, and 16 minutes. Their time in the air was 112 hours, 35 minutes, with only 13 hours, 41 minutes on the ground.

In the summer of 1966, while Joan and Robert Wallick were setting their record, Herman P. Miller III, president of an electronics firm in Stockton, California, decided to take a more leisurely trip around the world. He wanted to visit the 30 countries in which distributors sold the solid-state avionics equipment his firm manufactured. Also, Miller felt, a personal visit would give him the opportunity to evaluate personally the company's marketing capacity.

In a Piper Aztec, Miller flew from Stockton across the United States, then north to Iceland, across Europe, Africa, the Middle East, and Asia, with a stop in Honolulu before returning to Stockton. He traveled 45,000 miles in 91 days, logging a total of 250 flight hours. The final solo flight of 11 hours and 22 minutes was one of nine such flights more than 10 hours long.

With the reliability achieved by light aircraft by the mid-1960s, and especially after the Wallicks' successful flight, others were inspired to make round-the-world flights for record. Two physicians were infected by the fever. Francis X. Sommer, of Barbourville, Kentucky, and John Rieger, of Los Gatos, California, were confident they could set new records in a single-engine Beechcraft Bonanza S-35.

In January 1967, after adding extra fuel tanks and making some other modifications, Sommer and Rieger made a 2,400-mile shakedown flight from Louisville to Barbados, in the West Indies. That year marked the fortieth anniversary of Lindbergh's flight, and they wanted to commemorate

Drs. Francis X. Sommer (left) and John Rieger greet the cameraman by their Beechcraft Bonanza S-35 in May 1967. They completed a world flight in 132 hours elapsed time, not a world record. However, they did set three point-to-point records for their class of aircraft. (Beech Aircraft Co. photo)

the famous flight by duplicating Lindbergh's route before continuing around the world. Sommer and Rieger planned their departure for May 20, 1967, hoping to be airborne at the same minute Lindbergh had departed four decades earlier. The flying physicians admitted that the risk wasn't the same. Their aircraft, though also powered by only one engine, was equipped with a 14-channel VHF radio and had a range of 3,200 miles, with fuel for a flight of 26 hours. They also carried survival gear, including flotation equipment.

Sommer and Rieger arrived at Kennedy International Airport and began to prepare their Bonanza for the ocean jump. They estimated the flight would take 22 hours, compared to "Lucky Lindy's" 33 hours, 29 minutes, and 30 seconds. After conferring with Pan Am weather forecasters, however, they decided to leave May 19, when favorable winds were forecast over the North Atlantic, and thus revised their estimate of the flight time to 20 hours and 43 minutes.

The Beechcraft, looking small and vulnerable, taxied out to takeoff position on May 19, 1967, amid huge jet transports and took off. With ceiling and visibility good, the flight was conducted under visual flight rules. Sommer and Rieger landed at Le Bourget Airport within a few minutes of their estimated arrival time. After a brief rest, they flew on to Nice, then Rome, Athens, Istanbul, Teheran, Bombay, Bangkok, Hong Kong, Tokyo, and Barrow, returning to New York.

The flight had taken 35 days. Their total flight time was 132 hours. Although it wasn't a world record, they did set three point-to-point records for their class of aircraft: New York to Paris, Tokyo to Barrow, and Barrow to New York. Sommer said the most difficult moments were the landing at Tokyo in a thunderstorm and their arrival in fog at Barrow. "The fog was closing in at Barrow as we [got] close to it," he recalled. "We had fuel for about two more hours, but the nearest alternate airport was two to three hundred miles away. About 45 minutes after we landed, the fog closed in tight."

Despite the uncertainties and delays they experienced, due mainly to maintenance and flight clearances, they said their flight was the "most marvelous trip" they had ever taken.

The competition for records between Beech and Cessna continued in 1969, when Alvin Marks, 43, a psychologist and the president of Skymark Airlines, a commuter airline, attempted to set a new world record for light aircraft in a Cessna 210 Centurion. On April 3, Marks left Sacramento, California, with the announced intention of setting seven world, point-to-point records for single-engine aircraft, as well as eight more in other categories. His main goal, however, was to beat the round-the-world speed mark set by Sheila Scott.

Actually, Marks was making his second attempt. In September 1967, flying a Helio Courier, he was forced to abandon the flight in Karachi after electrical failures. He not only realized that goal on his second attempt but surpassed his own flight plan by 26 hours. Marks jumped far ahead of his schedule by flying two legs—Teheran–Karachi and Karachi–New Delhi—in one day. His flight route was from Sacramento to Wichita, then to Bermuda, the Azores, Madrid, Athens, Teheran, Karachi, New Delhi, Bangkok, Singapore, Manila, Guam, Wake Island, and Honolulu, returning to Sacramento. In his Cessna, *Semper Fly III*, he set point-to-point records on every leg. His total time was 13 days and 22 hours. "Everything went just fine," Marks said on his return. "I experienced a couple of weather problems out of Madrid and I didn't watch the fuel flow once, but the Cessna was absolutely perfect."

The success of the physicians Sommer and Rieger encouraged another flier to try to duplicate their feat in the same type of aircraft, but to do it solo. Dr. Hypolite T. Landry, flying a Beechcraft Bonanza, not only set a world-circling record but 13 point-to-point records as well. He left Baton Rouge, Louisiana, May 2, 1969, and returned on May 25, having flown 23,767 miles in 13 days, 9 hours, and 20 minutes. The only problem he had was a 48-hour delay in Bermuda because of weather.

During the next few months Beech airplanes were used in other world flights. One of the most significant was that of Trevor Brougham and Robert Dickerson, two Australians who flew Darwin-to-Darwin in August 1971. Flying a Beech Baron C-55, they covered approximately 24,800 miles in 5 days, 5 hours, 57 minutes, averaging 196.9 mph. Not only did they surpass the former record, but they added 31 point-to-point records during their trip.

Also during that summer, Edward Miller, a pilot for United Air Lines, and Diane, his bride of three months, decided to honeymoon by touring the world in Miller's single-engine Beechcraft Debonair. They started July 31, 1971, from Santa Rosa, California, and flew across the United States to Gander, Newfoundland, then across the North Atlantic to Shannon, Ireland. The route from there included stops in Scotland, England, the Netherlands, Belgium, Luxembourg, France, Switzerland, West Germany, Austria, Italy, Greece, Turkey, Iran, Australia, New Zealand, Fiji, the Gilbert Islands, and Hawaii.

Miller estimated that the Debonair, equipped with extra fuel tanks holding 170 gallons in addition to the 80 gallons normally carried, could stay aloft about 23 hours. Their longest leg, 17 hours from Tarawa to Honolulu, posed no difficulty. The honeymooners' baggage included survival equipment, a suit and tie for Miller, and a dress and accessories for Diane. "We like to dress comfortably," she said, adding that her usual blue jeans and green army shirt were appropriate when helping to service the plane in 100-degree heat in such places as Singapore.

Nearly perfect weather throughout the trip enabled the Millers, in warm climates, to often sleep under the plane. As they traversed the world, making about a hundred landings, improvisation became a way of life. Diane, who had earned her private pilot's license after taking instruction from her husband, did her share of the flying.

Edward Miller said he had no qualms about making the trip on the Debonair. He had owned the plane for five years and had previously flown it with another airline pilot to Hawaii, Wake Island, Samoa, and New Zealand. He had made national headlines a decade earlier when he piloted a Taylorcraft alone across the United States just after soloing at the minimum age of 16. The Millers logged 270 hours on their three-month honeymoon. "Our purpose was to see the world," Miller said. "We landed on grass strips and airfields in out-of-the-way places with the idea that we would try to see as much new country as possible. We . . . avoided the large cities. They're too accessible by the airlines. We had no strict timetable. I knew when I had to be back to work, and we estimated how long we could stay at each stop. That's as close as we came to being tied down to a schedule." They reported no trouble with the Debonair. Their only maintenance was to change engine oil every 25 hours of flying time.

Aircraft manufactured by Beech continued to set world-flight records. Again, two Australians, Dennis Dalton and Terry Gwynn-Jones, claimed a record for their country in October 1975. Their aircraft was a piston-powered Beechcraft Duke Model 60, powered by two 380-hp turbosupercharged engines. Dalton, a restaurateur, and Gwynn-Jones, a civilian flight examiner, set out to beat the Australian round-the-world record for this class of aircraft, then 125 hours and 57 minutes, set by Trevor Brougham in 1973. Flying from Brisbane to Brisbane via Tarawa, Honolulu, San Jose, Toronto, Gander, Gatwick, Beirut, Dubai, Madras, Singapore, Makassar, and Darwin, they bettered Brougham's mark by more than three hours, with a time of 122 hours and 17 minutes for the 24,494-mile flight.

"We could have broken his record by at least ten hours if we had not lost our radar immediately after takeoff from Honolulu and encountered other problems," Dalton told news reporters. "Fortunately, we did not need radar to London. But its failure to show the weather ahead cost us valuable time when we had to nurse the aircraft through bad weather later. In a 20-mile-wide corridor over Greece by the Albanian border, we flew into hail which knocked holes in the nose and engine nacelles."

Dr. Alvin Marks, right, psychologist and former president of a commuter airline, flew a Cessna 210 Centurion named *Semper Fly II* around the world in 1969. He completed the flight in 13 days, 22 hours and set point-to-point records on every leg. The man on the left is unidentified. (Cessna Aircraft Co. photo)

Because they were forbidden to fly outside the corridor, they had to go through the storm—at times with the landing gear and flaps down, to maintain a safe air speed. Delays were also experienced in obtaining high-octane fuel. At Makassar, the crew of an airliner operated by an Australian company came to their aid when they could not get fuel because of a documentation problem. "They let us siphon fuel from their aircraft to ours," Dalton said.

Despite the problems encountered, Dalton and Gwynn-Jones set a world-circling record for the weight class of their aircraft (6,600 to 13,320 pounds), as well as setting two point-to-point records, London to Darwin and London to Brisbane.

This attempt to set a world record wasn't the first for Dalton. Earlier in 1975, he had tried to break the world mark, but over Canada an engine failed, and by the time he reached Singapore, both engines needed extensive repair. Dalton did establish two point-to-point records on that flight, however—Honolulu to San Francisco and London to Singapore.

William and Priscilla Chester called themselves "nonprofessional" pilots. William was vice-president of an international company based in Milwaukee. Like many other pilots, he dreamed of flying his own plane around the world, "not as a race, nor alone, but as an aeronautical and cultural, once-in-a-lifetime experience." His boss was astounded when approached with the idea, but eventually gave his approval while recommending that the Chesters make the trip in a pressurized twin-engine turboprop, a Beech King Air 90.

William took an intensive course at the Beech factory, followed by a week of training at the TWA facility in New York, for corporate pilots flying the Atlantic. Priscilla joined him for a day of instruction in ditching and survival techniques.

They had fuel tanks installed in the cabin which would hold an additional 450 gallons and give the King Air more than twice its normal range. They also installed an HF radio receiver and a LORAN navigation set. As Priscilla said later, "This big step-up for us in equipment was a challenge to our relative inexperience as pilots. There were many firsts—higher altitudes, open oceans, foreign airports with unknown customs, approaches over mountains, desert, sea, often with frightening warnings on the maps bordering Communist or Middle East countries: 'Unidentified aircraft may be shot down without warning!'"

William and Priscilla set off from Milwaukee in June 1975, heading for Montreal, Newfoundland, Iceland, and Europe. They returned via Hawaii, San Francisco, and San Diego. On their 15-month trip, they logged 340 hours in the air and made 128 takeoffs and landings at 105 airports in 46 countries. They experienced two engine failures but each time managed to fly to a safe landing on one engine.

Cessna-made airplanes have continued to share fame in the seemingly endless round-the-world derby. Piloting a Cessna Centurion, Robert Mucklestone, a Seattle attorney and a keen student of aviation history, with his son Peter, set a world record in a single-engine aircraft by completing their flight in just under 12 days and 4 hours. On August 23, 1975, they took off from Boeing Field, in Seattle. They touched down again after 137 hours and 53 minutes of flight time, having bettered the mark of 13 days, 8 hours, and 41 minutes set by Alvin Marks in 1969 in the same type of aircraft.

Cruising at 11,000 feet most of the way, Mucklestone, to take advantage of a better tailwind, climbed as high as 22,000 feet during the final leg of the flight. The father-son team landed first in Milwaukee, then flew to Bangor before crossing the Atlantic. Their course took them over Europe to Turkey, then India and below the equator to Indonesia, before they swung north to Malaysia, on to the Philippines, Japan, the Aleutians, Alaska, and Seattle. According to Mucklestone, the trip took "an enormous amount of planning" over a nine-month period. Fuel stops had to be lined up and clearances obtained. He and his son had estimated their time of arrival in Seattle two months before the actual flight; they missed it by only six minutes, arriving 12 days, 3 hours, and 53 minutes after takeoff.

In 1974, Amos Buettell, another Cessna pilot, set out in his twin-engine Cessna 310 on a business trip that took him all the way around the globe. He covered 40,000 miles and took two months while making 25 stops to meet agents of his company. "I made reservations and appointments in advance of my departure and had no trouble maintaining my schedule in keeping all of them," he recounted later.

Buettell had only one minor maintenance problem—replacing a brake hose clamp—during his nearly 180 hours of flight time. A bonus of the trip was the establishment of four records for Cessna 310 aircraft.

Midway through the trip, Buettell set two world records, flying from Bombay to Singapore in 11 hours, 19 minutes, and 11 seconds, following this with another light-twin mark of 11 hours, 22 minutes, and 59 seconds, from Singapore to Perth, Australia. He concluded his trip with two more world point-to-point marks: Honolulu to San Francisco in 10 hours, 20 minutes, and 2 seconds, and two days later, 7 hours, 1 minute, and 55 seconds, San Francisco to Chicago. "The four international speed marks were a pleasant sidelight to my trip," he said; "but the flexibility and reliability the 310 [gave] me in the conduct of my business was the most satisfying factor."

The triumph of Robert Mucklestone and his son prompted Jack Rodd and Harold Benham, two pilots based in Colorado, to try beating the single-engine mark. Flying a Beech Bonanza christened *The City of Cortez*, they left Cortez, Colorado, October 29, 1977, following the route: Bangor (Maine), the Azores, Portugal, Munich, Teheran, New Delhi, Sri Lanka, Malaysia, Saipan, Wake Island, Honolulu, Santa Barbara (California).

Rodd, a private flyer with 35 years of flying experience, and Benham, a fighter pilot with service in World War II, Korea, and Vietnam, did indeed beat the record, making the flight in 11 days, 23 minutes, although they had hoped to make the trip in six days, give or take a few hours. According to Rodd, there were two "tight spots" on the trip. First was on the leg from the Azores to Portugal while flying on instruments in icing conditions. They were forced down to 200 feet over the ocean when their compass malfunctioned. "We [concluded that] we were flying west (back to the Azores) instead of east. We came in on radar from the Portuguese Air Force, and landed at Oporto, Portugal." There, the compass was replaced, and it performed fairly well until the Honolulu–San Jose leg. Then the compass went completely haywire, causing them to wander 700 miles off course. They radioed the U.S. Coast Guard that they had only about four hours' fuel left and were unsure of their position. The Coast Guard sent out a C-130 Hercules, which found the wandering Bonanza and escorted it to Santa Barbara.

After their return to Cortez, they were asked if missing the target of six days for the 23,800-mile trip had been a disappointment. "Yeah, it hurt a bit," Rodd replied. "We'll accept it though. Maybe we'll try it again, but not next week."

Philander Claxton had been a Green Beret in Vietnam. He had used his Army service to go to college under the GI Bill. By the time he was 30, Claxton had acquired a private pilot's license, two airplanes, and an MBA from Harvard and had founded the Watkins Corporation. He was also owner of the International House of Pancakes chain of restaurants.

Claxton got the idea of trying for the round-the-world record in 1975, when he read about Dalton and Gwynn-Jones's feat. He looked at their Beechcraft Duke and concluded that he could better the record with an Aerostar 601P, a plane with less horsepower than the Duke, but which was lighter.

He planned his flight carefully. In July 1976, he arrived in Washington, D.C. There, an elaborate array of communications and navigation gear was installed that cost nearly as much as the plane itself. He recruited

Steve Garfinkel as copilot. To commemorate the Bicentennial, they decorated the plane, christened *American Spirit*, in a paint scheme of stars and stripes. Their flight plan was ambitious: a 2,789-mile hop to Keflavik, Iceland, only 111 miles short of the Aerostar's range. They probably would have made it if the tailwinds forecast had held up and the fuel consumption had been as advertised. When the tailwind all but vanished over the Atlantic, Claxton realized they weren't going to make it. He had no choice but to change course for Greenland where he made a hazardous descent and threaded the fjords to a landing. As he checked the plane over on the ground, Claxton discovered something he had not taken into account: two of the tanks that had been installed to increase fuel capacity had collapsed like empty milk cartons. As fuel was consumed, the air hose to the tanks had apparently become clogged with ice, causing the pressurized air in the cabin to collapse the metal tanks. There was no way to continue the flight with the fuel capacity thus reduced, and the two dejected pilots returned to Washington.

On Labor Day weekend 1976, still intent on making his trip during the Bicentennial year, Claxton again took off but this time from Los Angeles. His copilot was John Cink, an officer of the firm that had installed the Aerostar's avionics. Although Claxton and Cink made it around the world on this try, they were delayed by red tape and fueling problems at

Phil Claxton (left) and Jack Cink (right) receive congratulations from Aerostar marketing executive Boyd Lydick upon completion of their 1977 flight in their piston-powered *American Spirit*. (Aerostar photo)

Istanbul and Karachi and had to make an emergency landing at Iwo Jima after tailwinds that had been predicted did not materialize. The Japanese, who controlled the island, put them through a prolonged but polite interrogation before letting them proceed. They made it to Los Angeles, with a total time of 125 hours, three hours more than the record they had hoped to beat.

Not at all pleased, Claxton decided to try again. In March 1977, with Cink as his copilot, he took off. This time, having hired a different firm to handle ground arrangements, Claxton wanted to shave the Australians' record by more than 20 hours. To save ground time, he and Cink ate in flight, consuming sandwiches, cookies, apples, and raisins. They swapped flying legs so one could sleep while the other flew. They were forced to give up the record try, however, on the penultimate leg, Wake Island to Honolulu, when they had to feather an engine because of low oil pressure.

Claxton and Cink did not give up, though. Three months later they were back in the air, only to suffer engine failure and have to abandon this, Claxton's fourth attempt.

It was on his fifth try, in November 1977, that Claxton finally succeeded. He and Cink had learned that they were pushing the Aerostar's engines too hard, that, when heavily loaded, they should cruise or climb more slowly to their cruising altitude of 24,000 feet. They decided to fly at a lower air speed and to make fewer stops. This proved to be a better strategy, and the record fell to them by more than 18 hours. They returned to Los Angeles in 104 hours, 5 minutes, and 30 seconds.

When Robert Mucklestone heard that Rodd and Benham had beaten his record, he decided to make another attempt. This time, however, he would fly solo. On May 19, 1978, he took off from Seattle in his Cessna Centurion. He returned 7 days, 13 hours, and 13 minutes later, to recapture the title. "I had people waiting with food, fuel, and oxygen almost everywhere I stopped," he said. Although he had planned to get 35 hours' sleep during the trip, he was able to average only three and a half hours each night he was gone. "I was pretty tired when I got back"—a remark often made by fliers seeking speed records around the globe.

Retired Air Force Lt. Col. Donald L. Rodewald didn't want to set a speed record. He just wanted to be the first paraplegic to fly solo around the world. He realized his dream in 1984, when he landed his red, white, and blue single-engine Piper Comanche 260 at Washington National Airport after a 35,000-mile trip that took him 230 hours of flying time and four months to complete. The two rear seats were removed and extra fuel tanks were installed to give the Comanche a 2,550-mile range. The copilot's seat was replaced by extra radio equipment, barely leaving space for his luggage.

Rodewald, who lives in Lake City, Colorado, had been an Air Force fighter pilot and had crashed while landing his F-80 at Andrews AFB, Maryland, in January 1954. The injuries he suffered left him paralyzed from the waist down, but that did not stop him from flying his specially-modified plane with hand-controlled rudder everywhere he wanted to go. "I hate to miss out on interesting things, although I do most things in life with my handicap in mind," he said. "I wanted to go places I'd never seen before, places Uncle Sam didn't send me. I just try to prove that if you want to do something bad enough, you'll do it."

Rodewald left Washington on August 2, 1984, and made stops in Canada, Iceland, and Europe. A former pilot with the famous Flying Tigers in China during World War II, he attended a reunion with former squadron mates whom he hadn't seen since 1942. He also flew to Australia to visit friends before making the flight across the Pacific. The longest leg was the 14-hour flight from Hawaii to Oakland.

The 32-stop flight was not without its trying moments. Although he had a clearance to overfly Pakistan, it was cancelled while he was en route from London, and he was forced to land at Karachi. Before he could leave, the airport authorities extracted $800 in landing fees from him. He flew across India to Calcutta at night, through bad weather, without ground-based radio aids. In Australia, he was placed in quarantine for five days with amoebic dysentery.

The plucky 66-year-old pilot attributed his stamina on the trip to his diet of water, crackers, cheese, peanut butter, and raisins. The trip cost him an estimated $30,000, some of it donated by old Air Force buddies.

"It is an outstanding demonstration of what anybody can do if they have the desire," said Donald R. Segner, associate administrator of the Federal Aviation Administration, after Rodewald's landing on November 30, 1984.

Did he have any regrets?

"I'm tired of flying solo," he told reporters upon arrival in Washington. "I'd like to have a pretty girl beside me from now on."

Although age and experience count, youth is no barrier to making a world flight. Chris Wall and Dan Dominguez of El Paso, Texas, can be added to the list. They were high school friends who dreamed of a world flight some day and planned for it while they were college students. Chris earned an airplane mechanic license, and Dan a commercial pilot license. They borrowed $15,000, found a 44-year-old twin-engine Aero Commander 580E in Guthrie, Oklahoma, named it *Dreamcatcher*, and put it back into the air after two years of hard work.

They then formed World Flight 2000 as a project of the Global Advancement Foundation to raise funds and support projects that benefit education, the environment, and communities around the world. The world flight portion was created entirely by students. They received their first donation from an executive of America Online, followed by gifts of cockpit essentials. The youthful, confident pair departed from Rochester, New York, for Bangor, Maine, on September 13, 2000. They had a large gas tank installed in the cabin and then flew to the Azores.

For the next three months, they flew to Spain, Italy, Turkey, Greece, Egypt, India, Indonesia, and Australia. Most flying was done at night when the air was calmer, while the days were usually spent on the ground doing minor maintenance, dealing with obstinate foreign customs officials, and planning the next legs of their flight. Working on a meager budget, they often slept in hammocks under the wings of the aircraft. Dan filed flight plans under instrument flight rules to ease the transition between control centers and also because they didn't have the money to buy all the visual flight rules (VFR) charts they would have needed.

The daring duo had only one serious emergency during the entire flight. That was in the Middle East when Dan had to shut down one

Dreamcatcher pilots Chris Wall (left) and Dan Dominguez. They resurrected a twin-engine plane from an airplane graveyard, made it flyable, and realized their dream of being the youngest pilots ever to complete a world flight. (Courtesy Dan Dominguez)

engine because of a magneto problem and landed at an Egyptian military base. Fortunately, Chris had a spare magneto in his parts kit, and they were able to proceed. As with other pilots, their greatest mental strain would be the overwater island-hopping legs ahead. By December 2000, they had flown the South Pacific via Vanuatu, Christmas Island, Kiribati, and Pago Pago in American Samoa to Hilo, Hawaii. The leg to San Francisco was made without incident.

Dominguez and Wall arrived at Rochester, New York, their official starting point, on December 15, 2000, via El Paso and Atlanta. They had been in flight for 220 hours without any serious mechanical difficulty that would have caused them to abort the trip. As with many other pilots, their problems were on the ground, not in the air. Refueling, clearing through customs, and filing flight plans delayed them the most.

The two young pilots appeared at the annual July 2001 EAA meeting in Oshkosh, Wisconsin, where they met the public, autographed a book about their experiences, and then paused to consider what they will do for their next adventure. When asked for advice about long-distance over-water flying, Dan's answer was, "Don't look down." He added, "Someone once told us, 'It takes three things to fly around the world: a great crew, a great airplane, and a lot of luck.' I think we had a lot of luck."

19

FIRST OVER BOTH ENDS

The first person to pilot an airplane over both poles was Bernt Balchen, a Norwegian-born pilot who specialized in Arctic flying. Although credit is often given to Adm. Richard E. Byrd, Byrd was not a pilot. His pilot over the North Pole was Floyd Bennett; his pilot over the South Pole was Balchen.

Colonel Balchen, who became a legend because of his many rescues of people stranded in the Arctic, was stationed in Alaska after World War II, in charge of a U.S. Air Force air-rescue unit. In May 1949, he received permission to fly a Douglas C-54 transport from Fairbanks, Alaska, to Thule, Greenland, via the North Pole. Although flights over the pole had become fairly routine by this time, Balchen's flight was to become a historic one, though he had no inkling of this at the time. In his biography, *Come North with Me,* Balchen tells how he circled the pole for two minutes before proceeding to Thule. After landing and filling out the flight log, he was approached by a mechanic on his crew. "Colonel, weren't you the pilot on the South Pole flight, too?" Continuing to write, Balchen nodded absently. "Ja, sure. Why?" "Doesn't that make you the first man to pilot a plane over both poles?" It hadn't occurred to him. "I guess it does."

It wasn't until the early 1960s that a flight over both poles, for record, was seriously considered. An anonymous operations planner in the U.S. Air Force got the idea. By that time, aerial refueling had become a routine operation. If necessary, the aircraft chosen could be refueled in flight for the long legs over the poles, thus demonstrating the Air Force's ability to fly quickly to any place on earth. If the flight was *not* successful, the whole world would know it, and the credibility of the U.S. Air Force, striving to convey the image of "Peace through Strength," would suffer; General LeMay, Air Force chief of staff, vetoed the plan, and it was never revived.

Such a flight had intrigued others, however. In 1965, two veteran TWA

217

pilots, Fred Austin and Harrison Finch, with the help of the Explorers Club, brought the project to reality. The chief sponsor was the Rockwell-Standard Corporation. The purpose of the flight was to be more than circumnavigation of both poles; it was to be a scientific expedition. The aircraft used would carry equipment and personnel to study cosmic-ray absorption and various aspects of high-altitude meteorology, including turbulence. Also to be tested were an inertial navigation guidance system never before used for cross-polar flights and 400-watt radio transceivers.

The flight route was planned meticulously. The aircraft chosen was a new intercontinental model of the Boeing 707, which was leased from the Flying Tiger Line. A special auxiliary fuel system was installed. Fuselage tanks held 4,000 gallons and were equipped with a unique surge-arresting and tie-down mechanism. As the tanks emptied, they were rolled up and stowed away. This system gave the plane a range of 7,000 miles. The plane was christened *Polecat*. Austin and Finch planned a flight that would follow as closely as possible the zero and 180-degree meridians. Stops for fuel would be made in Hawaii, London, Buenos Aires, and Christchurch. An additional stop at Lisbon was included because of a fueling problem in London.

As plans for scientific research gained momentum, various passengers were added to the manifest. Besides the crew of five pilots, three flight engineers, three navigators, and two radio operators, six film newsmen, and 10 scientists, 11 passengers were added, including Willard Rockwell, president of Rockwell-Standard; Edward Williams, a company vice-president; Balchen; Randolph Lovelace, the astronauts' physician; the official timers for NAA, Edward Sweeney and Bart Locanthi; and Lowell Thomas Jr., who kept in radio contact with his father throughout the flight. A renowned physicist, Serge Korff, led the team of scientists; it was their job to study cosmic-ray and upper-air phenomena in polar regions.

Sunday, November 14, 1965. Carrying 40 crew and passengers, *Polecat* lifted off from Palm Springs, California. After some three hours on the ground at Honolulu, they headed due north on the longest leg of the flight—the 7,400 miles over Alaska across the Arctic Ocean and North Pole to London's Stansted Airport. Lowell Thomas Jr. describes the first nonroutine event:

> We were passing over the northern coast of Alaska in the vicinity of Wainwright, flying at about 37,000 feet. . . . It was still dark outside, but the weather was essentially clear, with temperatures of about 60 below. At 12:15 P.M., Captain Finch was talking with Colonel Rockwell in the forward cabin area when a faint tinge of light blue smoke was seen coming from a fresh-air vent over a window. . . . Finch detected the smell of hot insulation, . . . a great deal of extra wiring had been strung through the

The crew and passengers of the first aircraft to fly around the world over both poles pose beside the long-range Boeing 707-320, *Polecat*, loaned by the Flying Tiger Line. Departure was made from the Honolulu International Airport. (Rockwell Corporation photo)

cabin to supply power for the scientific equipment, and Finch knew that some of these lines went right past the fuel tanks. . . . he hurried forward to the cockpit. . . .

"We seem to have an electrical problem," Finch told Valazza [the flight engineer]. ". . . maybe we'd better knock off the unessential power until we straighten it out."

Valazza immediately pulled the circuit-breakers, disconnecting all electricity except the power for flight instruments and the radio and lighting equipment. Larsen [the navigator] asked about the circuit-breakers for the Inertial Navigation System and Finch ordered the same procedure, . . . By now, the . . . forward cabin area was filled with . . . smoke . . . Finch . . . told Valazza to decrease the cabin pressurization and step up the air flow . . . to evacuate the fumes.

Within only a few minutes, Valazza pinpointed the trouble. A ventilating fan motor had burned itself up, probably because of a faulty bearing, . . . smoldering insulation had caused the . . . fumes. With the trouble isolated, all electrical power was turned on again, and the cabin pressure was returned to normal levels. . . . it became necessary to watch the operation of the scientific equipment very closely because some of it had [become] cooled . . . [when] the fan motor went on the blink. It also meant that the Inertial Navigation System could no longer give position information, because of a break in electrical continuity. But this loss was only temporary. The INS would be realigned and restored to normal working order as soon as we reached London. For the time being, . . . the *Polecat*'s human navigation was left without a confirming system.

As *Polecat* approached Scotland, an ice fog at Stansted Airport forced a change in the flight plan; they would land at Heathrow Airport, near London. This landing, in turn, led to another change. Because the runway at Heathrow was too short for the fully fueled 707, it would not be able to make a nonstop hop to Buenos Aires, as planned. Therefore, the plane would have to refuel at Lisbon before proceeding across the South Atlantic. By now, two point-to-point records had been set: Honolulu over the North Pole to London in 13 hours and 54 minutes; London to Lisbon in two hours and 19 minutes. Still another record was set, on the Lisbon–Buenos Aires leg, of 16 hours and 41 minutes.

They spent three hours on the ground, then took off for Christchurch, on the pioneering 7,000-mile leg over the South Pole. For Balchen, this leg brought back memories of his polar flight with Byrd in 1929. As *Polecat* crossed the polar plateau, he went forward to the cockpit to reminisce with the flight deck crew and to watch the inertial navigation system display the distance to the South Pole.

Just as the INS indicated they were precisely over the pole, the sky opened up as though commanded to do so. The crossing was confirmed by an observer at the U.S. Navy's South Pole Station, who spotted them at an altitude of 37,000 feet. Each of the five pilots circled the pole and thus shared the honor. The distance from the South Pole to Christchurch is about 3,000 miles. *Polecat* landed at Christchurch after dark. They were on the ground only two hours, departing for Honolulu, where they landed at 12:41 P.M. PST, November 17. It had been their intention to set five jet transport records; they set eight, covering 26,230 miles in 62 hours, 27 minutes, and 35 seconds. Their in-flight time was 51 hours and 27 minutes, only 33 minutes off the 52 hours announced before the flight by Finch and Austin. In addition to the overall record and the six point-to-point records, a mark for speed was established between the poles of 34 hours and 46 minutes.

20

CONQUERING THE FOUR CORNERS AND SEVEN CONTINENTS

After *Polecat*'s flight over the poles, it was only a matter of time before someone made the flight solo. That title belongs to Elgen Long, a pilot for Flying Tiger. As if that achievement weren't enough, Captain Long added four firsts:

The first to fly around the world and land on all seven continents.
The first to cross the equator at both the prime meridian and the 180th meridian.
The first to fly across the Antarctic solo.
The first to fly solo from Antarctica to Australia.

Long's flight demonstrated for the first time the progress made since 1924, when Army Air Service pilots first flew around the world. When Long decided to make the attempt, the plane, its engines, and the avionics aboard were a far cry from the days of open cockpits, no radios, and "guess-and-by-God" navigation. Long's background in aviation eminently qualified him for planning and piloting. Before becoming a commercial pilot, he had served with the U.S. Navy, completing courses in aerial navigation, radio, and radar. He became a captain with Flying Tiger after service as a radio officer and a navigator with the airline.

Besides a pilot's license, Long holds ratings as a navigator, radio operator, and FAA mechanic. He has extensive twin-engine experience in the Arctic, where he flew resupply missions to Air Force stations in areas where navigational, meteorological, communication, and other facilities are practically nonexistent. Meanwhile, he accumulated 25,000 hours of accident- and violation-free flying.

Until 1971, a global flight remained just a dream. Feeling that he at last had the resources and the ability to make the attempt, he told his wife that perhaps it was time to try, and with that, preparations began. The flight became a family venture: planning, letter-writing, meetings, preparation of equipment, the thousand and one things involved in such an undertaking. Long, his wife Marie, their son, and daughter tackled their jobs with a gusto. Marie served as logistics manager for the seven-continent flight, flying ahead by commercial airliner to arrange stops at London, Rio, Sydney, Tokyo, and other places. Eventually, she flew almost 10,000 miles more than her husband did.

Jointly, they christened the flight "The Crossroads Endeavor." Long planned to overfly the crossroads of time—the Greenwich meridian and the international date line, as well as those of geography, the North and

Capt. Elgen Long, pilot for Flying Tiger Line, became the first pilot to fly solo over "the four corners of the earth"—both poles and the equator at the 0-degree and 180-degree meridians. He is shown with his Piper Navajo, which was equipped with the latest navigation equipment. (Piper Aircraft Co. photo)

South poles. Harry, Long's 21-year-old son, composed a song by the same title to commemorate the flight. They realized early that the flight would require a lot of money. Eventually, the Longs raised the $50,000 that would be needed. Although it cleaned them out financially, Long thought the flight was "well worth it." A neighbor loaned them a plane, a white-and-blue Piper Navajo; the Flying Tiger Line contributed safety and survival equipment and helped make arrangements for assistance with other companies. American Telephone and Telegraph made its worldwide communications network available for calls during the flight. Delco Electronics provided the Carousel IV inertial navigation system, which proved extremely dependable. The autopilot came from Edo-Aire Corporation. Nystron Aviation readied the plane for flight and installed four additional fuel tanks, giving the aircraft a range of 4,000 miles, or 30 hours.

The flight, which began November 5, 1971, was surprisingly trouble-free; but it didn't start that way. Over the Gulf of Alaska, on the first leg, San Francisco to Fairbanks, Long encountered heavy icing which clogged the cockpit heater air inlet. The temperature in the cockpit dropped near the freezing point. "I put on my down-filled jumpsuit, boots and gloves, but my teeth continued to chatter for the rest of the trip," Long said. He reached Fairbanks 14 hours later.

After only five hours' sleep, he took off for the leg over the North Pole, then to Stockholm. But Long wasn't prepared for the awesome feeling of loneliness en route. "As you're going toward the North Pole—farther and farther away from everyone—you become just a speck, and the immensity of the ice cap starts to get to you. When you're planning a trip on maps and charts you understand what the mileages are, but until you actually find yourself out there in the middle of it, it's difficult to imagine its vastness and your smallness." The loneliness became even more pronounced when he lost radio contact for more than eight hours. There was also the malfunctioning heating system to contend with: "It just couldn't keep up with the extreme cold."

Long passed over the moonlit North Pole at 0320 Greenwich mean time, November 7. His sense of isolation was still strong: "I've never seen so much of nothing all in one place in all my life." He also found that being on top of the world produces something approaching hallucinations. "After I passed over the Pole, I actually got the sensation I was going downhill. And after flying along for just 200 or 300 miles, really an insignificant distance, I felt that if I looked down, I ought to see palm trees, . . . that I ought to be away from all that ice and snow."

After the pole crossing, Long made an unscheduled stop at Tromso, Norway, where he took on fuel. He also had reports of bad weather ahead. Two hours later, he was on his way to Stockholm. Later, when he had completed the flight of 3,454 nautical miles from Fairbanks, Long found that he had been awake for 34 consecutive hours. Nevertheless, he stayed in Stockholm only a short time; he was being reunited with Marie on his next stop, London. Long flew this leg, 782 miles, in 4.5 hours. In London, he and Marie shopped for another pair of thermal long johns and a heavy, long-sleeved shirt.

Leaving London on schedule, November 14, Long covered the 2,863 nautical miles to Accra, Ghana, in 20 hours and 1 minute. Throughout, the inertial navigation system functioned perfectly. He updated the system over Marrakech, inserting the latitude and longitude of Timbuktu. The INS flew him across the Sahara and brought him to within three miles of Accra's Kotoka International Airport. About five hours out of Timbuktu, as he crossed the Atlas Mountains, he encountered icing. "The trip up to now has been one long icing fantasy," he told his son over the phone after landing.

On November 15, Long left Accra and flew directly south for 337 nautical miles. This brought him to the second crossroads point on the globe—the prime meridian at the equator. He crossed zero degrees latitude, zero degrees longitude at 0744Z. With two goals down and two to go, Long already felt a sense of accomplishment. He wasn't lulled into overconfidence, however; he was aware that the most dangerous lap of the world flight lay ahead: the solo over Antarctica.

After his flight over the Atlantic to Recife, Brazil, where he arrived at 1958Z, November 15, Long reported everything in "apple-pie order." His Navajo functioned so well that after his arrival he would permit no one to touch it. The flawless mechanical performance was to continue throughout the trip, moving Long to boast: "In 215 hours I didn't even have to take the cowlings off the engines."

At noon the next day, he was airborne again, headed for Rio de Janiero, 1,007 nautical miles distant. Arriving 5 hours and 51 minutes later, Long commented that he was stiff from sitting so long. He had lost weight, but kept his energy up by eating space-food sticks and chocolate bars and drinking lots of water. Though tired, his attitude and motivation remained high. "It's been a grueling trip. I wouldn't wish it on anyone else. But one of the offsetting aspects is the sincerity of the good wishes coming from complete strangers. . . . For instance, in Accra, a little boy came up to me and gave me a St. Christopher's medal to protect me on the trip."

After a three-day stay in Rio, which he shared with his wife, Long departed for Punta Arenas, Chile, the southernmost city in Chile. It would be his jumping-off point for the 19-hour Antarctic flight to McMurdo Sound. His arrival in Punta Arenas on November 19 marked nearly the halfway point on his 36,000-mile world flight.

At long last, the make-or-break part of the flight had arrived: 2,942 nau-

tical miles over the continent of Antarctica. The journey from Punta Arenas to McMurdo Sound would be long and treacherous. Much of the
continent was inadequately charted, and there were vast areas for which
no weather information was available. Anticipating that cold would be
his worst enemy, Long donned three sets of thermal underwear and all
the survival clothing he had with him. "But I couldn't climb into the
plane with it all on," he said; "so I got into the underwear, then into the
plane and put the rest on inside. It's a good thing I did, because about
eight hours before reaching McMurdo I lost my heater altogether; then
the cockpit temperature really dropped."

Beginning the leg with good flight conditions, Long flew south, down
the 69-degree west meridian. He was thwarted, however, in his lifelong
dream of seeing Antarctica and the South Pole. "I had zero visibility and
was on instruments as I crossed the South Pole." Even though Long's INS
told him the precise moment that he crossed the pole (0255Z, November
22), realization of his long-held ambition didn't hit him until a Navy
C-130 in the area radioed congratulations. "That's the first time I felt I'd
accomplished something." Regret at not seeing the pole remained,
though. In a call to his wife after landing at Williams Field, McMurdo,
Long said: "I'm sorry, honey, but I missed seeing most of Antarctica after
waiting all these years." As it turned out, he was fortunate in getting in
and out of Williams Field at all. It closed down shortly after his arrival
and again soon after his departure.

Long's stay in Sydney, where he flew next, included a celebration with
his wife, who said: "I ordered a table for two on the terrace of our hotel
for a special Thanksgiving dinner. After all, we had something extra to be
thankful for this year—the flight was going perfectly." Long left for
Nandi, in the Fiji Islands, less than 24 hours after landing in Sydney.

On the next leg, Nandi to Wake Island, he was to overfly the fourth and
final crossroad of the world, the equator at the international date line.
Long left Nandi on November 27. During the early part of the flight, he
followed Amelia Earhart's planned approach to Howland Island. He conducted an experiment to determine whether the celestial navigation settings for Howland were correct. "After following the settings," he said,
"I looked down and saw nothing but overcast. Then through a break in
the clouds, I spotted Howland right where it should have been. That indicated to me that the celestial navigation approach may not have been Miss
Earhart's problem."

Long now turned west. At 0421Z, November 28, he crossed the equator
at the international date line, then continued to Wake Island. From there,
the schedule called for a Tokyo–Honolulu hop. Because he couldn't avoid
adverse weather en route, however, Long decided to land at Wake. It was

James Schwartz, left, presents the Piper-sponsored National Intercollegiate Flying Association trophy to Capt. Elgen Long at Purdue University in 1972 for his world flight. Mrs. Marie Long looks on. (Piper Aircraft Co. photo)

the second and last time in the world flight that Long had to depart from his original flight plan.

On the last leg, Honolulu to San Francisco, Long encountered strong head winds that put him three hours behind schedule. In a plane-side interview after the flight, he "apologized" for his tardiness, confessing that he had overslept in Honolulu. "I'm sorry to have inconvenienced all of you," he said; "the heart was willing, but the body was weak." Asked whether he was going after any other records, Long smiled and replied: "I may set one for sleeping."

In recounting his experiences, Long says: "There were an additional dozen or so world records that I could have claimed for the flight, . . . but what I prize most are some . . . unofficial comments. . . . a reporter remarked that the worldwide press coverage would have been even greater if I [had] had some emergencies along the way; then he said. . . . 'I know it was an extremely difficult flight that was made to look very easy,' and to an airline pilot there can be no finer compliment."

In an interview later, Long expanded on the difference between flying to reach a specific goal and professional airline flying. "[In] the kind of flying I do ordinarily, the safety factor is always first. If anything goes wrong, you take care of the emergency first. You don't worry about making the destination. But in this [flight], the only thing I had to remember was that it had to be completed: . . . I flew into a blizzard in Antarctica, and I knew full well that if an electromechanical device—the inertial guidance system—were to fail me, I would never make it to McMurdo. . . . It's not my way of thinking or flying—to leave things up to fate; but it had to be done."

William E. "Bill" Signs, an operator of an automobile service facility in Dallas, Texas, is a former corporate pilot, flying instructor, and licensed airplane mechanic. He began flying in 1969 at age 16 and has over 11,000 hours of flying experience. He served as a crew member on aircraft ranging from crop dusters and turbine-powered corporate planes to large four-engine transports. This experience has taken him to 73 countries in various types of aircraft.

Signs's first long cross-country flight in a light aircraft was in 1987 when he hopscotched from Dallas around the Caribbean in a single-engine Cessna 150 to most of the islands and Venezuela. He considered it one of the riskiest trips of his life at that time flying the overwater hops and over hostile jungles because of the plane's minimal fuel capacity and radio equipment.

In 1990, he outfitted a single-engine Mooney for extended flight capability and flew to 13 countries in Europe, thus crossing the North Atlantic twice. The following year, he began a series of "Friendship Flights" that he organized to promote international goodwill and friendship; he led a flight of 35 American and Canadian general aviation aircraft that flew across Alaska to the Soviet Union into far eastern Siberia and returned.

In June 1992, Signs flew the Mooney around the world in 30 days. It was a joint American-Russian flight commemorating, a year late, the fiftieth anniversary of the World War II Lend-Lease program. Signs and Russian navigator Yuri Kharitonov obtained permission to land at several Russian military bases, and their aircraft was one of the first general aviation aircraft to be allowed to cross Russia after the disintegration of the U.S.S.R. in 1991. Kharitonov was formerly vice president in charge of operations for civil aviation at Magadan, Russia. Having him aboard as a copilot and translator eased the way through customs at each stop. The only mechanical difficulty was the loss of a radio antenna that snapped off when overloaded with ice.

The following year, Signs organized "Friendship '93" and led a three-aircraft expedition to Russia and Mongolia. He had an extra aluminum

A single-engine Mooney flown by William E. "Bill" Signs and Russian navigator Yuri Kharitonov parks beside a giant Russian jet transport during a 30-day world flight in 1992. The Mooney had been modified for extended flight capability. (Courtesy William E. Signs)

gas tank installed in the cabin of a Cessna 210L Centurion and could fly for 15 hours, if necessary. For Friendship Flight '95, again using the 210, he was the first to fly a light aircraft from Chile to Marsh Base, Antarctica, and back without refueling. Side trips were made to the Galapagos and Falkland islands.

It was Friendship Flight '96 that put Signs firmly in the record books as the first to depart the United States with the expressed intention of landing on all seven continents. The 50-day expedition with the Cessna 210 included a total of 226 hours in flight and 30 stops. It began when he lifted off from Dallas's Love Field on December 31, 1995. Accompanied by copilot Ruth E. Jacobs, an experienced pilot from Anchorage, Alaska, they stopped briefly at Orlando, Florida, to visit Signs's mother. They experienced their only mechanical problem of the entire flight during the next leg to Puerto Rico when a specially designed alternator failed after 19 hours of flight. But Signs, a master aircraft mechanic, said there was no problem. "I just turned off the master switch and operated on standby power," he said. "I carried a big battery with me and had enough power to have up to 20 hours of communication and navigation capability even with the failed alternator."

Another alternator was obtained, and the two headed toward Ushuaia on the southern tip of Argentina. It was at this point that Signs almost lost his plane—not in flight but on the ground. There were no tie-down rings available, and winds gusting to 83 mph nearly blew the plane away. Fortunately, it survived, and the duo flew to Base Marambio, King George Island, Antarctica, where the temperature was about 20 degrees below zero. They placed the Cessna in a hangar overnight and left next day for Punta Arenas, Chile, then proceeded to Buenos Aires, Argentina; Rio de Janeiro; and Recife, Brazil. Next was a 1,650-mile, 11-hour leg to Cape Verde Islands off the west coast of Africa.

The duo proceeded from the islands to Spain, then over the Mediterranean to Malta. En route to Egypt, avoiding any landings in northern Africa, they flew within five miles of Libyan airspace, aware that they might be intercepted by Muammar Qaddafi's potentially unfriendly jet fighters.

Friendship '96 continued with stops at Luxor, Egypt; Muscat, Oman; and on to Bombay, India. "About 57 miles from Bombay," Signs recalled, "we descended into a brown, murky haze, and Ruth said, 'what is that smell?' It was Bombay. In the haze, visibility dropped to three-quarters of a mile."

Signs and Jacobs flew to Thailand, Myanmar, Malaysia, Singapore, Indonesia, and on to Darwin and Brisbane, Australia. It was on 400 miles of this last leg of the 1,600-mile flight that Signs recalls there were no trails, roads, houses, or ranches—nothing that could be used as checkpoints.

Friendship '96 continued to Guadalcanal, Kiribati, and Tarawa in the Gilbert Islands. "Tarawa was consistently one of the hottest places I've ever been to," Signs recalled. "It's just hot with no winds—just dead calm. And the folks there don't do much. They just lay around all day. It's so hot they don't even put sides on their huts. It's the only place I've been where even the chickens were lying on their sides because of the heat."

Signs and Jacobs departed Tarawa for Honolulu, a 14-hour flight. They spent four days resting there and then headed the faithful Cessna for Van Nuys, California. They were pleasantly surprised to be pushed along by the "pineapple express," a frequently encountered tailwind that gave them an additional 70 knots of ground speed. They covered the 2,554 statute miles in 12 hours.

Friendship '96 landed at Love Field on February 18, 1996, 50 days, 1 hour, and 16 minutes after departure. They had flown 39,543 miles at an average speed of 175 mph (152 knots). Gas consumption had been 3,153

The Cessna 210L Centurion poses beside a flight line of training planes in Russia during the Friendship '96 world flight by William Signs and Ruth Jacobs. The flight through Russian airspace required an accompanying Russian navigator. (Courtesy William E. Signs)

gallons, and 52 quarts of oil were used, including oil changes. The highest price they paid for gas in American dollars was $6.74 a gallon at Cape Verde; the cheapest was 89 cents a gallon at Bombay. The total cost of the flight was $50,000.

Signs and Jacobs share the honors as the first pilots to have landed on all seven continents during a single expedition. The National Aeronautic Association established for them a special record category for "Fastest Time to Visit All Seven Continents," and it remains unchallenged as this edition goes to press.

Signs was not finished with Friendship Flights after the grueling 1996 world flight. The following year, he commemorated the seventieth anniversary of the 1927 New York-to-Paris flight of Charles A. Lindbergh by duplicating the route of the *Spirit of St. Louis*. Signs departed San Diego on May 10, 1997, and flew to St. Louis and New York before flying to Paris nonstop for an arrival on May 21.

A final Friendship Flight took place in 1998 when Signs flew his Cessna 210 from Barrow, Alaska, across the North Pole to Spitzbergen to commemorate the seventieth anniversary of the historic cross-pole flight of Carl Ben Eielson, famous Alaskan bush pilot, and Sir Hubert Wilkins.

William E. "Bill" Signs points to the Antarctic destination where he and Ruth Jacobs landed in their quest to be first to land a single-engine aircraft on all seven continents during a world flight. Their success in 1996 caused the establishment of a special speed category by the National Aeronautic Association and Federation Aeronautique Internationale. (Photo by the author)

When asked why he began the Friendship Flights, Signs replied: "I wanted to make sure that I didn't portray an image of the 'Ugly American.' I wanted to make sure that wherever I went I would have something, a memento of the flight, to give to people that I met. So I had cards and pictures printed and hats made that I could give out wherever I went. As Americans we travel to so many countries now, and the only thing we do is take from them and demand prompt service. We have a tendency to travel to countries with a superiority attitude chip on our shoulders. When I go through customs or immigration, I'm the dumbest guy you've ever seen. I just don't know anything, and 'Can you help me?' becomes my most used phrase. Many of the government officials I deal with just shake their heads about how ignorant I am because I don't portray an image of superiority in any way. I always answer and respond, 'Yes, sir,' 'No, sir,' 'Si, señor,' 'No, señor,' and just be very polite. And I don't have any trouble."

Does Signs consider himself an adventurer? "Not at all," he told a reporter from *Texas Flyer* magazine. "I think of myself more as an expeditioner. My definition of the difference between an adventure and an expedition is planning. I don't cut any corners, and I know pretty much what's going to happen. There are firm plans laid out. So the difference between the adventurer and an expeditioner is lots and lots of planning. I don't go off 'half-cocked' and to date there have been no surprises. I've heard all those stories about the problems people have when they're flying around the world, and I didn't encounter any of them. If you get the *International Airman's Manual* and study it and do what they tell you, most of the problems never occur."

Signs has proved that it is possible to fly great distances in a single-engine aircraft safely provided a flight is preceded with thorough planning and careful attention to maintenance of a plane and its systems.

Signs hopes to make at least one more world flight. That will be when he is convinced that a diesel engine has been successfully mated with an airplane so that it is as reliable as one with a piston engine using aviation gas. He believes that time is not far off, and it will then be possible to make a world flight in a light aircraft with only one refueling.

21

BUSINESS AIRCRAFT
GO 'ROUND

One of the first types of business or executive jet-powered aircraft was the North American (later Rockwell) Sabreliner, a small twin-jet piloted by a crew of two and capable of carrying 2 to 10 passengers. Designed to meet Air Force requirements, it was first flown September 15, 1958.

In early 1965, J.F. Coleman, then marketing manager for North American Aviation, proposed a round-the-world attempt at the speed record to draw attention to the Sabreliner's capabilities as an executive transport. To serve as pilot, Coleman suggested Robert Fero, chief test pilot for the aircraft. He applied to NAA for 64 separate record sanctions, with a scheduled departure date of late April or early May 1965. For reasons that were never given, the flight was not attempted.

A competitor to the Sabreliner was the eight-passenger, twin-engine Lear Jet Model 23, which first flew October 7, 1963. Among the plane's earliest record-setting performances was that by John Conroy and Clay Lacy, who set three international speed records in a unique 5,005-mile flight from Los Angeles to New York, and return.

The capabilities of the small business jet quickly became known in aviation circles. W.R. Miller, president of AirKaman Company, applied for NAA sanction for a world flight, with himself as pilot. He proposed a departure date of November 1, 1965. The route would be Windsor Locks, the company's headquarters, to Greece via Newfoundland, the Azores, and Spain, including a stop in Saigon. The proposed route totalled only 20,525 miles, more than 2,300 miles short of the required distance for a record. This attempt was also cancelled.

On December 14, 1965, a Lear Model 23 carried seven people to an altitude of 40,000 feet in 7 minutes and 21 seconds, a feat that established a time-to-climb record for Class C. 1e jets weighing 6,614 to 13,227 pounds. The Model 23 was followed by the 24, a heavier plane, which placed it in the next class—C.1f (13,227 to 17,636 pounds). The 24 could carry 847 gallons of fuel, which gave it a range of 1,845 miles.

On May 23, 1966, a Lear Model 24 bearing the number N427LJ took off from Wichita, Kansas, with four aboard. It carried no extra fuel or special communication and navigation equipment; it was flown entirely within certified operation and weight limits. The announced purpose of the historic flight was to "demonstrate the great speed, flexibility, utility and dependability of today's modern business jet." Everyone in the crew was a qualified Lear Jet pilot: Henry Beaird; Rock King; and John Lear, son of the plane's designer, William P. Lear Sr. John Zimmerman, a writer for American Aviation Publications who was serving as official NAA observer, was making his fourth trip around the world but his first in a

The original world-girdling record for business jet aircraft was established in 1966 with a Lear Jet 24. Designer William P. Lear Sr., (second from left) and his wife, Moya, greet crew members John Zimmerman (left), official of the National Aeronautic Association; John O. Lear; Henry G. Beaird; and Richard "Rock" King. (Gates Learjet photo)

business jet. He reported no problems. Once, however, near the end of the Aleutian chain, a Soviet jet fighter intercepted them and flew close formation for five minutes, then peeled off, presumably because Zimmerman had put a telephoto lens on his camera. "It was a perfect example," he said, "of how businessmen can climb into a modern executive jet and conduct business on every continent of the Free World, following a minimum of careful flight planning and other detail arrangements. It's a little hard to conceive of a motor trip of one-tenth that distance going so smoothly."

Departing from Wichita on May 23, the Lear Jet made 16 stops, including St. Johns (Newfoundland), Teheran, Karachi, Singapore, Manila, Anchorage, and Seattle. Stops were also made at places not normally used on world flights: Windsor Locks, Connecticut; Barcelona; Osaka and Chitose (both in Japan); and Shemya, in the Aleutians. During the flight of 22,993 miles, just about every kind of weather was encountered, from the heat and humidity of Ceylon to the 40-below-zero cold of the Aleutians. All legs were flown at 41,000 feet, but even that altitude wasn't high enough for them to avoid detouring around a typhoon.

Total elapsed time was 65 hours and 39 minutes, with 50 hours and 19 minutes of that in flight. In addition to setting the world speed record for its class, the Lear Jet set another 17 records between cities. The crew claimed the distinction of being the first business-jet crew to circle the earth with FAI sanction. Zimmerman commented: "The flight of N427LJ was a . . . triumph from the standpoints of performance and world records . . . While performance records are relative and ephemeral, the contribution by the Lear team will serve as a landmark to the opening of a new era in business transportation . . . [that] era will be characterized by . . . little difficulty [and considerable] flexibility in scheduling, [by] increasing use, . . . and by intercontinental mobility . . . through use of corporate, private, jet-powered business aircraft."

An interesting sidelight of the flight was that William Lear, founder and president of the company, promised the crew a reward of $1 for every minute of the first hour under a total of 70 hours and a bonus of $5 per minute under the initial hour. Their arrival in Wichita, 4 hours and 20 minutes less than the 70 hours, earned each crew member $660.

The success of the Lear Jet immediately prompted competition from another manufacturer of jet aircraft, Aero Commander, a division of Rockwell-Standard. Actually, the plane's crew had wanted to race the Lear Jet 24; they had intended to leave New York on May 25, 1966, hoping to circle the globe in 53 hours or less. The day before they were to leave, however, three of the four pilots—Arthur Godfrey, Dick Merrill, and Karl

Four pilots who share a 1966 round-the-world record for business jets are shown beside their Jet Commander. Left to right: Karl Keller, Dick Merrill, Fred Austin, and Arthur Godfrey. En route, they set 21 speed and distance records for this type of aircraft. (Rockwell Corp. photo)

Keller—became ill, and the trip had to be postponed. Fred Austin, the other pilot, wasn't affected, nor was Jerry Jarmyn, an NAA observer.

The twin-engine executive jet transport, called a Jet Commander, was similar in performance to the Lear Jet. It, too, could operate at 40,000-foot altitudes, and it was not modified for the flight. The plane was equipped, though, with an experimental, single-sideband radio, which gave the crew voice contact with any place in the world. Finally, the U.S. Navy loaned them an experimental, lightweight, navigational device known as a GPL Doppler that measures drift and ground speed and gives pilots an instant readout of the correction needed to stay on course.

On June 4, 1966, Godfrey, Merrill, and Keller were pronounced fit for the flight. Godfrey and Keller flew the first leg, New York to Saint John's, Newfoundland, without incident. The second leg, Saint John's to Santa Maria, in the Azores—was flown by Dick Merrill and Fred Austin. Navigation on this leg was GPL Doppler navigation, following a precomputed

Great Circle Route. The weather was excellent. Keller and Godfrey then flew the first night leg to Madrid and ran into thunderstorms. Keller navigated around them, using his weather radar and following vectors from Spanish ground controllers. They landed in heavy rain at Madrid. The rain remained heavy until they reached Athens; they landed at dawn in excellent weather.

The flight continued to Teheran. The crew intended to fly on to Bombay; but shortly after crossing the border with Pakistan, they were ordered to land at Karachi, which they did during the night of June 5. The Pakistani government had not given overflight approval, though assurance had been given by its embassy in Washington before takeoff that clearance was granted. It took three precious hours to get approval.

Leaving Bombay early on the morning of June 6, with the crew rotating as usual at every stop, they flew to Colombo, Ceylon. Another deviation

Famous golfer Arnold Palmer (third from right) and his Lear Jet 36 crew are greeted with the traditional leis on arrival at Honolulu. Their record for the 22,985-mile flight was 57 hours, 25 minutes, 42 seconds. Left to right: James E. Bir, Lewis L. Purkey, Palmer, and aviation writer Robert J. Serling, pose with two unidentified hula greeters. (National Aeronautic Association photo)

from the flight plan was necessary; instead of flying to Singapore non-stop, they made a refueling stop at Butterworth, in upper Malaysia, because of head winds. This stop encouraged still another change of plan when permission was given by the Royal Australian Air Force to land at Labuan, Borneo, thus allowing them to bypass Singapore and permitting a straight-line course from Colombo to Manila.

The Aero Commander landed at Manila after dark on June 6, again during a thunderstorm. There, still another flight plan change was made. Due to strong head winds, a fuel stop would be made at Taipei en route to Tokyo, where, once again, approach and landing were in a heavy thunderstorm. The flight continued to the Aleutians. Because of a communications problem and inoperative runway lights at Anchorage International Airport, they landed at nearby Elmendorf Air Force Base. They flew on to Seattle, then through more thunderstorms, landing at Oklahoma City. The exuberant crew landed at La Guardia, June 7.

When the Aero Commander taxied up to the apron at La Guardia and the five crewmen stepped before the glare of TV camera lights, they claimed 21 speed and distance records for the aircraft. The flight had been made in 3 days, 14 hours, 9 minutes, and 1 second; over 23,373.6 miles at an average speed of 271.3 mph.

Although it was a spectacular achievement for the new business jets, the speed record previously set by the Lear Jet 24 was soon broken by a faster Lear Jet, the Model 36A. Another well-known personality, Arnold Palmer, was a crew member. Palmer is an extensive user of executive jets.

The idea of this world flight originated, almost casually, at a meeting of the National Business Aircraft Association in New Orleans in 1975. Palmer, a guest speaker at the meeting, was under contract to Gates Learjet Corporation for personal promotional services. Palmer suggested to associates that he publicize the new 36A by taking one to Europe for a golf tournament. "Why just to Europe?" someone asked. "Why not around the world?" "Fine," Palmer said. "When?"

The answer to this question was supplied by Jim Greenwood, a vice-president at Gates Learjet. Greenwood got the idea of tying the flight in with the U.S. Bicentennial celebration and the annual meeting of the Aviation/Space Writers Association in May 1976. The idea grew, becoming a major project. From the beginning, Greenwood envisioned a four-man crew: Palmer, two company test pilots, and a name writer as pool reporter. The route would be Denver–Boston–Paris–Amman–Colombo–Manila–Wake–Honolulu–Denver, Greenwood hoped they could get permission to land at Moscow and Peking, as a gesture of friendship by the Soviet Union and China to the United States on its anniversary, but he was unsuccessful.

The flight was planned meticulously. The reputation of the Gates company was at stake. In addition, the world's foremost aviation writers would be following the flight, and one of them, Robert Serling, would be aboard as the official NAA observer. The company pilots chosen were James Bir and Lewis Purkey.

The target time for the flight was "less than 60 hours." Using computers and the latest weather-forecasting resources, with emphasis on expected winds, the flight planners drew up a plan. Takeoff would be May 17, 1976. A pre-takeoff press conference was held at 8:30 A.M. that day. At 10:15, with Palmer in the left seat and Bir in the right—an arrangement they would follow 80 percent of the time—the brightly painted Lear Jet swung away from the ramp at Denver's Stapleton International Airport and headed down the runway. In the tower, John Slattery, secretary of the NAA Contest Board, wrote: "Takeoff: 10:24:16." The following narrative is adapted from "This is *200 Yankee*," a booklet prepared by the NAA.

N200 Yankee [climbed] . . . effortlessly to 33,000 feet—the initial assigned cruising altitude. At that point there was a modest tailwind of 25 knots, 11 knots weaker than what the [weather] forecast had indicated. As it turned out, it was the last tailwind *200 Yankee* was to enjoy until past Manila. . . .

Serling hauled out the inevitable spiral notebook of a reporter and began jotting down some . . . items . . . put on the airplane. . . . On the foreward bulkhead . . . were taped a silver dollar (from a Learjet mechanic), a Snoopy pin, . . . and Jeppesen's original United Air Lines pilot's wings. Palmer had taken along three old golf clubs and had agreed to carry a wood shaft putter that could have come out of a golfing museum. . . . Purkey and Serling surveyed the cabin in dismay—it was a [jumble] of boxes, cameras, food, paperback books and two six packs of Coors beer (which were never opened).

En route to Boston, it was strictly routine: *200 Yankee* was demonstrating the old saying that flying is hours of boredom punctuated by an occasional moment of stark terror. This, more than anything, summed up the 57 hours [of] the global flight.

Two hours out of Denver, the crew was informed of the first probable deviation from the carefully plotted trip. Palmer called Serling to the cockpit. "We've just been . . . refused permission to refuel at Djakarta, you'll have to certify we flew over [it] to stay on the sanctioned route and compile the necessary mileage."

"Where [do] we stop instead?"

"Singapore."

Purkey and Serling decided to bring order to the chaos in the cabin. Purkey rearranged the various boxes. He decided to put the Bicentennial flags and Declaration of Independence replicas in a place where they would be accessible to Palmer, who would dispense them at each stop. They finished the housecleaning a few minutes out of Boston, never suspecting that the chore would have to be repeated after each takeoff.

At Boston came the first of many news conferences. The questions seldom varied—"What will this flight do to your golf game?"—and neither did Palmer. He remained courteous, cooperative, and articulate. From there on, however, he would face the news media not only as a celebrity but as a Bicentennial representative and unofficial ambassador of the United States. At 2048 GMT, *200 Yankee* lifted off and streaked northeast. Paris was an estimated six hours and 55 minutes away, but at this point, they encountered head winds. Instead of a projected tailwind of 17 knots, *200 Yankee* encountered head winds up to 50 knots.

Palmer took a break about an hour out of Boston and went back to the cabin to relax and get something to eat. He was too excited to sleep. In a few minutes, he was back in the cockpit, conferring with Bir about the greater-than-anticipated fuel consumption. It was now dark. The Lear Jet seemed to be in its own self-sufficient world of metal, purring engines, and men. The lonely Atlantic crossing had suddenly brought home the solitude of flight and the magnitude of their adventure. Bir's unruffled manner masked his growing concern over fuel consumption. Although Bir thought there was no cause for alarm, he told Palmer it was possible they wouldn't make Paris nonstop. Palmer agreed; they should not take unnecessary risks by cutting corners. Serling, who had just entered the cockpit, inquired: "Have we passed the point of no return yet?" "Yeah," Bir said. "When we left Denver."

The head winds persisted—40 to 50 knots most of the way across the Atlantic. They finally shifted to the plane's left rear quarter, but the Lear Jet never made up the lost time. As *200 Yankee* approached Land's End, on the coast of Cornwall, the first VOR land fix, Bir rechecked fuel consumption. It was at that point that he realized their hopes of reaching Paris nonstop had faded to nothing. "Looks like we won't make it to Paris," he advised London control. "Can you advise which British airports might be open with fast refueling facilities?" "You might come into London," the controller suggested. "Negative," Bir ruled after a quick conference with Palmer; "That's almost as far as Paris." Finally, London control recommended Glamorgan, in Wales. "It's Rhoose Airport. It's open, and a fuel truck is available."

200 Yankee touched down at Rhoose after dawn, to be greeted by a young Welshman who gave their passports only a cursory inspection (except for Honolulu, it was the only time during the world flight that anyone asked to see passports) and reported that the fuel-truck driver was on his way to the airport. He apologized, saying, "I'll have to notify the customs inspector, of course."

The unscheduled stop at Glamorgan meant a delay of nearly two hours and added about 120 miles to the trip. Inconvenient as it was, the Rhoose stop provided relief from the monotonous routine of flying, for it involved decisions by Palmer and Bir and, in that sense, represented a challenge to their judgment, as well as furnishing that effective antidote for fatigue—humor. The aircraft had been refueled, a flight plan for Paris had been filed, and the crew, having inspected the nude calendars on the walls of the airport's offices, was awaiting Her Majesty's customs officer. "Where the hell is he?" Palmer finally asked. "Oh, I forgot to tell you, sir," said the pleasant young Welshman. "When I called him, he said he wasn't going to get out of bed just to check the passport of four silly blokes and that it was alright for you chaps to leave."

If the world flight was mostly routine, so was the pattern of each stop. Palmer would climb out first, hand a Bicentennial flag and Declaration of Independence plaque to an official, along with other items he had been instructed to present, patiently field questions from the press, and accept gifts from their hosts. Robert Lewis had written protocol instructions for Palmer at each city. Following is a sample, for Paris:

> Laurie Kassman (of Byoir, a public relations firm) is the contact here. She will meet you at the plane and escort you into the briefing room where she will introduce you to the Mayor of Paris or his deputy. You will present the letter from Mayor White to this man. The Bicentennial flag goes to the Bicentennial representative [introduced by] Laurie. The plaque goes to a representative of the French government. Tie tacs to government officials. Patches (Bicentennial) to press representative from papers and TV. A breakfast and refreshments will be available in the press reception room where brief interviews will be conducted with the French press.

The Robert Lewis Guide to Winning Friends and Influencing People was helpful—as a guide. In other words, it was not always followed. Arnold Palmer was, and is, his own man. Even so, the crew enjoyed reading his appraisals of what to expect or not to expect at various stops—for example, his explanation of why their reception in France might be less than thunderous. When Lewis was in Paris to make advance arrangements, a French official snapped: "Why should we welcome a Lear Jet? Look at what you're doing to the Concorde!"

When *200 Yankee* left Le Bourget Airport, it was two hours and three minutes behind schedule. To make matters worse, they promptly acquired a head wind. The forecast had been a 10-knot tailwind. "Maybe we should have gone east to west instead of west to east," Palmer observed wryly. Another hitch, though not unexpected, was the loss of communication between them and the Collins radio-relay point at Cedar Rapids. They had been greatly disappointed by the Defense Department's failure to approve use of Air Force frequencies in areas where normal reception was weak. The department did not refuse permission; it simply ignored the request. From England to Honolulu, communications between *200 Yankee* and Denver were haphazard. Trying to keep Denver informed, Serling, the NAA observer, turned to the more prosaic tele-phone. While Palmer was taking a helicopter to the Royal Palace in Tehe-ran, Serling managed to put through a call. Briefing Denver on the progress of the flight, he promised to phone again from Colombo. It was a promise he could not keep, neither there, at Djakarta, nor at Manila; it took too long to get calls through.

The Lear Jet raced through the night. Palmer later mentioned to the others that at no other time during the flight did he feel so alone and so insignificant, so aware that 41,000 feet under them was nothing but jungle or ocean. Over a jungle, it was as though the Lear Jet had slipped back in time and was suspended above a prehistoric world.

Thirty minutes out of Colombo, Ceylon, *200 Yankee* passed the halfway mark of its global journey, approximately 11,000 miles from Denver. They were some 27 hours into the flight. The welcome at Colombo's Bandara-naike International Airport ranked as the most colorful of the flight. Despite its being one in the morning, swirling native dancers met the plane, and Arnold Palmer, to please his hosts, climbed out of a million-dollar jet and onto the back of an elephant. He learned that Colombo's mayor and the U.S. ambassador had been waiting at the airport for three hours before giving up; but their absence didn't lessen the enthusiasm of the others. Impatient to leave, Palmer and Bir suddenly discovered that their flight observer was missing. Bir found Serling in the control tower, trying to talk a controller into placing a long-distance call to Denver. The controller kept smiling but shaking his head. Serling finally wrote out a message which a British Airways representative promised to teletype over his company's circuits for relay to the United States. Searching for some word of optimism about a flight now three hours and 18 minutes behind schedule, Serling ended his dispatch: "Palmer rode elephant. Ele-phant lost."

Another dawn. *200 Yankee* moved steadily toward Djakarta; permission to refuel there came through after they left Teheran. After more head-winds between Colombo and Djarkarta, this time up to 90 knots, Palmer sighed and said: "We sure aren't burning up the airways." Most of the time, they cruised at 41,000 feet, occasionally going up to 45,000 in an attempt to evade head winds. The flight was now four hours behind schedule.

Despite their difficulty getting clearance to land, the welcome at Dja-karta was warm. They took off, only to face another head wind. Palmer poked his head in the cabin. "Getting kinda crowded back there, Purk?" "Yeah—and smelly, too," Purkey drawled. Palmer laughed. "Well, when we hit Manila, we're gonna have a change of underwear." "No kidding?" Serling said. "Sure. I'm going to wear Bir's and he'll wear mine."

From the flight observer's log:

. . . as of takeoff from Djakarta, we've covered more than 13,000 miles. The guys seem a little depressed because we can't seem to make up any lost time, Arnie and Jim in particular. I mentioned to them that we've gone two-thirds around the world in 33 and a half hours—the . . . time it took Lindbergh to cross the Atlantic. I don't think the statistic cheered them up. . . . We're all pretty tired by now, and the word is we can expect a typhoon in the Manila area about the time we land. That's all we need. . . .

Typhoon Pamela and *200 Yankee* were speeding toward Manila simultaneously. The jet won. Low hanging clouds of the approaching storm were rolling in as Purkey supervised the refuelers. Palmer, unperturbed as usual, interrupted a news conference long enough to chat on the phone with President Marcos of the Philippines. In the operations room of Philippine Airlines, Bir concentrated on the weather forecasts, which were ominous. After his news conference, Palmer held a quick conference with Bir. He had been told that *200 Yankee* could avoid Pamela. Bir shook his head. "We're not going to avoid it, Arnie. Our real worry is how much ice we'll pick up climbing through it."

Indeed, ice was their biggest concern. Any accumulation would affect climb speed, which, in turn, would increase fuel consumption, and they faced an overwater leg of 2,632 miles. It wasn't that they feared ice as such—not with the Lear Jet's sophisticated deicing system; the system, however, drew its power from the engines, thus consuming more fuel. Another potential source of excess fuel consumption was icing on the fuselage, which would cause drag when the plane climbed.

Bir and Palmer decided to take off as soon as possible, stopping to refuel at Guam or Saipan if they couldn't make it nonstop to Wake. It is doubtful whether any of the four men aboard the Lear Jet will forget the departure from Manila. The rain was so heavy that, according to Purkey, "it was like being in a submarine with wings." Typhoon Pamela beat against the plane, but its Garrett engines never faltered. In less than three minutes, the sharp snout of the Lear Jet poked through the overcast, and they reached cruise altitude. Throughout the climb, Purkey constantly checked visually for ice. Although there was some talk of accumulation, it wasn't hazardous yet. The deicing system was coping well. At 41,000 feet, *200 Yankee* leveled off and headed for Wake. To everyone's relief, the flight would be nonstop, though there was some talk of stopping at Saipan. That was where, according to one version of Amelia Earhart's fate, she had been taken and subsequently executed by the Japanese.

The flight computer showed an ETE (Estimated Time Enroute) Wake of three and a half hours, and slightly less than five hours' fuel remaining. Of the crew, only Purkey had been there before. For Serling, the stop was a sentimental one. At each stop along the way, he had been passing out souvenirs—shoulder patches, tie tacs, Zippo lighters. Early in the flight, he glanced ahead at Bob Lewis's instructions for Wake and came across the sentence: "Try to save a couple of tie tacs and lighters for the guys on Wake. They lead a pretty lonely existence out there." Serling quietly appropriated about half the supply of tacs and lighters and kept them hidden until *200 Yankee* landed. When the welcoming ceremony was over, he gave them away.

They left behind them a special silver plaque from the Aviation/Space Writers Association honoring the heroes of Wake Island in World War II. Someone had given Palmer a lei made of golf balls. He got a fancier version in Hawaii, but he remembers this gift fondly.

200 Yankee was on its way to Hawaii—the ninth and last landing before the final leg to Denver. It was between Wake and Honolulu that the crew encountered the only mechanical discrepancy of the trip. The word *discrepancy*, rather than "malfunction," is deliberate. During one of his frequent fuel checks, Bir discovered that the selector knob on the fuel indicator had worked loose. Purkey tightened the knob with a screwdriver. If the Lear Jet was the epitome of reliability, it was also involved in an endurance contest; after 45 hours, it was still doing its job. It was the humans inside who were wearing down.

Palmer was so tired he was beginning to have spells; he had to get some sleep. Purkey took over. But when Serling went forward to ask Bir if they had picked up tailwind, he found that Bir, too, had dozed off. After some persuasion, he joined Palmer in the rear cabin. Serling, who used to joke that he held the world's record for crashing flight simulators, had finally gotten to sit in the cockpit. "Actually," he said, "my main job was to make sure Purkey didn't fall asleep, too. Just when I figured I was looking like John Wayne and [trying to remember] all I had learned from watching *The High and the Mighty* 12 times, Arnie came back to the cockpit. So much for Walter Mitty."

"I feel better," Arnie proclaimed. "You and Bir should have stayed away longer," Purkey said. "While you guys were asleep, we finally picked up a tailwind." They had indeed picked one up, though not enough to remove all their fatigue. Not even the pleasantries of the arrival in Honolulu lessened their impatience to get on with the last leg. That leg—3,353 miles—would be in daylight.

Despite Purkey's efforts to straighten up the cabin, it looked like the site of a garage sale. At Honolulu, he had to make room for more gifts and the most sumptuous food of the entire flight. The rear of the Lear Jet was crammed.

All the fatigue and lack of sleep, all the concentration seemed to evaporate as they took off from Honolulu. Hawaii to Denver would be the longest hop of the flight, but nobody cared. *200 Yankee* was heading home!

From the flight observer's log:

. . . somebody gave Arnie two bottles of champagne and a can of caviar at Honolulu. We taped the bottles to the inside of the cabin door to cool, but they are never opened and neither is the caviar. Everyone is too excited . . . the radio interviews . . . are in full swing, starting off with David Hartman of ABC TV's "Good Morning America" show. It's dawning on me . . . that the flight is really news. Arnie has been accepting each interview request with good-natured grace, even though he obviously would rather be concentrating on flight duties. . . . The questions are almost identical—where are you now? How do you feel? Any difficulties thus far? And the inevitable one, asked in a half-embarrassed, half-supercilious tone: Will this flight affect your golf game?

Purkey summed up the feelings of everyone as *200 Yankee* neared San Francisco: "You know, they say the romance has gone out of aviation. The hell it has—and we've just proved it!"

At 5:53 P.M. MDT, *200 Yankee* reached the west coast of the United States. They continued east, heading for Denver. As they passed from one air traffic control center to another, the unseen controllers got into the spirit of the flight. Salt Lake City, for example, acknowledged a transponder signal with: "Hey, Arnie—we've got a couple of good golf courses down here." This was followed by, "Say, *200 Yankee*, you have an SR-71 at nine o'clock. He'll cross about 50 miles ahead of you." Everyone aboard *200 Yankee* strained to see the SR-71, without success. "What kind of record is *he* after?" Palmer asked Salt Lake. "Don't know, but he's doing 1,679 knots at 60,000 feet." Suddenly the Lear Jet seemed almost obsolete.

Denver took over the world flight, adding its own invitation to come down there and play some golf. Forty-five minutes out of Denver, Palmer remarked. "It feels like we left San Francisco six hours ago." The fatigue was beginning to show again, but as they had on so many other occasions, the crew resorted to jokes to relieve the mounting tension of homecoming. During the approach to Denver, there was a last-minute flurry of communications, messages, and instructions—including a message from Palmer to the Gates factory in Wichita. "This particular airplane has something outstanding," Palmer told the workers at the plant. He wasn't just making a public relations speech; he had fallen in love with the Lear Jet 36A. To Bir and Purkey, both Learjet employees, the plane was something they took almost for granted. To Serling, it was part of a memory just beginning. To Arnold Palmer, *200 Yankee* was a living, breathing creature deserving of affection in the same proportions as its dependability on the world flight.

Among those waiting in Denver was a man who had as much, and probably more, at stake in the success of the flight as anyone, Harry

Combs, the genial president of Gates Learjet. Combs had much in common with Palmer's go-for-broke golfing strategy, and nowhere was it more apparent than in his approval of a flight that laid an airplane's reputation on the line. Having deliberately remained in the background before the flight, he could not resist indulging in banter with the crew as the world flight neared completion.

The Lear Jet began its descent. In the control tower at Stapleton, ATC gave *200 Yankee* both final approach clearance and clearance to make a low-level pass by the tower. The jet descended rapidly and flashed by the tower, heading west. It was 0149:48 GMT. They had flown around the world in 57 hours, 25 minutes, and 19 seconds. As Palmer put the plane in a climbing turn and headed for Arapahoe County Airport, the crew began to relax. Over loudspeakers at Arapahoe, as well as a public address system at the Gates factory in Wichita, came Palmer's voice: "This is two hundred Yankee. We have set a new course record!"

The crowd heard the Lear Jet before they saw it. Like a white-and-red meteor, *200 Yankee* made one pass, then another. Finally, it banked toward the runway, eased off, and touched down.

What had they accomplished by making the flight? "Exactly what we hoped to accomplish," Serling said in his log, written between San Francisco and Denver,

> starting with the speed record itself. We helped celebrate our country's 200th anniversary in a spectacular way—through the air. For what other industry, what other endeavor, so typifies the progress this nation has made over the past two centuries as aviation does? *200 Yankee* wasn't just an airplane but a symbol of technological progress, of a private enterprise achievement. We "showed the flag," . . . not in a chauvinistic sense. We didn't wave the Stars and Stripes—we flew them, in peace and with pride. We gave the Aviation/Space Writers Association meeting a sense of duty, of common interest, it never before had. We provided some prestige, some awareness of an organization dedicated to objective coverage of aviation. . . .
>
> We made . . . new friends for a nation that is too often misunderstood, misinterpreted and unappreciated. . . . this was due [in great part] to Arnie; he's an American who's also something of a world citizen. Conversely, we are taking back with us a new appreciation of a . . . fact too often forgotten: people are pretty much alike in all countries. . . . There was a common bond, demonstrated in the warmth, courtesy and open friendship with which we were received.
>
> Finally, the crew received much more than it gave. The friendship we felt at every stop was magnified [in] the plane. . . . Four strangers climbed aboard *200 Yankee* [on] May 17. Four comrades will be climbing off when we land. . . . Somehow, that seems more important to us than even the speed record we'll set. . . .

Aviation records are made to be broken, it seems. The world record for the class of business jets set by Palmer and his crew in 1976 was broken by a Gulfstream III. The twin-engine jet left Teterboro Airport, New Jersey, on January 9, 1982, and returned 47 hours, 39 minutes, and 3 seconds later. Christened *The Spirit of America*, the plane carried a crew of four and six passengers, and made stops at Geneva, Bahrain, Singapore, Guam, Hawaii, and Chicago. The crew experienced no mechanical difficulties and no problems caused by bad weather. Their distance was 23,314 miles, at an average cruising speed of 535 mph. This flight by Harold Curtis, William Mack, Robert Dannhardt (pilots), and Lee Weems (mechanic) reflects the state of the art of engines and aircraft at that point in aviation history.

As if to underscore this statement, a Piper Cheyenne III turboprop owned by the G and H Steel Service Company of Philadelphia and named *Steel Away*, departed on a record-setting global journey for its weight class

The crew of a Gulfstream round-the-world flight pose in the "front office" of their Gulfstream III business jet named *The Spirit of America*. They made their record trip in 1982 in 47 hours, 39 minutes, 3 seconds, accompanied by Robert Dann-hardt and Lee Weems. Shown are Harold Curtis (left), aviation department manager, and William Mack, both pilots for National Distillers and Chemical Corp. (Gulfstream American Corp. photo)

from the city of Brotherly Love for Goose Bay on March 19, 1982. It returned by way of the Marshall Islands, Hawaii, and San Francisco, landing at the takeoff point on March 23. The flight was completed in 109 hours, 23 minutes, and 7 seconds for an average speed of 215.67 mph. Crew members were Robert E. Reinhold, Donald Grant, and Frank Peruello.

At the Paris Air Show in 1985, Allen E. Paulson, chairman of the board of Gulfstream Aerospace Corporation, announced that his company was producing the Gulfstream IV, a new, sophisticated business jet and that he intended to fly it personally two years later to set a round-the-world speed record *westbound*, against the prevailing winds. He stated he would leave Le Bourget Airport in June, during the 1987 Paris Air Show, and return to Paris in less than 45.5 hours.

The odds were against Paulson carrying out his pledge. The Gulfstream IV was still in the preproduction phase and had not yet been flight tested. Besides, there would be strong head winds most of the way around in the Northern Hemisphere at that time of year. The challenge would be to seek the lowest head winds and the shortest route within the FAI/NAA rules, which require a minimum distance of 22,858.754 statute miles (19,851.44 nautical miles or 36,787.599 kilometers) to qualify for a record.

To keep the number of fuel stops to four, the G-IV had an extra fuel tank installed and the interior reduced to a couple of seats and a divan. Advance arrangements were made at each planned stop to ensure the fastest possible refueling and turn-around times; rehearsals were held with the ground crews that would be in place at each airfield. The route selected was finalized after experts made a long-range prediction of the weather and winds to be expected over the stages to be flown. At each of the chosen airfields, Gulfstream personnel were sent ahead to work with local organizations to ensure a minimum of delay in refueling and clearing customs.

Paulson; cocaptains John Salamankas, Jeff Bailey, and K. C. Edgecomb; and crew chief C.B. Allen, along with Everett Langworthy, the NAA observer, departed Paris on June 12, 1987. The planned stops were to be made at Edmonton, Canada; Midway Island; Kota Kinabalu, Malaysia; and Dubai, United Arab Emirates.

The flight was routine to Canada and Midway Island with turn-around times of 18 minutes and 21 minutes, respectively. There were some anxious moments on the next leg, however. After leaving Midway, the crew monitored weather reports from Singapore which showed fair weather at Kota Kinabalu, but an hour or so before the arrival time there, the local controller said that visibility was only 50 meters in heavy rain, much too low to attempt an approach. The alternate airport was Brunei, about 100

Allen E. Paulson, chairman and CEO of Gulfstream Corporation, is the first pilot to hold eastbound and westbound world-circling records. Flying his company's Gulfstream IV, he set the westbound record of 45 hours, 25 minutes, 10 seconds during the 1987 Paris Air Show. The following year, he set a new eastbound record of 36 hours, 8 minutes, 34 seconds. (Gulfstream Aerospace photo)

miles away; unfortunately, no advance arrangements had been made there for rapid refueling. Luckily, just before the decision had to be made to divert to Brunei, the weather cleared and the landing was made as planned.

The tired but happy Gulfstream executive and his crew returned to Le Bourget to the cheers of hundreds of air show visitors. The total elapsed time was 45 hours, 25 minutes, 10 seconds over the 22,886.451 statute-mile course. This established two records for speed around the world west-bound in Class C.1 and C.1k, Group III aircraft. No other round-the-world speed flight for a record in that direction had ever been attempted previously. In addition, the flight set 22 city-to-city world speed records. Paulson had not only set the record westbound but had beaten the east-bound, with-the-wind record set in a Gulfstream III by Brooke Knapp in 1983 (see Chapter 17). Paulson had proven that his new aircraft, the latest in the Gulfstream stable designed especially for business travelers, had the range and reliability for fast world travel.

The Gulfstream absolute speed record was not going to stay on the books for long. Clay Lacy, a friend of Paulson's, set a new eastbound record of 36 hours, 54 minutes, 15 seconds in a Boeing 747 in January 1988 (see Chapter 24). But Paulson was confident that the Gulfstream IV could beat it flying eastward as Lacy had done.

"The Boeing record made us knuckle down and do everything possible to cut that time. We knew the Gulfstream IV was faster, and we'd had experience in keeping ground turn-around times short on other record flights. We wanted to challenge Clay's record but without feeling cocky. Once you hold a record, you hate to see it go."

The edge to the Gulfstream would lie in the tailwinds, which are always greatest in the Northern Hemisphere in the winter. Paulson decided he would go in late February 1988, when the tailwinds were pre-dicted to be at maximum speed. Paulson chose as his cocaptains Robert K. Smythe, Jefferson M. Bailey, and John Salamankas. Again, Everett Lan-gworthy was the NAA observer. It was decided that no flight engineer would go along this time; instead, two mechanics and a pilot would be waiting at each stop. The schedule would be so tight that any deviation or slowdown at any of the four stops would cause the record to be lost.

The aircraft, taken off the assembly line at Savannah, Georgia, had only about 15 hours of flight time on it; it was modified as the other G-IV had been with the installation of an auxiliary fuel tank, a couch, and two reclining chairs. The galley was furnished minimally with cookies, dehy-drated soups, candy, and a large tank of drinking water. The aircraft was painted and christened *Pursuit of Excellence*, the Gulfstream company's motto.

The route this time called for a departure from Hobby Airport, Hous-ton, Texas, with stops at Shannon, Ireland; Dubai, United Arab Emirates; Taipei, Republic of China; and Maui, Hawaii. Again, the turn-around teams were rehearsed before departing for their four stop locations.

Paulson and his crew departed Houston on February 26, 1988. Flying northeastward on the 3,937-mile trek across the Atlantic, the hoped-for tailwinds did not materialize. The indicated Mach of 0.865 to 0.875 was not good enough. Could they cruise at a higher Mach number?

The Gulfstream IV, current holder of the world record for globe-circling. (Gulfstream Aerospace photo)

They did. After a smooth refueling at Shannon, the G-IV averaged 565 knots on the flight to Dubai, well above the average of 548 knots needed to eclipse the record for the rest of the flight, including turn-around time. It would still be touch-and-go, especially when the crew learned that Taipei was overcast at 900 feet, which would mean a night landing. The leg was flown over China, an advantage over previous world-flight attempts, because The People's Republic of China had consistently refused overflight permission. They flew this third leg at Mach 0.87, made an instrument approach at Taipei, and were able to make a 21-minute turn-around before they were off on the next and longest leg to Maui.

Tailwinds across the Pacific averaged over 100 knots and were as high as 150 knots for several hours. They averaged a ground speed of 591 knots and the record now seemed in reach. To make the final run of more than 3,500 miles from Maui, Paulson inched the throttles up to Mach 0.88 and streaked home for a landing at Houston on February 27, 36 hours, 8 minutes, 34 seconds after liftoff. Average speed, including ground time, over the 23,047-mile course was 554.16 knots (637.71 mph). Paulson had beaten his friend Lacy's record by 45.41 minutes.

Will this absolute speed record be beaten? Probably. But it will take an airplane as fast or faster than the Gulfstream IV, strong tailwinds, an efficient organization, and excellent flight planning to do it. And there is the FAI/NAA one percent rule to be considered. Whoever tries to beat the Paulson record will have to shave 22 minutes off his record time. Maybe, if someone could eliminate one fuel stop . . . ?

Einar S. Pedersen and Thor Tjontveit, Norwegians by birth, had a different reason for a world flight in a plane used normally for business purposes. "Our flight was not a record flight," he told the author, "but a commercial attempt to prove that a business airplane could be utilized over the Antarctic area as well as over the North Polar area safely if everything was well planned and operated by a crew with polar experience."

Both men had that experience. Pedersen had been a navigator with the Scandinavian Airlines System (SAS) since 1946 and became instrumental in encouraging the airline to fly over the polar regions to shorten the distances from Europe to the United States and the Far East. Test flights began in 1952 and continued through 1957 when two SAS DC-7Cs met over the North Pole, one having departed from Copenhagen and the other from Tokyo, thus proving that commercial flights could be made over the Arctic efficiently and on schedule. Pedersen gained considerable experience navigating the polar route and started classes in polar navigation for pilots and navigators of SAS and other airlines. He wrote a textbook on polar navigation, and a popular book about his experiences, titled *Polar Pathfinder*, was published in Norway and Sweden; the English version will be published by the University of Alaska Press.

During this period, he had wanted to fly in a small aircraft over the Arctic Ocean to study the polar ice from a low altitude and to determine if it might be possible for surface craft to transit the Arctic. He was transferred by SAS to its base at Anchorage, Alaska, in 1962 and navigated the route regularly from there to Tokyo and Scandinavia.

Pedersen married Ingrid Liljegran, a pilot since 1957, who had an Air

Transport License (ATP) and wanted to share her husband's love of arctic flying. They bought a single-engine Cessna 205, named it *Snow Goose*, and had extra gas tanks installed that gave it a fuel capacity to fly for 30 hours. On July 29, 1963, they departed Fairbanks, Alaska, flew over the North Pole, and landed at Station Nord on Greenland 21 hours later. Ingrid Pedersen thus became the first woman to pilot a plane over the North Pole. Next day, they made the 11.5-hour flight to Bodo, Norway.

Meanwhile, the Pedersens had met Thor Tjontveit, a pilot with Wien Alaska Airlines, who also became interested in polar flying. Thor asked Einar to navigate for him from Alaska to Norway in an amphibious Cessna 185 in 1965. This led to a number of ferry flights for Thor and Ingrid from the Cessna factory in Wichita to Norway. When Cessna produced the 206 model, Thor established a Cessna agency in Oslo, Norway. By this time, he had accumulated 8,000 hours of flying time, while Einar had logged 19,000 flying hours as a navigator, 9,000 hours of it over the SAS Arctic Ocean route.

Thor Tjontveit, pilot (left), and Einar Pedersen, navigator, pose before boarding their Cessna 421 for the flight from Invergargill, New Zealand, to McMurdo, Antarctica. (Courtesy Einar S. Pedersen)

Einar Pedersen poses beside the Cessna 421 at McMurdo Sound, Antarctica. Mount Erebus, a mildly active volcano, is in the background. They landed on all seven continents to establish an aviation "first" in 1970. (Courtesy Einar S. Pedersen)

In late 1969, Pedersen and pilots Tjontveit and Erik Sandberg decided to enter a race to celebrate the fiftieth anniversary of the original 12,000-mile London-to-Sydney air race in 1919 with a new Cessna 421, an excellent six-place aircraft for business travel, loaned by the company. The 421 had two turbo supercharged piston engines and was pressurized to give it a service ceiling of 25,000 feet. The latest available radio, weather radar, navigation, and survival equipment was installed. The understanding was that after the race they would attempt to fly over both poles. En route, they agreed to make demonstration flights for potential buyers of Cessna aircraft. Sandberg made the necessary arrangements for landing, overflight permissions, and refueling.

They named themselves *The Flying Vikings* and added the name Roald Amundsen, the famous Norwegian explorer, on the plane's nose. The race was arranged to give the 100 different competing aircraft calculated handicaps so that every plane would have a possible chance of winning. Mandatory stops had to be made at Athens, Karachi, Calcutta, Singapore, Darwin, Alice Springs, and Adelaide; intermediate stops were allowed for

Einar S. Pedersen (left) and Thor Tjontveit visit the barber's pole that marks the exact position of the South Pole, January 1970. (Courtesy Einar S. Pedersen)

the smaller aircraft with one hour allotted for refueling at every landing. En route they flew through violent tropical storms day and night which made the radio compasses all but useless, but Einar was able to steer courses around them with the help of their radar. Their Cessna, Air Race No. 107, landed on the grass field at Adelaide on December 22, 1969. They had logged 52 hours and 30 minutes of flight in an elapsed time of only 57 hours.

The trio placed third overall in the race among their class of planes with piston engines. They received a prize of 2,500 Australian dollars, enough to pay for the fuel to the South Pole. After a few days' rest, they left Sandberg behind, and Pedersen and Tjontveit continued to Auckland and Christchurch, New Zealand. They applied for permission to land at the McMurdo base where the U.S. Navy Antarctic Support Group was in charge of flying operations. But they were temporarily denied landing permission because Max Conrad, the famous "Flying Grandfather," was on his own world flight over both poles and had already been given permission to land at McMurdo. Because of failures on two previous attempts to fly over the South Pole, when Conrad took off for the third try, the Navy authorized a four-engine Hercules transport to escort him

The *Roald Amundsen* flown by Einar Pedersen and navigator Thor Tjontveit, known as *The Flying Vikings*, are welcomed at the South Pole base by Navy personnel. Their Cessna is believed to be the first aircraft to land and take off from the South Pole landing area on wheels. (Courtesy Einar S. Pedersen)

from Christchurch to McMurdo and then to the South Pole, even though the admiral in charge thought Max was not well enough prepared for such a flight. Pedersen and Tjontveit felt they were much better qualified because of their experience and more sophisticated navigation equipment. They asked for help from Walter Hickel, then Alaska's governor, to intercede with the Navy on their behalf in Washington to allow them to proceed.

After Max left New Zealand for Antarctica, the Pentagon approved the flight for *The Flying Vikings* when they demonstrated the considerable navigation capabilities of the plane and its occupants. However, Pedersen and Tjontveit had to agree that they would not depart New Zealand until Conrad had reached the South Pole station.

When word was received that Max was at the Amundsen-Scott South Pole station, *The Flying Vikings* flew to the McMurdo base and then to the pole airstrip in perfect flying weather. Conrad was still there but was asleep, and they didn't want to disturb him. They stayed for only two and a half hours. They were concerned that the engines would be difficult to start in the subzero temperature and that if the weather turned bad, they could be delayed for many days. They weren't able to meet Max Conrad before they left for the return trip to McMurdo, their departure point for Chile. They made a smooth takeoff and thus became the first to land an aircraft at the pole station on wheels and take off again safely.

The leg to Chile was the longest they would fly, and they were prepared for it. The normal range of the 421 was 1,520 nautical miles, not enough to fly the extra 1,200 miles to the airport in Punta Arenas, Chile. However, before departure from Oslo, they had two large tanks installed in the cabin to give the plane 21 total hours of flight capability.

Pedersen and Tjontveit were delayed at McMurdo for several days because of the weather and finally left on January 23, 1970. As they were en route from McMurdo, they heard a radio report about Max Conrad's crash at the South Pole station. (See his story in Chapter 14.)

The Flying Vikings landed at Punta Arenas's Chabunco Airport after 19 hours in the air. They continued to Argentina, Uruguay, Brazil, and via the West Indies to the Cessna factory in Wichita, then on to Seattle and through vicious snowstorms over the North Pole to Oslo in February 1970, two months and 172 flying hours after they had left on the air race to Australia.

"It had not been a record flight," Pedersen said. "But that had not been our intention. We just wanted to show that if a flight could be made safely over the Antarctic with a small twin-engine airplane, then there was every reason to start preparing for the commencement of the trans-Antarctic air route from Australia to South America and South Africa with modern business aircraft and passenger airliners."

22

DON TAYLOR AND JON JOHANSON: HOMEBUILT EARTHROUNDERS

If any prizes were given for tenacity, retired Air Force Lt. Col. Donald P. Taylor would certainly be in contention. He wanted to be the first pilot in history to fly a homemade airplane around the world. After retirement in 1965, Taylor decided he wanted his name in aviation's record books by doing something no one else had done. Building and flying his own plane wasn't enough. It had to be a first-of-a-kind feat.

Taylor's background in military aviation of 10,000 hours' flying time did not prepare him for building a plane, however, so he enrolled in a course at the Spartan School of Aeronautics, in Tulsa, to learn aircraft construction and small-engine theory, design, and repair. Then he spent six months checking all the available designs for homemade planes. Finally, he narrowed his choice to the T-18, an FAA-approved design by John Thorp. The T-18 was a single-engine "tail dragger" that had been one of the most successful homebuilts in general aviation.

Taylor visited Thorp, a former Lockheed aeronautical engineer in Burbank, California. He was impressed with Thorp's design. Built around a Lycoming 180-hp engine, the T-18 had two features that made it ideal for the hobbyist: a minimum of parts and simple assembly. Thorp opposed Taylor's purpose in building a T-18. "Those overwater legs are too dangerous and too long for this plane," Thorp said. "Besides, you can't get enough redundant equipment in it for safe instrument flight."

Taylor, who had heard that Thorp was the sort of engineer who underestimated his own designs, persisted. After all, he said, others had taken Thorp's basic set of plans and adapted the design. "I had to argue with

258

Former Air Force pilot Don Taylor flying his single-engine, single-seat Thorp T-18 after completing his 1976 world flight. Taylor's trip, the first in a homebuilt plane, took 31 days to cover 24,877 miles. The most dangerous leg was from Midway Island to Adak in the Aleutians. He made a later flight to Australia from California and return in this aircraft. (Don Downie photo)

him and really sell him on the project before he'd sell me a set of plans," Taylor said. "Even then he was skeptical. But I wore him down, and he finally modified the plans so I could take off safely with a load 100 percent over his original design."

Taylor began construction in a garage adjoining his private airport, near Hemet, California. Many of the plane's subassemblies were made in Thorp's shop. He bought a Lycoming engine from Thorp. Soon the plane had been built, and he was in the air giving the T-18 the FAA-required 50 hours of shakedown. His first long-distance flight was a 12.5-hour one from Hemet to Oshkosh, Wisconsin, where he attended a meeting of the Experimental Aircraft Association. After the meeting, he made several modifications. In August 1973, Taylor decided he was ready.

He christened his T-18 *Victoria*, for the only ship in Magellan's fleet to complete the historic voyage of 1622. He reached Japan in 63 days but was forced down in the Aleutians by fierce Arctic weather. Giving up the attempt, he disassembled *Victoria* and had it shipped home by boat.

His discouragement was only temporary, for Taylor made modifications based on his first experience. He decided, for example, that he would take more survival equipment, including oxygen, because he had nearly passed out over the Alps while on instruments above 17,000 feet.

His "survival kit" now also contained a two-passenger life raft, flares, a thermal blanket, and fishing gear. The normal 30-gallon fuel tank was supplemented by one of 115 gallons, bringing the total capacity to 145 gallons. The normal takeoff weight of 1,500 pounds was increased to 2,150. Three years after his first attempt, Taylor was ready to try again. Rechristening the 20.5-foot-long T-18 *Victoria 76*, Taylor decided to start and end his flight at Wittman Field, near Oshkosh. He painted the plane in gaudy colors so it could be seen against any terrain.

At 9:35 A.M., August 1, 1976, Taylor lined up on Wittman's Runway 18. Before him lay a flight of 26,200 miles. Takeoff was surprisingly easy for the heavily fueled T-18, and so was the 730-mile trip to Burlington, Vermont, where he remained overnight. The next day he pushed on to Moncton, New Brunswick, Canada. Clearing Canadian customs, he received permission to reenter Canada at the end of the flight. Taylor flew to Goose Bay, Labrador, where he was held up for two days waiting for the weather to improve. While he waited, he met some people who were flying to Europe in a light, twin-engine plane, and they all decided to take off together on the fourth.

The two planes were cleared to Narsarssuak, Greenland; it was the second-longest leg of Taylor's world flight. He compared the flight to a trip to Narsarssuak three years earlier:

> Last time I just sailed up the fjord, circled the field and landed. . . . This time I was IFR the last 100 miles in. I let down on the Sumatak beacon . . . turning back out to sea as I descended. I could see about half a mile, so I turned back into the beacon and flew back about half as long as I had flown out. I never was able to see the cliff walls of the fjord . . . so I turned back and headed out to sea again. I called Sumatak and told [the Danish controllers] I would have to divert to my alternate.

As he did so, Taylor radioed the plane he had left Goose Bay with. The pilot was holding at 9,000 feet to see if Taylor could make it into the fjord before trying it himself. "The twin kept asking how I was doing," Taylor said.

> I told him I couldn't make it, that I thought we ought to head north. He said, "Thank you" and started calling for a change in his clearance. The Danes instructed him to maintain 9,000 feet up the coast to the Kook Islands and from there to head inland to Sonderstrom; 9,000 feet is the minimum for overflying the Greenland ice cap, so I crawled up from sea level to that

altitude also and headed north. Pretty soon I began to notice some ice build-ing up [on] the airplane . . . then a little more . . . and then it began to snow.

Things were beginning to get uncomfortable. It was 400 miles to Sonder-strom and I couldn't tell the Danes about the ice because this would panic them. . . . I probably couldn't have gotten in a word anyway. The pilot of the twin had his wife and another couple on board and was really hollering about the ice he was picking up.

So I just turned 90° to the ice cap and went out and down for about 10 minutes. At about 4,000 feet the ice melted, just like that, and I finally broke out at 3,000. Off to the right were the Greenland cliffs. . . . I could see for four or five miles, so I turned and began to follow the coastline north. I was quite happy about how things were going, but my friend in the twin was still hollering! I called him (and the Danish controllers), saying I had found a hole and had descended to 3,000 where I was in the clear.

At the Kook Islands a Danish helicopter pilot came up on the radio say-ing he had just come over from Sonderstrom and that at 5,000 feet he could see five or six miles. He also told me the heading from the Kook Islands to Sonderstrom was 54°. I looked at my chart and found that it stopped at the Kook Islands! Because of the crowded conditions in the . . . cockpit, I stored the charts I wasn't using under the seat cushion and sat on them. At the weight I was carrying on this trip, I couldn't turn loose of the stick long enough to retrieve them. So, I had little choice but to . . . head up and over the glacier . . . and hope the helicopter pilot wasn't feeding me a line.

At this point I realized I hadn't asked how far it was to Sonderstrom, but it really didn't matter because I was committed. I had now been in the air for over eight hours and with the fuel I had left there was no going back to Canada. After about 30 minutes I tuned my ADF and hoped. Then "zip," the needle locked on and about 10 minutes later there the runway was—right over the next hill. What a beautiful sight!

Taylor stayed overnight at Sonderstrom. On August 6, he took off for Keflavik. He climbed to 10,000 feet, over the Greenland ice cap, then to 15,000, where he went on oxygen. "I was cruising along and everything was OK," he said. "But after a while a big cloud showed up right in my path. I didn't want to fly through it because I knew I would get icing again. But I couldn't get over or around it . . . when I looked back, clouds were building up there, too. Finally I noticed my outside air temperature and I read minus 27°. I . . . sailed right into that cloud. It was so cold, it . . . couldn't ice! All that happened there was . . . my toes were real cold. . . . After four hours I thought I was going to lose my toes."

He stayed overnight at Keflavik, then took off for Glasgow on what he hoped would be a point-to-point, record-setting leg. It was; his speed, helped by a brisk tailwind, was 160 mph for the 830-mile distance. After a night there, he flew to Leeds-Bradford, England, and the next day cleared for Venice. His departure from Leeds-Bradford was covered by

British television, which later paid off in an unusual way and contributed to the success of the flight.

Although Taylor had filed a flight plan for Venice, over Munich he encountered rain, which soon turned into sleet and then ice. Deciding the T-18 could not carry the extra load over the Alps, he landed at Munich. Three days later, after deciding to bypass Venice, he filed a flight plan for Brindisi, Italy, on the Adriatic. As he cruised down the west coast of Italy, the weather cleared. As he approached Brindisi, however, his itinerary suddenly changed. In fractured English an air controller was shouting over the radio what sounded like "No gassabrindisi! No gassabrindisi!" After several such messages, Taylor realized he was being told there was no fuel at Brindisi. He had a good reserve, so he refiled for Kerkira, Greece. After Kerkira, he flew to Larnaca, Cyprus, then to Diyarbakir, Turkey, and Teheran. All went well until he entered the traffic pattern. "Teheran was bad three years ago," he recalled, "but today it was even worse."

> Before, I had trouble getting in, but this time I darn near got myself killed! I was cleared for a final approach—and then was asked to make an ADF approach. . . . I didn't have the plate out and I didn't know the approach so I couldn't comply. So the controller said, "OK, go . . . go! Go!"
>
> All at once, swish, a . . . Hercules . . . went right under me! I turned and looked over my shoulder and could see two F-4 fighters coming around the corner . . . and a 747 behind them! I decided I better get . . . on the ground and out of the way. I got down and turned off in about 1,000 feet.
>
> Once on the ground I had a little trouble with my clearance, understanding the locals and in paying my bills . . . and then there was NOTAM 151100. Before I left the States I had been cleared to land at Teheran, but I was told I would have to comply with NOTAM 151100. The FAA tried for two weeks to find out what the NOTAM said but couldn't. I did [not] learn what it said until I landed. Then they tell me I can't park the airplane there overnight! . . . Here I am in the middle of nowhere and they tell me I can't stay overnight.
>
> Well, I just hid the T-18 under some large Iranian airplane . . . no one noticed me.

Taylor departed Teheran on August 17, cleared for Zahedan, Iran, a distance of 710 miles.

> Last time I had cleared direct to Zahedan right out over the desert. This time I . . . met an Irishman in Teheran who had been flying in there for about 30 years. He told me, "No way! You don't fly across that desert." Then he told me . . . horror stories about [it being] the worst desert in the world . . . I had cruised across without giving it a thought. . . . Now he had me worried. So, I took the Irishman's advice, overflying three cities on the way.

> At 15,000 feet I was in such turbulence that I almost lost the airplane. I've never seen anything like [the haze]. I was solidly on the gauges for about 500 miles. Most deserts are blessed with clear air, but this one . . . the Irishman was right, it *is* the worst desert in the world.

Taylor stayed overnight in Zahedan, then left for Karachi.

> Troubles start now. I'm back in the Middle East. . . . It's the same old thing, except that now they have improved their tactics! It took me three hours to get into Karachi and five hours to get out. It got so bad that finally I went to one of the guys there and said, "I just don't know how to get out of your airport." He took me to an "agent" who said, "Yes, I can get you out of here—for $30." He literally took me by the hand and led me through the bureaucratic obstacle course. . . . It took about an hour. The agent's fee . . . included a little grease for the palms of those officials who wouldn't give me the time of day when I was muddling through on my own.

From Karachi, Taylor flew to Ahmadabad, then Nagpur and Calcutta. At Calcutta, he encountered bureaucratic delays, and these too were cleared up when he hired an "agent."

The Calcutta-to-Bangkok leg was easy, as were those to Kuala Lumpur, Kuching, and Kota Kinabalu, all in Malaysia. On August 26, he flew to Zamboanga and Davao, in the Philippines. The next day, he departed for Yap Island. "Starting with this leg I began the long overwater flying. I couldn't get a forecast out of Davao, so I set out by dead reckoning. I flew to Yap by way of Palau—with a 30° correction to make when I finally raised Yap. Yap was my first landing on a coral runway. Only one airplane was based there. . . . The pilot let me put the [T-18] in his hangar that night."

The Yap–Guam leg was only 515 miles.

> The base commander put all of his facilities at my disposal for the maintenance I needed to do on the airplane. Members of the Guam-Agana Naval Aero Club couldn't do enough for me. Their mechanic actually made a set of brake pucks for the T-18!
>
> Finally, on the 31st, I headed for Truk. . . . I'm a fiddler. No matter how far out I am, I start fiddling with the ADF. . . . About 100 miles out of Guam I tried Truk and got nothing. . . . Then . . . I tried Guam. Again, nothing. I heard Guam's signal but the needle wouldn't track. I made the only decision I could make out there—return to Guam. I hated to do it, but there was no choice. The ADF was my lifeline. . . .
>
> Back at Guam I discovered the problem. . . . When I had installed the loop on the bottom of the airplane and had installed the plug [in] it, I [didn't] push it in all the way. . . . About one-eighth of the pins were

exposed, [and they] had corroded. The radioman there helped me clean everything up and it worked fine.

Taylor flew to Truk and then Ponape, where he learned something about the weather and local work customs:

> Just out of Ponape, I called in and was told the airport had light rain. I landed and the rain was light at the numbers. At midfield it was moderate. At the turnoff it was pouring so hard I couldn't see the nose of the airplane! I managed to taxi to the ramp . . . but the tower would not tell me where to park. Finally, I just stopped right in front of [a Continental airliner]. Then they told me what [to] do with it. Here educated people won't work with their hands, so no one would help me park. . . . The pilot and copilot of the jet finally helped me.
>
> The long legs were coming up now. My course was laid out to fly to Wake via Eniwetok, where the Air Force has a beacon. This way I would have a definite fix before heading out over a really long stretch of [water]. As I [approached] Eniwetok I was fiddling with the ADF again, listening to the identifier, when right in the middle of it—zap!—right off the air!
>
> Here I am, 300 miles from nowhere. My first thought was . . . the ADF had gone out on me. . . . I had been in contact with Guam, so I called and asked [them to] confirm that Eniwetok was off the air. They soon came back with the news that Eniwetok was . . . off the air. I said, "Please ask Eniwetok to put the station back on." Shortly came the news, "They are pedaling!". . . meaning they had rigged up a temporary generator and were on again which I was able to confirm as my ADF needle jerked into action.
>
> Over Eniwetok I talked to the Air Force and they assured me they would stay on the air until I was on the ground at Wake.
>
> I picked up Wake from 400 miles. . . . Wake is a nice little island manned by 20 Air Force personnel and about 200 Filipinos. . . . The facilities were great, but here my real problems were just beginning!

Taylor now confronted the most critical part of his flight. When he left the United States, he had not received permission to land at Midway, a military installation, or to fly from there to Adak, in the Aleutians, another military base. This was the only possible route, in view of the T-18's range. After Taylor left, friends tried unsuccessfully to secure permission. Now he faced the question, what to do? He could reverse course, or he could fly directly to Hawaii; but that would mean shipping the plane home again—and another failure. A third course of action would be to fly to Midway without clearance and take his chances. In order not to get the commander at Wake in trouble, Taylor filed a flight plan for Hawaii via overflight of Midway. He radioed the Navy in Hawaii one more time but was refused permission to land. He took off on September 5, crossing the international date line. Then, as he approached Midway, he was given landing instructions!

Taylor was immediately surrounded by Navy brass and accused of violating Midway airspace without permission. Arrest, fine, a jail term, and confiscation of his plane were possible, he was told. Messages flew back and forth. According to Jack Cox, editor of *Sport Aviation* magazine, "His plight went all the way back to the Joint Chiefs of Staff in Washington, to the FAA. . . . with pressure being applied by the Experimental Aircraft Association, the Aircraft Owners and Pilots Association, Don's . . . Congressman, his sponsor and many friends. . . . Finally, the Navy went to the National Aeronautic Association (NAA) . . . and worked out an arrangement by which persons on official NAA-sanctioned record flights would be [allowed] to land at Navy installations . . . Don would be the first to obtain such permission."

Shortly after he landed at Midway, Taylor met some British pilots who were flying two patrol bombers on a special mission with the U.S. Navy. One of them asked Taylor if he was "the bloke we saw on TV in England just before we left to fly out here—the one trying to fly around the world in some sort of backyard airplane?" Taylor allowed as how he was, and that he was glad to meet them. Another pilot asked when he was leaving for the Aleutians. "In the morning," Don said.

About an hour later, the British bomber took off. It returned seven hours later. Taylor asked them where they had been. "We just flew a little weather reconnaisance up to Adak and back," he was told. The British pilots had turned over to the Navy the report on their reconnaissance, which gave the winds for the entire 1,650-mile leg to Adak at altitudes of 3,000, 6,000, and 9,000 feet. The Navy made the report available to Taylor.

A few hours later, the crew of a U.S. Navy Lockheed P-3 patrol bomber told Taylor that they were preparing for a flight after his departure, also to Adak. They would overtake him and be in Adak when he arrived. A "coincidental mission," they called it.

The Midway–Adak leg, which replaced the Japan–Aleutians leg of his attempt in 1973, was the emotional high point of Taylor's world flight. Entirely over water, it was, at 1,650 miles, the longest leg by 500 miles. Thus, in addition to the physical distance, it was a significant psychological hurdle. "Jumping off from Midway with a [radio] fix," he recalled, "looking back over my shoulder watching that last speck of land vanish over the horizon, I did wonder . . . if I would make it."

A major obstacle to be overcome as far as navigation was concerned was the strong 10- to 50-knot crosswind Taylor encountered. With only the Navy forecast to rely on, he put a wind-correction factor in his heading for every five degrees of latitude, hoping that would be enough.

Hour after hour went by. Anchorage air traffic control center contacted

Taylor not long after takeoff from Midway and kept in touch every 30 minutes to ensure that he was still airborne. It was a grueling, 11-hour flight. Taylor entertained himself by fiddling with the ADF. When he finally raised Adak, he was within one degree of the proper heading for the airport. "That weather analysis I had received was . . . accurate," he said: "1,650 miles and right on the money!"

He landed at Adak with about a half hour of daylight left. Within minutes, fog rolled in and the airport was closed. After a short rest, Taylor flew to Cold Bay, an Air Force base in the Aleutians, where he stayed overnight. He filed a flight plan for Anchorage. "I pulled a boo-boo here," he said. "I tried to go up over the mountains between King Salmon and Homer, and got into icing conditions again. I was a pretty miserable rascal for about 20 minutes."

> The head of the FAA at Anchorage met me and introduced me to an attractive young lady and a very pleasant fellow. We talked for a minute or two and suddenly it came to me, "I know these people!"
>
> The FAA guy laughed and said, 'These are the two who followed you by radio all the way from Midway to Adak."

From Anchorage, Taylor flew to Whitehorse and Fort Saint John, flying "like the bush pilots—right down over the Alcan Highway." After an overnight stop in Edmonton, "I departed from the downtown industrial airport. . . . after about half an hour the engine got very rough. I turned back and with the situation getting worse by the minute, I decided to declare an emergency and take advantage of the 10,000-foot runway at Edmonton. . . . What a reception I got—the airport manager, the Royal Canadian Mounted Police—and seven fire trucks! In the shop . . . a . . . mechanic . . . diagnosed my problem . . . Fouled spark plugs. I had flown for the last 70 hours or so on 115/145 octane aviation gas, all I could get at the military bases [where I stopped], and the little Lycoming engine just couldn't handle the high lead content. [The] mechanic solved the problem by throwing away my plugs and selling me a good set out of his own airplane!"

Upon Taylor's arrival at Minot, North Dakota, he was welcomed with a party. Then, on September 30, with the wind and the weather in his favor, he flew to Oshkosh, Wisconsin. Cox, who was there, described what happened as Taylor's ETA was announced: "All eyes strained for the first glimpse of the T-18, and finally, there it was, lower than expected, aimed right for the tower. A cheer went up as Don cruised by. Thorp Delta Tango squawked on at 1:48 P.M., about 12 minutes ahead of his ETA, and the deed was done. Don Taylor had become the first person to fly a homebuilt airplane around the world. He was also the first to make the flight solo in a homebuilt and the first to do it in an airplane constructed by the pilot, each a separate entry in the record books."

Taylor's flight had taken 31 days and covered 24,877 miles. He spent 171.5 hours in the air.

Jon Johanson of Adelaide, Australia, probably has the most unlikely personal credentials for a record-setting, round-the-world pilot. He is a registered nurse and specializes in midwifery. He is also a carpenter, manufacturer of specialized aircraft components, author, and professional speaker.

Johanson's first flight was at age seven, when he admits he was immediately hooked on wanting to fly. However, he said he was never very good in grade school and thought he was not smart enough to learn to fly. After graduation he became a carpenter's apprentice. He had a friend who repaired wood gliders for an aero club, and Jon visited the airfield with him. Watching others, who seemed like they weren't much smarter than he was, fly small aircraft made Jon wonder if he could do it, too. Flying lessons were $25.00 an hour; he was making $27.00 a week. He managed to save enough to take lessons every two or three weeks and finally received his pilot license.

The carpentry business dried up, and he enrolled in a nursing course with a local hospital. He graduated with distinction and served two years as a nurse in Cambodia. Afterwards, he settled in Sydney where he worked in several medical clinics and returned to flying in his spare time. He earned an air transport rating and began flying passenger and freight charters all over Australia. He dreamed of owning his own plane and came upon a shop in Darwin where a small two-place, single-engine airplane powered by a 150-hp engine was being assembled. It was designated an RV-4 and could be built by anyone possessing the necessary tools and assembling it according to plans and with parts furnished by Van's Aircraft Company of Aurora, Oregon.

The RV-4 has two seats in tandem and space for baggage. It is designed for an engine of 150–160 hp although a 180-hp engine can be installed. It is capable of aerobatics, and its slow landing speed enables it to get into small airstrips with ease. However, its greatest capabilities are the cruising speed of 140 knots and range of 650 miles.

Caught up in the possibility of building one for himself, Johanson ordered a kit, meanwhile supporting himself as a midwife and studying for a college degree in nursing. Two and a half years later, he made the first test flight in his RV-4 and flew it every chance he got. He was impressed with it because it was "rugged, simple, went fast, went slow, could handle bush strips." He made longer and longer distance flights around Australia that led him to wonder how far the RV really could go if it were modified to carry additional fuel. Could it fly the Pacific from Australia to the United States so he could attend the annual gathering of homebuilt owners at Oshkosh, Wisconsin, the home of the Experimental Aircraft Association? If so, could it then fly around the world?

The RV-4's chief design engineer confirmed it could be modified safely to carry additional fuel, and in 1990 Johanson began to make the necessary changes. The entire backseat area was dedicated to holding a gas tank; the fiberglass wingtips were also converted to hold fuel; and additional space for small tanks was found in the wings, in the fuselage, and behind the instrument panel. The fuel available would thus be sufficient to allow him to stay in the air for more than 18.5 hours and would give the plane a range of 2,000 miles, compared to 650 miles when equipped only with the stock tank. Long-range radio and navigation equipment was installed, plus survival gear, aircraft supplies, and small parts. An oxygen system was installed so Jon could fly above 10,000 feet. The added weight was over the recommended maximum takeoff gross weight in the company's sales literature, but eventually Johanson's modifications were certified by the company's chief engineer for a onetime takeoff weight of 136 percent of the recommended gross weight.

On December 20, 1994, Johanson made a nine-hour, nonstop circuit of southern Australia as a test of the plane's capabilities. He then became the first pilot to fly a homebuilt across the Tasman Sea to Auckland, New Zealand. This success led to seeking sponsors to donate money for anticipated expenses or provide equipment for the flight to America and perhaps around the world.

Jon admitted it was very difficult to "sell" his dream to encourage private cash contributions, and still more difficult to obtain equipment from commercial manufacturers who were leery of publicly supporting the flight because of their concern for their corporate image if he should fail. "But what really touched me," he said, "was the small ten and twenty dollar bits that came from so many regular people. I had New Zealand dollars, Australian dollars, and American dollars, too."

But Johanson's performance and dedication to the idea prevailed. He received a GPS (ground positioning system), new tires, and an autopilot from manufacturers, along with a promise of free gasoline or reimbursement by a major international petroleum company regardless of where he landed. When he felt he had enough cash to pay expenses, he was ready to head to Oshkosh.

On July 2, 1995, Jon left Brisbane on Australia's east coast and flew to Nandi, Pago Pago, and Kiritimati (formerly Christmas Island) before heading for Hawaii. About four hours out of Hilo, the engine began to run rough. Jon says he did not panic. "Being so far from land made life easier," he said. "There was nothing to do but push on; no decisions to

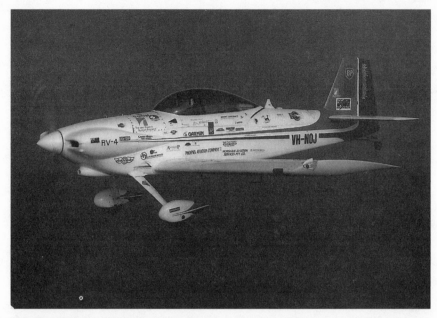

The Van RV-4, built by Jon Johanson over a 30-month period, was modified to hold sufficient fuel for a 2,000-mile flight. Johanson is a nurse with a specialty in midwifery. (Courtesy Jon Johanson)

make, no places to divert to." He reviewed his ditching procedure, checked the GPS readings to be sure he was on course, and flew on. He landed at Hilo on the large island of Hawaii without incident; the rough engine was caused by a cracked exhaust pipe, which was easily repaired.

He was too early for the opening of the Oshkosh air meeting, so he flew on to California where he tarried a few days and then headed north to visit the Van's Aircraft Company plant in Aurora, Oregon. Still early, he flew to Colorado and Missouri before arriving at Oshkosh to find himself a celebrity for having dared the Pacific from "down under" in a homebuilt.

Meanwhile, Jon had decided definitely to fly around the world. He left Oshkosh when the annual gathering of experimental aircraft owners was over, flew to Bangor, Maine, and blessed with good weather, proceeded to the Azores. It was next on to Spain, Britain, Crete, Dubai, India, Singapore, Darwin, and finally across Australia to Melbourne for a triumphant landing on August 31, 1995. For the world flight, he was clocked at a record speed of 18.25 mph (29.37 kmh) for the RV-4 class of light aircraft.

The entire flight was only a warm-up for the Australian nurse. He decided to make a westbound world flight from Australia the following year. He left on June 21, 1996, and crossed the Indian Ocean with stops at Cocos and Mauritius islands, then on to South Africa, Ascension Island, Brazil, Barbados, and the United States. There were stops in Florida, Texas, Colorado, California, and Canada before crossing the Pacific to Hawaii, Pago Pago, Norfolk Island, Sydney, and home to Melbourne on September 25, 1996. He was credited by the FAI with a speed record for his class of aircraft on the westbound world flight of 14.48 mph (23.31 kmh).

Johanson was not finished with flying around the world. He wanted to fly a new route that would take him over the North Pole. On May 16, 2000, he departed the Parafield Airport in Adelaide and flew to Canberra, Lord Howe Island, Tonga, Kiritimati (Christmas Island), and Hilo, Hawaii, where he stayed to rest for six days. He had difficulty with authorities there after he paid an agricultural inspection fee on the day he planned to depart. He didn't leave that day because of the weather and was supposed to pay the fee again the next day, even though the plane hadn't moved an inch from its parking spot. He took off anyway, half expecting to be intercepted by fighter planes, but he wasn't.

Jon Johanson holds the helmet he used on his world flights and his mascot bear "Kingsford" in front of his Van RV-4 homebuilt aircraft. He established eastbound and westbound world records for this type of light aircraft in 1995 and 1996. (Courtesy Jon Johanson)

Johanson's next stops were at Camarillo, California; Van's aircraft factory in Oregon; then on to Kamloops, Salmon Arm, and Eureka, Canada. From there he flew over the North Pole on June 8, 2000, to Spitzbergen. On that flight, with the temperature dropping to -28 degrees, the canopy cracked, and he was threatened with unbearable cold if it shattered. Fortunately, the canopy didn't disintegrate, and he had it replaced at the first opportunity. Looking back over the hundreds of hours of long-distance flying, he says his flight over the North Pole was one of the most perilous he ever made.

Johanson next flew to Norway, Denmark, France, and England. He spent three weeks in England and Scotland on holiday and then flew back to the United States via Iceland. He made a number of stops before revisiting Van's factory in Oregon and then headed for the Atlantic crossing via Bangor, Maine. He flew 2,000 miles to the Azores, followed by a stop at Tenerife in the Canary Islands and a landing at Accra in Ghana. He had difficulty obtaining oxygen to fill his bottle there but obtained help from Ghana Airways. He then found that he needed a liter of engine oil, and it took some time for sympathetic friends to find it for him. Next, he wanted to get off before dark to avoid a $250 charge for having the airport lights turned on.

"I was looking at the longest flight, timewise, I had ever tackled," he noted in his web site diary. "On top of that I had to get past Angola. I had heard many stories about Angola and none of them were good, but to get around their airspace would require me to go a long way out to sea. I had been told that the only safe way was to keep everything off—lights, transponder, etc.—and go overnight. I still filed my flight plan saying I was going around Angolan airspace but had every intention of going the shortest way possible.

"The reality in this part of the world is simple. You are on your own. I knew only too well that if I was to go for a swim no one would come looking for me, so the flight plan was simply to keep the paperwork in order." He paid the lighting fee and left after dark for Walvis Bay, Namibia, then flew south to Cape Town and four other stops in South Africa before heading for the islands of Reunion, Mauritius, Rodrigues, and Cocos in the Indian Ocean. He returned home to Adelaide via Karratha and Port Lincoln. He had traveled 47,576 meandering statute miles to complete his third world flight. He had been airborne for 332 hours.

Johanson applied for a world aviation record from Adelaide-to-Adelaide over the North Pole but the Australian Sport Aviation Confederation, the counterpart organization to America's NAA, refused to grant it, allegedly because he did not have an observer on the ground at the pole to affirm his passage. His last high frequency radio message reporting his position was 20 minutes short of the pole, but he was subsequently

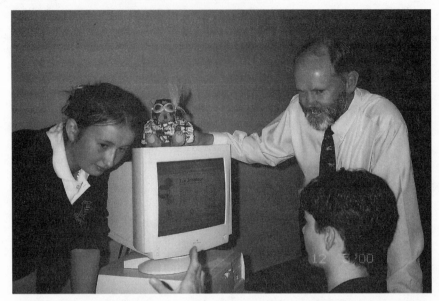

Johanson holds his good luck mascot "Kingsford" while talking with two high school students who maintained his web site during the world flights. The mascot is named after Sir Charles Kingsford-Smith, famous Australian distance pilot. (Courtesy Jon Johanson)

unable to contact anyone until reaching Spitzbergen after crossing the pole. He submitted video footage of two GPS readings in the cockpit as he went over the pole, but his claim has not been accepted.

Johanson did set three recognized point-to-point world records on this flight for Speed Over a Recognized Course in his class of aircraft. They were on the legs from Yellowknife to Eureka, Canada; Eureka to Longyearbyen, Norway, and Adelaide to Stauning, Australia.

Reflecting on his many long-distance solo flights, Johanson commented, "Navigation today is so simple; the real problems are political, especially in war-torn spots. There are places in Africa you shouldn't land; simply having a white skin would make you target practice, so you just don't go there. Where navigation was once the challenge, bureaucracy was not even considered, but now it's the major problem."

When asked if he worried about those long flights over water hundreds of miles from a landing strip, he replied that if a flight is planned properly, "there is nothing else to do but fly. Worry doesn't help. If you are a worrier, you shouldn't be making these kinds of flights."

The worst bureaucratic difficulty he had on any of his world flights, besides his experience in Hawaii, was in India where on one occasion, it took from ten in the morning until four in the afternoon just to file a flight plan. There was no malice in their lack of efficiency, he says, and he claims he never had to pay a bribe to get service.

Jon stated he would like next to make a world flight over the South Pole but realizes that finding a sponsor willing to provide $100,000 in Australian money will be difficult, even though he has proven he can do what he says he will do. He has found that many people think of his flying as a vacation and do not take him seriously. "It's not," he says. "It's hard work."

In the years of flying the RV-4 on such long flights, Jon Johanson was credited by the FAI with 43 point-to-point and two round-the-world speed records for his type of aircraft. Again, as Don Taylor had done, he proved that flying around the world in a kit-built single-engine aircraft is not only possible but can be accomplished safely with the proper navigation and communications equipment plus good preflight planning.

The flying accomplishments of the daring Australian are perhaps best summarized on the Van's Aircraft Company web site: "Those of us who fly could have had no better spokesman: a quiet—but no longer ordinary—man had safely and professionally flown around the world in an airplane he built himself in a rented shed."

Unfortunately, Johanson's two round-the-world speed records did not last long. Hans G. Schmid, a pilot for Swissair, Switzerland's national airline, eclipsed the eastbound and westbound records flying a Long EZ from Zurich in March and April 2000 and the following November. The FAI ratified a total of 164 world records for Speed Over a Recognized Course for Schmid.

23

GERARD MOSS AND HIS MOTOR-GLIDER

A combination of a glider with a small engine, called a motor-glider, entered the round-the-world flying picture in the summer of 2001 when Gerard Moss, a 46-year-old Brazilian mechanical engineer and ship-broker, began a solo world-girdling odyssey. He and his wife Margi had previously made a relaxed 32-month world flight and visited 50 countries between 1989 and 1992 in a Brazilian-built Embraer Sertanejo they named *Romeo*. They were the first South Americans to fly around the world, first to fly a light aircraft across the South Pacific from Australia to South America and first to choose that route for a round-the-world flight. In 2000, Gerard Moss became the first Brazilian pilot to land in Antarctica.

Gerard Moss, a private pilot with 2,500 hours of flying time, wanted to establish a new aviation "first" with a Super Ximango (pronounced "shimango") AMT-200S, a single-engine, two-seat motor-glider manufac-tured by the Aeromot Company in Porto Alegre, Brazil. Built of fiberglass and carbon fiber, it is 26 feet long with a 57-foot wingspan and is powered by a small Rotax 912S engine of 100 hp that can use automobile fuel or aviation gasoline. (Some pilots report that it runs better on the former.) It does not require a tow-plane to take off and can fly as a normal aircraft with a range of 650 nautical miles and a top speed of 110 knots. Its normal endurance is six hours, and can climb to a maximum of 18,000 feet.

What makes this aircraft different from others in its light weight class is that its wingspan provides a 31:1 glide ratio. This enables the pilot to have the option of switching the engine off and using the thermals to stay airborne for a longer time, thus saving fuel, or possibly loitering until the weather or air traffic clears. The wide-spreading wings are foldable for easier handling on the ground.

Moss took off solo from Sorocaba, Brazil, on June 20, 2001, during Aero Sport 2001, Brazil's largest annual aviation event, with a flight plan that called for at least 70 stops in 35 countries on five continents. He intended to fly only under visual flight rules during daylight hours.

Moss flew generally northwestward over the Americas with many stops to Nome, Alaska. He crossed the Bering Sea and with ex-Russian Air Force pilot Capt. Yakov Sabodin as navigator, proceeded to nine stops in Russia before flying alone to Niigata, Japan, which he reached during the first week of August 2001. The Ximango was intercepted by two jet fighters of the Japanese Air Defense Force when he strayed off course near Hokkaido after crossing the La Perouse Strait south of Sakhalin Island. The jets left after 20 minutes, satisfied by their controllers that permission to enter Japanese airspace had been obtained. Much relieved, Moss made several stops in Japan. During this period the autopilot malfunctioned, so he had to fly the aircraft manually until he could locate a repair facility or have a new one installed.

Moss continued to Macau, Hong Kong, and made two stops in Vietnam before fighting monsoon rains and head winds from Thailand, Myanmar, and four stops in India to Muscat, Oman. At one point, he had seriously considered parachuting out when the rains became so heavy and the turbulence so severe that he felt he had lost control.

Weather was not his only problem. During the pauses in India, he spent a total of 19 hours fighting the bureaucracy in order to clear customs and obtain flight clearances. He had flown through a sandy haze most of that time and found it exceedingly stressful, without a functioning autopilot, to keep his eyes focused on the instrument panel in order to maintain his heading at altitudes that varied between 2,000 and 10,500 feet.

The slow-flying Ximango was not approved for a flight across Saudi Arabia so Moss had to fly an unexpected 950 miles around the Arabian Peninsula to the Republic of Djibouti at the entrance to the Gulf of Aden, an exhausting 11½-hour flight. He then had a 12¼-hour flight at 100-foot altitude north over the Red Sea and then west to Luxor, Egypt, battling stiff winds and thick sandy haze. By this time, he had 252 hours in the air since departing Brazil and had covered more than 22,800 miles.

Thoroughly fatigued, Moss took two days to rest in Luxor, then flew for eight hours to the Greek island of Crete, followed by two stops in Italy. He hurried over the low Alps on August 29, 2001, to Saanen near Gstaad, Switzerland, to avoid a threatening cold front that smothered the mountains with snow soon after he landed.

Exhausted from loss of sleep at this point, he had the autopilot replaced, the UHF radio repaired and the engine checked at Grenchen in preparation for the 1,900-mile flight across the South Atlantic. Refreshed,

Gerard Moss poses beside his motorized glider at an airport in Rio de Janeiro, Brazil, before achieving an aviation "first" in this type of aircraft in 2001. He and his wife Margi helped establish an organization called Earthrounders for pilots who have flown around the world in light aircraft. (Courtesy Margi Moss)

he made a local test flight and then turned off the engine to glide while taking pictures of the Alps.

Moss left on September 5, 2001, for Aschaffenburg, Germany, then proceeded with diversions because of extremely low visibility to Worms, Germany, and Charleroi near Brussels and on to Persan-Beaumont and Amboise north of Paris, where he visited 80-year-old Rene Fournier, designer of the Ximango. He landed at Dieppe, then crossed the English Channel and flew over London. He shut off the engine and did some gliding over the city before landing at Denham on September 9 for a two-day visit.

Moss intended to leave England on September 12, but British Prime Minister Tony Blair grounded all commercial and private aircraft because of the World Trade Center and Pentagon terrorist attacks in New York and Washington the day before. However, Moss was able to file a flight plan for Madrid on September 13 and arrived there in excellent visibility but high velocity wind gusts that made a light plane difficult to land. Despite the security restrictions being imposed on worldwide aviation, he was able to continue to Cascais, Portugal, on September 14 and prepare for the flight to Africa. Again, high winds were encountered on landing, but Moss was able to handle them. A Cessna 172 landing behind him could not cope with the erratic gusts and crashed.

Moss left Cascais for Marrakech, Morocco, on September 16 flying in thick sandy haze similar to what he had encountered over the northeastern part of Africa. He stayed there a day then flew for more than eight hours to cover the 900 miles over the western Sahara to Nouadhibou, Mauritania. On September 19, he could not get permission to fly over Atar so headed directly for Dakar, Senegal. He flew at a low altitude and took many photographs of the strange land of pink flamingos, abandoned lighthouses, shipwrecks, and sand dunes. Instead of the three hours it should have taken to cover the distance, he took almost twice that. He departed Dakar for Praia, capital of Cape Verde, and arrived during a thunderstorm. The weather remained stormy for 48 hours but seemed to be clear enough to head for the island of Fernando de Noronha, a 1,500-nautical-mile flight through a wide area of huge cumulonimbus buildups. He made a takeoff in the dark because he wanted to make a daylight landing at Noronha.

Moss enjoyed a slight tailwind as he flew to his point of no return but shortly afterward he had his first serious battle with low clouds and rain. He deviated from his course and when the airspeed dropped to 85 knots, he became concerned that he was using up fuel too fast. He dropped from 2,000 feet to less than 50 feet to maintain visual contact with the ocean and pulled back the throttle to lessen the effects of the turbulence. He tightened his seat belt, put away all cameras and equipment, and prepared for the onslaught.

"I chugged along just above the waves, concentrating intensely," he reported. "A split second of inattention would be the end if the turbulence dipped one wing lower than the other. I struggled enormously to see through the rain pounding on the canopy.

"Suddenly I lost visual contact. Unhesitatingly, I started a 180-degree turn and climbed a few feet. This is the most dangerous moment. When banking tightly, the plane is prone to stall and the wing comes dangerously close to the water."

Moss was in touch with Andre Sampaio, a ham radio operator in Noronha, who passed weather information to him and words of encouragement. He returned to his course after deviating several times and finally managed to break through the thunderstorm area. "When at last that peak of Noronha appeared on the horizon," he said, "I was unspeakably happy. I declare it my favorite island of all time! Perhaps no one was more surprised than me that I had made it across that ocean."

Moss couldn't resist circling the island before touching down at dusk 12 hours, 30 minutes after takeoff. He flew on to Recife on the mainland

Gerard Moss flies over the Brazilian jungle in the Ximango, a motor-glider, in which he completed a world flight in September 2001. Several times he shut the engine off and glided to view the landscape and take photographs. (Courtesy Margi Moss)

in good weather for a joyous reception. To relax, he did some gliding over the mountains along the coast and arrived back home in Rio de Janeiro, Brazil, on September 28, 2001, exactly 100 days after his departure in June. When asked if he would do it again, he told the waiting press, "The Ximango is ready to go around again, but I need a rest."

Moss made 94 stops on his solo flight, flew 29,949 nautical miles (55,497 kilometers) and spent 407 hours in the air. He pointed out that the flight had a scientific purpose other than establishing an aviation "first" for a motor-glider. The Ximango carried special air filters and ozone sensors to monitor the atmosphere at the relatively low altitudes it flew and provided data on air pollution, global warming, and climate change. The ozone sensor was designed at the Center for Atmospheric Science at Cambridge University in England which analyzed that data, along with the Sao Paulo State University in Bauru, Brazil. In a separate study, sponge filters picked up persistent organic pollutants for analysis at England's Lancaster University. Research data was transmitted directly from the aircraft by satellite to these universities.

In a postflight message to the author, Moss compared his two experiences and gave advice to others contemplating a global flight in a light aircraft: "I have flown around the world twice. The first time ten years ago, with my wife, visiting 50 countries along the way in leisurely fashion, requesting flight clearances directly ourselves when we were ready to move from one country to the next. Our objective was to see the world, not just a string of airports.

"The second flight in 2001 was a difficult aviation challenge taking a motor-glider around the world for the first time. The plane had to fly exclusively by visual flight rules (VFR) and this caused problems. Also, I had [scientific] commitments along the way so I was bound by pre-organized clearances with limited leeway which can complicate life when flying VFR. Sadly, I think aviation authorities around the world are increasingly going to demand that you fly IFR (instrument flight rules) and stay strictly on airways.

"So, my advice is go now and take all the time you can. Treat your plane like a sailboat, except you don't have to cook and sleep in it. If you are lucky enough to fly a light aircraft to distant exotic lands, go to small out-of-the-way airstrips as well, see unique things, meet the people. It will be an unbeatable experience."

Moss did not apply for FAI sanctions for his flight so will not be credited with any point-to-point speed records for his aircraft's weight class. However, he deserves everlasting credit as the first pilot to conquer the globe in a motor-glider. He is a candidate for the Paul Tissandier Diploma and Air Sports Medal of the Federation Aeronautique Internationale (FAI) and the Santos Dumont Medal from the Brazilian Civil Aviation Authority.

24

THE FASTEST PASSENGERS

After the first airplane crossed the Atlantic, in 1919, there were predictions that in only a few years passenger and freight service across the oceans would be commonplace. The world flight of the U.S. Army Air Service fliers in 1924, Wiley Post's two flights, and the earth-circling, passenger-carrying flights of *Graf Zeppelin* made the likelihood of the prediction coming true even more likely.

The Pacific Ocean, the last great barrier, was first flown nonstop by Pangborn and Herndon. This flight was followed by flights to Hawaii from the United States and, in 1928, by Charles Kingsford-Smith's multi-stop flight from California to Australia and his return flight in 1934.

In 1934, Pan Am, encouraged by the U.S. government, considered establishing a transpacific air route to the Orient. To avoid complications from foreign governments and to tie the route only to U.S. possessions, a route was chosen which, starting at Alameda, California, would include Hawaii, Midway, Wake, Guam, Manila (then under U.S. control), and Canton, China. The leg from Alameda to Honolulu—2,400 miles—was the longest.

A Sikorsky S-42 four-engine flying boat was built specially for the route, and on April 16, 1935, it began test runs to Hawaii, with Edwin Musick at the controls. As outlying stations were constructed, Musick made practice trips to them, carrying Pan Am officials and supplies. By late summer he had flown 8,000 miles from Alameda to Manila, including all the stops. On November 22, 1935, *China Clipper* flew the first air mail from the United States to Manila. The mail delivery time of three weeks by ship was cut to five days by airplane.

In recognition of his pioneering feat, Musick was awarded the Harmon International Trophy for 1935. What was once an adventure was soon routine. Passengers would enjoy "Pullman car service" across the Pacific.

Now that Pan Am had inaugurated transpacific air service, it was possible to travel around the world almost entirely by air. As one writer commented, "A round trip from one's hometown back to one's hometown [can be made] in less than three weeks."

To test the feasibility of such a flight, and to get some journalistic mileage out of it, three groups of American newspaper publishers, in 1936, proposed that each group select a reporter as a contestant in an air race. The expenses of the winning reporter would be paid by the losing groups. Three reporters were chosen, all based in New York: Herbert Ekins represented the Scripps-Howard *World-Telegram*; Leo Kieran was from the North American Newspaper Alliance and wrote for the *New York Times*; and Dorothy Kilgallen represented the New York *Evening Journal* and the International News Service.

The reporters began their journey together aboard the German dirigible *Hindenburg*, September 30, 1936. Throughout the summer, the dirigible had been making trips between Europe and the United States. Each contestant wore everyday clothes and carried a typewriter and one traveling bag. Connecting schedules with various airlines had been planned. It was agreed that no airline would wait for any reporter, nor would a pilot be asked to increase the speed of his aircraft to help a reporter make a schedule. The race was intended as a fair test of commercial air service around the world.

The selection of Kilgallen recalled Nellie Bly's feat in 1889, when she was sent on a similar trip by her paper in an attempt to beat the time of Jules Verne's fictional Phineas Fogg, who took 80 days to circle the globe. This time, the idea originated with the Scripps-Howard newspaper chain after Pan Am announced that its *China Clipper* would be carrying passengers from Manila to San Francisco, October 16, 1936.

Scripps-Howard's *World-Telegram* announced that Ekins would make the trip so as to coincide with the inaugural eastbound departure of *China Clipper* from Manila. Ekins said he was confident that he could better the record set by John Henry Mears and Charles B.D. Collyer, of 23 days and 15 hours, "by means of regular transportation services."

The day after the *World-Telegram* headlined that its reporter would "girdle the globe by regular airlines," the *New York Times* announced that its reporter, Leo Kieran, would make a similar trip to demonstrate the globe-circling possibilities for the ordinary traveler. Coincidentally, the New York *Evening Journal* announced that Dorothy Kilgallen would make the trip in competition with the other two reporters. Caught up in the sensationalist competitive journalism of the time, Kilgallen, age 23, had already built a reputation as an aggressive reporter. She was good at getting stories, which she wrote up in a sensational style.

All three contenders took the *Hindenburg*; it was still the only way to cross the Atlantic quickly by air. On the evening of September 30, 1936, after logging their exact time of depature with the National Aeronautic Association, the journalists drove to Lakehurst, New Jersey, and boarded the dirigible. Just before departure, several telegrams were delivered to Kilgallen. One was from Amelia Earhart: "I know you can make it, Dorothy, but you must follow your normal schedule of eating, drinking, and sleeping even though on such a trip. Forget you are flying and you won't even get air weary. Imagine you are back in the *Evening Journal* office and stick to one brand of bottled water throughout."

The *Hindenburg* lifted off at 11:17 P.M. The three reporters had dinner together. They chatted amiably, but no one was revealing his or her plans for crossing Europe and Asia, to make the departure of *China Clipper* from Manila on October 16.

Three airlines were operating between Europe and Asia: Air France; KLM of the Netherlands; and Britain's Imperial Airways. Kilgallen wasn't sure which airline she would use; she had depended entirely on her newspaper's staff to make the arrangements. While on the *Hindenburg*, she received a radiogram telling her that she was booked on Imperial Airways to Manila.

The *Hindenburg*, not noted for speed, progressed sedately across the Atlantic at less than 100 mph, arriving in Frankfurt six hours behind schedule. Kilgallen debarked well ahead of the other passengers. When she filed her story, the Hearst papers proclaimed: DOROTHY WINS FIRST LEG OF AIR RACE.

It was at this point that the rules of the race were bent. It had been agreed that the race would be a realistic test of round-the-world commercial air service. The *World-Telegram*, for example, had announced that Ekins would travel "over *routes* available to anyone"; the newspaper had avoided the wording "*planes* available to anyone." The significance of this wording increased when the *Hindenburg* moored in Frankfurt. Without saying a word to his competitors, Ekins retrieved his suitcase and walked across the airport to a KLM DC-2. Within minutes he was airborne, heading for Athens. It was the last time Kieran or Kilgallen would see him during the race. What annoyed them was that Ekins had *chartered* the plane, though he was flying a regular KLM route between Frankfurt and Athens.

Kilgallen booked a flight to Munich, then took a series of trains to Brindisi, Italy, where she caught an Imperial Airways plane. She arrived in Brindisi at four in the morning of October 5, tired, dirty, and angry at Ekins.

Kieran took trains from Frankfurt to Brindisi, arriving two hours after Kilgallen. Independently, they decided to stay at the Hotel International and rest while waiting for the Imperial airliner, then six hours behind schedule.

Meanwhile, Ekins had reached Athens. He was now several hundred miles closer to Manila than Kilgallen and Kieran. Having checked the on-time departures of both KLM and Imperial, he had concluded that KLM was the likeliest to keep him on schedule. Over the next few days, he made stops at Alexandria, Baghdad, Karachi, Jodhpur, Bangkok, Medan, and Singapore.

Kilgallen had intended to take Imperial from Brindisi to Bangkok; since there was no air service between Bangkok and Manila, she would take the steamship *Franklin Pierce* to Manila. Kieran planned the same itinerary.

As Kilgallen and Kieran traveled east, filing their stories by radiogram, Kilgallen's readers were told that she was braving desert storms, swamps, oceans, disease, and the world's most ferocious animals and vipers to get her stories through to them. Kieran kept his stories low-key. When they reached Karachi on October 9, they learned that Ekins was far ahead. They had assumed that he would fly from Singapore to Hong Kong, then catch a ship to the Philippines; but instead, he had flown to the Dutch East Indies. Ekins told his readers that he would leave Batavia (later, Dja-karta) "swing north again, crossing the equator for the second time in two days, and with luck . . . be in Manila Saturday. How? I'll let you know in a future dispatch. I can say only what I have said all along, that I expect to fly all the way to Manila."

In 1936, the China Sea was the sole remaining gap in round-the-world air service. Once again, Ekins bent the rules. KNILM, a KLM affiliate airline, had permission to fly from Tarakan, on the northeast coast of Borneo, to the Philippines. The airline was making survey flights to acquaint crews with the route. Ekins found out about the survey and talked his way aboard a flight. He reached Manila on October 10, six days before the scheduled departure of *China Clipper*.

Kilgallen and Kieran, still together on Imperial airliners, could not close the gap. Both were frustrated by the pace of their journey through India, and their disgust—with red tape, hotel accommodations, and delays—had crept into their stories. Arriving in Rangoon, they were informed that Ekins had already reached Manila and moved on. Once again, he had not played fair. Instead of waiting for the *China Clipper*, he would book a flight to the United States on *Hawaii Clipper*, an airliner also on a survey flight, not a scheduled one.

Warmly received in Manila, Ekins finagled a visit with President Quezon, to whom he presented letters from President Roosevelt, Fiorello LaGuardia, and Roy Howard, co-owner of Scripps-Howard. Pan Am officials, eager for publicity, allowed Ekins to sign on *Hawaii Clipper* as a crew member, again breaking the rules by using transportation not available to ordinary travelers.

In his book, *Around the World in Eighteen Days*, Ekins rationalized his tactics: "Thanks to the typhoon which had blown me into Manila, the *Hawaii Clipper* still tossed at her moorings out at . . . Cavite Naval Base, 25 miles away, and I proposed to be aboard her when she made her delayed departure. There was actually no reason why this should not be. The *Hawaii Clipper* was even then a regularly licensed passenger seaplane and the service in which she is now being used had been inaugurated three days earlier, when the *China Clipper* left Alameda Marine Base at San Francisco with a party of newspapermen."*

Kilgallen was furious. Upon their arrival in Bangkok, and saying nothing to Kieran, she rushed to the offices of the Aerial Transport Company. She, too, would bend the rules. Kilgallen plunked down traveler's checks and tried to charter a plane to take her across the China Sea to Manila in time to catch *Hawaii Clipper*. She also asked for an American pilot. No American pilot was available, nor was any plane available with that range. Instead, she was told she could charter a plane to Hong Kong, where she might be able to catch a ship that would get her to Manila in time. Kilgallen agreed to this alternative, and on the morning of October 12, pilot Luen Phongsobhon, who could speak no English, taxied his Puss Moth out to the end of the grass strip with Kilgallen in the front seat.

By the end of the first day of flying, they had reached Hanoi. Kilgallen stayed in a hotel and went shopping. The next morning, they took off, heading southeast. En route, they landed in a rice paddy; Phongsobhon hadn't liked the sound of the engine. Deciding that it was a fouled spark plug, he got out his tool kit and changed the plug. They took off again. Later, Phongsobhon got lost and landed for directions. Throughout, Kilgallen tried to keep up with what was going on, but received only shrugs from her pilot. She was getting worried. She had hoped to be in Manila by now, and time was running out. Not only might she not reach the Philippines by air, she might not even get to Hong Kong to catch the *Franklin Pierce*, en route from Bangkok to Manila. But her luck held; she arrived in Hong Kong just before the ship was scheduled to depart.

Kieran, rested and relaxed, welcomed her aboard. As they sailed out of Hong Kong harbor, they were informed that Ekins was still in Manila, where *Hawaii Clipper* was waiting out a storm. As they cruised to the Philippines, Ekins radioed that he would be off on October 14th. Adding insult to injury, he congratulated Kilgallen for her courage in chartering the Puss Moth and invited them to dinner in New York at his expense when they returned.

---

*Ekins, *Around the World in Eighteen Days*, New York: Longman, Green, 1936.

Kilgallen, still furious with Ekins and feeling sorry for herself, wrote in her diary: "I think I deserve a break. Maybe the *China Clipper* will overtake the *Hawaii Clipper* in mid-ocean. Maybe something will happen. I really would like to win this round-the-world jaunt."

Arriving in Manila, she and Kieran were entertained and asked to speak on a radio program that would be relayed to the United States. Her father, following her trip with more than passing interest, heard the broadcast and cabled: YOUR BROADCAST SPLENDID. YOU HAVE DONE A KNOCKOUT JOB AND HAVE STOLEN THE STORY ALL AROUND.

China Clipper finally arrived, and on Monday, October 19, Kilgallen and Kieran boarded for the 8,200-mile, five-day flight to San Francisco via Guam, Wake, Midway, and Honolulu. En route to Wake, they learned that Ekins had reached New York and claimed a new world record for passenger travel around the world—25,794 miles in 18 days, 10 hours, 26 minutes, and 4 seconds, measured from Lakehurst. Not only that, but he became the first passenger to circle the globe entirely by air over established passenger *routes*.

China Clipper arrived in San Francisco on October 24. Jim Kilgallen flew with his daughter to New York. They were driven to the New York office of the *Evening Journal* for formal check-in with the timer and a welcome-home breakfast. Ekins had beaten Kilgallen by six days. She placed second, completing the trip in 24 days, 12 hours, and 51 minutes. Kieran, without a special plane, arrived at his office only an hour behind her. Like Ekins, he had flown regularly scheduled air routes from San Francisco. In his story about the trip, he reminded his readers that, although he finished last, he was the only one of the three who had not resorted to transportation unavailable to ordinary travelers.

Kilgallen claimed to be the first woman to fly across the Pacific, but she had forgotten about Lady Grace Drummond-Hay, who flew the Pacific in *Graf Zeppelin's* flight in 1929. Kilgallen's trip did, however, bring her publicity far beyond that of her male rivals. Her dispatches were published in *Girl Around the World*, and a song, "Hats Off to Dorothy," honored her feat. She appeared on radio programs and posed for magazine ads for Camel cigarettes.

Despite the disagreement over the rules, it was Ekins who was credited with finishing first. Upon his arrival in San Francisco, he boarded a United Airlines Boeing 247, made an unscheduled stop at Bakersfield because of weather, and then flew to Burbank. He flew to New York via Wichita, Kansas City, and Pittsburgh, arriving October 19, 1936. In New York, Ekins persuaded the pilot to circle over Lakehurst so the NAA official on the ground could time his arrival. He was adjudged the new record-holder, with a time of 18 days, 11 hours, and 14 minutes, measured from the time he left his New York office until he returned to it. With the exception of the dirigible flight to Frankfurt, all flights were made in American-made aircraft. He finished some 10,000 miles and more than six days ahead of his rivals.

Ekins never made good on his promise to treat Kieran and Kilgallen to a dinner upon their return. After a six-day round of luncheons, dinners, and speaking engagements, he hurried out of town to "fulfill the first of my list of lecture dates. I was sorry that I was unable to carry out my plan to greet my competitors when they arrived . . . but as every newspaperman knows, an assignment is an assignment. They are both splendid company and I know that neither cherishes any resentment against the one who 'got the breaks.'"

As we have noted throughout this book, records are made to be broken, and the round-the-world record for a passenger was broken three years later. On June 28, 1939, Mrs. Clara Adams, of New York City, left Port Washington, Long Island, on *Dixie Clipper*. She returned to Newark, New Jersey, July 15, having made the trip in 16 days, 19 hours, 8 minutes, and 10 seconds. With war clouds gathering in Europe, however, circling the earth by commercial aircraft became inadvisable, if not impossible.

Pan Am was the first airline to offer round-the-world, scheduled, commercial air service. Its success with the Clipper service showed that most of the navigation and communications problems had been solved. Pan Am's plans for worldwide service were halted by World War II. What service there was came from the long-range planes of the U.S. Army Air Forces.

A worldwide military network was formed in December 1941. Originally called the Army Air Forces Ferrying Command, it soon became the Air Transport Command (ATC). The embryo unit was assigned 11 converted Consolidated B-24 *Liberators*, an equal number of Boeing and Martin flying boats, and five Boeing *Stratoliners* from TWA. Most of the pilots were airline pilots under contract to the government. Because of the war's scope, the ATC grew; by V-J Day, 1945, it encompassed 750,000 men and women who operated 3,000 aircraft. Each day, 38 flights were made across the Pacific, and 28 were made over the Atlantic.

The largest aircraft flown by the ATC was the four-engine Douglas C-54, *Skymaster*, known commercially as the DC-4. With a normal range of 3,000 miles, it was used on transcontinental and transoceanic routes. The plane had a capacity of 44 passengers and a crew of five, and some military versions seated as many as 54.

The end of the war, in August 1945, brought the dismemberment of the largest air force that the world had ever seen. Anticipating this, and taking advantage of the availability of ATC crews and aircraft, Lt. Gen. Harold George, ATC commanding general, ordered his staff to plan a round-the-world flight for selected members of the press, using a relay of six ATC C-54s. The purpose of the flight was not only to set a record for passengers but to demonstrate the reliability of the aircraft and the efficiency of his operation.

On August 28, 1945, Mrs. George stood on a grandstand at Washington National Airport and cut a ribbon that released balloons, thus christening a C-54, *Globester Crescent Caravan*. Besides four AAF officers, the passenger manifest included Fred Othman, United Press correspondent; Paul Miller, reporting for the Associated Press; and Mrs. Inez Robb, correspondent for the International News Service. A few minutes later, the C-54 departed, dipped its wings in salute, and disappeared, flying northeast. On September 4, the passengers returned, having covered 23,279 miles in 6 days, 5 hours, and 44 minutes, including 33 hours and 21 minutes on the ground.

Although the flight was reported by the news correspondents on

Globester Crescent Caravan, a U.S. Air Force C-54, is christened at National Airport, Washington, D.C., on August 28, 1945, before the start of its world flight. The purpose of the flight was to emphasize the long-range capability of passenger-carrying aircraft. (U.S. Air Force photo)

board, it received little publicity. Nevertheless, the flight showed that it was possible to circle the globe on a preestablished schedule with passengers traveling in relative comfort. It wasn't until 1949, however, that the ATC, now called the Military Air Transport Service (MATS), set round-the-world schedules, which it referred to as "embassy flights." Operating from several bases and over various routes, flights linked U.S. embassies around the globe, enabling State and Defense Department couriers to travel conveniently between countries.

After World War II, scheduled, commercial airline flights around the world were contemplated by several airlines. Pan Am, though, appears to have beat the rest. The airline inaugurated round-the-world service in June 1947. That flight, made in a Lockheed Constellation, a sleek four-engine transport, had a passenger manifest of 18 prominent newsmen, the mayor of San Francisco, a representative of the U.S. State Department, an artist, and Juan Trippe, Pan Am's president. The Constellation had a crew of nine men and a stewardess. Christened *America*, the Constellation would not attempt a speed record but merely get extensive press coverage of Pan Am's projected world routes.

Departing June 17, 1947, from La Guardia Airport, the group's itinerary was Gander, London, Istanbul, Dhahran, Karachi, Calcutta, Bangkok, Manila, Shanghai, Tokyo, Guam, Wake, Midway, Honolulu, San Francisco, Chicago, and New York.

Although plans called for a flight of 93 hours, maintenance problems twice forced the Constellation back. In addition, the stop at Chicago was not in the original itinerary; it was made because of a special invitation from the city's mayor, to pay tribute to the group's circumnavigation of the globe.

The Constellation landed at La Guardia June 30, after a flight of 101 hours and 32 minutes. During the 13-day flight, it visited 10 countries, stopped at 17 cities and airports, and covered 22,297 miles.

Now that Pan Am spanned the oceans routinely, the airline could set passenger schedules and that would make it possible to break the records. Pan Am advertised a seven-day world flight, and the fever to set passenger speed records caught on. In late 1948, Edward Eagan, chairman of the New York State Boxing Commission, flew around the world in six days, three hours, and 40 minutes. Eagan's record stood for a year. In 1949, the Air Force Association promoted an "Aviability" program to dramatize the progress of aviation in the 46 years since the Wright brothers' flight at Kitty Hawk. Tom Lanphier Jr., a World War II fighter pilot, was chosen to make the trip, which would advertise the program by flying around the earth on regularly scheduled commercial aircraft. Carrying a letter from President Truman commemorating the forty-sixth anniversary of powered flight, Lanphier followed an itinerary that called for departure from New York's La Guardia Airport, December 2, 1949, and travel via Gander, London, Brussels, Basra, Karachi, New Delhi, Bangkok, Hong Kong, Okinawa, Tokyo, Midway, Honolulu, Los Angeles, Chicago, and New York, in 4 days, 23 hours, and 50 minutes.

To the credit of Pan American, United and American Airlines [Lanphier reported to the Air Force Association upon his return] I made the global flight three minutes ahead of schedule. . . . Ahead of schedule at almost every stop, I rode 83 hours, 43 minutes flying time on five separate planes during the trip. Pan American's Constellation *Paul Jones* took me all the way from New York to Hong Kong, I rode a Pan Am DC-4 to Tokyo, a Pan Am Boeing *Stratocruiser* to Hawaii, a United DC-6 to Chicago, and an American Airlines DC-6 for the final leg to La Guardia.

Understandably, I had little time for close-up sightseeing . . . though I did . . . get downtown to London, Karachi, Hong Kong, Tokyo and Honolulu long enough for a bath or at least a *Reader's Digest* look at the town. Altogether, of the five days I was gone, I spent about a day and a half on the ground.

All I saw of much of the earth was a sort of blurred succession of airports, most of them in darkness, several of them in the rain. I . . . saw thousands of miles of ocean and undercast. I did, however, experience and note a few things about flying around the world in this air age which might be news to those who haven't had a similar opportunity.

For instance: It costs $1,548.75 to fly completely around the world. . . . For baggage, I carried a camera, a handbag, a typewriter, [and] a suitcase. . . . [I also carried President Truman's] letter in a huge envelope which I had stamped by postal officials in each of the 12 countries and territories visited. The whole outfit . . . weighed 72 pounds, . . . well within the limit of 88 pounds allowed the round-the-world traveler.

Lanphier had cut 27 hours and 28 minutes off Eagan's record. His record would be difficult to beat until the advent of commercial jet airliners. It stood until 1953, when Horace Boren, a public relations officer for Braniff Airways, had an idea: How about celebrating Braniff's twenty-fifth anniversary and the fiftieth anniversary of the Wright brothers' flight by going after Lanphier's record?

On June 21, 1953, Boren took off in a TWA Constellation from New York, en route to London. After 16 stops, and using three different airlines, with three different planes—the Constellation, a BOAC deHavilland Comet jet airliner, and a Northwest Airlines Stratocruiser—he deplaned in New York with a record for passengers of 99 hours and 16 minutes.

Boren's record stood for several years, but eventually it was broken. In March 1978, Alec Prior and Terry Sloane, flying east out of Sydney,

Australia, made the *Guinness Book of Records* with a time of 53 hours and 34 minutes, using available commercial routes.

On January 8, 1980, David Springbett, a 42-year-old insurance broker and travel agent living in London, departed from Los Angeles, flying east. His successful attempt to break Prior and Sloane's record included booking passage on a BOAC supersonic Concorde from London to Singapore. At this writing, Springbett is the record-holder, having completed the world flight in 44 hours and six minutes.

What was Springbett's motivation for the 23,068-mile flight? He said he wanted to promote business travel, show that airlines do meet schedules, investigate jet lag, and fly just for the fun of it. The cost of $8,288 was covered by a $10,000 bet he had made before the flight.

25

AROUND THE WORLD WITH PAN AM AND UNITED

The word *World* in Pan American World Airways took on special meaning in May 1976. Within two days, a Pan Am 747SP circled the globe and set an official world speed record for commercial airline aircraft. The feat was unique in that it was accomplished with passengers who paid for their tickets solely to take part in a modern flying adventure.

Even in today's jet age, the statistics of the flight are impressive. Christened *Clipper Liberty Bell*, the 747 lifted off from Kennedy International Airport on May 1, 1976. Thirty-nine hours, 25 minutes, and 53 seconds of air time later, it touched down again. With only two stops (New Delhi and Tokyo), the total elapsed time from takeoff to return was 46 hours and 50 seconds, and the distance flown was 23,137.92 miles.

The previous record for round-the-world flight by a commercial aircraft was 62 hours, 27 minutes, and 35 seconds, established in November 1965, by a Boeing 707-320C, which flew over both poles. The Pan Am 747SP globe-circler was another in a long line of Pan Am commercial aviation firsts in that 98 passengers were carried. Passengers in first class paid $2,912; economy-class tickets were $1,838. The trip paid for itself; it wasn't just a public-relations gimmick.

The idea of the flight was, in many ways, a by-product of the highly successful, pilot-led Pan Am Employee Awareness Program, which brought management and employees together in an unprecedented show of cooperation and solidarity. Employees were encouraged to submit worthwhile suggestions for improving the company's image and its income. One such suggestion was submitted by Lyman Watt, a Pan Am

291

Passengers on the *Clipper Liberty Bell* pose beside the Pan Am 747SP at New Delhi Airport, India, on their record flight in 1976. Although the flight set a record for commercial jet aircraft, it could have been completed in less time except for a two-hour strike by Japanese ramp crews at Tokyo's Haneda International Airport. (Pan Am photo)

captain: Could Pan Am revitalize its image as a world airline by attempting a commercial round-the-world record, and tie it in with the Bicentennial? The newly acquired 747SP would make it possible to circumnavigate the globe, using only two regular Pan Am stops. Certainly, the existing record of 62.5 hours could be beaten. If paying passengers were taken, the trip would be cost-effective.

In the next few weeks, Watt's idea was found not only feasible but an excellent way to give Pan Am some favorable publicity. Watt had suggested departure from Washington, with stops in Karachi and Guam; it was decided that the flight would leave New York and make stops at New Delhi and Tokyo. Thus it would consist of three nearly equal segments. Besides, the NAA requires that a world flight for record must be a minimum of 22,858 statute miles. To be sure the minimum distance is flown, most record-seekers deliberately plan to fly more miles than are required, in case their computations are inaccurate.

While Pan Am operations and maintenance people worked out details of the flight, the public relations and marketing departments geared up for publicity and sales. Ads were run and brochures were sent to Pan Am offices.

At 5:40 P.M., on May 1, 1976, the one-of-a-kind flight began, with Watt part of the crew. Capt. Walter Mullikin, Pan Am's vice president and chief pilot, headed the 15-man cockpit team, consisting of three five-man crews. Clipper 200—*Liberty Bell Express,* as the flight was designated, headed east and flew to Land's End, England, then proceeded across Europe via Paris, Munich, Istanbul, Ankara, and Teheran to New Delhi, a distance of 8,081 miles—the longest leg of the flight. Air time was 13 hours and 31 minutes, a city-to-city record. The average speed was 598 mph.

There was a two-hour layover in New Delhi, for refueling. Passengers deplaned and were treated to a warm welcome by sari-wearing women, who gave each passenger and crew member a garland of flowers and a dot of red paint in the middle of the forehead. The next destination was Tokyo. To ensure that the minimum mileage required was flown, the leg was not a direct flight. A new crew took over the flight deck, but the original five-man crew, including Captain Mullikin, stayed aboard. NAA rules require that the original crew go all the way around in order for the new record to be official. Also at this time, two passengers bound for New York came aboard.

The flight moved southwest to Bombay, then to Tokyo via Singapore, Djakarta, and Manila. This leg of 7,539 miles, was covered in 14 hours and 1 minute. Adverse winds reduced the speed to a relatively low 536 mph, but another city-to-city record went into the record books.

A two-hour fuel stop was planned for Tokyo, but a work slowdown by ground crews at Haneda International Airport nearly spoiled the historic flight. To focus attention on their demands, ramp personnel parked their vehicles three and four deep behind the 747 just as the captain signaled for a pushback. It took Pan Am negotiators two hours to persuade the ground crews to allow the plane to depart. This delay prevented Clipper 200—*Liberty Bell Express* from setting an elapsed-time record for all types of aircraft, a record held by three B-52s that circled the globe nonstop in 45 hours and 19 minutes in 1957, by refueling in flight.

Choosing the best winds available across the Pacific, Clipper 200, now being flown by its third crew, headed east. It made landfall at Vancouver after dawn. Through FAA cooperation, the crew obtained a nearly direct route to New York, using INS. Its speed for the 7,517 miles was calculated at 641 mph; the air time was 11 hours and 53 minutes, still another city-to-city record.

When the plane had docked at JFK, Pan Am's new president, F.C. Wiser, came aboard to welcome the world travelers. They had set new marks in the jet age and their names had gone in the history books as the first public group to accept an invitation to participate in such a trip. Captain Mullikin, a veteran of 25,000 hours with Pan Am, praised the passengers. "I have never seen such a team-spirited group of passengers who were so keenly interested in aviation and in the flight of the *Liberty Bell*," he said. "In all my years with Pan Am, this flight is the high point of my career."

For its golden anniversary in 1977, Pan Am decided to emphasize the word "World" again and establish new international speed records as it had in 1976. This time the flight would take the same 747SP (renamed *Clipper New Horizons*) over both poles with paying passengers aboard and would begin on the official fiftieth birthday of Pan Am—October 28, 1977.

The crew members of Pan Am's fiftieth anniversary round-the-world flight of 1977 are congratulated by company vice president James O. Leet. Crew members in uniform are: Capt. Walter H. Mullikin; Capt. Albert A. Frink; First Officer Stewart W. Beckett; and Flight Engineers Frank D. Cassaniti and Edward L. Shields. Looking on are Capt. James C. Waugh (holding map) and Mrs. Audrey S. Balchen, widow of famous Arctic pilot Bernt Balchen, first to pilot an aircraft over both poles. (Pan Am photo)

Just as in 1976, Pan Am advertised in major newspapers for adventurous passengers to help celebrate its midcentury milestone "by doing what no airline has ever done before." The ads announced the "first round-the-world passenger flight over both the North and South Poles: Pan Am's one-time-only Flight 50." Fares were $3,333 for first class and $2,222 for economy class.

Within three days after the ads appeared, the maximum number of paying passengers allowed had signed up and a standby list was begun. There was no further need for advertising. Thirty-eight Flight 50 passengers were alumni of the *Clipper Liberty Bell* Bicentennial flight. They wanted to be aboard another one-of-a-kind flight that would make aviation history. The route of flight would be from San Francisco to London over the North Pole; to Cape Town, South Africa; over the South Pole to Auckland, New Zealand; and then return to San Francisco. This would be an attempt to beat the record set in November 1965, of 62 hours, 27 minutes elapsed time by a Flying Tiger Boeing 707 cargo plane.

Capt. Walter H. Mullikin, vice president and chief pilot, was again put in charge of making all operational arrangements. This time a total of 20 flight deck crew members would be aboard—five for each leg.

While the necessary NAA forms were accomplished and coordination with foreign governments was being conducted, Mullikin and his staff put internal wheels in motion to have maintenance personnel, flight crews, and station agents in position. In-flight meals were decided upon and menus printed. Special arrangements had to be made at Cape Town because it is not a normal Pan Am stop. The station manager in Rio de Janeiro was sent there to assure prompt ground service would be available.

As the departure date approached, Pan Am Board Chairman William T. Seawell explained why the company was putting its reputation on the line again and chancing a failure if plans went awry: "The flight is intended to focus world attention on the scope, capability and human and technical achievements of today's global air network, which has developed over the past half-century to serve the world under the leadership of the U.S. Flag airlines and U.S. aircraft and engine manufacturers," he said. Not only Pan Am but the entire U.S. aviation industry stood to gain if the flight were a success.

On the morning of October 28, 1977, passengers, crew members, press representatives, retired pilots, company officials, relatives, and friends gathered in the Pan Am gate area at San Francisco International Airport. A large anniversary cake was placed in a prominent position; catering personnel set up tables for refreshments. By noontime, the bon voyage party was in full swing with speeches by Pan Am and city officials. News reporters interviewed passengers and the most commonly asked question was: "Why do you want to fly around the world?"

The answers were as varied as the backgrounds of the interviewees:

"Because it's one aviation record-setting event that I can take part in."

"Just so when somebody asks me on Monday morning, 'What did you do over the weekend?' I can say, 'Flew around the world. What did you do?'"

"Because I had so much fun last time that I don't want to miss this one."

"Because my wife says I never take her anywhere."

"My husband had too much fun on the last trip. I wanted to see what goes on."

"I wanted to get away from it all for the weekend."

"Beats working."

There were 126 male and 46 female passengers aboard *Clipper New Horizons* including 14 husband/wife couples, two father/daughter and two father/son combinations, and one grandfather/grandson pair. Most of the 50 states were represented plus Japan, England, Trinidad, Italy, New Zealand, Uruguay, and Canada.

The aircraft departed on a course to the North Pole over Eugene, Oregon; Seattle; Vancouver; and Fort Nelson, Canada. En route, one passenger celebrated his fiftieth birthday; another noted it was his wedding anniversary. A Gucci style show was held near the top of the world and a guitarist broke into song as the countdown began near the magic point where there is no time or dateline. When the zero point was crossed, the passengers cheered and toasted the event with champagne. One passenger pulled Santa Claus whiskers, wig, and hat out of his carry-on bag and paraded through the aisles passing out candy canes and wishing all welcome to "his" domain. Pan Am personnel stamped passports with a special inscription.

Clipper New Horizons circled the pole briefly and then proceeded down the 5° meridian to Bergen, Norway, and then to London. There the passengers debarked and were welcomed by the Lord Mayor of Hillington, the nearest town to Heathrow Airport. The distance of this leg: 6,289 statute miles.

Airborne again two hours later, the aircraft flew south over France, northern Africa, and across the equator. At this point, Capt. Lawrence N. Brown announced on the PA system: "Welcome, ladies and gentlemen, to the bottom half of the world."

The landing at Cape Town was at 11 P.M. local time after covering a distance of 6,022 statute miles from London. The passengers debarked to tight security and were met by a large group of South Africans for whom the arrival was a very special event. The mayor of Cape Town welcomed the group to "the finest cape in all the world" and invited all to return "when you can stay longer."

At takeoff from Cape Town two hours later, it was now October 30. The aircraft proceeded toward the South Pole and as dawn approached, all aboard were treated to a smogless, virginal sunrise. As the day brightened, the solemn grandeur of the Antarctic continent was revealed as few have seen it. Glaciers, mountains, and thousands of square miles of ice and snow sparkled in unspoiled splendor. It was, as one passenger remarked, "The rarest treat for the eyes that there is."

The South Pole was crossed under a bright sun. The crossing was verified by precise navigation instruments in the cockpit. Below, a team of U.S. Navy scientists were beginning their summer observations. A C-130 of Squadron VXE-6, based at McMurdo Sound, was parked on the 14,000-foot strip monitoring the Clipper's transmissions and standing by for search-and-rescue operations should there be a problem. The South Pole crew said they could see the 747 as it passed overhead at 41,000 feet. The Navy also assisted with weather forecasting and by providing flight-following services.

After the aircraft passed the pole, it was October 31. Two flight attendants were awarded their Pan Am Gold Wings in a brief ceremony; another announced that it was now her birthday, which she could celebrate once more when she crossed the international date line en route to San Francisco. Passports were again stamped and toasts offered. The skies darkened after leaving Antarctica and the landing at Auckland was made in a driving night rainstorm. The 7,541 miles covered was the longest leg of the trip. It was 3 A.M. local time but the early hour and the rain did not dampen the enthusiasm of the native dancers and the welcome ceremony that followed.

Airborne for the final leg, passengers were treated to movies and another fabulous sunrise. The international date line was crossed near Tahiti, and it became October 30 once again.

The 6,537 miles to San Francisco were covered in 11 hours and 34 minutes. This leg of the trip had special significance for Capt. Jake M. Marcum. It was his last flight before retiring under FAA's age 60 rule.

When the aircraft touched down at San Francisco, seven national and world speed records had been established. Total elapsed time for the trip was 54 hours, 7 minutes, and 12 seconds. The previous elapsed time record by the modified Flying Tiger 707 cargo aircraft had been eclipsed by more than eight hours and *Clipper New Horizons* had flown 114 miles farther.

Wayne W. Parrish, former aviation publisher and special assistant to Pan Am's president, was aboard both flights and can claim a special honor of his own. He is the only person in the world to have been on two bipolar, record-setting flights.

While Pan Am now chalked up more aviation firsts and records in its corporate logbook, the fact that such a flight could be planned and executed so flawlessly is a tribute to the U.S. aerospace industry that had made the flight possible. Mechanical perfection and flawless professionalism had combined once more to make aviation history.

Because "records are made to be broken," Clay Lacy, a United Airlines captain, decided to go after the Pan Am record in another Boeing 747SP "loaned" to him by his airline. The purpose, in addition to setting a new eastbound record, was to raise funds for the Friendship Foundation, a charity for children. As with the Pan Am flight, Lacy planned to make only two stops: Athens and Taipei.

The happy crew of *Friendship One* on the Athens-to-Taipei leg of their 1988 trip, which was made in 36 hours, 54 minutes. Shown left to right: Capt. Clay Lacy, pilots Gary Meermans and Bob Jones, and flight engineer Al Clayes in foreground. (Friendship Foundation photo)

The 141-passenger list included Neil Armstrong, first man to walk on the moon; Bob Hoover, famous aerobatic pilot; Edward Carlson, former United Airlines president; retired Air Force Gen. Laurence Craigie, America's first military jet pilot; and Moya Lear, widow of William Lear, maker of Lear Jets. Passengers donated a minimum of $5,000 for their seats.

Friendship One departed from Boeing Field, Seattle, on January 28, 1988, and returned on January 30. The 23,125-mile flight riding the winter high-altitude jet stream went off without a hitch and established a new "absolute" speed record of 36 hours, 54 minutes, 15 seconds with an average speed of 625 mph. Over the Atlantic, the flight reached a top speed of 805 mph; at one time, the tailwinds were recorded at 210 mph above the Pacific. The former absolute round-the-world speed record was 45 hours, 26 minutes, 55 seconds set by Allen Paulson in a Gulfstream IV in June 1987. The United Boeing 747SP had surpassed the east–west Pan Am mark by 10 hours.

The Friendship Foundation netted more than $500,000 for children's charities. As one passenger commented afterward, "I didn't get much sleep. It was a nonstop party." Another said, "It was the longest cocktail party I've ever been to." Still another said, "It was like flying around the world in a luxurious mobile home."

Capt. Clay Lacy, leader of the 18 crew member volunteers, including three other pilots and two flight engineers, knew he was going to set a record before takeoff. "And I'm confident this record will stand for years," he said afterward. He added that the passenger list included 80 pilots with over 540,000 hours of flying time. "This gave us a lot of 'backup' in the cabin," he said.

26

VOYAGER:
THE ULTIMATE FLIGHT

They dreamed about it, planned for it, raised the money, and built the airplane in five years. Burt Rutan, one of America's most innovative aircraft designers and aeronautical engineers, came up with the concept: Construct an airplane strong enough yet light enough to fly around the world nonstop and nonrefueled. It would be a one-of-a-kind airplane made with space age composite materials that could carry five times its weight in fuel. A specially designed, liquid-cooled engine or engines would be required to propel the craft, using synthetic oil that would not have to be changed for 1,000 hours.

The design of the aircraft was kept secret as Rutan labored over the numbers that would make it possible to build a plane that would be able to make the ultimate flight. "What was required," according to Rutan, "was what every designer strives for: low drag, efficient propulsion, and stringent weight control." Slowly, the design emerged and took shape in a hangar in the Mojave Desert of California.

In order to cut drag, Rutan decided on an exceptionally long, narrow wing, similar to a sailplane. He provided a canard, a lifting surface that helps improve the aerodynamic efficiency of the aircraft. Mounted between it and the main wing are three streamlined bodies: the fuselage and two outrigger fuel tanks that made the aircraft look like a trimaran mounted on a wing whose length was 34 times its average width.

To reduce weight, Rutan used advanced composites: graphite, Kevlar, and fiberglass over a Nomex paper honeycomb core. Strangely, he decided that the trailing edge of the wing should be made of fabric and balsa wood because "weight is the enemy," Rutan said. When the aircraft was finally ready, it weighed only 938 pounds yet it could carry 8,400 pounds of fuel in 17 tanks. Its takeoff weight would be 9,750 pounds, counting the crew and crew supplies. Landing weight would be as low as 2,200 pounds.

With such an aircraft, it was expected that a round-the-world flight would take 12 days. When the aircraft was heavy, the true airspeed would be about 130 knots; however, as the fuel was burned off, the speed could be reduced to as low as 70 knots and the plane would require less than 25 horsepower at a fuel burn rate of only a few gallons per hour.

Finding a pilot was no problem. Dick Rutan, Burt's brother, was the logical candidate. A retired Air Force fighter pilot with 325 combat missions in three tours in Vietnam, he was the production manager and chief test pilot for his brother's planes and had set six world distance and speed records in them. He had shared in the development and construction of the round-the-world plane, along with Jeana Yeager, a former draftsman and long time pilot friend, whose own weight of 100 pounds was an added asset. (Dick Rutan, more than six feet tall, weighed 167 pounds.) Jeana held four speed records in a Rutan Long EZ, one of several Burt Rutan–designed planes.

It was the design of the fuselage and cockpit of the plane that provided some concern to the two pilots. The maximum internal width of 39.5 inches and the maximum height of only 33 inches meant that there wasn't much more room than there would be in a bathtub. The only seat was for the pilot. The other position was a bed. The flight would not be a comfortable one, especially if it lasted for 12 or more days. As one pilot said, "Weight reduction was so critical, the cabin size was reduced to about the size of a phone booth lying on its side. Weight reduction also virtually eliminated any backup systems."

After months of struggling with the construction of the various parts, frustrated by many failures and disappointments because of lack of funds, the day finally arrived for the first test flight. On June 22, 1984, Dick and Jeana taxied out, took off, and began an exhaustive test program. There were hundreds of frustrating problems and equipment failures ahead. The aircraft was unstable and had strange flying characteristics that both pilots felt were dangerous. The aircraft "porpoised" continually. The wings flexed excessively, and the two pilots took a beating from turbulence. They began to make longer and longer flights, however, and set an absolute closed-circuit distance record of 11,593.68 miles in July 1986. The flight took 111 hours.

Dick Rutan, Jeana Yeager, and a group of unpaid volunteers slowly licked the gremlins that threatened to defeat their best efforts at every turn. They had to make an emergency landing after one of the two propellers broke off in September 1986, on what was to be the last test flight before the record attempt.

In their postflight book, Dick Rutan admitted there was a time when he hated the plane. "It was the only airplane I had ever been afraid of," he wrote. "I had never gotten used to its flailing wings . . . It was a gnawing, grinding fear, and it never went away."

It was two more months before they felt reasonably sure enough of the aircraft and their own abilities to make the attempt. Meanwhile, they had trained themselves mentally and physically and had gradually become more confident that they could make the ultimate flight. Only they know how to manage the strange undulations of what had been named the *Voyager* by Jeana. And only they knew whether their bodies and minds could take the nearly two weeks of mind-dulling flight cooped up in a plastic cylinder in pursuit of an aviation "first."

At 8:02 A.M. PST on December 14, 1986, the strange-looking craft departed from Edwards Air Force Base, California, on the 15,000-foot runway, the longest in the world. *Voyager* took 14,200 feet of it for takeoff and narrowly escaped disaster when the elongated wings, loaded with fuel, scraped along the tarmac. The right winglet eventually broke off cleanly, but the left one was left dangling for the remainder of the flight. Rutan circled over the base twice, then continued when he found no problems with the controls. Eighteen inches had been sheared off the left wing, 16 off the right.

Climbing slowly, *Voyager* headed west across the Pacific. The plane flew over Hawaii the next day, pushed by strong tailwinds, and crossed the international date line. The pilots adjusted their flight path to avoid areas of scattered thunderstorms.

On December 16, the third day aloft, *Voyager* skirted the northern edge of Typhoon Marge, which was then centered over the Marshall Islands and packing winds up to 80 mph. Safely past this threat, they shut down the front engine to conserve fuel. "At that point we thought the mission was lost for sure (because of excessive fuel use avoiding the storm)," Rutan said later. The original flight plan was to fly as much as possible in the Southern Hemisphere, but weather conditions kept them north of the equator for almost all of the trip.

Rutan had stayed in the front seat for the first 24 hours and all but six of the next 24. The flight surgeon for the flight, Dr. Jutila, ordered Rutan to take more rest. From that point on, the two tried to follow their planned cycles of flying and rest. (Rutan flew the aircraft about 85 percent of the time.)

They skirted Southeast Asia and then followed a westerly course over Sri Lanka. Turbulence and thunderstorms confronted them continually. Crossing the Malay Peninsula, they were forced to make several 180-degree turns to avoid storms. Over the Indian Ocean, they surpassed the previous record of 12,532 miles for nonstop unrefueled flight set in 1962

Dick Rutan and Jeana Yeager pose beside the uncowled rear engine of the *Voyager* after their world-beating unrefueled "ultimate flight" in 1986. The engine was a specially designed, liquid-cooled engine manufactured by Teledyne Continental Motors Corp. The duo completed the 24,986.727-mile flight in 216 hours, 3 minutes, 44 seconds. (Courtesy Jeana Yeager)

by an Air Force B-52. South of Indochina, the crew turned the plane around and climbed to a higher altitude to avoid storm systems they could see ahead. When they reported their fuel gauge readings to the mission communications center at Mojave, Burt Rutan expressed his concern that such detours were depleting their fuel supply, making completion of the flight doubtful.

Keeping in continuous touch with a communications trailer at Mojave, weather forecasters, and air traffic controllers using NASA and Defense Department satellite links, they crossed the east coast of Africa over Somalia. Concerns over shortage of fuel were lessened when the command trailer determined that a fuel gauge may be giving false readings.

Fatigue began to overwhelm them as turbulence jolted *Voyager* day and night and threatening weather dogged them continually. As they approached the middle of Africa, they had to don nasal oxygen masks and climb to 20,000 feet to clear mountain ranges and violent storm systems. Their discomfort was aggravated by the deafening noise despite the fact that both wore earplugs and an electronic noise-dampening device had been installed. Doctors on the ground at Mojave expressed concern that their hearing might be permanently damaged.

After leaving the west African coast, *Voyager* trundled along at about 110 mph and turned northwest toward the Caribbean to avoid storms over the Gulf of Mexico. Over the Atlantic, they forgot to make the six-hourly check on their liquid-cooled rear engine, and it nearly overheated. When the warning light came on, indicating low oil pressure, they hurriedly pumped in additional oil until pressure and temperature were normal.

Midway across the Atlantic, *Voyager* was tossed around violently and at one point, with Rutan piloting, was flipped into a 90-degree bank. Rutan made a hasty detour and radioed, "I almost lost it!"

As they passed north of South America on the seventh day, the amount of fuel left became a new threat. The pump that drew fuel from tanks on the right side malfunctioned. Fuel crossover valves were adjusted, and the faulty pump was bypassed. This threat added much anxiety to their fatigue. Instead of taking a direct course across the Gulf of Mexico, *Voyager* crossed Central America between Yucatan and Costa Rica before heading northward toward California.

Although the goal looked in sight at the end of the eighth day off the west coast of Mexico, head winds prevailed and, to make matters worse, the rear engine's fuel pump failed; the engine coughed and died. Because the engine had no self-starters, Rutan had to dive the aircraft from 8,500 to 5,000 feet before he could make the front prop turn over in a windmill start. The aircraft's front pump, which was being used after the previous fuel transfer problem, was not strong enough to feed fuel to the rear engine when Rutan began a slow descent toward California.

Their worries were not over. Their volunteer friends on the ground at Edwards AFB, called VIPs (for *Voyager*'s Important Persons), were concerned that fuel had leaked into the cockpit where some electrical wires were housed. Exhausted and weak from eight days aloft, Dick had to reroute a fuel line located in the cockpit under his left knee.

Fuel worries still dogged the pair as they neared their goal, but shortly after 8:05 A.M. on December 23, 1986, on the ninth day of their flight, one day ahead of their original schedule, *Voyager* landed at Edwards Air Force Base to the cheers of thousands of spectators. Rutan and Yeager had successfully completed a nonstop flight measured at 24,986.727 miles for record purposes in 216 hours, 3 minutes, 44 seconds after takeoff. Their speed averaged 115.646 mph. When they landed, there was 18 gallons of fuel left in the tanks, enough to fly an additional 396 miles.

This flight established or surpassed more aviation records than any previous world flight. Rutan and Yeager broke two absolute world records, broke four World Class records, and established two others.

President Reagan awarded Dick Rutan, Jeana Yeager, and Burt Rutan Presidential Citizens Medals in Los Angeles on December 29. The following May, they received the prestigious Robert J. Collier Award for 1987, presented by the National Aeronautic Association for "The greatest achievement in aeronautics or astronautics in America, with respect to improving the performance, efficiency or safety of air or space vehicles, the value of which has been thoroughly demonstrated by actual use during the preceding year." Dawson Ransome, airline president and veteran pilot, was one of the many who nominated the trio. He said:

> The round-the-world, nonstop, nonrefueled flight of the *Voyager* is the single most achievement since the Lindbergh flight in 1927. Only Dick Rutan and Jeana Yeager, who flew the flight, and Burt Rutan, who designed the aircraft, truly knew how tough it was to, first, design an aircraft capable of the flight, and then to successfully fly the aircraft nonstop, nonrefueled around the world for the first time.
>
> From the time Burt, Dick, and Jeana first conceived the idea over lunch in the Mojave, there were tremendous obstacles to overcome. They were to attempt to do what the world's total aerospace industry, including the military, had never been able to do, and they did it without the use of unlimited resources with which to work. Unlimited resources would have resulted in a *Voyager* that would have permitted the crew to sit back in the lap of luxury and cruise serenely around the world, high above the turbulent tropospheric weather below them . . . they did not have that luxury.
>
> . . . For Dick and Jeana to even get to the point of taking off on a world flight meant long years of creating an organization, begging corporations

The *Voyager*, made of advanced composite materials, was designed by Burt Rutan, Dick Rutan's brother. The forward engine was feathered in flight to conserve fuel. Average speed for the trip was 115.646 mph. The flight almost ended on takeoff when the wingtips scraped the ground. However, there were no control problems so the plane continued to a successful landing over nine days later. The aircraft was never flown after the world flight. It hangs in a place of honor in the National Air and Space Museum, Washington, D.C. (Photo courtesy of Jeana Yeager)

for materials and equipment, building an airplane, acquiring a hangar big enough to house something with a 110-foot wingspan, capturing the imaginations of enough people willing to donate funds sufficient to rent so large a hangar and pay the other bills, build the necessary offices, provide for a minimum staff, do flight test evaluation, and attend to tens of thousands of other day-to-day problems. And they would have to do all this while educating themselves in each of the phases of meteorology, communications, navigation, airframe, powerplant and propeller technology, aeromedicine, business, public relations, and everything else—like keeping themselves healthy and sane—necessary to make the round-the-world attempt possible.

In adding his nomination to that of many others, NASA Administrator James C. Fletcher called the *Voyager* flight "an unparalleled achievement" and said its new records "will expand the imaginations of those in the aeronautical community throughout the world."

A group of eight other aviation enthusiasts, in their combined nomination of the Rutans and Yeager for the award, stated that the *Voyager* team had "extended the technical parameters of airframe design, engine design, the use of composite materials, the sophisticated use of computers, and gave new insight into vital elements of human physiology and psychology which had not been previously measured. The flight of the *Voyager* is far more than expression of the best in the technical advancement of aeronautics (and) far more even than an expression of the best of the American spirit. It is an evocative, moving, tribute to the best of the human spirit, an example not only for the United States but for the world."

In their book, entitled *Voyager*, Rutan and Yeager answer the questions asked by many everywhere they went: Would they do it again and was it worth it?

"No, once was enough," they say to the first question. And "Yes" to the second. They say it was worth the years of work, discouragement, sweat, physical discomfort, and danger. And yes, it was worth the heartache, strain, and "the distance it put between us and the other paths of life we didn't take, and the imprisonment and the fear and the reduction of life to a hangar and then a cockpit-sized space."

And they say it was worth it "even if we had failed or lost the *Voyager*, or lost our lives."

"This was the last first in aviation, we had always said, a milestone, and that made it unique."

"Would we do it again? No one can do it again. And that is the best thing about it."

27

THE CHOPPERS
GO 'ROUND

The helicopter is a rotary-winged flying machine whose greatest asset is its ability to hover, land, and take off vertically. After several decades of steady progress since the first successful flight of the Sikorsky VS-300 before World War II, the helicopter eventually became a sophisticated vehicle with long-range capability and improved instrumentation for operations in bad weather and in-flight refueling. In August 1956, a U.S. Army H-21 helicopter was flown nonstop coast-to-coast, and nonstop flights were made later across the Atlantic Ocean. It was only a matter of time before someone would attempt a world flight in an "egg beater" and achieve a new aviation first.

It was Ross Perot Jr. and Jay Coburn who opened up a new speed-around-the-world category in the NAA (National Aeronautic Association) and FAI (Federation Aeronautique Internationale) record books. Perot, son of the wealthy entrepreneur who started Electronic Data Systems, Inc. in Dallas, Texas, had checked out in helicopters in 1981. He conceived the idea to make a try for the record on August 6, 1982, when he read in the newspaper that Dick Smith, an Australian helicopter pilot, had departed Fort Worth the day before in an attempt to be the first to fly a helicopter around the world. Smith, flying solo, planned to take a year to make the trip.

"I didn't think a guy should have a world record and take a year to get it," Perot said later. "I thought America ought to have this record." He thought such a flight could be made in less than 30 days.

Perot received the reluctant blessing of his father, who told him that he would support such a flight only if it were planned in "a very, very safe and efficient manner." The younger Perot then teamed up with Coburn,

Ross Perot Jr. and Jay Coburn opened up a new speed-around-the-world category in the record books with the flight of a Bell 206 Long Ranger helicopter named *The Spirit of Texas*. In 1982, they covered 25,000 miles in 29 days, 3 hours, 8 minutes. Dick Smith, an Australian, began a 30,168-mile world solo helicopter flight the same year but had no intention of setting a speed record. He made the trip in two stages with a five-month break in between. (Bell Textron photo)

Jay W. Coburn, a Bell helicopter test pilot, had participated in the successful 1979 rescue of Electronic Data Systems employees imprisoned by the Iranians. He was reportedly on the Iranian "wanted" list as a war criminal. (Bill Textron photo)

a veteran Vietnam helicopter pilot and test pilot for the Bell helicopter company. They chose a Bell 206 Long Ranger 2 and had it modified within 10 days to include extra fuel tanks to stretch the range to eight hours of flying time. Navigational avionics, high frequency radios, and an automatic pilot were also installed. All unnecessary weight was stripped from the aircraft, and it was painted in high-visibility colors. Meanwhile, Perot and Coburn made a trip to Washington to seek advice and information from the Defense Intelligence Agency, National Weather Service, *National Geographic* organization, National Aeronautic Association, Air Force, and Navy. They took survival training at the U.S. Navy's Pensacola helicopter facility and conferred with Bob Mucklestone, former round-the-world light plane record-holder. They took ground school training on the new navigation and communication equipment, studied geography, and made many familiarization flights in the modified Bell.

A Lockheed C-130 transport plane was chartered and filled with spare parts and engines, food, and a 50-day supply of water. Dubbed the "Mother Hen," it was to precede and then follow the helicopter, named *The Spirit of Texas*, around the entire route. On board the C-130 was a four-man crew, a helicopter mechanic, the trip coordinator, a represenative of the elder Perot's company, and two trained rescue specialists who could parachute over desert or arctic areas if the helicopter went down.

The route all the way around the world was well within the range of the Bell helicopter. There was one exception. The helicopter had to stop somewhere between Japan and the Aleutians for fuel. Ideally, the stop would have been on the Kamchatka Peninsula in the Soviet Union: the request, made through the Soviet ambassador in Washington, was denied.

Young Perot's father solved the dilemma. He arranged for an American President Line cargo ship, the *President McKinley*, to position itself between Japan and Shemya on the Aleutian chain. The ship was outfitted with large platforms on top of its cargo load. Underneath the platforms was a tank containing jet fuel and pumps.

Perot and Coburn left Love Field in Dallas on September 1, 1982, landed at Terre Haute, Indiana, and proceeded to Montreal through their first encounter with low visibility. It was a 12-hour day of flying. Their subsequent flights took them to Greenland, Iceland, United Kingdom, France, Italy, Greece, Egypt, Saudi Arabia, Pakistan, Burma, Thailand, Singapore, Philippines, Taiwan, Japan, Alaska, and Canada. They crossed 26 countries and 17 seas and oceans. The trip took 29 days, 3 hours, 8 minutes to cover 25,000 nautical miles. They were in the air 246.5 hours; average altitude was approximately 1,000 feet above ground level.

Perot and Coburn had their adventures. As one reporter wrote later, "The Eskimos thought they were spies. The French thought they were crazy. The Egyptians pointed guns at them. The Pakistanis made them

Jay Coburn, left, and Ross Perot Jr. take survival training before their epic flight. They announced that they would complete their flight in "less than 30 days." They did, with 21 hours to spare. (Bell Textron photo)

apologize. And there were army officers in Burma who almost arrested them."

In Greenland, they got their first taste of bureaucratic red tape and stubbornness. They had approval to land and refuel at Kulusuk on the eastern side of Greenland but were a day earlier than their flight plan showed. The airport operator had let his staff off to go hunting and fishing and refused to give them landing clearance. "He told us we were supposed to go through procedures and thought he should teach us a lesson, so he refused to let us land," Perot said later. They landed at the village of Angmagssalik where Greenland Air, a small Danish airline, had a helicopter pad and fuel.

The French also gave them problems. "We couldn't speak French," Perot said, "and they refused to speak English. We kept trying to understand what their air traffic controllers were saying but we couldn't even pronounce the French city names."

In their trek through the Middle East, they ran into "a real raging" group of soldiers who surrounded them, made them fill out reams of papers, and asked a multitude of questions. "You can tell you're in the Middle East," Perot said. "The guards and the military come out to the runway with all their guns. It's very intimidating."

Coburn was especially concerned when they flew within 134 miles of the Iranian border. He had participated in the successful 1979 rescue of Electronic Data Systems employees who had been imprisoned by the Iranians. The rescue had sparked the escape of 11,000 other prisoners, the largest jailbreak in history. Coburn was wanted by the Iranians as a criminal.

The biggest scare came in Burma. They had requested permission to land in Burma, but it was refused. Perot and Coburn decided to take off anyhow. Their diary says simply: "The Burmese Air Force sent two jets to follow us on takeoff. Thunderstorms caused route changes and forced us to land at Mergui, Burma, for fuel. They did not want us there, and it created quite a lot of excitement."

As they neared the town, the air traffic controller yelled over the radio. "No land! No land! You have no permission. We forbid." Perot declared an emergency and landed amid a large band of troops and villagers. They were allowed to leave only after giving out all their food, candy bars, and cigarettes and writing out an apology to the Burmese army.

"Those people in Burma made us feel like prisoners of war," Perot told his father in a telephone call from the Orient. "But the most dangerous part of the trip so far has been riding in the taxicabs in India."

A typhoon, named Ken, was developing between the Philippines and Taiwan, and the two intrepid airmen decided to try to beat it. Despite head winds of 50 mph, they managed to get around it. They flew 12 hours and 40 minutes that day. The Taiwanese required that they fly no lower than 5,000 feet and only along the airways.

The most dangerous part of the trip lay ahead after landing in Japan. A last-minute appeal to the Russians to land on their territory to refuel was again denied. Accordingly, Perot talked with the captain of the *President McKinley*, now at sea, and confirmed that he would be in position on September 26th. Their diary relates what happened next:

> Back into our wonderful rubber suits and cold weather gear this morning. We made HF radio check with ship at 1:30 A.M. and depart at 2:00 A.M. It is a miserable early morning—dark, rainy and winds have shifted to southeasterly. Typhoon Ken has caught up with us again!
>
> Ceilings are about 700 feet, and for the first 100 miles of trip we are only 500 feet above the water. We have to go in an easterly direction for first part of trip to avoid Russian airspace and our ground speed is terrible. Things start to improve at daybreak, and we are making excellent progress after turning more northerly. We have radio contact with the *McKinley* and tell her to remain in current position which will allow a shorter second leg. We pick up her beacon at 250 miles out, and she is reporting clear skies, seas at 12 feet, wind is 35 knots but steady. We made HF radio contact each 30 minutes with the ship and she is finally in sight!

One pass around the ship and then approach 300 yards from rear. Wind is 20 degrees off starboard bow. We slide slightly off to port side at 500 feet and begin descent to pad. The landing deck is on the bow and 45 feet above water line.

We take a high hovering position and begin to settle downward trying to get a feel for ship's motion. About 45 seconds later, we are firmly on deck and signal crew to secure us to the deck. We are still full RPM, and the pitch of boat is same as when we were hovering, and you really have to fight off the tendency to try to control the aircraft. Finally secured to the deck we shut down. We had about 30 minutes' fuel remaining. A short visit with the captain, refuel, and off for dry ground, Shemya."

At this point an Air Force C-130, code-named "King 86," took over from Mother Hen to shepherd the chopper to the island chain. The diary picks up at that point:

About two hours into this leg, it is apparent we don't have sufficient fuel to make Shemya and begin to search for alternatives. King 86 inquires about ships in the area for us and about 3 hours into leg we hear it is possible that a destroyer and an aircraft carrier can give assistance. They will not give location to us but would be available. The forecast for winds indicate a calming trend as we get closer to Shemya. We hope they are right and press on, straight line for Shemya.

About 2 hours out from Shemya things start to improve, and at the 1^1/$_2$-hour out mark, it appears we will make it with a 10-minute reserve. It is dark now and the weather is good for another night landing on unfamiliar terrain. But at least it is over terrain and not water! Our fuel situation had improved more as we now had a 15-minute reserve.

They landed at the Air Force base at Shemya and logged 14 hours, 25 minutes for the 1,390-mile flight over the Pacific. There was still more flying ahead as they flew down the Aleutian chain to Anchorage, Alaska, and Whitehorse, Canada. They had to climb to 14,500 feet to get over the mountains into Whitehorse and found themselves over a thick deck of clouds. They spotted a hole in the clouds, dropped down to 500 feet above the ground and followed a riverbed and the Alcan Highway to the city's airport.

On the next leg, they encountered snow showers, low visibility, and low ceilings. On the flight from Fort Saint John, their diary noted: "Creeped along with ceilings less than 50 feet at times until darkness caused us to land. Found Shell gas processing plant at Simonette, Canada, and spent the night. Just landed near road and walked into plant to find very surprised workers."

Perot and Coburn, tired and dirty, landed at Love Field, the official end of the flight, on September 30, 1982, where their families were waiting.

The Spirit of Texas, modified to carry extra fuel, was assisted by a chartered Lockheed C-130 cargo plane filled with spare parts and supplies. Two trained rescue specialists were on the C-130 crew to parachute if the helicopter went down. (Bell Textron photo)

Ross Perot Sr. had a barber on hand and told the pair "the city's been nice enough to have a reception for you downtown, and you're not going there looking like a couple of bums." An hour later, they made the short flight to City Hall and official welcome home ceremonies.

The cost of this epochal flight was no doubt enormous but the family has never revealed any dollar amount. Only someone with a lot of financial backing could afford it. No doubt about it, their aviation first and its accompanying mark will stand for a long time.

But what about Dick Smith, the Australian fellow who gave Perot the idea in the first place? He had left first. How could he afford it?

Smith, 39, is a highly successful businessman in Sydney. In his early twenties, he had started his own radio repair shop and by age 30 had built up a multimillion dollar electronics business, largely by taking advantage of the CB radio boom of the 1970s. He wrote a book about electronics that sold more than 100,000 copies.

He had learned to fly fixed-wing aircraft in 1972 and competed in the 1976 Perth–Sydney Air Race. He learned to fly helicopters in 1978 and made a record-setting 640-nautical-mile flight from Sydney to Howe Island and return. He ventured away from electronics when he organized a charter operation to fly tourists over Antarctica. He flew with the Royal Australian Air Force to Antarctica and produced a film about the trip.

Smith broke his flight plan down into three stages: Fort Worth to London; London to Sydney, Australia; and Sydney to Fort Worth. He wanted to fly the entire distance under visual flight rules (VFR) only. To do this, he had to cross the North Atlantic in August and the Pacific in June. In addition to sight-seeing, he intended to make it into a business trip by taking still photos for a photo essay book and videotapes for television documentaries.

Smith's trip wasn't any easier than that made by Perot and Coburn, even though he planned to take a year to complete it. His life was threatened several times by animals, nature, and people. Forced by foul weather to land on a rocky ledge overlooking the Hudson Straits in Canada, he slept under the helicopter in a sleeping bag. The next morning, he flew to a nearby Eskimo village and was told that he had camped at a spot that was on a favorite route of polar bears.

En route east over Greenland, someone shot at him with a rifle. He didn't realize it until he landed in Scotland, but he recalled a strange whistling noise in flight and found bullet holes in a fuel tank and the cockpit. One of the latter was within inches of his seat.

At another stop in the Far East, Smith landed on a beach during a heavy rainstorm. The sand was soft. One wheel sank down, and the rotor blades came dangerously close to hitting the ground.

After completing the second phase of his flight in Sydney, Smith took a five-month break to prepare his photo essay book and two documentaries for Australian television. He made a third video after completing the last leg.

Smith rarely flew higher than 500 feet and frequently set the craft on automatic pilot so he could photograph the sights below. He, too, arranged to have a freighter meet him halfway between Japan and the Aleutians for refueling.

It isn't known when he conceived the idea of flying around the world alone in a chopper. "I wasn't out to test technology," he told the press afterward. "I just wanted to make the flight for selfish reasons. I wanted to see if I was up to the challenge of it. I did it for the same reasons the early aviators did it: to test themselves."

"There's no way I could compare my flight with the flights of Lindbergh and (James) Mollison, the first men to fly solo across the Atlantic, Mollison flying east to west," Smith told the press afterward. "For them it was staring death in the face. I had all the avionics and navigation equipment they didn't. But I was much like them in that over the water we all had just one engine. It goes out and into the drink we go." He had no Mother Hen or group of experts standing by to assist if he got into trouble on the 30,168-nautical-mile flight. He said the trip was extremely tiring, often lonely, and sometimes frightening.

Smith estimated that the trip cost him $150,000, some of which was offset by proceeds from the three documentary videos and the photo book. He also had financial help from Qantas, the Australian national airline, and Mobil Oil Co.

Would he do it again?

"Never. Had I known what I know now, I would not try it. I would advise anyone considering such a trip who would listen to me not to attempt it. You just can't rely on the weather. I really shouldn't have done it. I pressed my luck too far. But I learned a lot about myself."

Dick Smith didn't set a speed record on his historic solo world-girdling flight—a record that someone might beat some day. He did better than that. He established three aviation firsts—first solo helicopter flight around the world, first solo helicopter crossing of the Atlantic, and first solo helicopter flight across the Pacific—something no one can take away from him.

28

SPACE-AGE GLOBE-CIRCLERS

The Space Age began October 4, 1957, with the launching of the world's first artificial satellite by the Soviet Union. Its speed of five miles per second carried it around the earth once every 92 minutes. *Sputnik* weighed 184 pounds and was 23 inches in diameter. A month later, *Sputnik II* was sent into orbit. It weighed 1,120 pounds and carried a dog, the first globe-circling space passenger. Since then, many satellites have been placed in earth orbit.

Challenged by the Soviet success, the United States began a space program of its own. On January 31, 1958, it launched *Explorer I.* In the fall of 1958 a group of engineers and scientists working in the newly established National Aeronautics and Space Administration (NASA) were given the job of designing and launching a series of manned space capsules into earth orbit to study humans' ability to live and work in space. Project Mercury was established, and a number of astronauts were chosen and trained. First, however, a three-year-old chimpanzee went for a ride in space that lasted 18 minutes.

Then, on April 12, 1961, the Soviet Union launched a manned spaceship-satellite into orbit around the earth. The cosmonaut was Yuri Gagarin. To Gagarin goes the honor of being the first human to circle the earth in space. In his message to the Soviet leaders, President Kennedy called it "an outstanding technical achievement," adding: "The exploration of our solar system is an ambition which we and all mankind share with the Soviet Union . . . this is an important step forward toward that goal. Our own Mercury man-in-space program is directed toward the same end."

The Soviets next sent Gherman Titov aloft. Titov orbited the earth, August 6–7, 1961, spending 25 hours and 18 minutes in space. The United

318

States "replied" by putting Alan Shepard into suborbit. The first complete orbital shot in the U.S. space program came November 29, 1961; again, it was a chimpanzee.

Behind the scenes, around the country, Project Mercury personnel were working feverishly to catch up with the Russians. On February 20, 1962, John Glenn Jr. made three orbits of the earth. He landed after 4 hours and 56 minutes of orbital flight, having covered 81,000 miles. Project Mercury was followed by Project Gemini, in which two-man teams were sent into orbit around the earth. Project Apollo followed, and on July 21, 1969, astronauts Neil Armstrong and Edwin Aldrin Jr. landed on the moon. By this time, 52 Americans and Russians, including one Russian woman, had orbited the earth. Six men had orbited the moon. Earth orbiting has since become almost routine, though all space flights are inherently dangerous.

In January 1972, it was announced that NASA would continue development of a reusable, low-cost Space Shuttle. The system would be the main component of U.S. space research and its applications for years to come. The purpose of the Space Shuttle would be to carry payloads into earth orbit. On a standard mission, the Orbiter remains in orbit seven days, returns to earth with the flight crew and the payload, and lands like an airplane. It is then readied for another flight.

The requirement that the Shuttle "land like an airplane" made it different from all previous space ventures. Once in space, the Shuttle is maneuvered like a spacecraft, but it becomes an aircraft once it enters the earth's atmosphere. It lands on a runway at about 200 mph.

The first Shuttle, *Columbia*, was readied for launch in the spring of 1981. The astronauts were John Young and Robert Crippen. Both had undergone extensive training. Young has logged more time in space than any other astronaut. He flew two Gemini missions, came within 69 miles of the moon as Apollo 10's command module pilot, and landed on the lunar surface in 1972 as the commander of Apollo 16. Crippen had been in astronaut training for 11 years but had not made a space flight. Along with Young, he had spent more than 1,300 hours in a simulator, practicing and testing his reactions.

In a sense, flying the Space Shuttle can be as nerve-racking as flying the planes used in early round-the-world flights. Jammed with electronic gear, it is one of the most complex machines ever built. Almost anything can go wrong. It isn't placement in orbit that is so risky; it is reentering the earth's atmosphere and landing.

The maiden flight of the Space Shuttle was made April 12, 1981, 20 years to the day after Gagarin made the first manned space flight. The countdown ended, and the two rockets ignited; 6.3 million pounds of thrust forced the 18-story, 4.5-million-pound rocket off the launchpad at Kennedy Space

Center. Two minutes later, the boosters dropped off and *Columbia* floated over the Atlantic. Eight and one-half minutes after blastoff, the main tank was thrust off and disintegrated in a shower of sparks over the Indian Ocean. The orbital engines were switched on and with a series of short bursts carried the Shuttle into orbit 150 to 170 miles above the earth.

Marine Col. John Glenn Jr., wearing an astronaut's pressure suit, poses beside his *Friendship 7* space capsule in 1962. Glenn, now a U.S. senator, was the first American to orbit the earth in a space vehicle. (NASA photo)

John W. Young, left, and Robert L. Crippen were first to orbit the earth in space and return in their vehicle for a normal aircraft landing. They are holding a model of their space shuttle *Columbia* after their successful flight in 1981. (NASA photo)

The flight plan of *Columbia* called for a 54.5-hour, 36-orbit mission. As the craft began its third orbit, Mission Control found that all systems checked out, and the flight was "go." There were some tense moments, however. Some of the spacecraft's 30,000 silica tiles had fallen off during launch. Loss of the tiles could doom the craft and its crew. But Mission Control, viewing the outside of the craft by remote television cameras, determined that the tiles were in a noncritical area and that their loss would not interfere with a safe return.

Young and Crippen settled into a routine of prearranged housekeeping duties. They ate their first space meal of "rehydratable" turkey tetrazzini and "thermostabilized" frankfurters. Everything went smoothly during the first few hours, then minor problems began to develop. During their first "night" in space, the temperature in the cabin dropped to 37° Fahrenheit. When the astronauts complained, Mission Control sent a signal from earth that caused warm water to be pumped into the system, and the cabin temperature was raised to a comfortable level. Next, a faulty flight data recorder ceased operation. When the astronauts tried to open its cover with a screwdriver to repair it, they found that it had been screwed down too tightly. They switched to a backup recorder.

During the final orbit, Young fired several thrusters. He then fired the orbital engines to reduce the Shuttle's speed and let the earth's gravity pull it down. At 400,000 feet, a series of hypersonic S turns signaled by the computers were made, and reentry into the earth's atmosphere began. Over the dry lake bed at Edwards AFB, *Columbia*, now a 120-ton powerless glider, made a 180-degree turn for its final approach to the five-mile runway. As *Columbia* came out of the turn, it was in a steep dive—seven times steeper than the approach of a commercial airliner—traveling at 400 mph. At 1,800 feet, only 30 seconds from touchdown, Young pulled the nose up, and their airspeed dropped to 180. At 19 seconds from touchdown, he dropped the gear and floated to a tire-squeaking landing. As *Columbia* rolled to a stop, a local radio station played "The Star-Spangled Banner." From Mission Control in Houston came an exuberant "Welcome home, *Columbia!* Beautiful. Beautiful."

For the record, *Columbia*, the world's first aerospace craft capable of

The Orbiter *Columbia* is about to touch down at Edwards Air Force Base, California, after the historic first full test of the Space Transportation System. (NASA photo)

operating both in space and in the atmosphere, was in flight 54 hours, 20 minutes, and 52 seconds. Its maximum altitude was 130 miles. Today Shuttle crews are routinely sent into orbit, where they carry out scientific experiments and launch or repair satellites. One day they may begin assembling interplanetary manned spacecraft for exploration beyond earth.

29

BALLOONING'S GREATEST ACHIEVERS

An entirely new era for the original flying vehicle—the hot air or gas balloon—began during the last half of the twentieth century. By then, the sport of free ballooning had reached more highly sophisticated levels because of satellite navigation equipment, more precise high altitude wind predictions, satellite communications systems, improved space-age envelope materials, and pressurized gondolas that made longer flights at high altitudes possible and less hazardous.

The North American continent was first spanned in a free balloon May 8 through 12, 1980, by Maxie Anderson and his son Kristian. In their 200,000-cubic-foot balloon *Kitty Hawk*, they covered 2,832 miles from Fort Baker, California, to the province of Quebec on the southern tip of eastern Canada in 99 hours and 54 minutes to establish a coast-to-coast record and become the first to cross any continent by balloon.

On October 9, 1981, balloonists John Shoecroft and Fred Gorrell sought to surpass that record time and lifted off from Costa Mesa, California, in *Superchicken III*, a ten-story-high, helium-filled balloon. It took them 55 hours, 25 minutes to make the ocean-to-ocean flight of 2,515 miles from Costa Mesa, California, to Blackbeard Island, off the coast of Georgia.

The Atlantic Ocean represented a longtime challenge for those who chose to fly in the unguided gas bags. Such a flight had been considered by balloonists since the mid-1800s, and the first actual attempt was made in 1873 from New York City; but that flight came to grief in the Catskill Mountains. The Atlantic was eventually conquered a century later by Maxie L. Anderson, Ben L. Abruzzo, and Larry M. Newman during a five-day period, August 12 to 17, 1978. They flew *Double Eagle II* from Presque Isle, Maine, to Miserey, France, a distance of 3,107 miles in 137 hours, 5 minutes. It was this achievement that whetted Anderson's desire for the ultimate balloon flight—circling the earth. He teamed up with Don Ida of Boulder, Colorado, and planning began soon after the transatlantic venture.

Anderson's plan was to launch their craft, christened *Jules Verne*, from a base in Egypt and ride the winds at altitudes of 25,000 to 30,000 feet. At these altitudes, they hoped to average ground speeds of 100 mph and perhaps reach as much as 150 mph. If so, Anderson believed he could make 20,000 miles in 8 to 10 days. He hoped to circle the globe nonstop but said, "We will complete the voyage even if forced to land a time or two. It should be the longest, fastest, highest balloon flight ever."

Anderson and Ida chose Egypt as their launching point because they thought it would give them the best chance of going all the way around. "We think we can reach the Pacific from there without flying across Afghanistan, Iraq, Iran, or the Himalayas," Ida told the press. "Once over the Pacific, we believe we can fly back to Egypt or to a point along the same longitude without crossing any of the same geographical or political barriers. The 6,000 miles from Egypt to the Pacific should be the toughest part of the flight."

The two planned to depart from Luxor, about 350 miles south of Cairo. From there, they hoped the winds would carry them over the Red Sea, Saudi Arabia, Pakistan, India, Myanmar (Burma), and possibly China before reaching the Pacific south of Japan. They then expected the *Jules Verne* to drift far north, possibly to Alaska, before floating across Canada, the United States, and the Atlantic back to North Africa.

The early trajectory of the flight was extremely important, according to Anderson. It was essential that the craft remain south of the Himalayas to avoid the extreme turbulence over the mountains. If the balloon headed in that direction, they felt they would have to abandon the flight.

Jules Verne was launched from Luxor on January 11, 1981. They flew according to plan until they were over India. Their concern about flying over the Himalayas was well-founded. The enormous silver balloon, 11 stories high, drifted toward the world's highest mountain range. After 47 hours, 30 minutes of flight, the balloonists decided to abort the flight. They descended near Murchpur, 90 miles west of New Delhi. They had flown 2,763 miles.

Others were considering world-circling at the same time, and those interested sensed that a race was on to meet ballooning's greatest challenge. However, many felt that the ultimate flight had to be preceded by the experience to be gained at shorter distances.

In February 1981, Rocky Aoki, owner of the Benihana restaurant chain; Ben L. Abruzzo; Larry M. Newman; and Ron Clark made the first transpacific balloon flight in *Double Eagle V*. They traveled 5,208.67 miles from Nagashima, Japan, to Covelo, California, in 84 hours, 31 minutes.

By this time, no hot air balloon had successfully crossed the Atlantic, so Richard Branson and Per Lindstrand decided it would be a "first" they wanted to achieve. They did, in 1987. They then set the distance and duration record for a hot air balloon January 15 through 17, 1991, on a flight across the Pacific in the *Pacific Flyer*, the largest hot air balloon ever flown. They caught a high altitude jet stream during their 48-hour flight and reached an estimated 145 mph. These flights were made in contemplation of making a world flight as soon as they could.

Although the Atlantic had been crossed by the team of three balloonists in a helium-filled balloon in 1978, it had not been accomplished solo. Joe W. Kittinger, a former U.S. Air Force fighter pilot, decided to try. He had ridden a helium-filled balloon to a record altitude of 102,800 feet in August 1960 before leaping from its open gondola to test a new type of parachute. It was the greatest height from which anyone had ever parachuted.

Kittinger's transatlantic solo flight in *Rosie O'Grady*, a helium-filled balloon, took place September 15 through 18, 1984. He departed Caribou, Maine, and made a crash landing at Montenotte near Savona, Italy, to establish a distance record of 3,544 miles that still stands as the longest solo balloon flight in his class of balloon.

Steve Fossett, a Chicago businessman, completed the first solo crossing of the Pacific in February 1995. His route of flight was from Seoul, South Korea, to Mendham, Saskatchewan, Canada.

There were several aborted attempts for a world flight in the following years. Larry Newman, Richard Abruzzo, and Vladimir Dzhanibekov tried in 1993 in *Earthwind 1* but crashed shortly after takeoff from Reno, Nevada. The following year, Newman, Abruzzo, and David Melton tried again in *Earthwind 2*; but a relief valve froze, and they had to land the same day after covering only a few miles. Newman, Melton, and George Saad made a final attempt in 1995 with *Earthwind 3*; but their anchor balloon burst during the initial climb, and they had to abort.

Richard Branson, Per Lindstrand, and Alex Ritchie went aloft for a world flight attempt in the *Virgin Global Challenger* on January 7, 1997, from England; but they had to land in Morocco after 19 hours aloft. Other attempts were made that year. Dr. Bertrand Piccard and Wim Verstraeten took off from Chateau d'Oex, Switzerland, in the *Breitling Orbiter* on January 12 but came down in the Mediterranean because of a massive fuel leak after only 6 hours of flight.

Three days later, Steve Fossett lifted off alone from St. Louis in the *Solo Spirit*, crossed the African continent and landed in Sultanpur, India, after setting a duration record for his class of balloon of 6 days, 2 hours, and 44 minutes, and a distance record of 10,361 miles.

In December 1997, Richard Branson wanted to try once more from England, again with Per Lindstrand and Alex Ritchie in a craft named *Virgin Global Challenger*. However, the craft's envelope broke away from the gondola before they could board it and flew on its own to eventual destruction.

Steve Fossett had not given up after his long-distance, record-setting solo flight. He left St. Louis on January 8, 1998, in the *Solo Spirit 2* but was forced to land in Krasnodar, Russia, after covering 5,802 miles in 108.5 hours. A week later, Bertrand Piccard, Wim Verstraeten, and Andy Elson attempted to take off in the *Breitling Orbiter 2*, again from Switzerland; but the envelope deflated, and they had to abort the takeoff. Only a day later, January 9, 1998, Dick Rutan and David Melton left Albuquerque, New Mexico, in the *Global Hilton*; but the balloon burst, and the two pilots had to parachute out of the gondola to save their lives.

By January 28, 1998, Piccard, Verstraeten, and Elson were ready to try again, but landed ten days later in Myanmar (Burma) after flying 5,266 miles. They had been forced to land because of an unexplained fuel leak and lack of permission to fly over China. Although it wasn't a distance record, they did set a duration record of 233.5 hours in flight.

Steve Fossett still refused to give up his dream of a solo world flight. On August 7, 1998, he lifted off in the *Solo Spirit 3* from Mendoza, Argentina, for a flight in the Southern Hemisphere. He seemed headed for a successful completion ten days later when he was caught in a violent thunderstorm that ruptured his balloon and dropped it into the Coral Sea about 500 miles east of Australia. He had been cruising at an altitude of 29,000 feet when flames from the burners melted the fabric of the envelope, and he landed in the water upside down. He was able to free his life raft from the capsule just as the propane fuel tanks exploded. He was unhurt and was located the next day by rescuers who were guided to the location by the craft's emergency locator beacon. However, he had set a new world balloon distance record of 14,236 miles.

On December 18, 1998, Richard Branson, Per Lindstrand, and Steve Fossett lofted from Morocco in the *ICO Global Challenger*, made the first crossing of the Asian continent, but had to ditch seven days later in the Pacific Ocean off Hawaii. They had flown 12,404 miles in 177.5 hours.

Two new attempts by Americans were made in January 1999, but both failed because the Chinese would not give clearance for them to fly through their airspace. The next month, Andy Elson and Colin Prescot took off from Almeria, Spain, on February 19 in the *Cable & Wireless*, but were forced to ditch off the Japanese coast because of bad weather on March 7 after flying 11,496 miles and setting a new duration record of 425 hours, 41 minutes.

Bertrand Piccard by now had failed twice to fly around the world with the Breitling watch company of Switzerland as his sponsor. He persuaded the company's officials to allow him to try once more—but with the understanding that there would be no fourth time.

The Piccard name had been noted before in ballooning history. Bertrand's grandfather was Auguste Piccard, a Belgian physicist known for his two balloon ascents into the stratosphere to study cosmic rays. He invented the pressurized capsule that enabled humans to survive the ascent. In May 1931, accompanied by Paul Kipfer, Auguste Piccard launched from Augsburg, Germany, and lofted to 55,500 feet. The two thus became the first to reach the stratosphere and also the first to see the curvature of the earth. After World War II, Piccard made ocean dives in a bathysphere of his own design. His son Jacques in a bathysphere reached a depth of 35,800 feet in the Pacific Ocean to establish a world mark. Their scientific breakthroughs led to pressurized aircraft, space capsules, and safer submarines.

Bertrand, born in 1958, heard the details of these pioneering events from his father during his early years and developed a keen taste for adventure. He learned to fly a hang glider and at age 16 took up aerobatics in it, which gave him a feeling of self-awareness he had not experienced before. He decided to become a physician "to explore the human condition—the mind and soul—rather than the physical world." He specialized in psychiatry, but he continued to fly hang gliders and progressed to motorized gliders and microlights. He gave demonstrations in them at air shows and became a European aerobatic hang glider champion. One of his acts was to go aloft dangling in a hang glider from a balloon. He would be released at about 6,000 feet and perform loops, spins, and wingovers on the way down. Although he went aloft this way many times, he had no desire to go ballooning. He considered it an "absurd" sport for a long time because of the uncertainty of a definite destination and a safe landing.

A chance discussion with the veteran Belgian balloonist, Wim Verstraeten, changed his outlook. Verstraeten suggested that since Piccard was a physician, he would make an excellent copilot for him on the Chrysler Transatlantic Challenge in August 1992, the first transatlantic balloon race. Sensing a new opportunity to test himself, Piccard agreed to go. He learned the fundamentals of ballooning, and after five days and nights in an unpressurized gondola, the two succeeded in crossing from New England to Spain to win the award. As a result, the duo had an audience with Belgian King Baudouin. When the king asked Piccard what they were going to do next, he answered offhandedly that they would attempt a flight around the world. He was surprised at what he had said so brashly, but felt obligated to follow through on the remark.

It was this thought that led Piccard to contact Breitling's chief executive to see if the world-famous Swiss aviation chronometer firm would consider sponsoring such an effort. They had gratuitously displayed Breitling's logo during the press conferences that had followed the Chrysler race, and the publicity was much appreciated by the watch-making firm's top executives. The company's answer was a wholehearted affirmative, and thus began the tasks of designing and constructing a capsule and balloon; studying the possible routes; and forming an organization to handle weather forecasting and reporting, visas, overflight permissions, and overseeing the innumerable details of launch, flight following, and air traffic control.

Many lessons had been learned during the two previous *Orbiter* attempts. Most important was the necessity to obtain official government permission to cross China, because the vagaries of the eastbound jet winds could easily put the balloon over its borders. Chinese officials had refused to give permission for overflights after a British balloon had drifted over Chinese restricted areas without prior authority, and because of the resumed bombing of Iraq by allied forces. However, in August 1998 Piccard flew to Beijing with Swiss foreign service officials, and the Swiss diplomats gained approval for the flight with the understanding that the balloon had to remain south of the twenty-sixth parallel, an admittedly difficult feat for a free-floating balloon.

For his copilot, Piccard chose Brian Jones, born in 1947, a former aircraft and helicopter pilot and loadmaster with 13 years' experience in the British Royal Air Force and extensive survival training. He became interested in ballooning in 1986 and bought one for himself. Gaining experience, he became an instructor and flight examiner, and formed a partnership that operated balloons for corporate publicity. By November 1998, he had accumulated 5,000 flight hours, of which 1,200 were logged aboard a balloon.

Jones helped organize Breitling's 1997 and 1998 round-the-world balloon attempts. He was the on-the-ground project manager responsible for the construction of the balloon's flight system and gondola. Heavily involved in the flight's preparations, he manned the control center during the flight, and Piccard credited his calm demeanor and humorous messages for maintaining the crew's morale during the flight. When the flight ended in Myanmar, Jones efficiently organized the recovery of the gondola and the balloon. Piccard was impressed with his performance and confidently appointed him as his copilot for the *Orbiter 3* attempt.

The failures of the first two flights caused many engineering changes to be made in the envelope and gondola, manufactured by Cameron Balloons, a British firm. The balloon, Model R-650, was a Rozier design, with the lifting power of a combination of hot air and helium. Many computer simulations were made to investigate fuel consumption, and the consensus was that the best technique was to keep the balloon as cool as possible during the day. An insulated envelope, increased in size and shape over the former one, was made of aluminized, double-skinned Mylar fabric, and a new burner system was designed and installed after Piccard decided to switch from kerosene to propane fuel. More computer simulations were run to determine if the changes were adequate; however, until it flew, no one could know exactly how the new engineering features would perform.

The 18-foot floatable gondola, which could be pressurized to rise to 40,000 feet, was equipped to sustain two pilots for a four-week flight. It contained one sleeping bunk, a cockpit, kitchen, survival equipment, and food storage. Oxygen and nitrogen tanks were carried; filters were installed to remove excess carbon dioxide and recycle the air. Fuel controls in the cockpit enabled the pilots to operate the burners, switch fuel tanks, and drop empty tanks. Electrical power was obtained from batteries that could be recharged by solar panels suspended from the balloon. The latest communications systems were installed, including a computer, fax machine, satellite telephone, and a ground positioning system (GPS).

The question of where to launch *Orbiter 3* had to be decided early so that launch preparations could begin. North Africa, which other balloonists had used, was a possibility. America was also considered; but that would mean that the Pacific Ocean would have to be crossed last, and they wanted to cross it as early as possible. In addition, an American launch would have made it more difficult to avoid flying over south China because of the usual west-to-east winds in the northern latitudes. In both cases, the logistics of transporting the balloon, its equipment, and the personnel for a command center would be expensive and difficult. Finally Chateau d'Oex in the Swiss Alps was chosen because it was relatively close to the equipment manufacturers and because Piccard had been impressed with the "enthusiasm and friendship of the villagers" they found in the previous attempts.

Piccard and Jones took intensive survival training over the next several months that included decompression chamber practice and water and fire survival instruction. The possible success of the Branson team gave urgency to the *Orbiter 3's* preparation. When they failed, the chances for a Piccard-Jones success with an early spring 1999 departure seemed brighter.

Since permission to overfly parts of China was assured and the forecasts by their expert meteorologists Pierre Eckert and Luc Trullemans seemed encouraging, the 180-foot-tall balloon lifted off under clear skies from the snow-covered ground of Chateau d'Oex at 8:05 A.M. on March 1, 1999. Their liftoff was ten days after the British *Cable & Wireless* balloon flown by Andy Elson and Colin Prescot. The race with them for the elusive balloon "first" was on.

The wind took *Orbiter 3* slowly over the Alps and southwestward over Spain as planned. Two days later, they "turned the corner" and slowly drifted eastward over the Sahara Desert, exactly as their weather experts had forecast. At one point, Piccard had to exit the gondola to chip ice away from the envelope with an ax. The "skywalk" could have been dangerous, but he felt so safe that he didn't wear a harness. Both made several EVAs (extravehicular activities) later. Piccard commented, "I must admit the sight of the empty space was very impressive."

The balloon gradually picked up speed and raced over Libya at about 90 mph. There was concern that they were going so fast that the winds would eventually swing northeastward and take them toward the Himalayas. They were advised by the control center to drop to a lower altitude to get winds that gradually took them on a more southerly route to avoid no-fly zones in Egypt and Yemen.

On March 7, the news was flashed to them that Elson and Prescot of the *Cable & Wireless* crew had been forced to ditch their craft in the sea 60 miles south of Japan due to problems with electrical power and bad weather. Without power, they could not transfer kerosene from the tanks to the burners and could not communicate with their control center. Fortunately, the pair was rescued, and Piccard and Jones were relieved that their rivals had survived. They were not pleased with someone else's failure and a near tragedy. However, Elson and Prescot could take some comfort in the fact that they had set a duration record.

The lower altitude recommended by the *Orbiter* ground crew was followed, and it was a wise decision. During the next few days, the balloon drifted over southern Egypt, Saudi Arabia, Yemen, Oman, Bangladesh, and India toward Chinese airspace. While British balloonists had not been given permission to fly over China because of previous airspace violations, the *Orbiter* crew with Swiss registry was the first to gain authorization—provided they stay south of the twenty-sixth parallel. As they drifted within 25 miles of the restricted zone and it looked like they were going to drift beyond it, Chinese authorities ordered them to prepare for an emergency landing.

A landing was not necessary. The wind increased and drifted them back on track so that they crossed through the permissible Chinese airspace in a surprising 15 hours. Then came the supreme test of the hundreds of miles of the Pacific that lay ahead.

The ground crew in Switzerland checked various computer models based on the high altitude winds and weather conditions and advised that they should not consider going northward toward North America as originally thought but head toward the equator where a jet stream was

The *Breitling Orbiter 3* in flight over the Alps en route to Africa on the first day. The initial route southwestward was planned to avoid drifting eastward over forbidden territory in China. Winds then caused the balloon to take a generally eastward direction, but they had to avoid no-fly zones over Egypt and Yemen. (Courtesy Bertrand Piccard and Brian Jones)

expected to form several days later. It meant avoiding Hawaii and the United States completely and crossing land over Mexico. This would be a flight of about 10,000 miles over water, an extremely long stretch, but they were assured by their ground crew in Switzerland that they had no other safe options.

The flight southeastward seemed interminable. They crossed two hundred miles south of Guam over the Mariana Trench, the deepest ocean spot on the planet, where Piccard's father, Jacques, had steered his bathysphere to a record depth of 35,800 feet in 1960. The clouds seemed continually threatening as the hours passed. Small, puffy clouds in the mornings developed into huge cumulonimbus clouds in the afternoons, but disappeared in the early evenings. They followed the advice of their ground crew in Switzerland to maintain an altitude and trajectory that would keep them away from or above the tops of the clouds. They frequently saw thunderstorm clouds developing to the north that could rip the balloon to shreds if they drifted into them. They descended from 13,000 feet to 5,000 feet four times to melt ice on the balloon, depressurize the gondola, or cause their course to be changed to catch more favorable winds.

The expected tailwinds did not evolve as they slowed down to about 25 miles an hour and covered less than 3,000 miles of the anticipated distance to land. Both men admitted their fear of having to ditch in the world's greatest ocean far from rescue vessels. In an article in *National Geographic*, Piccard said, "This immense expanse of ocean has become a mirror in front of which it is impossible to fool myself. I feel naked with my emotions, my fears, and my hopes. We'd like to be farther on in our flight, but all we can do is accept being where we are, drifting in a lazy wind over the biggest ocean on the globe."

Jones expressed his concern about an ocean ditching inside the top-heavy gondola in their book titled *Around the World in 20 Days*: "If we found ourselves upside down in the ocean, our only chance would be to pile all loose equipment at the front and hope that the gondola would tilt nose-down at a steep enough angle to bring the rear hatch clear of the water. Even then, we might easily drown trying to escape with a hatch open; the gondola could fill with water and sink, taking us to the bottom with it. If we had to parachute from a height—forget it. We were six, seven, eight days away from rescue; the chances of anyone finding us in time to save our lives were extremely remote, and even if an aircraft managed to locate us and drop a large life raft, there was no guarantee we would survive until a ship arrived."

Their mutual concern was heightened when they found that as they flew closer to the equator, their ability to communicate was affected because the aluminized balloon blocked facsimile and satellite communi-

Bertrand Piccard, a medical doctor, son and grandson of two famous Swiss scientists, adjusts one of the radios in the balloon's pressurized capsule. An air recycling system added oxygen and removed carbon dioxide. Solar panels recharged batteries. The capsule was designed to keep two pilots comfortable for four weeks. (Courtesy Bertrand Piccard and Brian Jones)

cations with the team in Switzerland. There was nothing they could do but drift as the winds decided. Remarkably, they wove in and out of the clusters of storms without being blasted helplessly aloft in any of them. The vertical winds in the towering clouds could have ripped the balloon to shreds.

As they reached the halfway mark on March 13, they opened the sealed hatch for the first time in more than a week to breathe fresh air. They passed the time with household chores and cleaning out the gondola. On March 16, they surpassed Steve Fossett's distance record of 14,236 miles; the next day, they crossed the international date line.

The balloon continued to float lazily for hours. Then finally the jet wind predictions of the meteorologists in Switzerland suddenly proved comfortably accurate. They were thrust into a powerful eastbound jet stream and sped toward Mexico at 115 miles an hour. But new threats arose. The outside temperature dipped to 58 degrees below zero and caused the water inside the gondola to freeze, requiring more fuel to be burned. The balloon slowly drifted out of the jet stream, crossed over the

Mexican coast, slowed down and headed southward. They did not notice or care that they had become the first balloonists to cross the Pacific during a nonstop, round-the-world attempt.

The two pilots were exhausted and found it difficult to breathe. They put on their oxygen masks and took turns sleeping. It seemed their dream of victory would be unobtainable if the slow drift toward South America continued. In desperation, Piccard decided to rise as high as they could to try to catch the jet stream again, even if it took a large amount of fuel. As they rose, the balloon slowly took a northeastward track over the Caribbean. They passed over Jamaica and found that they were turning eastward again headed toward Africa at a speed of more than 100 miles an hour. They crossed the African coast during the night of March 19. That day they had broken the duration record set by Elson and Prescot in the *Cable & Wireless* of 17 days, 17 hours, 41 minutes. They were over the Sahara Desert on March 20 at the 26,050-mile mark and crossed the longitudinal line of 9 degrees, 27 minutes, which was the exact geographical point where they had turned and headed east and thus could officially claim their nonstop world global record.

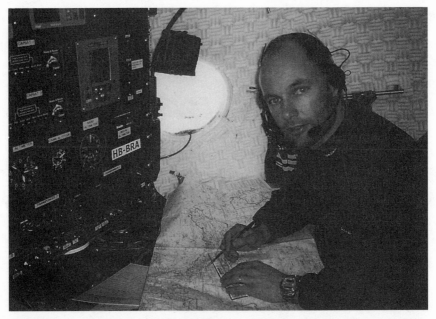

The two-man crew was in continual radio and facsimile contact with their base in Switzerland. Here Brian Jones checks a map to verify readings on the ground positioning system. The pilots could operate fuel burners and gas tanks or jettison fuel tanks from inside the capsule. (Courtesy Bertrand Piccard and Brian Jones)

The *Orbiter 3* continued eastward, and as dawn broke on March 21, a Breitling jet plane with reporters and TV cameramen aboard circled and filmed the descent toward a landing. At 5:52 A.M. Piccard and Jones officially landed the *Breitling Orbiter* safely at Mut near Dakhla, Egypt. Seven hours later, a Russian-made Egyptian rescue helicopter arrived and whisked the two happy world-circlers on the first stage back home.

The two men had spent 19 days, 21 hours, and 47 minutes together on their 25,360-mile odyssey and achieved what so many others before them had dreamed, dedicated their fortunes, and risked their lives to realize. Piccard and Jones had their moments of doubt and misery cooped up in the gondola that was not much larger than an ordinary bedroom, but the moment of victory was worth it. As they told the press later, "We took off as pilots, flew as friends, and landed as brothers."

The happy pair won the Budweiser Cup and a million-dollar prize awarded by the Anheuser-Busch Corporation, which was supplemented by a donation from the Breitling company, with the understanding that half of it would be used to create the Winds of Hope Foundation, a Swiss charity they favored. The foundation is dedicated to combating unusual,

Safely on the sands of Egypt, Jones and Piccard wave happily for the camera. They had been in the air 19 days, 21 hours, 47 minutes and could claim an historic ballooning "first" that had eluded others for many years. (Courtesy Bertrand Piccard and Brian Jones)

disregarded ailments and diseases such as noma, a devastating gangrene caused by malnutrition that disfigures the face and causes intolerable mutilations.

Piccard and Jones returned to Europe amid continuing world acclaim for their singular achievement. Britain's Queen Elizabeth presented them with the Charles Green salver, a silver tray first given to the balloonist of that name in 1839. They also received the award of the Olympic Order from Juan Antonio Samaranch, president of the International Olympic Committee; the Gold Medal of the Aero Club of France; and the French Gold Medal of Youth and Sport. They were honored in America with other awards such as the Explorers Club Medal and the George E. Haddaway Medal for Aeronautical Achievement sponsored by the Frontiers of Flight Museum of Dallas, Texas. Their gondola was put on exhibit at the Smithsonian's National Air and Space Museum in the nation's capital where it shares honored space with other air and space craft that have circled the globe. It is the only piece of equipment on display that is not American.

In the book about the *Breitling Orbiter 3* flight, Piccard predicted that someone, perhaps Steve Fossett, would make a solo flight around the world, the last great balloon challenge. That possibility has long intrigued J. Stephen "Steve" Fossett, president of a Chicago investment company, who has the distinction for being the most pertinacious balloonist in the world with a single mind-set. He tried four times to make a solo world flight and failed but did score several balloon "firsts": the first flights across the continents of Africa, Asia, and Europe, and across the Indian and South Atlantic oceans.

Fossett's quest for adventurous diversions is legendary. He holds ten official sailing records, including those for crossing the Pacific Ocean single-handed, circling Great Britain and Ireland, and sailing from Newport, Rhode Island, to Bermuda. He also holds eight boat racing records. Fascinated by endurance sports, he has swum across the English Channel, run the Iditarod dogsled race in Alaska, participated in the Ironman Triathlon in Hawaii, and driven in the Le Mans sports car race in France.

Fossett has also established several aircraft speed records in a Cessna Citation X jet, including U.S. transcontinental records in both directions. He also set round-the-world speed records in both directions for this class of aircraft in February 2000 and November 2000.

On June 17, 2001, he was ready to make a fifth solo world attempt in a free balloon. As his 140-foot silver balloon *Solo Spirit* was being inflated at the airport in Kalgoorlie, Australia, winds ripped it apart before he boarded it, and his hopes were dashed once more. The balloon was so badly damaged that it had to be returned to Britain for repairs.

To no one's surprise, Fossett tried again only six weeks later. A new *Solo Spirit* departed Northam, Western Australia, on August 4, 2001, for still another attempt in the Southern Hemisphere. His intended route of flight was eastward across the South Pacific to South America, across the Andes and then the South Atlantic and Indian oceans to as near the take-off point in Australia as possible. His mission control team was located at Washington University in St. Louis, Missouri.

The *Solo Spirit* control center director, Joe Ritchie, Fossett's friend of more than 30 years, was confident he could do it. "He is one of the most indomitable, determined, cheerful adventurers that you could imagine," he said on the *Solo Spirit* web site. "I think it's fun the way he's trying to do it—with a relatively paper-thin budget, lower altitude, unpressurized, all by himself, down below the jet stream where he has to dodge thunderstorms. It's more exciting than a high-tech, high money approach."

As Fossett crossed Australia, the balloon and its equipment tested perfectly, so he headed out over the Pacific full of confidence. It took him nine uneventful days to cross the world's largest ocean, much of the time above 20,000 feet and on oxygen. As he reached the coast of southern Chile on August 15, he had to rise to 28,000 feet to be sure he would clear the Andes Mountains. During that leg, he encountered strong, turbulent winds which could cause a balloon's envelope to rupture. He put on his parachute as a precaution and burned extra fuel to control the balloon's altitude.

The turbulence increased when he approached the eastern Argentina border at night. A cold front had stalled in the vicinity of Montevideo, Uruguay; thunderstorms were still building and could be seen ahead. They did not dissipate as expected, but Fossett was able to slip by some of them briefly until *Solo Spirit* drifted into an area that produced freezing rain, snow, and more severe turbulence.

The weather reports over the South Atlantic were even more ominous. To continue, Fossett would have to descend to 15,000 feet or less and expose the balloon to more dangerous weather that could rip the balloon apart. The route across the South Atlantic was now blocked by a severe weather system that the control center meteorologists predicted would not budge for at least three days. There was no alternate route around the weather for a balloon. "It turned out to be a minefield of thunderstorms," Fossett lamented in a postflight interview.

Senior members of the staff in the control center at Washington University in St. Louis advised Fossett to terminate the flight, and he reluctantly agreed. He landed at dawn on August 17, 2001, on a cattle ranch about 30 miles from the city of Bage in southern Brazil, close to the border of Uruguay and about 150 miles from the Atlantic Ocean.

A plane circling the scene reported that the balloon was deflated and the gondola seemed to be undamaged, although it had been dragged over the ground for about a mile before it came to rest. Fossett suffered a few bruises but was otherwise unhurt.

Fossett had been in the air for 12 days, 13 hours and had flown more than 12,695 miles. It was the longest solo balloon flight made to date, in terms of the distance traveled and time spent in the air. The last great balloon challenge of a solo world flight remained to be mastered.

"I thought I did have a chance to make it to the end," he said in a tele-conference with the *Solo Spirit* control center. "But you have to assess the risk."

Would Steve Fossett try again?

He said he didn't want to speculate. "I've tried so many times before. I'm afraid my luck will run out if I try it again." However, those who have followed him through all his other daring adventures believe he will.

And he did. When asked why he was going to try a sixth time, he replied, "This is important to me, I'm just not likely to let go."

On June 18, 2002, he lifted off from the Northam Aerodrome 60 miles east of Perth in western Australia in the 10-story-tall *Spirit of Freedom* and headed east. He estimated the flight would take 20 days and there would be enough fuel aboard to last for 27 days. This time his capsule featured an autopilot that maintained a constant altitude by controlling the burner through means of an external pressure sensor and a vertical speed indica-tor. He planned to fly at 20,000 feet and eventually reach 30,000 feet but would reduce the altitude when necessary to take advantage of better winds. He would be on oxygen for most of the flight. Outside tempera-tures at those altitudes in the Southern Hemisphere would vary from − 30 degrees Fahrenheit to − 50 degrees.

The flight proceeded easily over Australia and New Zealand at speeds of 80–100 miles per hour in a robust jet stream at altitudes of about 25,000 feet until June 23. To steer clear of severe storms looming ahead over the Pacific Ocean, mission control meteorologists advised Fossett to lower the balloon to 900 feet above sea level, an unusual request. He descended but downdrafts forced the balloon to within 400 feet of the ocean in heavy rain squalls. To stay aloft, he ran his burners on full flame and climbed back to 25,000 feet when the skies cleared ahead. He said it was "the most crucial day" of the flight.

Fossett flew eastward, crossed South America and the Atlantic Ocean at various altitudes to escape thunderstorms or achieve better flight direc-tion. He was able to sleep about four hours a day and at one point had to climb outside the capsule in temperatures far below zero to change fuel tanks or repair burners.

He crossed the southern tip of Africa and headed over the Indian Ocean. At one point he caught a jet stream that propelled the balloon at

200 miles per hour. As he approached his goal of 117 degrees east longitude over western Australia, the line from which he had set off nearly two weeks before, he climbed the balloon to 34,700 feet above clouds and snow flurries. By the time he reached this point, he had traveled 19,428.6 miles to achieve his goal.

He gradually lowered the balloon to slow it down for a landing in daylight. Just when it seemed all was well, he had to leave the capsule in the freezing temperature of the Australian night to put out a fire caused by a loose burner hose. He was able to put it out by shutting off a valve connected to the propane fuel tanks. It was the most dangerous incident of the whole flight.

After dawn, he hoped for a light wind to make a landing but it was still 20 mph when he landed near a dry lake in the Australian Outback near Birdsville, about 870 miles northwest of Sydney. The capsule was dragged roughly over the ground for about 15 minutes before he could detach the balloon. He emerged unhurt and was picked up by ground team members who had been following in a chase plane.

Fossett had accomplished what many said was a "Mission Impossible." Not only was he the first to complete a solo world flight, but had set a record for the longest distance flown by a single person in a balloon and broke the record for flight duration by a single person by staying in the air for 14 days, 20 hours. Soon after he landed, he received confirmation that the *Spirit of Freedom* capsule would be displayed in the Smithsonian's National Air and Space Museum next to the *Spirit of St. Louis*.

EPILOGUE

Even though it might seem that interest in round-the-world flying would be waning because it appears to be so much easier now, there are still many pilots who dream of making such a flight alone, with a crew or with others in groups of planes. In 1977, an organization was formed in Australia to sponsor what it called "The First World Air Race." It was to take place during a 21-day period, June 15 to July 6, 1980, to commemorate the fortieth anniversary of the Battle of Britain. Entries were divided into aircraft weight classes and assessed against the performances of other aircraft in each class. Entrants could start anywhere they chose, provided they landed at Stansted Airport, 30 miles north of London, sometime during the race period. However, the race was postponed indefinitely when sponsors said they did not "feel comfortable that the event could count on the high levels of technical and organizational support necessary." The world oil crisis, as well as unrest in various parts of the world at the time, were also cited as reasons for canceling the race.

Another world air race was planned to begin in May 1985 with single- or twin-engine aircraft in the weight category between 1,102 and 13,227 pounds. Starting points could be Paris, New York, or Singapore with seven mandatory stops. Maximum time allowed at each stop was 36 hours. The winner would receive $30,000. This race was canceled for reasons never explained.

The idea of a world air race was revived in 1991 when the government of Russia changed after 70 years of communism. Instead of individuals competing on their own, Bernard Lamy of France organized the Arc-en-Ciel World Air Rally made up of operators and passengers of 28 light aircraft and four chase planes led by the organizers that would traverse the previously restricted airspace of the former Soviet Union and continue around the world. The planes ranged in size from two-seat experimental composite Glasairs to twin-engine Beech King Airs.

The rally began with participants from 13 countries on June 20, 1992, from Geneva, Switzerland. Mandatory stops along the 16,500-nautical-mile course were required at Helsinki, Finland; Moscow, Irkutsk,

Yakutsk, and Anadyr, Russia; Nome, Alaska; Victoria, British Columbia; Fresno, California; Washington, D.C.; Godthab, Greenland; and Cannes, France. Intermediate refueling stops were made, depending on individual aircraft capabilities.

The following month, 12 aircraft departed Santa Monica, California, for a similar world air rally. Organized by Marcel Large, the route of flight was also through Russia. Nine of the aircraft were flown by American pilots, the others by pilots representing Canada, Italy, and France. The completion date was July 24, 1992.

Another round-the-world air rally, again organized by Bernard Lamy, was held beginning May 1, 1994, and ending May 24. The route was from Montreal to the Azores, Marrakech, Istanbul, Dubai, Agra, Ho Chi Minh City, Okinawa, Petropavlovsk, Anchorage, and Calgary. Eighteen aircraft and pilots from seven nations participated.

The exact number of pilots who have circled the globe is uncertain, because there is no world flight database, and the FAI does not record all such flights, only those who declare they will seek a record beforehand and agree to adhere to the rules. But a study of known world flights was made in July 2000 by Austrian pilot Johann Gutmann, who had completed a world flight in a Glasair IIS in 1996. He initiated invitations through the Experimental Aircraft Association (EAA) to the pilots of single- and twin-engine light aircraft that have made successful world flights to attend a meeting during the annual EAA fly-in in Oshkosh, Wisconsin, in July 2000. About 40 pilots showed up; in addition to the United States, other countries represented were Australia, Brazil, Canada, France, Germany, Great Britain, Korea, Mexico, and New Zealand. Claude Meunier of Australia, Margi Moss of Brazil, and Gutmann, all world-circlers themselves, decided that there was a sufficient number of light plane world pilots to form an organization called Earthrounders. At the Oshkosh meeting, attended by more than 50 earth-circlers, it was decided to meet again, and the second meeting was held in Vienna, Austria, for four days in June 2001. Meetings are scheduled for the summer of 2003 in Australia and beyond.

A web site (www.earthrounders.com) has been established as a register for pilots who have flown around the world in light aircraft. It will also provide a communications medium where past, present, and future world-circlers can exchange information, announce the progress of those making new attempts, and "inspire others who have similar flying dreams."

At the end of 2001, the Earthrounders listed the pilots of 102 single-engine aircraft and 40 twin-engine aircraft as having made world flights since the original U.S. Army Air Service fliers made the first one in 1924.

They also list pilots of seven helicopters, ten homebuilts, and two micro-lights as successful world-circlers.

At press time, the FAI was considering an Earthrounder Badge "to recognize the significant achievements of pilots of powered aerodynes making around the world flights." The proposed requirements are that a maximum of 20 control points be used; all flights must be completed within 365 days; applicants must have been on board the aircraft during the entire flight; and the same aircraft must have been used. The wings and fuselage may not be replaced, but replacement of engines and other components would be permitted. Non-pilots, passengers, or others not actively engaged in the flying of the aircraft will not be eligible. Badges will be issued with one to four diamonds, indicating whether the flights were eastbound, westbound, polar, or nonstop. Badges will not be awarded posthumously.

A lighter-than-air controllable vehicle—the dirigible or blimp—has the potential to fly around the world, but the only one to make such a flight was the German-built *Graf Zeppelin* under the command of Dr. Hugo Eckener in 1929. (See Chapter 4.) Its modern-day offspring, the nonrigid blimp, used mostly during World War II for submarine patrol and now for advertising at major athletic events, has not made a world flight, probably because their manufacturers have not deemed such a trip worth the risk or expense. The makers or operators of the tilt-wing, tilt-rotor, and autogiro types of flying machines have also not yet made any world flight attempts.

There are no official NAA or FAI world records shown for a seaplane flight around the world as of this writing, but Thomas Casey, of Everett, Washington, flew a Cessna 206 on floats 27,000 miles eastbound from Lake Washington near Seattle around the world in 1991. He landed the *Liberty II* more than 75 times on rivers, lakes, and the open ocean in the 20 countries he visited during a 188-day period. Originally proposing to make the flight in 60 days, he was hampered by delays in obtaining over-flight clearances, bad weather, mechanical difficulties, and a hospital stay for back surgery.

Casey's route of flight took him across the United States to Labrador, Greenland, Iceland, and Scotland. He had planned to land on the Thames River where British newsmen were waiting, but permission was denied, so he flew on to Italy, Greece, and Egypt. After three weeks in Saudi Arabia, recovering from surgery for herniated disks, he gained permissions to fly through the Middle East to India, Thailand, Malaysia, the Philippines, Okinawa, and on to Japan. Unable to get permission to land in Russia, he made a 12-hour flight from Lake Memanbetsu, Hokkaido, Japan, to Massacre Bay at Attu, the longest leg of the entire trip.

While en route to his next stop in the Aleutians, Casey made an emergency landing in the rough waters of the North Pacific, reportedly because of an engine malfunction due to using automobile fuel, and was rescued by the *Judy B*, a private fishing boat, and the U.S. Coast Guard. The Cessna was hoisted aboard the boat and taken to the military base on the island of Shemya. Three weeks later with a new engine shipped from the factory, he found he could not take off from the ocean because the seas were too high, so the plane was placed on float dollies and towed to the runway. This enabled him to depart from the airport by flying with the floats off the dollies. He returned to the bay at Attu and then resumed his flight so he could claim a world flight with takeoffs and landings only on water. He then made water landings at Atka, Dutch Harbor, Kodiak, Cordova, Ketchikan, and Campbell River, British Columbia, before touching down on Lake Washington, the departure point.

Casey was not granted a world record for this flight; however, he deserves to claim this solo flight in a light single-engine seaplane as an aviation "first."

There are no world records on the NAA or FAI books for amphibians, either. However, Reid W. Dennis, the pilot-in-command of the Grumman Albatross chase plane that accompanied Linda Finch on her world flight, can rightfully claim this aviation "first" for amphibians. (See Chapter 16.)

Since the first flight of the British-French supersonic Concorde on March 1, 1969, it was speculated that the pilots of either British Airways or Air France would eventually persuade their management officials to allow them to seek some worldwide publicity for their respective airlines by making a global flight in record time. Air France decided the time had come in December 1986. Ninety-four passengers boarded an Air France Concorde at Charles de Gaulle Airport in Paris on November 14 and returned 18 days later. The total flying time for the trip was 31 hours, 51 minutes. The flight was not made in a quest for an official round-the-world speed record, but it did prove that such a record could be easily set if that were the objective of the flight.

That time came in October 1992, when Air France authorized Capt. Claude Delorme to depart Lisbon westbound to seek a record with passengers and proceed to Santo Domingo, Acapulco, Honolulu, Guam, Bangkok, and Bahrain. The Concorde's return to Lisbon, after 32 hours, 49 minutes of flight, was on October 13, 1992. Its speed for the westbound record in the Unlimited Class was 764.98 mph (1,231.12 kmh).

The U.S. Air Force decided to enter the speed record books in 1995 again with a new nonstop global flight with in-flight refueling. A Rockwell International B-1B bomber departed Dyess Air Force Base, Amarillo, Texas, on June 2, 1995, eastbound for a war-simulation mission around

Air France and British Airways Concordes arrive for the inauguration of service in conjunction with Braniff Airways at the Dallas-Fort Worth Airport in January 1979. The supersonic transports were prohibited from flying at Mach 1 over land areas. (Courtesy Capt. Ken Larson)

A Braniff Airways flight attendant smiles beside the Machmeter in the passenger cabin indicating that the Concorde has reached twice the speed of sound. Concordes fly at cruising altitudes of 50,000 to 60,000 feet. (Courtesy of Capt. Ken Larson)

the world. Refueling in flight, the crew of four flew for 36 hours 13 minutes and averaged 631.16 mph, shattering previous world records for its class of aircraft in time, distance, and speed. The crew, led by Col. Douglas L. Rasberg, was awarded the Mackay Trophy for "the most meritorious flight of the year."

That same year, Air France Capt. Michel Dupont departed New York's John F. Kennedy International Airport in the Concorde and flew his 98 passengers and crew members to Toulouse, Dubai, Bangkok, Guam, Honolulu, and Acapulco before returning to New York on August 16, 1995. His average speed in flight was 811 mph (1,305.93 kmh), and the elapsed time of 31 hours, 27 minutes established a new eastbound speed record for commercial aircraft. Those on the plane saw three sunrises and three sunsets. The interior of the Concorde was refurbished for the flight with a special crew rest area—10 seats and three bunks—at the rear of the cabin. British Airways did not choose to try to beat the Air France records for a world flight, but like Air France, British Airways has established a number of point-to-point records over their respective commercial air routes.

A British Airways Concorde takes off with the nose visor down for maximum pilot visibility while taxiing, landing, and taking off. Concordes of Air France and British Airways have established speed records between cities over their respective commercial routes. However, Air France aircraft are the only ones that have officially established round-the-world speed records. (Courtesy Capt. Ken Larson)

Besides a motorless glider or human-powered aircraft, the most unlikely aircraft to make a world flight might seem to be the hang glider, motorized ultralight, or microlight types of aircraft. However, Jim Campbell, a flight instructor, and Patricia Trust planned to try it in two ultralights in the spring and summer of 1984. After completing a 3,300-mile flight from Watsonville, California, to the East Coast in very short hops, they continued to Canada but got no farther.

In 1998, Brian Milton and Kenneth Reynolds of Great Britain flew a Trike microlight eastward around the world via Russia in 121 days. On the Russian portion, P. Petrov joined the aircraft as navigator. Colin Bodill, flying a Mainair Blade 912S microlight, accompanied Jennifer Murray, both of the United Kingdom, in a Robinson 44 helicopter as they flew eastward in 1997 and circled the globe in 99 days. Michel Gordillo, a pilot for Iberia, Spain's national airline, completed a world flight from Salamanca in an MCR 01 on August 2, 2001. Brian Milton, who had previously flown a Trike microlight around the world with Kenneth Reynolds, attempted to fly an ultralight alone across the North Atlantic from Newfoundland in June 2001, but Canadian authorities refused to grant him clearance. His ultralight was not equipped for instrument flight.

A world flight in these smaller types of aircraft is a difficult undertaking. They are limited in range, and because the pilot in most types is exposed to the elements, flight in the northern latitudes can be extremely uncomfortable and dangerous. However, there is no doubt that others will attempt to have their names added to the record books in the future.

There are two other types of aircraft that may be engaged in a world flight someday, but the technology is not that far advanced at this writing. One of them is a solar-powered aircraft. A national altitude record of 96,500 feet was established in an AeroVironment Helios on August 14, 2001, at Lihue, Hawaii. The unmanned flying wing stayed aloft for 27 hours. No flights to establish a distance record have yet been made, and no manned flights with solar power have yet taken place.

The other type of vehicle that might accomplish a world flight in the future is also unmanned. One of these is in the NAA record books now in a special category. It is a Teledyne-Ryan Firebolt that has reached 103,000 feet and was clocked at Mach 4.1 or more than four times the speed of sound. However, with no human at the controls of either of these vehicles in flight, establishing records for such aircraft seems insignificant and pointless except for their possible military and atmospheric monitoring capabilities.

APPENDIX 1: THE FAI
AND THE NAA

When the dirigible, and then the airplane, came into being and long-distance flight became possible, an urge to set records developed. Fliers wanted to fly higher, faster, and farther than anyone else. Shortly after the Wright brothers' flights at Kitty Hawk, it became clear that some organization was necessary to make rules and keep records to ensure fairness and accuracy among claimants.

On June 10, 1905, the Olympic Congress, meeting in Belgium, passed a resolution calling for the creation of a "Universal Aeronautical Federation" to regulate aviation and the sport of flying. Each nation was encouraged to form its own association and participate in the development of standards for record-keeping and setting. The result was the founding of the Federation Aeronautique Internationale (FAI) in October 1905. Today, the organization includes the aviation associations in 70 nations and acts as the governing body for all official aircraft and space records. The sole representative of the United States is the National Aeronautic Association (NAA).

The rules of FAI and NAA are administered to ensure equal opportunity for all competitors; competent, unbiased judging; and scientific, accurate records. Certified observers and timers are required; only the latest electronic time and altitude measuring equipment is used. Distances flown are confirmed by precise techniques of measurement. National records are sanctioned and certified by the NAA. Only the FAI may certify world records; the NAA forwards potential entries for the world record books to FAI for consideration.

It is the FAI, then, that lays down regulations for evaluation and comparing performances of aviation vehicles. Throughout its history, FAI has defined, controlled, and approved world aeronautical and astronautical records and set sporting codes and regulations that permit fair and scientific comparison of performance and that aid education in aviation, promote world air travel by noncommercial aircraft, encourage proficiency

349

and safety in flight, and confer medals and diplomas on people who have contributed significantly to achievement of these goals.

Information concerning classes of records, as well as applications for official sanction of attempted record flights, can be obtained from the NAA or FAI. The NAA's main office is located at 1815 North Fort Myer Drive, Suite 500, Arlington, VA 22209. The telephone number is (703) 527-0226, and the facsimile number is (703) 527-0229. The NAA e-mail address is www.naa-usa.org. The headquarters of the FAI is located at Avenue Mon-Repos 24, CH-1005 Lausanne, Switzerland. Telephone: 41 21 345 1070. The FAI e-mail address is www.fai.org.

APPENDIX 2

Round-the-World Speed Records
(As of September 1, 2001)

ABSOLUTE SPEED AROUND THE WORLD RECORDS

Classes C, H, M and N

(Open to all classes of airplanes
regardless of type of power)

Speed Around the World, NonStop, NonRefueled (USA)
Richard Rutan
Jeana Yeager
Voyager
115.65 mph, 186.11 kmh
Edwards AFB, California
12/14/86–12/23/86

CATEGORY RECORDS

Piston Engine Aircraft

Class C-1 (Unlimited), Group 1

Speed Around the World, Eastbound (USA)
Philander P. Claxton
John L. Cink
Aerostar 601P
Los Angeles
219 mph, 353.57 kmh
11/4/77–11/9/77

Speed Around the World, Westbound (USA)
Max Conrad
Piper Aztec

Miami
123.19 mph, 198.27 kmh
3/8/61

Speed Around the World Over Both the Earth's Poles (USA)
Elgen M. Long
Piper Navajo
San Francisco
57.82 mph, 93.05 kmh
11/5/71–12/3/71

Class C-1.a, (661–1,102 lbs / 300–500 kg)

Speed Around the World, Eastbound (UK)
Colin Bodill
Blade 912
Brooklands, UK
10.27 mph, 16.53 kmh
9/6/00

Class C-1.b (1,102–2,205 lbs / 500–1,000 kg)
Group 1

Speed Around the World, Eastbound (Switzerland)
Hans G. Schmid
Long-EZ
Zurich, Switzerland
43.41 mph, 69.87 kmh
3/28/00

Speed Around the World, Westbound (Switzerland)
Hans G. Schmid
Long-EZ
Zurich, Switzerland
43.49 mph, 69.99 kmh
4/29/00

Class C-1.c (2,205–3,858 lbs / 1,000–1,750 kg)

Speed Around the World, Eastbound (Canada)
Donald F. Muir
Andre Daemen
Cessna 210N

Montreal
151.46 mph, 243.75 kmh
8/1/82–8/7/82

Speed Around the World, Westbound (USA)
Charles Classen
Phillip Greth
Beech Bonanza G-35
Waukegan, Illinois
54.37 mph, 87.50 kmh
5/27/88–6/6/88

Class C-1.d (3,858–6,614 lbs / 1,750–3,000 kg)

Speed Around the World, Eastbound (Australia)
Trevor K. Brougham
Beechcraft Baron B55
Darwin
197.77 mph, 318.28 kmh
8/4/71–8/10/71

Speed Around the World, Westbound (USA)
Max Conrad
Piper Aztec
Miami
123.19 mph, 198.27 kmh
3/8/61

Speed Around the World Over Both the Earth's Poles (USA)
Richard Norton
Calin Rosetti
Piper Malibu
Paris
8.72 mph, 14.04 kmh
1/21/87–6/15/87

Class C-1.e (6,614–13,228 lbs / 3,000–6,000 kg)

Speed Around the World, Eastbound (USA)
Philander P. Claxton
John L. Cink
Aerostar 601P
Los Angeles

219.70 mph, 353.57 kmh
11/4/77–11/9/77

Speed Around the World, Westbound (Qatar)
Hamad Al-Thani
Piper Aerostar 601P
San Jose, California
82.03 mph, 132.02 kmh
4/17/92–4/29/92

Speed Around the World Over Both the Earth's Poles (USA)
Elgen M. Long
Piper Navajo
San Francisco
57.82 mph, 93.05 kmh
11/5/71–12/3/71

Turboprop Aircraft

Class C-1. (Unlimited) and Class C-1.e (6,614–13,228 lbs / 3,000–6,000 kg)

Speed Around the World, Eastbound (USA)
Joe Harnish
David B. Webster
Gulfstream Commander 695A
Elkhart, Indiana
304.80 mph, 490.51 kmh
3/21/83–3/24/83

Class C-1.d (3,850–6,614 lbs / 1,750–3,000 kg)

Speed Around the World, Eastbound (France)
Jacques Lemigre Breuil
Nicolas Gorodiche
Oliver Waisblet
Socata TBM 700
250.43 mph, 403.03 kmh
6/13/93–6/17/93

Jet Engine Aircraft

Class C-1. (Unlimited)
Group III (Jet Engine)

Speed Around the World, Eastbound (France)
Michel Dupont
Claude Hetru
Concorde
New York
811.46 mph, 1,305.93 kmh
8/16/95

Speed Around the World, Eastbound (with refueling in flight) (USA)
Col. Douglas L. Rasberg
Capt. Ricky W. Carver
Capt. Gerald V. Goodfellow
Capt. Kevin D. Clodfelter
Rockwell International B-1B
Abilene, Texas
631.16 mph, 1,015.76 kmh
6/3/95

Speed Around the World, Westbound (France)
Claude Delorme
Jean Boye
Concorde
Lisbon
764.98 mph, 1,231.12 kmh
10/11/92–10/13/92

Speed Around the World Over Both the Earth's Poles (USA)
Capt. Walter Mullikin
Capt. Albert Frink
S. Beckett, F. Cassini, E. Shields
Pan American World Airways
Boeing 747SP
San Francisco
487.31 mph, 784.31 kmh
10/28/77–10/31/77

Class C-1.e (6,614–13,228 lbs / 3,000–6,000 kg)
Group III (Jet Engine)

Speed Around the World, Eastbound (UK)
M. Naviede
Cessna 550

Las Vegas
278.51 mph, 448.22 kmh
5/10/91–5/13/91

Class C-1.f (13,228–19,842 lbs / 6,000–9,000 kg)

Speed Around the World, Eastbound (USA)
Mark E. Calkins
Charles Conrad, Jr.
Paul Thayer
Daniel Miller
Learjet 35A
Denver
467.60 mph, 752.53 kmh
2/12/96–2/14/96

Class C-1.g (19,842–26,455 lbs / 9,000–12,000 kg)

Speed Around the World, Eastbound (USA)
Arnold Palmer
James E. Bir
Lewis L. Purkey
Robert Serling
Learjet 36
Denver
400.23 mph, 644.11 kmh
5/17/76–5/19/76

Class C-1.h (26,455–35,274 lbs / 12,000–16,000 kg)

Speed Around the World, Eastbound (USA)
J. Stephen Fossett
Darrin L. Adkins
Alexander M. Tai
Cessna 750 Citation X
Los Angeles
559.89 mph, 901.07 kmh
2/10/00

Speed Around the World, Westbound (USA)
J. Stephen Fossett
Alexander M. Tai
Pierre F. d'Avenas

Cessna 750 Citation X
San Jose del Cabo, Mexico
500.56 mph, 805.59 kmh
11/24/00

Class C-1.i (35,274–44,092 lbs / 16,000–20,000 kg)

Speed Around the World, Eastbound (Saudi Arabia)
Aziz Ojjeh
Challenger 601
Nice, France
467.11 mph, 751.70 kmh
7/22/84–7/24/84

Class C-1.k (55,116–77, 162 lbs / 25,000–35,000 kg)

Speed Around the World, Eastbound (USA)
Allen E. Paulson
Robert K. Smyth
John Salamankas
Jeff Bailey
Gulfstream IV
Houston
637.71 mph, 1,026.26 kmh
2/25/88–2/28/88

Speed Around the World, Westbound (USA)
Allen E. Paulson
K.C. Edgecomb
Jefferson Bailey
John Salamankas
Colin B. Allen
Gulfstream IV
Paris
503.91 mph, 810.93 kmh
6/12/87–6/14/87

Speed Around the World Over Both the Earth's Poles (USA)
Brooke Knapp
Gulfstream III
Los Angeles
334.83 mph, 538.83 kmh
11/15/83–11/18/83

Class C-1.q (330,693–440,924 lbs / 150,000–200,000 kg)

Speed Around the World, Eastbound (with in-flight refueling) (USA)
Col. Douglas L. Rasberg
Capt. Ricky W. Carver
Capt. Gerald V. Goodfellow
Capt. Kevin D. Clotfelter
Rockwell International B-1B
Dyess AFB, Texas
631.16 mph, 1,015.76 kmh
6/3/95

Class C-1.s (551,155–661,386 lbs / 250,000–300,000 kg)

Speed Around the World, Eastbound (USA)
Frank P. Santoni, Jr.
Richard A. Austin
John E. Cashman
Charles A. Hovland
Isham Ismail
Joseph M. McDonald
James C. McRoberts
Rodney M. Skaar
Boeing 777–200
Seattle
552 mph, 889.20 kmh
4/2/97

Class C-1.t (More than 661,386 lbs / 300,000 kg)

Speed Around the World, Eastbound (USA)
Clay Lacy
Verne Jobst
Boeing 747SP
Seattle
623.59 mph, 1,003.53 kmh
1/29/88–1/30/88

Speed Around the World Over Both the Earth's Poles (USSR)
Lev V. Kozlov
Yuri P. Resnitsky
Oleg I. Pripuskov
Anatoly V. Andronov

Antonov 124
428.18 mph, 689.10 kmh
12/1/90–12/4/90

Helicopters

Subclass E-1.c (2,205–3,858 lbs / 1,000–1,750 kg)
Group 1 (Piston Engine)

Speed Around the World, Eastbound (UK)
Jennifer Murray
Quentin Smith
Robinson R44 Astro
Denham, UK
10.55 mph, 16.99 kmh
5/10/97–8/8/97

Subclass E-1.c (2,205–3,858 lbs / 1,000–1,750 kg)
Group II (Turbine Engine)

Speed Around the World, Eastbound (USA)
Joe Ronald Bower
Bell JetRanger III
Hurst, Texas
40.99 mph, 65.97 kmh
6/28/94–7/22/94

Speed Around the World, Westbound (USA)
Joe Ronald Bower
John W. Williams
Bell 430
Hurst, Texas
57.01 mph, 91.75 kmh
8/17/96–9/3/96

Subclass E-1.d (3,858–6,614 lbs / 1,750–3,000 kg)
Group II (Turbine Engine)

Speed Around the World (USA)
H. Ross Perot, Jr.
J.W. Coburn
Bell 206 L-II Long Ranger
Dallas, Texas

35.40 mph, 56.97 kmh
9/1/82–9/30/82

Subclass E-1.e (6,614–9,921 lbs / 3,000–4,500 kg)
Group II (Turbine Engine)

Speed Around the World, Westbound (USA)
Joe Ronald Bower
John W. Williams
Bell 430
Hurst, Texas
57.01 mph, 91.75 kmh
8/17/96–9/3/96

ABSOLUTE WORLD RECORD—BALLOONS

Shortest Time Around the World (Switzerland/UK)
Bertrand Piccard
Brian Jones
Cameron Balloons R-650
Chateau d'Oex, Switzerland to Dakhla, Egypt
370 hours, 24 minutes
3/1/99–3/21/99

BIBLIOGRAPHY

Boase, Wendy. *The Sky's the Limit*. New York: Macmillan, 1979.

Bruce, Mary. *The Flight of the Bluebird*. London: Chapman and Hall, 1931.

Buegeleisen, Sally. *Into the Wind*. New York: Random House, 1973.

Cleveland, Carl M. *'Upside Down' Pangborn*. Glendale, Cal.: Aviation Book Co., 1978.

Earhart, Amelia. *The Fun of It*. Chicago: Academy Press, 1977.

Ekins, H.R. *Around the World in Eighteen Days and How to Do It*. New York: Longmans, Green, 1936.

Fraser, Chelsea. *Heroes of the Air*. New York: Thomas Y. Crowell, 1940.

Friedlander, Mark P. and Gene Gurney. *Higher, Faster and Farther*. New York: William Morrow, 1973.

Glines, Carroll V. *Around the World in 175 Days*. Washington, D.C.: Smithsonian Institution Press, 2001.

Glines, Carroll V. and Stan Cohen, *The First Flight Around the World*. Missoula, MT: Pictorial Histories Publishing Co., 2000.

Heinmuller, John P. V. *Man's Fight to Fly*. New York: Funk & Wagnalls, 1944.

Israel, Lee. *Kilgallen: A Biography of Dorothy Kilgallen*. New York: Delacorte, 1979.

Kilgallen, Dorothy and Herb Spiro. *Girl Around the World*. Philadelphia: David McKay Co., 1936.

Klotz, Alexis. *Three Years Off This Earth*. Garden City, N.Y.: Doubleday, 1960.

Mattern, Jimmy. *Cloud Country*. Pure Oil Co., 1936.

Mears, John Henry. *Racing the Moon*. New York: Rae D. Henkle Co., 1928.

Moss, Margi. *Freedom of the Skies: Adventure Around the World in a Light Aircraft*. Shrewsbury, England: Airlife Publishing Ltd., 1997.

Nichols, Ruth. *Wings for Life*. Philadelphia: Lippincott, 1957.

Pellegreno, Ann Holtgren. *World Flight: The Earhart Trail*. Ames, Iowa: Iowa State University Press, 1971.

Penrose, Harold. *British Aviation: The Adventuring Years, 1920–1929*. London: Putnam, 1973.

Piccard, Bertrand and Brian Jones. *Around the World in 20 Days*. New York: John Wiley & Sons, 1999.

Post, Wiley and Harold Gatty. *Around the World in Eight Days*. New York: Rand McNally, 1931.

Scott, Sheila. *Barefoot in the Sky*. New York: Macmillan, 1973.

Thomas, Lowell. *The First World Flight*. Boston: Houghton Mifflin, 1925.

Thomas, Lowell and Lowell Thomas Jr. *Famous Flights that Changed History*. Garden City, N.Y.: Doubleday, 1968.

Von Koenig-Warthausen, F. K. *Wings Around the World*. New York: G. P. Putnam's Sons, 1930.

Wells, Linton. *Around the World in Twenty-eight Days*. Boston: Houghton Mifflin, 1926.

Yeager, Jeana and Dick Rutan. *Voyager*. New York: Alfred A. Knopf, 1987.

INDEX

Note: *Italic* page references indicate information contained in photographs or illustrations.

ABOUT THE AUTHOR

Carroll V. Glines is a former U.S. Air Force colonel, has served as an editor for numerous aviation magazines, and is the author or coauthor of 34 books, including Jimmy Doolittle's autobiography, *I Could Never Be So Lucky Again*. His numerous writing awards include the prestigious Lauren D. Lyman Award for "outstanding achievement in aviation writing" from the Aviation/Space Writers Association. Colonel Glines lives in Dallas, Texas.